Racism and Anti-Racism in Europe

WEEK LOAN

Racism and Anti-Racism in Europe

Alana Lentin

Pluto Press
LONDON • ANN ARBOR

First published 2004 by Pluto Press
345 Archway Road, London N6 5AA
and 839 Greene Street, Ann Arbor, MI 48106, USA

British Library Cataloguing in Publication Data
A catalogue record for this book is available from the British Library

ISBN 0 7453 2221 2 hardback
ISBN 0 7453 2220 4 paperback

Library of Congress Cataloging-in-Publication Data
Lentin, Alana.
  Racism and anti-racism in Europe / Alana Lentin.
    p. cm.
  Includes bibliographical references.
  ISBN 0–7453–2221–2 – ISBN 0–7453–2220–4 (pbk.)
    1. Europe, Western – Ethnic relations. 2. Racism – Europe,
  Western. I. Title.
D1056.L46 2004
305.8'0094—dc22   2003025962

10 9 8 7 6 5 4 3 2 1

Designed and produced for Pluto Press by
Chase Publishing Services, Fortescue, Sidmouth, EX10 9QG, England
Typeset from disk by Newgen Imaging Systems (P) Ltd, Chennai, India
Printed and bound in the European Union by
Antony Rowe Ltd, Chippenham and Eastbourne, England

For Louis and Ronit

Contents

Acknowledgements

Writing on themes related to 'race' and racism in Europe at the continent's intellectual heartland requires a great deal of support; academic, emotional and material. A number of people have assisted and encouraged me in the course of researching and writing this book, and for this I owe them my heartfelt gratitude. Firstly, my thanks to my PhD supervisor at the Department of Political and Social Sciences of the European University Institute in Florence, Peter Wagner. The opportunity opened up to me by our arrivals in Florence in the same year is undeniable. His ability to help me see the connections between the specificity of my research interests and the broader questions thrown out by the social and political theory of the European state are what helped make this work what it is and keep me 'puzzled' over the years as it gradually came to fruition. The external members of my thesis defence committee, Zygmunt Bauman, Cathie Lloyd and Barnor Hesse are warmly thanked for their insightful and encouraging comments and the support they have continued to show me.

I have benefited immensely from the comments of a number of people. First and foremost, my gratitude and love go to my mother, Ronit Lentin. She has read every single version of every single paragraph of this work and has never failed to return with her remarks on everything from concept to style. Her unwavering commitment to anti-racism and anti-colonialism has been a beacon through the harder times. Others who took time to read and comment on my work include Etienne Balibar, Craig Calhoun, Roland Erne, Paul Gilroy, David Theo Goldberg, Karma Nabulsi, Jean Terrier and Eléni Varikas. I would like to particularly thank Etienne Balibar and Zygmunt Bauman for their unwavering commitment to the fight against racism and nationalism and for their generosity towards young scholars, from which I have been so lucky to benefit.

Without the following people, conducting this research would have been made an arduous process. Udo Enwereuzor and Mercedes Lourdes Frias must be thanked for the invaluable introduction they gave me to Italian anti-racism. Friends and family provided me with accommodation and sustenance during my research missions to France, Britain and Ireland: Flora Bernard in Paris, Lars Nyctelius and Peter Lauritzen in Strasbourg and Louis and Ronit Lentin in Dublin. Special thanks to my brother, Miki, whose flat in London must at times have seemed like my permanent second home.

A final word must go to the friends, old and new, whose company or voices on the other end of the phone have helped make the last four years exceptionally enjoyable. To Yael Ohana: the special qualities of our relationship bore their mark here too as they do throughout many aspects of my life. Others with whom I have seen these times through together and whose friendship and solidarity I value enormously are Benoit, Chiara, Eeva, Hakim, Irene, Jean, Joerg, Nicolas, Punky, Roberto, Sandrine, Sylvain, the members of the EUI Women's Running Club, those of the Collettivo IUE, the Grays, and of course my Savta Lia.

Most importantly, to the protagonists of this book, the anti-racist activists, for your words, thank you.

List of Interviews

Anti Nazi League (ANL)
A broad-based mass organisation involved in direct campaigns against the far Right

Campaign Against Racism and Fascism (CARF)
Independent anti-racist magazine

National Assembly Against Racism (NAAR)
Black community-led anti-racist organisation

National Civil Rights Movement (NCRM)
Nation-wide network for racial justice against institutional racism

National Coalition of Anti-Deportation Campaigns (NCADC)
Voluntary organisation that provides assistance for running anti-deportation campaigns

Newham Monitoring Project (NMP)
Emergency service for victims of racial violence and police harassment

The 1990 Trust
National organisation for the protection of the interests of black communities

FRANCE

Agence pour le développement des relations interculturelles (ADRI)
Assistance for the integration of people of non-French origin

Association des travailleurs maghrébins en France (ATMF)
Organisation for the protection of the interests of the Maghrebi population of France

La lettre pour la citoyenneté
Campaign for citizenship and voting rights for 'foreign residents'

La maison des ensembles (MDE)
Autonomous collective of sans-papiers in the Parisian 10th District

Les Sans-papiers
National Coordination of the Sans-papiers in France

Ligue contre le racisme et l'antisémitisme (LICRA)

Organisation against antisemitism and racism with a strong legal emphasis

Ras l'Front
Anti-fascist organisation established to oppose the *Front national*

Réseau pour l'autonomie des femmes immigrées et réfugiées (RAJFIRE)
Feminist collective for the rights of immigrant and refugee women

SOS Racisme
Youth-based national anti-racist organisation

IRELAND

Association of Refugees and Asylum Seekers in Ireland (ARASI)
Campaigning organisation of refugees and asylum seekers

National Federation of Anti-Racism Campaigns (NFARC)
Umbrella organisation for groups campaigning for the rights of asylum seekers and immigrants

National Travellers' Women's Forum (NTWF)
Organisation of Traveller women and their supporters

Pan-African Organisation
Network of African communities

Residents Against Racism (RAR)
Direct action campaign for the rights of immigrants and asylum seekers

Sport Against Racism in Ireland (SARI)
Campaign against racism through sport and education

'Žena Project' – Bosnian Community
Project for the integration of Bosnian women refugees

ITALY

Arci Nuova Associazione (ARCI)
Social organisation based on mutual aid and solidarity

Comitato per lo Sviluppo dei Paesi Emergenti (COSPE)
Development organisation running anti-racist projects including training and the coordination of Italy's membership in the European Network Against Racism (ENAR)

Associazione Rom Firenze
Organisation for the rights of Roma people in Florence

La Rete d'Urgenza contro il Razzismo
Emergency hotline for the victims of racial violence in Turin

Why write this book? No one has asked me for it.
Especially those to whom it is directed.
Well? Well, I reply quite calmly that there are too many idiots in this world.
And having said it, I have the burden of proving it.
Towards a new humanism...
Understanding among men...
Our coloured brothers...
Mankind, I believe in you...
Race prejudice...
To understand and to love...
From all sides dozens and hundreds of pages assail me and try to impose their wills on me.

Frantz Fanon (1967:9–10)

Introduction
Anti-Racism, Sociology and the Political

What is anti-racism? What is the place of the discourse of anti-racism and the practices of anti-racist organisations in the political arenas of western Europe? These questions have very seldom been answered in a wide-ranging literature preoccupied with the study of 'race' and racism, 'ethnicity' and discrimination in the social sciences. Treating anti-racism seriously from either an historical or a sociological point of view is hindered by the predominance of polemics and prescriptions, arising from the tendency to mobilise a common sense depiction of anti-racism as simply the inverse of racism: 'Racism and ethnic discriminations are under continuous historical and sociological examination. But anti-racism is consigned to the status of a "cause", fit only for platitudes of support or denouncement' (Bonnett 2000:2).

'The construction of a scientific object requires first and foremost a break with common sense' (Bourdieu and Wacquant 1992:235), in particular as it is reflected in 'institutions and thus present both in the objectivity of social organisations and in the minds of their participants' (ibid.). Constructing the object of my research – the discourse and practices of anti-racism in Europe – requires both a deconstruction of its relegation to the realm of the commonsensical, and so its omission from that of serious scholarship, and a reconstruction of the reasons for which this appears to be the case.

As a consequence of the empirical study of the discourse of anti-racism and the practices of anti-racism organisations carried out in this work, it is possible to offer a theorisation of anti-racism as existing along a continuum of proximity-to-distance from the public political culture of the nation-state. The discourses and practices developed by anti-racist activists in the post-war period are not explicable outside of an analysis centred on the histories of European states and the political processes they engender. By challenging the persistence of racism in European societies of the post-*Shoah* and post-colonial era, anti-racism constructs a discourse that

1

necessarily fixes the nation-state in its gaze. What is entailed by public political culture and in what way is it possible to construct the continuum along which I propose anti-racism is arranged?

Public political culture is a concept that emerges from a view of the specificities of democratic societies. It is an aggregate of the dispersed elements of political thought that, even in the daily life of its citizens, are associated with the idea of democracy as a principle ordering the modern, western state. It is principally a set of 'familiar ideas' (Rawls 2001:5), some 'more basic than others' (ibid.) which 'play a fundamental role in society's political thought and how its institutions are interpreted' (ibid.:6). Rawls, in his 'theory of justice', proposes that these ideas culminate in the overriding principle that a 'well-ordered' democratic society is founded upon the idea of social cooperation guided by recognised rules. What is central to my reinterpretation of Rawls's certainly very different intentions, is his depiction of the origins of these rules in a publicly shared understanding of the tenets of a public political culture: 'It is assumed that citizens in a democratic society have at least an implicit understanding of these ideas as shown in everyday political discussion, in debates about the meaning and ground of constitutional rights and liberties, and the like' (ibid.:5).

The ensemble of ideas captured by the notion of public political culture is, according to Rawls, encapsulated by the central guiding principle that citizens are regarded as 'free and equal persons' (2001:7), which in turn governs received notions of justice and fairness.

I want to argue that this principle, and the ideas with which it is generally articulated, are fundamental to an anti-racist world view. In a game of word association, anti-racism could easily conjure up any of the following: democracy, solidarity, freedom, equality, tolerance, respect and dignity. What creates a continuum of proximity-to-distance from this conceptual package, commonly thought of here as public political culture, is the extent to which it is seen as inherent to the state. Put in another way, further word associations for anti-racism could include emancipation, empowerment, resistance, liberation and self-determination, all of which, when contextualised historically, denote a critique of the state's readiness to guarantee freedom and equality, justice and fairness. I will therefore consider proximity to public political culture as descriptive of a position which relates the principles of anti-racism to the historically constructed ideologies of the democratic European nation-state.

Although such anti-racism may involve the criticism of individual state actions, such criticism is perceived separately from a general belief in the just nature of the principles upon which the dominant political thought is founded. Furthermore, this positioning incorporates historical moments in the struggle against racism into a generalised view of public political culture. The defeat of Nazism, *la Résistance* or anti-slavery are portrayed as national legacies, demonstrative of the democratic principles on which the state is purportedly built. Contemporary anti-racist speech recalls these moments and advocates a return to the principles which gave rise to them, considered to be inscribed in national public political culture.

In contrast, associating anti-racism with emancipation or resistance implies a distancing from public political culture that is cognisant of its complicity in the modern phenomenon of racism. Far from supposing an extension of rights and freedoms, democratic political thought is regarded as existing in an historically ambivalent relationship with their parallel denial to certain groups, known as 'inferior races'. Anti-racism in this view necessarily contains a critique of modern nation-state histories, which are as much narratives of colonialism, fascism, Nazism and the suppression of immigrants' rights as they are those of universal suffrage, the defence of human rights and the suppression of totalitarianism. The forms of anti-racism founded upon this view constitute the other extreme of the proposed continuum, marking their distance from the elements of public political culture deemed relevant by other anti-racisms and incorporated into their discourse. Very often, the anti-racist position of distance from the public political culture of the nation-state is grounded in a belief in the importance of the self-organisation of anti-racism by the actual or potential victims of racism, that in Europe developed out of the recognition of the anti-colonial struggle and the interrelated call to black resistance.

In contrast, a position of proximity habitually relies upon a discourse of human rights and meritocracy that orients anti-racism in a perspective of 'justice and fairness', to use Rawls's terms, that considers the democratic state and its institutions their principal guarantors. In practice, anti-racist actors often blend these discourses together, influenced by transformations in the wider politics of social movements or the non-governmental sphere. However, an analysis of the discourse produced by anti-racism organisations that constitutes the research for this work clearly reveals their differential positionings along the continuum, signalling an original elaboration of ideas and political standpoints that creates a profound heterogeneity among what is generally known as anti-racism.

Through its analysis of the historical unfolding of anti-racist discourses and the practices of contemporary anti-racist organisations, this book demonstrates the theoretical power of the continuum through the generation of the competing languages of culture, class, blackness, memory, universalism, lived experience, majoritarianism, self-representation, internationalism, localism and alliance. Throughout, this often conflicting vocabulary, taken as a whole, shall be shown to constitute the various discourses that together constitute the language of anti-racism.

It is only possible, in this light, to speak of a variety of anti-racisms, often competitive or even conflictual, the heterogeneity and disunity of which mirror the often painful transformation of European societies, from the myth of monoculturalism to the reality of diversity. The story of anti-racism, its accompanying discourses of solidarity and paternalism and, in opposition, the struggle for its appropriation by the racialised, is also the story of the metropolises of western Europe and of a creeping cosmopolitanism which, since the birth of nationalism, competes for its original place alongside democracy.

WHY ANTI-RACISM?

The world of my childhood included the incomprehensible mystery of the Nazi genocide. I returned to it compulsively like a painful wobbly tooth. It appeared to be the core of the war, and its survivors were all around us ... It was clear, too, that some Jewish families had opened their homes to West Indian students who had been shut out from much commercially rented property by the colour-bar. I struggled with the realisation that their suffering was somehow connected with the idea of 'race' that bounded my own world with the threat of violence.

Paul Gilroy (2000:4)

I came to research anti-racism in Europe convinced I myself was an activist. I came to writing this book believing in the possibility, indeed the necessity, of combining theory and praxis. I would continue being an anti-racist. I soon came to understand that the myriad of personal questionings of anti-racism itself – as a 'good' – to which the research process gave rise, meant for me that what I then thought of as 'hands-on' activism was to take a back seat, at least for the time being. The frustration that this created in me soon gave way to acceptance and understanding. The question of why I had chosen to embark on the path of research in the first place, rather than actively searching for work in an anti-racist organisation, was answered. It was answered through an historicisation of my own experiences and the juxtaposition of such with the first impressions from these early interviews.

I had chosen to construct anti-racism as an object of research, rather than career, because of a need to know why belonging to an entity known as an anti-racist movement often led more to feelings of unease than conviction. I looked back to my own involvement, notably in Europe-wide campaigns financed and coordinated under the auspices of the European institutions, and remembered the anger of black people at the lack of representativity, the platitude of slogans in black and white – 'All Different-All Equal' – and of institutional promises of practical 'followup' that materialised only in the glaring orange-coloured posters produced two years later for the European Union Year Against Racism. Images and symbols – half black face, half white; slogans – 'Racism, its all the same shit!'; media awards, 'ethnic' food fests, Cheb Khaled: they'd solve it. What made some anti-racisms like this? Why did this emphasis on culture as a one-stop-shop solution to racism's persistence win the institutional support that the local organisations with their constant, plodding insistence on institutional racism or voting rights never seemed to attract? Why, on the other hand, was it clear that as a white, Jewish, middle-class person, for some I would never have anything useful to say about anti-racism. Indeed, for many, being half-Israeli made me a Zionist, and so part of the racist problem itself. Why was culture, colour and increasingly religion so central to anti-racism for some and so utterly irrelevant, or even dangerous, for others? What political dividing lines marked out the platitudes of institutional responses from the hardness of local realities and where, between the growing hold of 'identities' and the privileged knowledge they claimed, did I fit in?

The urgency of these questions was quelled by the research process. My shift from activism to research that seeks to be politically grounded, but which recognises the importance of avoiding 'the trap of a speaking position which ultimately can be reduced to a form of advocacy' (Back and Solomos 2001:386), enabled this. By remaining committed to the struggle against racism, but allowing the research to reveal the extent of anti-racism's heterogeneity, the impossibility of speaking about anti-racism as a unitary or unproblematic phenomenon was made clear. It also revealed the importance of contextualising a study of anti-racism in the political transformations that have marked the period over which the research was carried out, culminating most emphatically with the political swing rightwards that has accompanied its final twelve months, from mid 2001 until mid 2002.

This study was being brought to its conclusion at a time when the majority of western European states were governed by the Right or by a barely distinguishable Centre-Left. Several countries have been recently marked by the unprecedented successes of far right-wing, anti-immigration political parties in general elections. Since September 2001, the western world has launched a new 'war of peace' (Roy 2002), of 'good' over 'evil', against 'people that we don't know who massacred people we know'[1] (ibid.:7). And all the states of western Europe are building detention centres for the indefinite confinement of migrants, asylum seekers and refugees. The people that 'we don't know' have come to our place, but unlike the early decades of the post-war period, we did not invite them. Our cities are already cosmopolitan and multi-racial/ethnic/cultural. The 'right mix' should not give way to a 'swamping'.

This context poses several crucial questions for anti-racism, not least the unparalleled mounting of Islamophobia as a previously overlooked form of racism, grounded in a concomitant racialisation and Islamicisation of all Arabs, but now also of undifferentiated South Asians (Fekete 2002). The discourse generated by Islamophobia is inextricable from the parallel growth of the political (and academic) discourse of security, reaching new heights in the runup to the second Gulf War. This is linked to the purported threat posed by the new 'illegal' immigration – the clandestinity provoked by the almost total sealing of its legal channels – and to the perceived failure of a third generation of 'old immigrants' to integrate into the European societies which nevertheless are its only homes. In Oldham and Bradford, like in Marseille and Paris, these rioting, car-burning grandchildren of guest workers and colonial subjects are too often tarred with the single brush of radical Islam. The criminalisation of immigration and the demonisation of Islam is welded together by the overriding vocabulary of security that rejects the opening of the borders of both states and city centres: immigrants not yet in are kept out or temporarily detained before deportation, while those already 'born in' may at least be confined to the *banlieues*, the council estates, the low-ranked schools and the unemployment office. The rehabilitation of the language of swamps, floods and waves that some may have considered safely confined to the history of 1970s neofascism and anti-immigration (Barker 1981), is today used by some for a crucial reorientation of the discourse of anti-racism.

The contextualisation of this study in these emerging developments is vital to a scholarly orientation in the implications of wider political processes beyond its apparently immediate concerns. Of particular concern is the reconceptualisation of anti-racism as compatible with a securitarian discourse that increasingly targets Islam and focuses on the purported return of antisemitism, or the 'new Judeophobia' (Taguieff 2002). This has been most evident in France where the 2002 presidential electoral campaign was accompanied by Israel's intensified assault upon the Palestinians of the occupied territories, symbolised by the killing of hundreds at Jenin. These events gave rise to a series of inexcusable attacks on Jews, synagogues and Jewish schools in France, Belgium, Germany and Britain.

Public anti-racists in France condemned the acts. The proposal that antisemitic attitudes are increasing among the descendants of Muslim North African immigrants was related directly to a generalised discourse of 'delinquency', that marked the presidential campaign, and for several years in France has targeted North African youth as principally responsible for anti-social behaviour, violence and drug-related crime. This was embodied by the so-called feeling of insecurity, evoked by the left- and right-wing in their electoral efforts, which made 'youth' a euphemism for North African, thus establishing a racialised code for all society's fears. Alternatively, but not wholly irreconcilably, violence against Jewish targets was proposed as proof of the 'new Judeophobia' that 'never, in the France of the post-war ... has circulated in as many social milieus, meeting as little intellectual and political resistance' (Taguieff 2002:11). The specificities of recent French events are merely evocative of the particular challenges facing a study of anti-racism that seeks to expose its internal contradictions in the present political context. Taguieff's (2002) book, *La nouvelle judéophobie*, is a larger exposé of his already well-known views on the subject, namely that an antisemitism promoted by a 'communitarian' (read Islamist), left-wing anti-Zionism is the real threat posed by racism in contemporary Europe. According to Taguieff, Judeophobia is epitomised by the belief that 'the Jews are all more or less disguised Zionists; Zionism is a colonialism, an imperialism and a racism; so the Jews are declared or unspoken colonialists, imperialists and racists' (ibid.:12).

This form of racism, a global phenomenon due to its wide diffusion by means of the new technologies, is indicative of a more general anti-Americanism, the 'transnational political orthodoxy that dominates the world after 1989' (Taguieff 2002:16), which creates the categories of 'Jewish-American' or 'American-Zionist imperialism'. Taguieff creates a conspiratorial web of anti-Jewishness, shared by Marxists and 'tiers-mondistes', the far Right and Islam that, he proposes, is at the vanguard of contemporary radicalism.

The proposal of a 'new Judeophobia' would reorient anti-racism against its purported mobilisation 'like in the old "anti-Semitism" in the strong sense of the word, [of] an absolute hatred of the Jews' (Taguieff 2002:13). Indeed, anti-racism would have to be entirely reformulated because, as shall be discussed in Chapters 2 and 4, Taguieff sees it as the construction of a left-wing, culturally relativist 'communitarianism'[2] that rejects the universal principles of colour-blind human rights as the basis for combating racism. The threefold attack implied by Taguieff's work – on Islam, on the radical Left and on anti-racism – poses a significant problem for my positioning as a Jewish researcher of anti-racist discourse and praxis under present political conditions. How to recognise the persistence of antisemitism – rather than 'Judeophobia' – alongside the undoubtedly more acute racisms against non-white, non-national and non-Christian Others in the public spheres of Europe? I felt that, by claiming that Judeophobia is based on an equation of all Jews with Zionism, Taguieff was paradoxically presenting Jewish anti-racists with a choice: reject his proposals or accept the belief in the existence of the phenomenon and, unavoidably, equate one's own Judaism with a Zionism that the acceptance of the new formulation of anti-semitism as Judeophobia forces upon us. For Taguieff, it is little more than hypocritical for an anti-Zionist to call herself an anti-racist because, in his opinion, anti-Zionism is the epitome of contemporary antisemitism, and so tantamount to racism. This leaves no room for a position of Jewish anti-Zionist anti-racism, because to claim such a stance would for Taguieff be a contradiction in terms. By essentialising Jews in this way, Taguieff's own 'Judeophobia' comes to the fore, because is it not the impossible choice that he offers us which is much more significant of present-day Jew hatred; that waged, as it always has been, by elites, including those within the academy?

The contemporary political climate as well as the paucity of study into the history and contemporary sociology of anti-racism enable the unproblematic reception of Taguieff's ideas (Redecker 2002). His theorisation of 'Judeophobia' can be heard in a European political sphere where trite public expressions of remorse for the *Shoah* may still be expected. Taguieff's separation between 'old antisemitism' and 'new Judeophobia' provides society with respite from the past and, by focusing on acts of violence committed by the powerless, a means of turning attention from the ongoing, unseen racisms that, paradoxically because of the tragedy in our past, Jews no longer endure on a daily basis. Recognising the exclusivities and disunities that an espousal of Taguieff's propositions would engender – between Jews on the one hand, and the ostensible Judeophobes of anti-racism and the Left on the other – this work is grounded in a commitment to transcending what are often presented as being 'incompatible identities' (Gilroy 2000:98). It is inspired by Paul Gilroy's description of the childhood origins of his motivations for theorising 'against race'.

HISTORICISING ANTI-RACISM

Contextualising anti-racism in a way that reveals the interstices of its discourse with the vocabulary of public political culture, beyond an analysis of present-day political transformations, requires its historicisation. The process of historicisation as I refer to it in the discussion of anti-racism involves a sociological reconstruction of the historical emergence of anti-racist discourse and praxis in a way that gradually reveals its contemporary complexities. Therefore, events in the development of anti-racism since the beginning of the twentieth century shall not be told chronologically in the form of historical narrative. Rather, they are used alongside the information gathered from the interviews with contemporary anti-racist activists as a means of telling a more complete story that draws connections between anti-racism and the changing political, institutional and societal contexts that accompanied its elaboration over time. Most importantly, this work of historicisation is used in order to fully develop the theorisation of the continuum of proximity-to-distance from the public political culture of the nation-state along which the research suggests anti-racism may be arranged.

I propose firstly, that anti-racism cannot be researched sociologically without a concomitant and interrelated historicisation of the political idea of 'race' and the rise of modern racism. Secondly, the depiction of the development of anti-racism's internal contradictions which lead us to talk of a variety or heterogeneity of anti-racisms, involves an historicisation of this very complexity. In other words, following Joan Scott (1989:681), 'history is inherently political'. It is therefore necessary to reveal how politics, or what we may call public political culture, intervenes in the reconstruction of both racism and anti-racism in a way which leaves both certain interpretations and certain people out of its writing. The work of historicisation that I propose is cognisant of the importance of adding different world views and experiences to the writing of history and rejects the insistence that 'there is one past ("our past") and only one way to recount it' (ibid.:685).

The historicisation of the rise of the 'race' idea and racism as its political ideology in modern Europe is fundamental to a full understanding of the political project of anti-racism. This is so because, in order to deconstruct the common sense interpretation of anti-racism as the opposite of racism, or as its counter discourse, it is necessary to understand what precisely anti-racism seeks to oppose. Because an anti-racist approach, to scholarship or activism, has provided us with most of our present-day definitions of 'race' and racism, this has very rarely been questioned. One of the principal arguments of this book, by means of which the theorisation of an anti-racist continuum is moulded, is that the anti-racism which emerges in the post-war period as a project of the international institutions, principally UNESCO, and subscribed to by the European states, does not propose a relationship between racism and the nation-state. By introducing alternative explanations of human difference, notably 'culture', this form of hegemonic anti-racism marginalises the role played by the modern states of Europe in racism's development. Preferring behavioural and psychological analyses of racism that individualise it as a set of isolated practices, this approach glosses over the utility of the political ideology of 'race' for the accomplishment of the imperial project (Fanon 1963), the consolidation of national state borders (Noiriel 1991), the suppression of the internationalist working class (Balibar 1991), the building of strong armies (MacMaster 2001) and the ultimate annihilation of the Jews of Europe (Bauman 1989).

Chapter 1 therefore analyses the growth of racism as a modern phenomenon in a way that negates the widely accepted view that the processes of racialisation and racist oppression, particularly those within Europe, are inconsistent with a political philosophy of the democratic European nation-state. This view, still largely accepted, would see the *Shoah* as an aberration, 'an interruption in the normal flow of history, a cancerous growth on the body of civilised society, a momentary madness among sanity' (Bauman 1989:viii). On the contrary, 'race' and racism, following central authors such as Bauman, Arendt, Voegelin and others is shown, not only to be a particularity of modernity, and specifically of the mid-nineteenth century on, but also to be grounded in what Gilroy (2000:59) calls a 'statecraft' which at a particular historical moment requires a notion of racial hierarchy as the legitimating framework for its actions.

It is important to note that, despite the wide and highly respected scholarly sources of this argument, it is not to be taken for granted that it embodies the general anti-racist perspective. Historicising anti-racism's own definition of racism entails recognising the very different relationships that are constructed between 'race' and state within anti-racist discourse. Chapter 2 reveals the unfolding of these competing explanations. It shows how the isolation of racism as prejudicial behaviour supports the efforts of western states and international institutions in the post-war era, and later during the process of decolonisation, to establish themselves as the protectors of externally defined injustice, a mission that takes on even more importance following the start of the Cold War and the displace-ment of the embodiment of 'evil' from Nazism to Communist total-itarianism. Early anti-racisms committed to the memory of the *Shoah* or to the equal treatment of non-whites also gave preference to the possibility of overcoming individual prejudice through the spread of cultural knowledge and tended to neglect the ideological content of racism.

It was not before the emergence of an anti-colonialist critique in the 1950s and 1960s and its influence upon the development of a discourse of black resistance in Europe's metropolises via the US by the 1970s, that these depoliticised explanations of racism were chal-lenged. The growth of black self-organisation, in response both to institutionalised 'everyday' racism and to the paternalist solidarity of so-called 'white left' anti-racism, focused on the state and capital as the main conditions for the persistence of racially conceived oppres-sion. The tension to which the opposition of state-centred and cul-ture-centred explanations of 'race' and racism gives rise is a key factor in the creation of the proposed continuum. The disunity which char-acterises anti-racism, and to which many observers continue to attest, is inexplicable without an historicisation of the development of the conflicting discourses which I suggest are at its core.

Revealing the tensions around which the heterogeneity of anti-racism develops historically assists us in seeing how an anti-racism that positions itself closer to public political culture has been involved in a writing of anti-racist history that excludes 'competing' interpretations of the history of racism and the orientations of anti-racism. As I shall show in Chapter 4, a so-called 'majoritarian' discourse of anti-racism established itself as the defender of the humanist principles of European public political culture, and in so doing worked to exclude an anti-racism grounded in the recognition of 'difference' and against an ideology of colour-blindness and meritocracy. By referring to the anti-racism grounded in the experiences of the actual or potential victims of racism as 'communitarian' or particularist, 'generalist' anti-racism assumes the inability of the racialised to participate in the construction of an anti-racism that is 'acceptable' to all, and so uprooted from the specificities of lived experience (Fanon 1967). Furthermore, by emphasising explanations of racism that display caution in relating 'race' to state, 'hegemonic' anti-racist discourses monopolise the telling of racism's history, in turn marginalising the history of the evolution of state-centred accounts.

In contrast, this study insists on a political sociological approach to the explanation of racism and the sociological analysis of anti-racist discourses and practices that places the state at the centre. However, not privileging an examination of culture-centred approaches would result in an inability to demonstrate how such politically grounded perspectives have often been underemphasised in the construction of 'mainstream' anti-racism. Therefore the historicisation of anti-racism's diversity proposed here prioritises both the 'different voices' that are often neglected and the political reasons for which this has been so.

ANTI-RACISM AND EUROPE

The historicised approach proposed by this study establishes itself around a particular relationship to western Europe as the privileged political space in which the research was conducted. The process of unveiling the internal complexities of anti-racism is permanently accompanied by a questioning of what could be meant by a specifically European anti-racism. In this sense, a sociology of anti-racism in western Europe is inextricable from the latter's legacy as the birthplace of nationalism and modern racism, imperialism and the *Shoah*. It is also the intellectual space in which the notions of cosmopolitanism and liberty, with which anti-racism is closely bound, originated but whose potentialities were masked by the 'consistent endorsement of "race" as a central political and historical concept and ... the grave violence done to the central image of man by the exigencies of colonial power' (Gilroy 2000:65).

The study of anti-racism discourse and praxis I propose takes four western European states as its focus: Britain, France, Italy and Ireland. Their choice was made on the basis of practical as well as theoretical considerations. Firstly, they were selected due to my knowledge of their three languages and relative familiarity with their political systems and societal particularities. The choice of these four countries allows for a certain symmetry in the research design that represents a more general overview of the western European political sphere and enables me to make a wider argument about the nature of European anti-racism.

In this design, France and Britain are taken to represent the old colonial powers and the traditional receiving countries of immigration. Italy and Ireland on the other hand are the former 'sending' societies for whom incoming migration becomes a noticeable reality only following the beginning of the 1990s. France and Britain have both accepted Irish and Italian immigrants. However, Britain's old relationship of colonial domination over Ireland creates an interesting third dimension in this symmetry because of the way in which that relationship informs current Irish perceptions of the experience of immigration, framed by the end of its own emigration and the racisms that accompanied it. Further complexifying this symmetry, Italy's own internal and external immigration is juxtaposed with the colonial and fascist histories that appear to disable Italian anti-racism from mobilising the discourse of past victimhood that often accompanies the construction of anti-racist empathy. The construction of anti-racism and its relation to public political culture is explicated in Chapter 3, a country-by-country perspective on the specificities of French, British, Irish and Italian anti-racisms.

The ambivalence of western Europe's historical position as the locus of colonial power and the universal measure of 'progress' is a constant presence in anti-racism, and so must inform its analysis. To this end, the research design purposefully includes these four spaces of anti-racist activism to the exclusion of a wider perspective on Europe as a continent, because of the specificity of the historical process of nation building in the political arena now known as the European Union. By focusing on three of the states in which the rise of the idea of 'race' was located historically – France, Britain and Italy – and juxtaposing the analysis of such with a contemporary political sociology of anti-racism, the centrality of the ambivalent relationship to past racisms in these national polities is revealed. Both Ireland and Italy, whose trajectories of migration have generated the societal myth that indigenous racism does not exist, display unease towards anti-racism's deconstruction of such founding narratives of national identity. Beyond the historical falsity of the myth of a racism-free society, the inconsistencies that the diffusion of anti-racist discourse throw out imply that the idea of Europe as the guarantor of 'liberty, equality and fraternity' must be continually questioned (Hall 2002). In this light, the focus on western Europe is also cognisant of the contemporary preoccupation with the construction of a European identity, a 'political Europe' to accompany the by now consolidated monetary union. Anti-racism that positions itself closely to the public political culture of the nation-state is also underpinned by a wider conception of Europe and the West as the general birthplace of the so-called 'rights of man'. This reworking of the commendable project to overcome narrow nationalisms and to replace them with any one of a number of possibilities for a supranational Europe must nonetheless be cognisant of the failure to dispute the value of Europeanness. This is particularly important in the effort to describe the struggle for the recognition of the impossibility of severing the history of racism from that of modern western Europe that is implicit in the state-centred anti-racist critique.

Multiple comparability

An awareness of the inequalities at Europe's centre also bears upon the sociological perspective in which this study has been conducted and informs one of its key methodological choices. Researching the evolution of modern racism and its anti-racist responses sociologically necessitates the recognition of sociology's historic complicity with the event of imperialism. As Connell (1997) reminds us, early sociologists, due to the political context into which the discipline emerged, organised their research into societal processes around the foundational ideas of 'progress' and the 'difference between the civilisation of the metropole and an Other whose main difference was its primitiveness' (ibid.:1517). The predominance of the conditions of empire as a central organising mechanism for viewing internal and external societal differences meant that sociology as a 'science of society' could not evolve independently of this racialised political context. Indeed, it set itself the task of gathering up 'the information yielded by the colonising powers' encounter with the colonised world' (ibid.:1519). The centrality of notions of human hierarchy and differential levels of progress to early sociology reveals the extent to which it, as much as the more frequently cited examples of statistics and demographics, was complicit in the installation of the system of bio-power; the uniquely modern alliance between science and the state (Foucault 1978). However, its construction as a 'science of progress that claimed the world as its province' (Connell 1997:1530) failed, because of the abstract equality created by the comparative method, to admit its own reliance on the conditions of imperial domination.

For Durkheim, the comparative method was at the core of sociology itself and that which distinguished it from other sciences. It enabled 'assembling examples of the particular social "species" under study and examining their variations' (Connell 1997:1523). The primacy of comparison for sociology was, as Connell makes clear, determined by the colonial situation which enabled the construction of the method as 'a one-way flow of information, a capacity to examine a range of societies from the outside, and an ability to move freely from one society to another' (ibid.). Comparative sociology, as it was understood by Durkheim and his contemporaries, has remained dominant in contemporary sociological practices, due particularly to the value placed on national comparative studies enabled by larger research budgets, not least those afforded by the EU. This study chooses to prioritise a perspective on western Europe over one on the comparison of its four national settings, in recognition of the sociological legacies to which Connell draws our attention. A focus on the comparability of national societies may be unable to avoid the reification and externalisation of society, as a 'unit of analysis', that the process already involved at the turn of the twentieth century. Societies are viewed as internally homogeneous for the purposes of being contrasted to other undifferentiated societies according to a predecided level of controlled comparability. Rather, this study advocates the use of comparison at a number of levels, notably between anti-racist discourses and practices, both across and within individual states. By questioning the superior utility of nationally based comparison, I hope to reveal both the problematic legacy of this methodology in terms of its relationship to the construction of racial categories in the imperial context, and the difficulty it has today in exposing the complexities of the diverse societies that European anti-racist discourse reflects.

One of the central structuring ideas for the type of multilayered comparison with which the book operates is that of *time*. In other words, beyond the many different spaces in which anti-racism is elaborated – neighbourhoods, cities, national and international 'levels' as well as the virtual space of the Internet – it proceeds at a variety of tempos. To a great extent, these temporal differences are in fact shaped by the national contexts in which a particular anti-racist discourse is formulated. But neither does this constitute the whole picture.

Anti-racism certainly originated at different times in all four of the study's settings. Britain and France saw anti-racism emerging mainly with the end of the Second World War, as a reaction against fascism and antisemitism, and soon after in solidarity with non-European immigrants. However, to only emphasise this period when, it is true, anti-racism as a publicly recognised form of political organisation emerged, would be to negate the preexistence of a myriad of self-help groups established mainly by Jewish immigrants in France between the wars, or the importance of the Pan-African Conference to Britain since the turn of the twentieth century as precursors to contemporary anti-racism. In other words, by concealing the various times at which differential anti-racisms emerge a picture is painted of a linear progression of anti-racism from the post-war to the present day which disguises its rather more halting and manifold progression.

Similarly, Italy and Ireland witnessed the first purposefully anti-racist organisations in the early 1990s in response to racism against immigrants who, for the first time, began to arrive in these countries in significant numbers. Nevertheless, the introduction of several Irish activists to anti-racist practices as migrants in Britain demonstrates how anti-racism was actually embedded in the Irish experience before it became a reality within the borders of the Republic itself (McVeigh 2002a). The recognition that different temporalities overlap is vital for the construction of an overview of anti-racism in each of the four settings as well as between them.

The centrality of time is also reflective of another level at which comparisons have been drawn between anti-racist discourses in the production of my research. The amount of time for which a given organisation has been in existence is often significant of its positioning along the continuum of proximity-to-distance from the public political culture of the nation-state. In particular, the longevity of activists' experiences was revelatory of their differential capacities to recount their version of the story of anti-racism. A marked difference may be noted between organisations of citizens or long-term residents of a given country, and those established by more recently arrived migrants and asylum seekers. The length of time for which an organisation has been in existence is determinant both of its political confidence and of its capacity to analyse anti-racism's societal implications. The tendency of established organisations to contextualise their work within national public political culture and the exigencies of contemporary political conditions is contrasted with that of newer activists to refrain from 'being political' and to remain at the level of either technicalities or 'values'. The variable possibilities of alliance, and manipulation, to which this difference gives rise should be taken into account in the effort both of representing the heterogeneity of anti-racism and its specificity to Europe in the book. The important structuring effect of time is linked also to the trajectories of immigration that mark the various societies of western Europe, creating and recreating with each arrival new agendas for anti-racism that must be negotiated with the preexisting 'ways of doing things' that each anti-racist 'time' constructs.

INTERCONTINENTAL INFLUENCES

While this is a book about racism and anti-racism in Europe, I do not assume that this is a unique political space which does not bear comparison with other contexts. On the contrary, I aim to contribute to the cross-fertilisation, ongoing since the work of those such as Du Bois and Boas, of European and North American anti-racisms. Europe and the United States have always been sites of influence upon each other, not only in the obvious realms of politics and culture, but also in the ways in which racism and anti-racism have interacted with governmentality and affected individuals' lives. Nevertheless, the proposed specificity of the way the idea of 'race' has taken hold and fundamentally shaped US society and politics has often obscured useful possibilities of comparison, in particular with Europe which some influential voices, most famously perhaps Richard Wright

(Cobb 1979; Gilroy 1993), assumed was free of the problem of the 'colour line'. With regard to anti-racism too, the view from Europe that US anti-racisms have been subsumed under a wave of identity politics which swept aside alliance-based struggles, breaking them down into a panoply of particularities, has made it difficult to find similarities with the European context. In contrast, I propose that there are three main areas in which a reading of this study of racism and anti-racism in Europe may point towards reopening the dialogue between the US and Europe on a subject that, in light of globally consolidated approaches to asylum and immigration, is increasingly affecting all areas of the North in strikingly similar ways.

Firstly, there has been a tendency in writings on 'race' in the United States to treat it as constituting a problem which is incomparable with that in other societies. This assumption is of course grounded in the reality of the particular history of slavery, segregation and stratification which has, since the birth of the American nation-state entrenched the divisions between blacks and whites. However, it appears that it is this precise distinction, which reifies blackness and whiteness as two irreconcilable extremes, that makes the US relationship to 'race' appear so incompatible with racisms as they have affected other areas of the northern hemisphere, especially Europe. Within this situation of opposed polarities it seems difficult to talk about racism as divorced from skin colour and to take on board the proposal that racialisation constitutes a much more subtle process that does not always play by the rules laid down by so-called phenotype. Nowhere can this challenge be seen more clearly than in the treatment of Travellers and Roma in Europe. While Travellers in Ireland, for example have spearheaded the anti-racist campaign, in the US it appears that the power of the black–white dichotomy forces other racialised groups to have recourse to 'identity', each fighting for the recognition of its oppression as racism.

Furthermore, Kushnik (1998) has spoken of the tendency to reduce class to 'race' in US discussions of social stratification. This is based, to a large extent, on the reality in which 'institutional racism determines resource allocation: access to goods and services and housing assures that, compared with blacks, whites get privileged access to scarce resources' (ibid.:46). However, as Kushnik demonstrates, white working-class racism, based on the benefits of institutional racism against non-whites in US society, is not inherent. In contrast, at several points in white working-class history, responses other than racism were possible that were ultimately unsuccessful due to the elite mobilisation of 'race' as consistent with anti-Communism in the context of the Cold War. For this reason, there was strong resistance to black attempts to develop political projects that linked 'race' with class which negatively affected the potential for alliance between the historical white and black working classes.

The suppression of alternative political responses to class subordination across black–white divides in the US has also made its mark upon the possibility for intercontinental dialogue. While, as we shall see, in Europe too the discourse which promotes the equivalence of ' "race" and class' is a problematic one which has obscured racism's ability to cut across socioeconomic divides, its unifying potential has not been conceived with such difficulty in the European context. The fact that, within anti-racist circles in Europe, 'race' is not reduced to class, as it often is in the US, may allow for discussions of the institutionalisation of racism that go beyond an emphasis on attitudes and behaviours which contributes to obscuring the analysis of racism.

In particular, the analysis I am proposing here, explicated in Chapter 1, is that 'race' as a political idea develops under specific conditions enabled by the concomitant expansion and internal rationalisation of modern nation-states. In order to understand the extent to which racism continues to shape contemporary political realities, I propose that it is important to understand that western states in the aftermath of the Holocaust and colonialism treated racism as an external force, coming to divert the course of democracy. It was proposed, therefore, that with a return to the principles upon which modern nation-states are founded that racism would, naturally, disappear. The alternative to racism, as shall be shown in Chapter 2, was generally conceived throughout the West in terms of the idea of 'racelessness' (Goldberg 2002). In the United States, this has most importantly taken the form of colour-blindness which, in its aim to overcome 'race' by ignoring it, on the contrary, compounds racism by 'conjur[ing] people of colour as a problem in virtue of their being of colour, in so far as they are not white' (ibid.:223).

By showing how 'racelessness' takes hold throughout the West in the aftermath of the Second World War, under various guises but nonetheless following similar patterns, it is possible to show how it may not always be necessary to consider the US as entirely separate from other contexts in this regard. Indeed, under conditions of increased globalisation, we may witness a similarity of states' reactions to racism as well as anti-racist responses across a variety of settings. As stated in the previous section, this study shows how anti-racism may be compared across time in recognition of the temporal gaps between the evolution of racism and the responses to it across national and regional contexts. Therefore, taking the discussion outside of the US context, yet reading about European racisms and anti-racisms from a US perspective, may assist the American reader to consider the similarities between Europe and the US as a means of emerging from the impasse into which the 'race' debate in North America sometimes runs.

Secondly, and in relation to the importance of the similarities between the history of racism's development across western contexts, the US debate on anti-racism can also be informed by an engagement with European discourses and movement forms. In an era in which it is no longer possible to talk of political and social processes as existing entirely separately from each other on a global scale, the case of anti-racism appears an interesting study of the way in which such interconnectivity functions. Indeed, the domain of anti-racism can be seen as a precursor to the development of common thinking on issues of injustice within the Global Justice Movement today. US, European and colonial settings have influenced each other's thinking on 'race' since the days of the anti-slavery movement in the late 1700s. Furthermore, to a great extent, the inter-war years represented a period of greater cooperation on anti-racism between Europe and North America than any since, due to the influence of the migration of European anti-racist intellectuals to the US such as Franz Boas and Gunnar Myrdal.

Thinking about rejuvenating such cooperation may benefit from briefly considering the historic importance of anti-racist interconnections. It is well known that US-based anti-racisms have had a strong influence over their European counterparts. For example, Lloyd (1996b) has shown how the American model of civil rights, and in particular the notion of internal colonialism, was used by the movement against colonialism and anti-immigrant racism in France in the 1960s. Similarly, several authors (Mullard 1985; Gilroy 1987) have demonstrated the symbolic importance of African American resistance to racism, such as the Black Power movement, for the emergence of black political consciousness in Britain of the 1950s and 1960s. However, to what extent have European influences upon the US perhaps become lost due to the predominance of North American reference points in the reconstruction of the defining moments of anti-racism?

Two examples of the importance of European responses to racism that predate the contemporary period are the anti-slavery movement, on the one hand, which at the end of the eighteenth century was an important force in both French and British civil society (Lloyd 1998), and the Pan-African Conference, on the other. As I shall show in Chapter 2, the Pan-African Conference, first held in London in 1900, constructed Europe in the ambivalent position of both colonial metropolis and as a site for anti-colonialist resistance. What is interesting about these two instances of historical anti-racism is the way both were always constructed in relation to the ever-present reference to Africa, both as symbolic of colonialism in general and as the source of slavery, in a way that created a triangular relationship between Europe, Africa and America. The power of this relationship has been diminished due to the increasing localisation of anti-racism brought about mainly by the pressing nature of the problems of racism in individual societies. Further, the end of anti-colonialism and the death of Pan-Africanism that accompanied the birth of the post-colonial era also led to the disappearance of internationalism, which had its roots in this triangular cross-fertilisation, as a guiding principal of anti-racist thought.

It may be interesting to consider how a return to internationalist ideals may be achievable in the present-day context in which increasingly, progressive politics are being informed by international dialoguing. While, as I shall show in Chapter 5, the new 'movement of movements' has so far demonstrated a problematic relationship to racism and anti-racism, tending to mirror much of the paternalism of anti-racisms past, it is constantly evolving in this regard. Many of the ways in which the Global Justice Movement works with the usefulness of applying learning from other contexts to the local level is mirrored in the profound effect that Europe had on black intellectuals over the course of the twentieth century. For example, Small (1994) refers to several black American leaders, such as Frederick Douglass and Booker T. Washington, who visited Britain, remarking that 'historically, Blacks and whites went to England to learn lessons and gain experience about "racialised relations"' (ibid.:2). Similarly, Gilroy (1993) examines the influences of British, American, African and Caribbean cultures upon the construction of contemporary western black culture(s), seeing them as fluid sites of anti-racist resistance.

W.E.B. Du Bois, James Baldwin, Richard Wright, C.L.R. James and Paul Robeson were, each in their own way, fundamental to the understandings of racism developed in the West. Each moved between the US and Europe and, in the specific cases of Du Bois, James and Robeson, intervened in Africa and/or the Caribbean, contributing to the internationalisation of the struggle against racism and colonialism. In each case, the particular lived experience of racism in the US, as citizens or passers-through, had a profound impact upon their interpretation of racism in either the colonial, the post-colonial or the European context. The analysis contributed by these authors was often sharpened by the particular acuteness and directly obvious nature of racism in the US, in contrast to its often more subtle dimensions in the Europe of the post-war period. Indeed, the US, in the period of anti-colonial resistance of the 1950s and 1960s, often acted as a conveyor for the interpretations of colonialism that could not be heard in the European metropolises.

It is striking to note, for example, that Frantz Fanon's analysis of racism in the colonial context in *The Wretched of the Earth* became a key text, not for the French under whose domination he wrote, but, beyond the colonised world, for the American proponents of Black Power. It is only through their adoption of Fanon's thesis, upon the translation of *The Wretched of the Earth* in 1965 (Macey 2000), that his work was returned to Europe through the influence of Black Power upon British self-organised anti-racism. The neglect of Fanon's memory in France highlights the importance of this work of translation afforded by the US. Europe itself is often too close to colonialism and to the *Shoah* to come to terms with its own racism. As Macey (ibid.:15) notes, 'Fanon had been forgotten because France wanted to forget something else, namely a war in Algeria that lasted for eight years.' It is due to the fact that it had such resonance for US readers that Fanon's work became 'one of the classics of decolonisation' (ibid.:17).

Finally, a consideration of the potential interconnections between the US and Europe in thinking about racism and anti-racism is of particular importance in the current political climate. The gradual spread of a global social movement, comprising diverse components of progressive politics, is a reaction to a concomitant consolidation at world level both of economic processes and of strategies of state power. In this climate, multiculturalism and identity politics, previously seen by many as emancipatory, are now being challenged as viable means of coping with racialised oppression. In Europe, the breakdown into a variety of individualised campaigns for the recognition of individual communal identities is often criticised as a North American import which denies anti-racism access to the mainstream (cf. Taguieff 1992). More importantly, identity politics may be critiqued for confining groups to reified communities and denying the possibility of interethnic alliance as well as of a structural analysis of racism which eschews the pull of racial authenticity and separation.

The interviews carried out with anti-racist activists in four European settings, on which this book is based, demonstrate the extent to which these protagonists have developed a significant analysis of the limitations of identity politics. All place significant emphasis on the importance of alliance building. In consideration of the influence of the new global movement upon North American social-movement politics since 1999, the discussion of the drawbacks of the identity model for resisting racism in Europe may go towards informing the US debate. If it is increasingly being recognised that the struggles of Latino migrant workers for just treatment in California, for example, is inextricably linked to the campaign for globalisation from below, so too must it be increasingly clear that anti-racist politics may no longer be thought of as divisible by community.

The immediacy of the challenges facing progressive social movements including anti-racism in the current political situation is exemplified most clearly by the case of Islamophobia. The effects of the global 'war on terrorism' at the local level is the targeting of Muslim populations in the West as guilty by association for the crimes of the eleventh of September and Middle Eastern suicide bombings (Said 2002). In the US, under multicultural arrangements, the obvious difference of veil-wearing Muslim women for example has, until recently, not provoked any particular reaction. The vehemence towards ordinary Muslims residing in the United States as a consequence of the causal relationship drawn between terrorism and Islam, described in civilisational terms, by the state has, therefore, engendered a sudden concern with Muslim dress practices. The recent case of a Florida woman denied a driver's licence because she refused to remove her veil for the official photograph demonstrates the change in American opinion on the place of Islam in the public sphere. Before the 9/11 attacks, the woman held a driver's licence that pictured her wearing the veil.

Debates on similar cases have recently arisen once again in France but have been a staple of discussions on racism and the perceived dangers of multiculturalism there since the early 1990s. Whereas in France, the outlawing of the veil in official public spaces, such as schools, is linked to the historical centrality of secularism to French public political culture, in the US Islam is increasingly being opposed to Christianity in a crusading discourse of civilisation versus savagery. Therefore, the responses formulated by anti-racist groups in the French context, while necessarily different, are informative for US activists confronting the problem for the first time. Indeed, the variety of reactions to Islamophobia across European settings is exemplary of the need for increased dialogue between anti-racisms at a global level which takes into account the growing consolidation of state action in response to what is being constructed as an Islamic 'problem'.

As Balibar (2003) has pointed out, since the election of the Bush administration in the US there has been a call from the US addressed towards so-called European intellectuals to formulate an alternative to the political project being put into action by the American regime and which is increasingly stifling dissent. Balibar surmises that the opposition constructed between the US and Europe by these thinkers is a false one. Today, he writes, 'undoubtedly Europe and America are not separated spaces, any more than Europe and Eurasia, or Europe and the Middle East' (ibid.:23). In this spirit, it is important to note that encouraging an engagement with racism and anti-racism in Europe is not intended to imply that the European setting holds solutions to the specific problems faced in the North American context. Rather, continuous cross-readings may enable the discussions already begun with the global movement to be extended to the realm of anti-racism, a domain which, due to the acuteness of its localisation, has become increasingly removed from the principles of internationalism. Opening a debate between Europe and the US with regard to the lacunae in the way in which racism and anti-racism are approached by both scholars and activists may be a step towards reinvigorating the themes of alliance and delocalisation that were central to the protagonists on whose work this book is based.

THE INTERPRETATIVE CAPACITY OF ANTI-RACISM

Anti-racism, in its variety of forms, is interpreted in this study according to a historically contextualised methodology that gradually reveals the development of its internal diversity. These differences take in a number of political and experiential factors that help to position anti-racism vis-à-vis public political culture. The hierarchisation of discourses to which this diversification may also give rise reveals the importance of temporality and political location in determining the variable ability of competing anti-racist discourses to assert the dominance of their position. The success of anti-racist discourse is often judged internally by its ability to institute the interpretations of 'race' and racism that it offers. As Chapter 2 reveals, an anti-racist perspective in both scholarship and in the collective action of organisations has determined conflicting explanations of racism that continue to emphasise profoundly different reasons for the persistence of racism in European society. The construction of an anti-racist approach to scholarship in the fields of 'race relations' or 'ethnicity and racism studies', as it has variably been known (Barot and Bird 2001), has had an important influence over the language used to write and speak about 'race' today. Rather than using them indiscriminately, the concepts constructed by an anti-racist approach to the study of 'race' and racism need, as several authors suggest (Gilroy 1998, 2000; Varikas 1998; Barot and Bird 2001) to be problematised and contextualised.

It is today acceptable to consider that the majority of studies carried out into racist discrimination, 'ethnic identities' or 'multicultural societies' are done so in an anti-racist perspective. The willingness to prescribe solutions for, or at least to question, the continued relevance of what are perceived as 'race' differences and their resultant inequalities shapes research carried out in a number of social scientific fields. Since at least the inter-war period, this work has generated the conceptual tools of the trade used by writers on 'race', 'ethnicity' and racism. Nevertheless, these very terms cannot be used unproblematically and, to a great extent, continue to have currency because of the inability of researchers to finitely agree on their renunciation. Two main introductory points can be made about the use of such terminology in this study. The first regards the usefulness of the term 'race' itself and its relationship to the concept of racialisation, that appears to many contemporary scholars to much more succinctly describe the processes involved in the naming of groups and individuals as Other. Secondly, the problematisation of such concepts has rarely been carried out in an international or multilingual context. The reliance in this study on four national arenas and three different languages necessitates an awareness, particularly for the writer in English, of the very different reception of this vocabulary across academic publics and linguistic divides.

The persistence of the term 'race' as explanatory of the 'lived experience of many people' (Barot and Bird 2001:601) is based upon the unwillingness of a scholarly anti-racism to undermine what is perceived to be the feeling of belonging that 'race' still evokes. The unproblematic way in which 'race' is referred to in American popular and academic speech is proof of the completeness with which racial categories have become embedded in daily discourse long after the official refutation of the existence of actual human 'races' (UNESCO 1968). For many, this is confused with the idea that what has been disproved is the superiority of some 'races' over others. The success of the relativist dictum has paradoxically permitted the continued use of 'race' as a descriptive signifier. For example Patricia Williams's discussion of the problems of colour-blindness calls for a problematisation of whiteness but confuses this as a problem of 'race' by referring to the ' "exnomination" of whiteness as racial identity' (Williams 1997:7):

> Whiteness is unnamed, suppressed, beyond the realm of race. Exnomination permits whites to entertain the notion that race lives 'over there' on the other side of the tracks, in black bodies and inner-city neighbourhoods, in a dark netherworld where whites are not involved.

While Williams's analysis of US black–white divides rings poignantly true, her 'racialisation' of whiteness refuses the historical point that 'race' indeed only concerns the Other because, as Fanon reminds us, 'not only must the black man be black; he must be black in relation to the white man' (Fanon 1967:110): 'Race', rather than a colour-coded fact, ignored by some and accepted by others, is an imposition born of domination. Although the situation is rather different in Europe, 'race' has not disappeared from the scholarly vocabulary for mainly anti-racist reasons. Many writers are unprepared to give up 'race' because of the origins of its contemporary use in a stance of pragmatism or negritude that informed the emergence of black political consciousness following the anti-colonial critique.

In contrast, Gilroy (1998, 2000) has proclaimed that ' "race" ends here', or in other words that despite its past value in reappropriating the language of oppression, the term has been stripped of all interpretative capacity under present conditions. Gilroy bases his argument upon the importance of contemporary developments in technology which create 'new histories of visuality and perception' (Gilroy 1998:839) and radically transform notions of 'absolute identity' from which new and competing subjectivities emerge.

Gilroy (2000) discusses the meaning of Fanon's notion of 'epidermilisation' as the means by which racial identities are entrapped within the skin. Simplistic interpretations of Fanon's writings on the black colonial experience have led to an adoption of a ' "race"-entrenching pragmatism' (ibid.:42) that deny even those who seek to stamp out racism the ability to overcome 'race' thinking. Gilroy's argument is that to insist on the primacy of such epidermal identities, in other words to accept the eternal relevance of the racial markers of difference invented by racial pseudo-scientists, is to fail to recognise the profound changes that the western view of 'race' has undergone.

The biotechnological innovations Gilroy explores are metaphors for the more generalised perspective on racial difference as altogether more profound than skin-deep. To understand the contradictions that allow for the persistence of racism alongside the possibility of popular images of blackness as a 'vital prestige' (Gilroy 1998:844), Gilroy introduces the concept of 'raciology', 'the lore that brings the virtual realities of "race" to dismal and destructive life' (Gilroy 2000:11). The history of the complicity with the colonialist 'race state' that is implicit in Gilroy's use of the term points to the depoliticisation of analyses and responses which he proposes the continued insistence on 'race' has engendered. By accepting the terms of definition imposed by racism, anti-racist scholarship limits the scope of its critique. In response, Gilroy (1998:839) suggests that 'the proposed renunciation of "race" might also represent a reactivation of political sensibilities in a field from which politics has been banished, and where the easy invocation of 'race' is a regular confirmation of the retreat of the political.'

In this light, where 'race' is used in this work it refers to its persistence as an explanatory term within much anti-racist discourse, rather than in acceptance of its potential political utility. Where the term 'minority ethnic' is applied to the description of groups of non-national origin in European societies, it is used in recognition of the historical anti-racist project to replace 'race' with 'ethnicity' as a non-hierarchical means of describing difference (Anthias 2002). The ease with which ethnicity is employed in unique reference to the Other requires problematisation in light of this process of historical construction in which the racialised themselves generally played no role.

Gilroy's raciology is a useful concept that blends together the idea of the continuing pervasion of 'race' as an accepted identity and that of racialisation as a process of domination. The term 'racialisation' is used in this work to denote the relationship of power involved in the assigning of inferiority and its codification using visual signifiers. While I accept the undeniable relationship to blackness that Fanon (1967) introduces in his connection of racialisation to epidermilisation, there is an undeniable racialisation of the Other which functions according to different perceptual codes, beyond those of the skin. Barot and Bird (2001) suggest that the current popularity of the term masks its historic usage by racial scientists, particularly in relation to its inverse, 'deracialisation', the possibility 'of the loss of the physical and cultural distinctiveness of races' (ibid.:604), which fascinated biologists and geneticists in the early twentieth century. Barot and Bird show that British sociologists of 'race relations' take up the term in neglect of this earlier history, as an attempt to side-step 'race' as a politically problematic and mythical concept: 'racialisation is reintroduced into sociology as a more *useful* term' (ibid.:606; italics in original). They do not reject this utility, but caution us to be aware of its very different origins in either mainstream writings, represented by British students of 'race relations' such as Banton and Miles, and in those of the periphery, notably Fanon.

While the earlier history of the term 'racialisation' may indeed have been masked, its contemporary usage consistently attributes its origins to Fanon. However, Barot and Bird suggest that neither Banton nor Miles endows racialisation with the epidermal or corporeal meaning in Fanon. On the contrary, unable to break with the centrality of 'race' as a general organising principle, they suggest that racialisation is a process that affects both self and other. Indeed, Miles sees the process as a dialectical one in which individuals are biologically assigned to a racialised category. As Barot and Bird rightly point out, describing racialisation as dialectical would assume that racism and production mutually structure each other, leading to both 'a largely redundant idea of racialisation and a form of class reductionism' (ibid.:611). In contrast, Fanon's use of racialisation implies both a resistance to it, including the recourse to violence he advocates in *The Wretched of the Earth* (1963), and its centring on the body, and therefore on the direct experience of being racialised. Fanon's relationship of racialisation to lived experience negates its use, by those who Barot and Bird think of as sociologists at the 'centre', to think about racism in abstracted terms that ignore the physical violence that in reality it often entails.

Nonetheless, in that the use by sociologists of the concept of racialisation represents an attempt to emancipate the discipline from that
of 'race', Barot and Bird consider that it has not altogether succeeded. As they precipitously point out, ' "race", or whatever term
we use – takes on a spurious concreteness and validity which it does
not really have and the common experiences of those who are
racially oppressed seem to disappear from view' (ibid.:616).

Caution as to the use of terminology has, despite these problems,
been consistently proposed by students of racism and racialisation
in the Anglo-American literature. The attempt in this work to
develop a thesis of European anti-racism, requires a brief look at
these problems beyond their use in the English language. The term
'racialisation' has been introduced into France by Balibar (1991) and
has entered into scholarly usage also in Italy (Zincone 1994). Yet,
particularly in French, a different relationship to the terms 'race',
'ethnicity' and racism has been constructed that requires attention
when writing in English, yet in a wider European perspective. Two
main problems may be observed. Firstly, as Varikas (1998) makes
clear, there is a reticence to use the word 'race' in France borne out
of a mistrust of 'the Anglo-American studies that make use of this
category' (ibid.:91). Instead, inverted commas are used around the
word 'race' when it cannot be avoided, not as a means of recognising its 'important role in popular thinking' (Barot and Bird
2001:613), but as a means of designating its interpretative empti-
ness. Varikas points out two paradoxes in this that draw on international examples but are aimed at motivating a debate in France.
French studies of racism and discrimination are often couched in
the language of 'migration' or 'ethnic relations' (Simon-Barouh and
De Rudder 1999). They are often carried out in an ethnological
perspective that, by concentrating on micro-level analyses, often
results in the depoliticisation of their findings.

For Varikas, the tendency to replace 'race' with 'ethnicity', as a
less politically problematic term, ignores the historical fact that the
two were developed together. The root of the term 'ethnicity' is the
word 'ethnic' which designates 'anatomical characteristics' (Varikas
1998:91) and was originally associated with the adjective 'racial'.
The scientific status attributed to 'ethnicity' as a replacement for
'race' contributes to the neglect of the persistence of racism in contemporary society. The second paradox Varikas points to refers to
the claiming of the term 'race' by black scholars in a deliberately
provocative effort to refute biologically or genetically essentialist

explanations of difference. This was not the case of 'ethnicity', which remained a western conceptualisation. The use of 'race' in this way constitutes a naming of oppression and a reclaiming of its signifiers, in the pragmatic vision which Gilroy now calls upon us to reject.

The interest in Varikas's article, which in Anglo-American terms reintroduces old arguments, is the fact that is written in the French context. In particular, the preference for the term 'ethnicity' is critiqued, not in order to replace it with pragmatic 'race', but to demonstrate that it has been unilaterally applied to those of non-French origin. As Varikas makes clear, although formal definitions apply to French ethnicity, those of so-called 'French stock' 'are not perceived or treated as an ethnie in France, whereas French Muslims or those of Maghrebi origin are' (Varikas 1998:94). The reluctance to recognise these inconsistencies arises from what is referred to, often with pride, as the 'French exception'. According to Varikas, the fact that the terms of her discussion are widely unknown or unacknowledged in French academia is not because they lack relevance to French history, but paradoxically because of the very pertinence to France's 'colonial crimes and its responsibility for the genocide of the Jews and Gypsies' (ibid.:97). The dominant mode in French scholarship may only treat these histories by concomitantly proclaiming the superiority of France's national culture over imported 'Anglo-Saxon' references from unrecognised disciplines such as women's or black studies. Critiquing Jacques Julliard's rejection of 'American style feminism' (ibid.:97), Varikas reminds us that,

> his 'argumentation' testifies to an approach to difference which is all the more widespread and persistent in the social sciences because it is the expression of a cultural particularism with universal pretensions: the expression of an 'ethnicity' that does not name itself as such.
>
> (ibid.:97)

The second problem of categorisation that applies to such a multinational study emerges, again in France, from the differential use of the term 'racism'. It refers to the tendency to construct a wide-berthed popular and academic usage of the term to cover a range of discriminatory phenomena. Racism becomes a catch-all concept that is deracinated from the racialisation process and becomes a euphemism for all forms of oppression, real or imagined. Therefore, Wieviorka (1997) calls our attention to the use of formulations such as 'anti-youth' or 'anti-worker' racism. More recently, an important change in the use of racism in this way by the Left was influenced by its adaptation by the far Right. Right-wing discourse often refers to 'anti-French racism' in order to propose that the indigenous majority ethnicity is threatened by the presence of the incompatible cultures of non-French immigrants. This shift has led to a parallel tendency in progressive discourse to replace the overused concept of 'racism' with the euphemistic notion of 'discrimination'. An unwillingness to refer to racism because of a fear of the Right's retort that 'reverse racism' has inverted black–white antagonisms leads to the proposition of 'discrimination' as an equalising discourse that brings all sufferings to the same level, and at once disconnects them from their historical origins.

WRITING A SOCIOLOGY OF ANTI-RACISM

The material on which this book is based has been gathered from a range of sources. These include, most importantly, the interviews with anti-racist actors, but also the documentation produced by organisations, including leaflets, magazines, newsletters, reports, posters and websites, in addition to the scholarly literature. This material will be used together throughout in order to reconstruct the discourse of anti-racism and reveal the means through which it is represented by its protagonists.

The central component of the research process involved interviews with anti-racist activists in Britain, France, Italy and Ireland carried out between November 1999 and September 2001. Twenty-seven organisations were interviewed for the study (see list in the front matter of the book). I did not attempt to secure an equal number of interviewees for each national setting. This is undeniably because of the longevity of anti-racism in France and Britain as opposed to Italy and Ireland, which therefore represented smaller 'samples'. Furthermore, I restricted the number of organisations, rather than choosing to do more and shorter interviews, because of a qualitative focus that prioritises the utility of the information generated by the research over its ability to represent the whole spectrum of anti-racism in any given context. Although the ability of the organisations selected to provide an overview of the anti-racist arena in each national setting was considered important, I did not attempt to cover the gamut of anti-racism in each country. This was based on a considered decision to focus on associations, rather than on government bodies or state-run projects.

The interviews were open-ended and did not therefore rely on prearranged questions. Nonetheless, four broad themes were established before beginning the research process which covered my central preoccupations. These were:

- Representation: To what extent did activists consider it important that anti-racism be represented by the actual or potential victims of racism?
- Alliance: How important is it for anti-racist organisations to establish links with those involved in similar activities in order to construct a movement?
- The European or international dimension: Do activists evaluate their work as belonging to a wider European or global movement with consequences beyond the local or national level? To what extent is this a practical possibility?
- The institutional relationship: Do anti-racists believe that they have a right to state funding and to participate in state-run anti-racist initiatives at local, national and international levels or do they believe that doing so would jeopardise their independence vis-à-vis the state's institutions?

These four areas of interest are reflected in my discussion of contemporary anti-racism in Chapter 5, revealing that they were indeed of central concern to almost all interviewees. The interview was initiated by a general question on the origins of the organisations. The activists were asked to 'tell the story' of their organisation. This often meant going back to before the interviewee's own involvement, meaning that the narrative became much more one of anti-racism as a form of collective action, as demonstrated by the specific history of a given organisation, than the personal story of the individual activist. The extent to which a discussion of the various elements of public political culture with which anti-racism intersects emerged in activists' own discourse testifies to the utility of this concept. A variety of interpretations of public political culture were offered and constitute the discussion in Chapters 4 and 5.

The knowledge produced in the research process allows anti-racism to be conceptualised as a set of discourses that, far from existing only for themselves, are a window on a wholly more complex range of political processes. The construction of the research object in relation to the theorisation of the anti-racist continuum of proximity-to-distance from the public political culture of the nation-state demonstrated how much anti-racism reveals about the state and political processes more generally. The positioning of the various anti-racist discourses vis-à-vis an interpretation of European public political cultures showed how the ideologies that politically structure our lives as citizens take on wholly different meanings in relation to the degree of inclusion or exclusion which groups and individuals enjoy in the polity. The extent to which the state, represented by its public political culture, is seen as benevolent or oppressive and the impact that these differential interpretations have on anti-racist praxes is fundamental to a complete understanding of anti-racism.

Interpreting the research

The transcribed interviews were interpreted according to the main criteria identified in the research process: the relationship to issues of representation, institutional relations, alliance building and international activity. Particular attention was paid to the way in which public political culture was represented or negated in this discourse, often witnessed in the way interviewees spoke about the 'state', national histories or the importance of memory and education. This is particularly evident in Chapter 4's analysis of contemporary anti-racist representations of public political culture. The information generated by each of the interviews was subdivided into individual passages that referred to the main areas of concern prioritised in this work. This enabled the use of the interview material as text, rather than as purely the speech of individual anti-racist activists.

I chose to focus interpretatively on the power of these activists to generate anti-racist discourse. The text of their speech is used alongside a reading of secondary documentary sources, produced both by anti-racist organisations themselves and in the academic literature. The discourse constructed by the interviews is used in different ways throughout the book, either to tell anti-racism's story, as is emphatically the case in Chapter 3, on the construction of anti-racism in each of the study's four national settings, or in the theorisation of the continuum of proximity-to-distance from the public political culture of the nation-state. This is interpreted in a variety of ways throughout Chapters 2, 3, 4 and 5 in which citations from the interviews are juxtaposed with references to the relevant literature in the effort to build an empirically grounded account that may inform the theorisation of anti-racism that I propose.

The discourse produced by the anti-racists interviewed for this work is interpreted as a 'collective story' that, taken as a whole, relates the complexities of European anti-racism and helps to focus its internal heterogeneity, where before the picture remained grainy. What is afforded by this approach is an emphasis on the importance of activists' own words, not only as subjects, but as agents in the production of an anti-racist discourse that takes on a relevance beyond the domain of the single anti-racist group. The sophistication of much of this discourse reveals a level of self-examination and political analysis, the absence of which in previous research represents a critical lack. The tendency of anti-racist scholars to neglect the historical origins and contemporary meanings of that anti-racism has meant that its theorisation has occurred in the absence of a grounding in research. This study attempts to counterbalance this lack and to reveal the discursive capacities of anti-racism as a means through which several central questions about the nature of 'multi-racist' societies (Cohen and Bains 1988) may begin to be answered.

1
'Race and State': European Modernity and the Political Idea of 'Race'

The knowledge of man has come to grief.

Eric Voegelin (1933b)

Reading the history of racism correctly means also pondering the history of Europe with which it is so closely intertwined. Too often racism has been brushed aside as unworthy of serious study, as a simple and naïve world view that can be laid to rest, a mistaken faith, while historians turn to more sophisticated and fascinating subject matter. Yet to exorcise this evil, no occult powers are required, but merely to integrate the study of racism within our study of the modern history of Europe. We must never neglect to seek the whereabouts of the scavenger until we have stripped his disguise and found him – even where there seemed to be only virtue, goodness and truth.

George Mosse (1978:236)

The ambivalence characterising the development of European political ideas in the period thought of as modernity – principally that since the Enlightenment – shapes our understandings of the wholly modern notion of 'race'. The ambiguity of a modernity, at once liberating and repressive that is disguised by the efficiency of discourses of science and rationality, has often resulted in the dismissal of racism as phantasmic or as a behaviour born of individual prejudice. The psychologisation of racism, as much on the level of common sense as on the intellectual plane, has hindered explications that root it, rather, in the history of European political thought. The persistence of racism beyond the *Shoah* and the official refutation of 'race', for many, beg analyses of racism as perennial, or even primordial. In such thought, even state policies are reduced to the actions of individual governments and, therefore, considered in purely behavioural terms. An anti-racism that seeks to relate racist practices to the disciplinary constitution of modern states, by means particularly of an emphasis on violence and institutionalised discrimination, is often thwarted by a depoliticised discourse that culturalises, psychologises and individualises them so as to relegate them to the societal margins. Policies created to combat racism during the post-war era in Europe, most notably both the assimilatory and the multicultural models, as well as much of the anti-racism of progressive social movements, have contributed to the development of a view of racism as disconnected from public political culture if not also the practices of the democratic state.

What follows intends to lay the ground for one of the central propositions of this book: that a constitutive force in the development of anti-racist discourse and praxis, mainly in the aftermath of the *Shoah*, fails to historicise the interrelationships between the consolidation of the political idea of 'race' and the exigencies of the modern European nation-state. Such a failure engenders both the diversity and the disunities that characterise anti-racism and, more critically if only partially, the inability to curb the endurance of racism in Europe.

If anti-racism may be shown, through this research, to exist along a continuum of proximity-to-distance from the public political culture of the nation-state, what is the relationship between such a conceptualisation and anti-racism's understanding of 'race'? By offering an analysis of racism that separates between the phenomenon and the evolution of the idea of 'race' 'within the field of nationalism' (Balibar 1991a:37), an anti-racism that sees its discourse as compatible with public political culture fails to unveil the utility of racism for the consolidation of state power. On the other hand, the tendency of some anti-racisms to reduce racism to nationalism or vice versa complicates efforts to elucidate precisely the interaction between racism as a modern political project and the European nation-state. Moreover, it strengthens the argument of those who would portray racism as irrational and, as a consequence, irreconcilable with state practices that, it is commonly agreed, are increasingly constituted in terms of rationality with the progression of modernity. In contrast, it is vital to specify the ways in which 'race' and state, by the end of the nineteenth century, become mutually dependent and by what means elements of this interrelationship have continued to determine the perseverance of racism as an everyday reality of European societies. An historicisation of these linkages points up the failure of some forms of anti-racism to engage with them in the formulation of their discourses and lays the foundation for the theorisation of anti-racism's diversity as determinable by the degree to which it contains a critique of the nation-state.

In order to locate *what* precisely post-war anti-racist discourse fails to address, this chapter develops an historically grounded theorisation of what, by the end of the nineteenth century in western Europe, may be thought of as the embeddedness of a language of 'race' in that of politics (Hannaford 1996) and resultant state-sanctioned practices. It does so, firstly, by offering a general theory of the rise of the political idea of 'race' as an important tool in the consolidation of the nationalist project. Two central directions taken towards the achievement of this ever-closer relationship are elucidated.

Firstly, I argue that the acceptance of 'race' as a fundamental organisational principle of national societies by the end of the nineteenth century is related to the growing reliance on the internal rationalisation of populations and, in a second step, the external fortification of the nation-states in which they lived. This was governed, on the one hand, by the perceived threat of external defeat in international war, often conceived of as wars between 'races', and on the other, by the fear of the internal degeneration of the national population, again seen to constitute a distinct 'race'. While the obsession with Social Darwinist 'race' strengthening initially targeted the 'inferior' working classes, the increased pace of the imperialist project and the beginning of immigration on a significant level at the turn of the century shifted the focus onto the non-national Other. The passage from fear, stoked by political opportunism, to the introduction of policy, particularly in the realms of social welfare and immigration, reveals the extent to which 'race' was central to the development of methods for the organisation of modern state and society. Secondly, the ability of 'race' to take hold precisely within the democratic nation-states of western Europe indicates the ambivalence of the modern political project. It is because of the possibility of egalitarianism, proffered by the revolutionary ideal of universalism, that racialisation becomes a viable political tool. Both the emancipation of the European Jews and the anti-slavery of the Enlightenment radicals brought with them a concomitant drive to uniformisation that, paradoxically, made more obvious the differences between human groups previously kept apart. The persistence of domination, this time under the guise of assimilation or the 'mission of civilisation', created the conditions for the racialisation of Jews or blacks that, despite initial intentions to the contrary, focused on hierarchies of progress that, due to the primacy of scientific rationalisation, saw the concept of 'race' as the principal reason for their existence.

I have chosen in this chapter to focus on an anti-racist interpretation of the rise of 'race' and modern racism in Europe, and so uniquely on the work of authors writing against racism rather than on the original production of racist thought itself. It therefore does not attempt, in the manner of the intellectual historian or political theorist, to reveal the purported racism of the philosophers or political thinkers of the eighteenth and nineteenth centuries, nor go back to the texts of racial science. On the contrary, by examining the works of several writers, from a variety of intellectual traditions, it is possible to reconstruct an anti-racist account of racism that links its growth to the demands of a modernising nation-state. To this end, I shall draw upon authors who have rarely been considered together. This intermixture of accounts which nonetheless reveals a high degree of concordance between the various authors, attempts to unite the numerous strands of anti-racist thought for the construction of a uniquely anti-racist theorisation of 'race' that also highlights the need for a reconsideration of the lacunae between anti-racist discourse and an historicisation of 'race'. Furthermore, the diverse backgrounds of these authors assists in the formulation of a theoretical-historical view of western Europe, beyond the specificities of individual states, as the main locus for the development of modern racism.[1] This will form the basis for a critique of the widespread understanding of racism as an aberration of the European norm of democracy rather than as a foundational moment in its development.

'RACE' AND RACISM, NATION AND STATE

[R]ace is not simply a peculiarity of certain nations; it is a phenomenon of expansive nations and the emotional borderlines set by the laws that define and constitute nations. People were turned into races when nations extended and defined their political hegemony through conquest and expropriation. Race and nation were born and raised together; they are the Siamese twins of modernity.

Philip Yale Nicholson (1999:7)

The title of this part of the chapter, which sets out a general theorisation of the incremental embedding of the political idea of 'race' in the western European nation-state, is cognisant of the potential conflict between a focus on either nation or on state in discussions of 'race' and racism. While the distinction should not be overplayed, the choice of different authors to prioritise nationalism as a political movement over the modern nation-state per se in their analyses of the relationship to racism reveals important varieties in approach. Most significantly, such differences point to authors' variable willingness to concretise a relationship between nationalist ideology and the nation-state and, as a further step, racism.

In the work of Eric Voegelin (1933a, 1940), 'race' is described as a 'body idea' central to the construction of political communities since well before the birth of the nation-state. While Voegelin's interpretation of the idea of 'race' as crucial for the understanding of modern political ideas as they inform the actions of states serves as a vital framework for an account of the growing reliance of state logics upon 'race', it may be unable to wholly explain why it is only with the consolidation of the nation-state that racism flourishes. A further possibility is extended by Etienne Balibar (1991a). Although entitling his chapter on the subject 'Racism and Nationalism', Balibar overcomes the problematic sharpness of the distinction between nationalism and the nation-state in other writings by pointing out the futility of such a separation. Balibar makes it clear that, due to their invented nature, nation-states may not be based on the common ethnic origins of their populations. Therefore, nationalism may only be ethnocentric to the extent that it fabricates a mythical ethnicity which is compared with the equally fictitious character of other nations. In other words, nationalism is a tool of the state and it is only in this relationship that racism joins with nationalism. Such a state-centred account is capable of considering the role played by nationalism by shedding light on the relationship of reciprocity it constructs with racism, not as an independent movement but as a structuring ideology of the nation-state.

The theorisations of Voegelin and Balibar provide stronger arguments for linking racism to nationalism, both propelled by the state. Voegelin in particular makes a strong case for the separation of the theorisation of 'race' as a scientific concept from 'race' as an idea and political symbol. The greater emphasis placed on the political utility of 'race' signals Voegelin's refusal to engage with the proposition of racism as a science. In other words, 'race' should be contradicted on political rather than on the scientific grounds being addressed by his contemporaries (mainly anthropologists and biologists). Voegelin's work *Race and State* (1933a) is therefore a very early example of a work of political anti-racism that rejects the very possibility of critiquing 'race' as science and is therefore, at least in the European context, several decades ahead of its time.[2]

The political idea of 'race' is one of a set of so-called body ideas and, therefore, 'one of the elements producing political communities' (Voegelin 1933a:1). While the 'race' idea is a well-ordered system of political dogmas with real life application in National Socialism, the 'race' concept has no bearing on reality, in Voegelin's terms. This is not to say that Voegelin did not consider that scientific racism directly informs the political idea of 'race'. His invocation of 'real' ideas as opposed to 'false' concepts needs to be assessed within the context of the time of writing, when racial theories were widely accepted to be scientifically viable, a situation which necessitated a clear statement of the socially constructed nature of scientific racial categories. Voegelin's *Race and State* is a work stemming from a larger project on the 'theory of the state', a discussion of the significance of body ideas to the construction of polities. Body ideas are defined as 'any symbol which integrates a group into a substantial whole through the assertion that its members are of common origin' (Voegelin 1940:286).

Voegelin prioritises the 'race' idea as central for the development of a theory of the state. The 'race' idea is emphasised not because of his interest in it as such, but because of what an examination of 'race' may tell us about the state. The 'race' idea is separated completely from its concept in order to show that 'race' is not a unique notion emerging from the 'findings' of racial scientists. It is, firstly, one of many body ideas. Secondly, although modern in terms of its political formulation, its development can be traced to two preceding body ideas, the Greek *polis* and the Mystical Body of Christ, formative of the emergence of contemporary European polities. Modern racism is related to gradual changes in the understanding of a variety of constitutive notions about the nature of human beings since Antiquity. That is not to say that racism, in the way that we understand it today, existed before the onset of modernity. Rather, Voegelin's point is that in these two ideas there are elements which can help elucidate why it is possible for an idea such as 'race' to later emerge.

Voegelin understands the theory of the state as primarily concerned with the problem of the 'justification of the phenomenon of
law' (1933a:3). Law is grounded on two experiences, that of the
individual and that of the community; the first moral, the second
universalising. Voegelin sees the laws pertaining to the community
(state) as being based on those grounded in the individual's experience. The laws governing the community comprise the problem
of the 'form' of the state. The state's form is made up of ideas, or
so-called models,

> in which the reality of the political community is built up for the
> members of the political community. These ideas are not a science of
> the state but an essential part of the reality of the state itself. The con-
> tents of these state ideas essentially originate in the fundamental
> human experiences already mentioned – they are ideas pertaining
> either to persons or to communities.
>
> (ibid.:4)

In other words, Voegelin sees the actions taken by the state as
being based on the vision created of the type of people that make
up its political community and the kind of moral experiences that
they, collectively, have had. This is the essence of the notion of
'body ideas' to which 'race' is central: 'person and community are
grounded essentially in the body, and therefore body ideas will
always share significantly in the structure of the reality of the state ...'
(Voegelin 1933a:5).

For Voegelin the 'race' idea is the most important of the body ideas
for 'any understanding of the modern world of political ideas'
(Voegelin 1933a:8). Moreover, a discussion of the idea of 'race' is of
particular importance at the time of the book's publication due to the
sense of the 'extraordinary' that it evoked for many people. The only
historical difference between 'race' and other body ideas is that it is
not purely a political idea but relies on scientific justification, thus
adding to the degree of myth building that puts it beyond the realm
of political or legal theorisation. Concretely, in order to prove the
importance of the 'race' idea to the self-vision of communities, which
he sees as grounding a theory of the state and informing the actions
of governments on behalf of polities, Voegelin traces the development of some of the core political theories of 'race'. His aim is to
highlight the extent to which thinking about humanity in terms of
racial categorisation becomes the norm in the nineteenth century.

He therefore contrasts the work of Klemm and Gobineau; the former a liberal democrat, the latter an aristocrat. Klemm saw racial divisions as playing a role in creating an equal society, the conquest of passive 'races' by the active (European) one bringing about a symbiosis that, through their amalgamation – compared to marriage between the strong man and the weak woman – brings about a unified, egalitarian society. In other words, during migrations, the smaller active 'race' subjugates the passive 'race' leading to the establishment of monarchical societies. However, interbreeding provokes the disappearance of the strong 'race' which, in turn, quells domination and brings about a societal uniformity. Klemm's antimonarchism led him to use a discourse of 'race' in the theorisation of a positive alternative to the view of 'races' as necessarily hierarchical. Gobineau, who also believed in the existence of two 'races', one weak and one strong, in contrast to Klemm, negatively perceived the disappearance of the strong 'race'. He saw the 'bastardisation' of the 'race' as ultimately leading to the downfall of the nation, because without the dominance of the strong 'race' over the symbiosis, the cultural values upon which the society depends disappear as, in turn, does the state within which the nation can no longer rule. The contrast between Klemm and Gobineau's positions marks, for Voegelin, the 'aporetic' structure of the 'race' idea and its ability both for great optimism as to the benefits of 'race' mixture and the deep pessimism that became politically dominant.

Beyond this ultimately crucial difference, Voegelin's interest is in showing the extent to which the notion of strong and weak, or passive and active, 'races' takes hold as a fundament of the theorisation of the emergence of modern nation-states. For example, Ratzel contrasts two tribes – one of agriculturalists, the other herdsmen and hunters – the meeting of which is at the origin of 'the established organisation of states and all higher civilisation' (Voegelin 1933a: 177). Herdsmen and hunters have the ability to build states which is lacking in agricultural tribes. So, when the former conquer the latter, 'a firm structure develops "because the conquering and cohesive force of the nomads here becomes wedded to the industry of the agricultural people, who by themselves do not form states" ' (ibid.:178; citing Ratzel 1887). Ratzel, a leading member of the radical right-wing Pan-German League, in 1901 developed the concept of *Lebensraum* in which the human struggle for existence so central to Darwinist thinking is reinterpreted as a 'struggle for space' that justifies colonial expansion as the natural entitlement of the strong 'races' (Lindqvist 1992). The point in these types of theories is that the rise of the state is determined by a natural process originating in pre-modern societies by which a strong group is destined to win over a weaker one and to shape the construction of the state as a vehicle for the power of the 'race'/nation.

The facility with which the 'race' idea becomes the dominant paradigm for a theory of the state – whether it is positively or negatively perceived – stems from the crucial changes in the writing of history brought about by the birth of the nation-state. This change was essential to Klemm, for whom the 'political orientation of history' (Voegelin 1933a:159) came, following the French and American revolutions, to dominate universal history so that, like theology at an earlier time, politics is now the 'subject everything else must serve' (ibid.). Klemm observed that this new epistemology of history saw each phase of politics as successively culminating in the 'perfection' embodied by the 'Fichtean idea of the German state' (ibid.). His personal rejection of history's political mission failed to overcome the fact that the nationalisation of history also created the conditions for the development of 'race' due to the split between a political history of the 'civilised peoples' (ibid.:160) and the ethnographical or anthropological sciences of the 'primitive' 'with whom the former kind of history could not really connect' (ibid.).

Voegelin offers us a clear view of how a social scientific fixation on 'race' is able to contribute to a functional theory of the state with the advent of nation. The replacement of theology with politics, which also enables the later shift to polygenesis, turns the purpose of history to the business of theoretically founding the 'race nation' (Hannaford 1996). The state is crucial in that it is only through nationalism's realisation through it that the concrete differences between nations and 'races' could be operationalised. With the strengthening of the western European nation-state, particularly following the stepping up of rampant imperial competition towards the end of the nineteenth century (MacMaster 2001), nations and 'races' within Europe become synonymous and further consolidate the embeddedness of 'race' in state.

The means by which 'race', via nationalism, becomes a central 'body idea' of the state is sharpened by Balibar's exposure of the interrelationships between nationalism, nation and racism. His view is based upon the proposal that modern racism emerges in societies that are considered egalitarian, a condition not of the state per se but of the 'modern (nationalist) nation-state' (Balibar 1991b:50). The equality purportedly assured by the nation-state is determined by political citizenship, and so by nationality. Therefore, Balibar fuses nationalism and nation by deconstructing the received notion that nationalism as an ideology may be opposed to the 'reality' of nation. Nations are indeed 'invented' (Hobsbawm and Ranger 1983), an historical process which is witnessed through the state's official use of nationalism which, in turn, creates racism in the modern sense. The relationship between official state nationalism and racism is one of 'reciprocal determination' in that it assists the national objective of imposing political and cultural unity over the population of the nation-state. Therefore, where groups could not be assimilated so as to be classified in nationally acceptable terms, racism intervened to oppress them 'as if the domination of a culture and a more or less fictively unified nationality ... over a hierarchically ordered diversity of "minority" ethnicities and cultures marked down for assimilation should be "compensated" and mirrored by the racialising persecution of an absolutely singular *pseudo-ethnic* group ...' (Balibar 1991b:52; emphasis in original). Racism as necessity was formulated in this way with regard to the Jews and was determinative of modern antisemitism.

Like Voegelin's focus on the effects of the 'race' idea on a theory of the state and the role played therein by the social sciences, history in particular, Balibar emphasises the utility of a perspective on the 'field of nationalism' in the analysis of modern racism. The examination of the 'historical articulation' (Balibar 1991a:50) of nationalism/nation to the state and the nation-state to racism in the modern era is crucial for a politicised theorisation of the idea of 'race'. A clear delineation of such relationships, which are not causal but reciprocal, is an important means of rejecting biological and psychological explanations of racism. In other words, locating racism within the history of the nation-state 'confirms, without doubt, that racism has nothing to do with objective biological "races" ' (ibid.:37). Furthermore, it demonstrates how the psychology of racism is itself explained in psychological (individual and behavioural) terms which reveal nothing of its political, and therefore non-naturalistic, origins. Finally, such a project rejects the attempts of some historians to place racism beyond the domain of nationalism in a view that purposefully neglects the importance of racist movements for the functioning of imperialism in particular. What a view of the reciprocal relationship between nationalism and racism as made possible by the apparatus of the nation-state offers us is not a simplistic argument that racism and nationalism are direct consequences of each other. On the contrary,

> [R]acism is not an 'expression' of nationalism, but a *supplement of nationalism* or more precisely *a supplement internal to nationalism*, always in excess of it, but always indispensable to its constitution and yet always insufficient to achieve its project, just as nationalism is both indispensable and always insufficient to achieve the formation of the *nation* or the project of a 'nationalisation' of society.
>
> Balibar (1991b:54; emphasis in original)

What Balibar stresses by rejecting any argument of inevitability or of causality is to leave open the possibility, important to any historicisation, that there may have been alternatives to the historical 'articulation' which made racism necessary to nationalism. Due not least to the demands of imperialism and its accompanying wars, as well as industrialisation, urbanisation and immigration, history reveals the undeniable mutuality of racism and the nation-state. For historical reasons therefore, the claim that this was the alternative that resulted from a potential variety of forms that the modern state may have taken deserves serious consideration. Such a project calls for a placing of 'race', as Voegelin and Balibar insist, in the realm of the political as it is expressed under the specific conditions of the modern European nation-state.

Science as a source of political justification

The positions of Voegelin and Balibar enable a politicised theorisation of modern racism which refuses analysis according to the terms established by 'race', namely those of 'science'. Due to its precocity, Voegelin's work is particularly important because it points out the mistaken nature of early anti-racism's refutation of 'race' on scientific grounds. By treating 'race' as a science to be disproven, the twentieth-century anti-racist scientists set themselves an easy task, as 'race' could indeed be shown to have no measurable basis. What is offered us by an analysis of the link between 'race' and state in modernity is a view of how the primacy of science – as opposed to metaphysics – from the Enlightenment on was increasingly posited in the legitimation of political practices, so creating the conditions for 'race' to emerge.

'Race', from its beginnings as an object of the new science of physical anthropology, gradually takes on a political meaning that is not the intention of its protagonists until at least the middle of the nineteenth century. Indeed, Hannaford (1996) separates the rise of the 'race' idea into three periods, beginning in 1684[3] and culminating in the so-called Golden Age of racism (1870–1914), an era which marks the emergence of the 'race state', the birth of modern antisemitism, rampant imperialism and the belief within politics, exemplified by Benjamin Disraeli, that 'race is everything; there is no other truth' (Hannaford 1996:352). These stages are characterised by the growing reliance of politics on a discourse of science that emerges from the methodological realignment, occurring during the first stage (1684–1815), that led to the replacement of theological and metaphysical depictions by 'a more logical description and classification that ordered humankind in terms of physiological and mental criteria based on observable "facts" and tested evidence' (ibid.:202).

Nevertheless, during this time, initial interest in the classification of human beings, motivated to a large extent by the increase in travel, was reconciled with a monogenetic outlook that continued to subordinate scientific discovery to the primacy of Creation. A shift to polygenesis is enabled by the advent of political Romanticism and the ideology of nationalism during the second period proposed by Hannaford, from 1815 to 1870. The growth of nationalism as a secular religion which promoted the essentialist character of particular communities replaced the religious tradition grounded upon the idea of human beings' common origins. The possibility for racism to emerge with the advent of nationalism, as a revolutionary project for the organisation of populations in the state, is indicative of 'race's' position at the cusp of a central tension in modernity. On the one hand, it is the novel interest in rationality and progress emerging with Enlightenment – as well as the possibilities bred by advances in technology – that engenders a scientific fascination with 'race' as a tool in the classification of different groups of people. On the other hand, the complete shift to a discourse of polygenetic racial hierarchy is only made possible with the concomitant rise of the idea of separate and unique nations that emerges from an anti-Enlightenment movement: political Romanticism.

We may see, therefore, how 'race' intervenes as a bridging device between the apparently oppositional tendencies of tradition and progress. Romanticism's rejection of the Enlightenment notion that 'reality was ordered in terms of universal, timeless, objective, unalterable laws which rational investigation could discover'

(Malik 1996:78), could not be developed without recourse to the epistemology enabled by this very principle. In other words, the notion that essential differences existed between peoples that compelled them to live apart as part of separate communities was precipitated by the idea, resulting from the 'investigations' of Enlightenment scientists, that the world was indeed racially ordered. From this only a short step was necessary from a monogenetic to a polygenetic position, the precursor to the belief in racial hierarchies. The primacy of polygenesis was brought about by the displacement of the religious perspective within nationalism which was in turn enabled by the previous questioning of the supremacy of religious explanations that accompanied the revolutionary era.[4]

The outcome of the intersection of Enlightenment methodologies and Romanticist ideology may be characterised by the 'timely' development of the 'race' idea. Nevertheless, modern racism, in the contemporary terms in which it is now thought of, is not a 'natural' progression of the shift from universalism to nationalism. A marriage of science and politics is necessary in order to bring racism as 'itself a singular history' (Balibar 1991b:40) into being. In other words, because 'race' existed previously as an object of new scientific methodologies and later as a legitimatory discourse in the growth of nationalist ideas, following the mid-nineteenth century it could come to formulate its own theory: racism. This ability was fundamentally due to the emergence of Social Darwinism, an undeniable case of the complicity of scientific practices and political ends. The utility of Darwin's theory of human evolution to the project of nation-state building is encapsulated by the possibility it offers of conceiving of state and society – comparable to individual human beings – as organic entities following the laws of evolution.

The application of Darwinism to society by racial theorists such as de Lapouge and Galton in the latter half of the nineteenth century was enthusiastically received in political circles due to the growing international tensions between European states, due most importantly to the intensification of imperialist competition. This competition led to the quest, common to each of the leading western European states, for the 'integral nation' (MacMaster 2001) which would 'assure the external strength of the state in international conflict only through an internal cohesion based on racial purity' (ibid.:24). 'Race', as translated by the Social Darwinists, provides a useful analysis of both the challenge facing the nation, in international conflict and imperial conquest, and of the obstacles with which it was confronted due to the presence of 'inferior' peoples within its borders.

The malleability of the racist theory enables its use both as an underpinning of the nation's superiority and as a legitimate excuse for any failure which, it could be argued, remained inevitable as long as the 'race' was threatened by internal impurity. Undoubtedly, it is on the basis of such logic that modern political antisemitism evolved during the third phase of racism's development, following 1870. The efficiency of the amalgamation of science and politics epitomised by Social Darwinism, indeed the infusion of politics with a language of (scientific) 'race', laid the foundations for a reworking of the old religious scapegoating of the Jews into a scientifically grounded theory that ultimately justified their extermination. The linking of political antisemitism to the eugenicist project of purification that led to the *Shoah* could only have been considered possible due to the completeness with which politics had, by the beginning of the twentieth century, been subsumed under a discourse of 'race':

> From the middle of the nineteenth century all aspects of legal right, feeling, justice, treaty, compromise, settlement, conciliation, arbitration – the essential components of political society – were eclipsed, and then obliterated, by a doctrine of force that saw each matter primarily in terms of its natural evolutionary course. This doctrine would finally express itself in the language of biological necessity, managerial efficiency, and effectiveness in a science of eugenics.
>
> Hannaford (1996:276)

Hannaford argues that 'race thinking in its antisemitic form appeared when there was a fundamental collapse of political thinking' (Hannaford 1996:316). In other words, the success of what he calls the 'new, unhistorical concepts of the social realm' (ibid.) of the natural and social sciences in subjugating politics as it was developed under the antique state is what enables modern racism, the most appealing of these ideas, to take hold. In particular, Hannaford claims that of these notions, the two 'autonomous entities' (ibid.) of society and the commercial world compounded the decline of the political state. This hints at the importance of the internal rationalisation of societies, on the one hand, and the growing quest for imperial gains of unconstrained capitalism on the other, both of which are central directions taken in the application of racism by the turn of the twentieth century. In the following section, a theorisation of these dimensions shall be proposed as essential to the understanding of the embeddedness of 'race' in the modern nation-state.

INTERNAL RATIONALISATION/EXTERNAL FORTIFICATION

[T]he modern notion of race, in so far as it is invested in a discourse of contempt and discrimination and serves to split humanity up into a 'super-humanity' and a 'sub-humanity', did not initially have a national (or ethnic), but a class signification or rather (since the point is to represent the inequality of social classes as inequalities of nature) a caste signification … Thus it is clear that, from the very outset, racist representations of history stand in relation to the class struggle.

Etienne Balibar (1991c:208)

In the above quotation, Balibar further reveals the extent to which, preceding discussions of the relationship of racism to nationalism which as we have seen become crucial, 'race' must be seen to function within the logics of the state and capital. Modern racism begins to take shape as a tool for maintaining the status quo of aristocratic privilege increasingly threatened by 'proletarian revolt' (Balibar 1991c:206). It also serves as a justification for the subjugation of slaves in the colonies without whom the various imperial companies could not assure a maximum exploitation of the conquered territories. What may be observed therefore, is a shift in the use of 'race' from the unique classification of groups ('castes') as racially inferior, to one which created an analogy between 'race' and nation. In the first period, the racialised group often belonged to the national society, as was the case most notably with regard to the racialisation of the working classes that was developed in reaction to the spread of the notion of class struggle. In a second step, following 1900, racism was principally directed at the non-national Other (MacMaster 2001).

This shift was brought about by two interrelated moves; firstly, the upscaling of imperial competition sought legitimacy from a discourse of the European nation-states as 'races' competing for the control of the 'primitive' populations, and the resources of their lands. Secondly, the need for internal consolidation in international conflict and, in particular by the First World War, the requirement of a mass civilian army largely recruited from the working class, led to a shift from a discourse of the 'savage and animalistic "race within" of the common people' (MacMaster 2001:56) to a Social Imperialism which employed welfare nationalism to bring about the 'racial unity of all social classes' (ibid.). The emergence of modern political antisemitism at this time is not unrelated to this shift, as the image of the Jew as the internal cosmopolitan enemy of the nation could be mobilised in the effort of quelling the internationalisation of class conflict. The seemingly contradictory portrayal of Jews as both 'the key agents of capitalism (bankers, stock-market traders) as well as of revolutionary socialist organisations that sought to overturn capitalism' (ibid.:88) served to warn the working class of their subversion by a force which actually sought their exploitation.

Linking these two periods of the adaptation of racist discourse from the mid-nineteenth century on is the growing importance of the image of the black 'native' as a source of threat within the interior of European societies. The myth of a 'black peril', stoked by media accounts of the viciousness of the colonised peoples, particularly in Britain (MacMaster 2001), functioned firstly as a metaphor for the ' "race threat" offered by the working class' (ibid.:64). In parallel, the reaction of popular radicalism was to use the image of the black slave as a metaphor for the condition of the European worker. Later, the fascination of European publics for 'primitive societies', largely induced by the international fairs held since 1870 that exhibited black people captured in the colonies as subjects of curiosity, contributed to a confirmation of 'inherent white superiority' (ibid.:73) that united the classes. Beyond the presence of small pockets of black communities in Europe for several centuries, particularly in port towns, anti-black racism in the metropolis served metaphorically to compound society's preexistent 'race' fears rather than to redirect racist attitudes against black people per se. Indeed, as the image of the inferior, but also dangerous, African was used analogously to the threat posed to the 'race' by the 'underclasses', so too did it serve in the racialisation of the Jews as black. This is not to underplay the existence of widespread anti-black racism at this time nor to deny the crimes of colonialism, but to point out that, for the European societies which are our object, black people mainly remained abstract – either as distant 'natives' or freak show exhibits – and so mainly came to symbolise more familiar threats.

From 'race war' to 'class war' and back

The move from a racialisation of the proletariat to the 'racing' of the nation itself, in opposition to the equally racialised external Other, embodies the consolidation of modern racism as a project of the nation-state. It is a process which also witnesses a strengthening of the reliance of politics on a discourse of science and an ability, with the perfection of such, to relate old societal fears and hatreds to new methods for banishing them by proving the superiority of the (national) 'race'. In the following, the passage from the internal rationalisation of European societies to the external fortification of the frontiers of national states against racial contamination shall be explained. The shift to this second stage is impossible without the foundations laid during the former. In particular, the analysis proposed here of an ethnicisation of racism that shifts its focus from intrasocietal degeneration to the threat posed from the outside, emphasises the preceding rise of the state's control over the 'efficiency' of populations; that which Michel Foucault has called bio-power.

The use of a discourse of 'race' in the description of the 'danger-ousness' of the working classes by European elites constitutes itself as a reaction to the rise in class consciousness and the beginnings of a mass workers' movement from the mid-nineteenth century onwards (Balibar 1991c; Foucault 1997; MacMaster 2001). Although self-referential racism – the aristocratic categorisation of itself as a 'race' apart – began by the early nineteenth century, in the imperial context with reference to the colonised (so already revealing the relationship between racism and the accumulation of capital), the same process began in Europe only later and with reference to the proletariat (Balibar 1991c). The working classes become gradually syn-onymous with 'degeneracy'. Firstly, they are pathologised by an obses-sive procedure of racialisation that analyses their poverty in biologised terms, pinpointing 'criminality, congenital vice (alcoholism, drugs), physical and moral defects, dirtiness, sexual diseases ...' (ibid.:209). The theorisation of the proletariat as a degenerate 'race' is, in a sec-ond step, posed as a danger for the weakening of the national 'race'. The invocation of danger is undoubtedly linked to the rise of a political consciousness amongst the working classes due to which physical degeneracy is added to by the threat of moral subversion. Not only did the poverty of the working class – presented as a natu-ral condition – disable its participation in the strengthening of the 'race'; its growing adhesion to an internationalist anti-capitalism threatened the foundations of the nation-state as the sole vessel in which the 'race' could flourish.

The development of modern racism, as opposed to what Foucault has called 'race war' – the notion of the existence of a plurality of opposing 'races' at the core of the 'race' idea – is linked inextricably to the preexisting imposition of 'class war'. The advent of 'race war', in Foucault's terms, marks the end of Antiquity and the beginning of a new historical consciousness based on the discovery of this new means of classifying human differences. It may, therefore, be thought of as a counter-history in the sense that it alters the course of political history from then on. The success of the notion of 'race war' in transforming the preexistent (antique) view of politics by founding itself upon a purportedly historical quest for national glory is fundamentally challenged by the advent of class consciousness. Foucault conceives of this challenge as the catalyst for the transformation of the discourse of 'class war' into the practices of modern racism, or the racialisation of populations and their domination by the state as such. Racism in this contemporary sense is developed when the discourse of 'race war', part of the revolutionary ideal of national destiny, was at the point of being overtaken or converted into that of 'class war'.

The relationship between 'race war' and aspirations to nobility that rejected the successes of the bourgeoisie, observable most clearly in Gobineau, is threatened by a discourse of class struggle that poses itself as a serious contender for the people's support. By challenging the continuing determination of an upper class to prove its aristocratic privilege through the mobilisation of a theory of its racial superiority, 'class war' emerges as a competitive counter-history to that of 'race war'. Faced with destruction, the notion of 'race war' is reinvented by the removal of its historical dimension. This is replaced by a vision of biologically incompatible 'races', pitted against each other. Mosse (1978) and Noiriel (1991) both see the aristocracy, or aspiring aristocrats such as Gobineau, as playing a leading role. Using the work of racial scientists, French racist thinkers, such as Gobineau and de Lapouge in particular, translated the idea of the existence of different 'races' into organic terms in a purposeful attempt to reroute revolutionary discourse away from the unifying factor of class. The battle of the 'races' is no longer thought of in the warlike terms of conflicting nations. It is now racialised in the biological sense along the lines of Social Darwinist interpretations of the 'survival of the fittest'.

The racialisation of the working classes, which can be thought of as the first form taken by an institutionalised modern racism in the internal arena of European nation-states, rather than their colonies, must be seen in light of the increasing egalitarianism of these

societies. As Wagner (1994:89) remarks with regard to the establishment of political citizenship, 'limits to who can consider themselves
as political beings can also be set *inside* a political entity.' Such was
the aim of the suppression of the proletariat through their classification as racially degenerate, and so as incapable of 'political "com-
petence" ' (Balibar 1991c:210). The call, since the French Revolution,
for political equality created a paradox between what Balibar considers the increasing juridical and moral difficulty of claiming a
natural difference between individuals, and the perception of a
concomitant political need to do so. The threat posed by the working
class to 'social order, property and the power of elites' (ibid.) made
it imperative for the latter to deny their right to political citizenship. Modern racism in the biological and technological sense with
which it began to be used by states since the end of the nineteenth
century, albeit unevenly, was formulated precisely against the rise of
class struggle as a means of contradicting the political principle of
'equality of birth [with] that of a hereditary inequality which made
it impossible to re-naturalise social antagonisms' (ibid.).

The seeming paradox between the political notion of universal
equality that emerged with the French Revolution and constituted
a continuing struggle at the heart of European modernities, and the
naturalisation of inequality that sought to deny it is captured by
W.E.B. Du Bois. He contrasts the internal stratification of European
societies with that of the racialised inequality between the coloniser
and the colonised that long preceded its application to the 'lower'
social classes of the European states themselves. As the European
political class became increasingly convinced of the utility of a 'science of race' in the suppression of so-called degenerates, so too the
white man – as any white man in the colonies could constitute
himself as a member of the modern nobility (Balibar 1991c) –
created a racial hierarchy with reference to the 'native' population.
Furthermore, the degree of racialisation of the proletariat was
relativised in terms of the colonial system which pitted white
against black so that, despite the oppression of the working class in
Europe, generally 'the white people of Europe had a right to live
upon the labour and property of the coloured peoples of the world'
(Du Bois 1946:312).

Unifying the 'race nation'

The beginnings of such a hierarchy of racial superiority that looked
beyond the confines of the state may be associated with the

intensification of imperial competition and the threat of inter-European war, on the one hand, and with the demands of industrial capitalism, on the other (MacMaster 2001). The strength of the working class was required in order to ensure the nation's fitness in conflict. What MacMaster calls 'the racialisation of European nationalism' (ibid.:40) is developed primarily with reference to the Franco-Prussian war and is perfected by the time of the First World War. By the beginning of the twentieth century therefore, the focus is turned away from a shunning of the working class. It is rather nurtured in the interests of the 'race nation' as a whole; a process that still necessitates the proletariat's domination. While at first, the influence of the eugenics movement proposes the gradual demise of the working class through the halting of public and private charity, this is replaced by a belief in the utility of national welfare programmes in improving the nation's efficiency, not least so as to curb the revolutionary Left and ensure industrial productivity (MacMaster 2001). The success of this move that stressed 'new forms of corporatism, "solidarism" or organic unity' (ibid.:56) of the entire nation lay also in the fact that it went beyond Left–Right cleavages, with a growing tendency among Socialists embracing eugenicist ideas of the 'technocratic and biological engineering of the unified race-nation' (ibid.). The totalising control over the indi-vidual, practised by means of the extension of welfare nationalism, is enforced by the state in its effort to render racially coherent the population under its jurisdiction. Its principal tools include the sci-ences of demography and statistics, crucial to the operationalisation of Foucauldian bio-power.[5]

The 'racing' of the nation is central to the general implementation of the systems of bio-power from the turn of the century on. For Foucault, racism becomes a fundamental mechanism of power that makes it impossible for any modern state not to pass through racism at distinct times. Racism, under the conditions of bio-power, has two functions in the state. Firstly, it introduces a rupture that divides those who may live from those who must die. The taking of control over the biological realm by state power and the introduc-tion of 'good' and 'inferior' 'races' serves to pit groups against each other. Racism's second function is to make work what Foucault terms the positive relation of the old warrior mentality of ' "if you want to live, the other must die" ' (Foucault 1997:227–8). The posi-tive link made between killing/letting die and the survival of the 'race' means that annihilation of the Other goes beyond protection of the self; it becomes the logic of killing, rejecting or expelling the Other in the name of self-improvement (the self understood as being one's own 'race'). Racism becomes the justification for the state's murder of others who have become dispensable or who pose a threat, not only to the survival but to the betterment of the 'race'. The couching of this logic of racism's necessity in the language of biology legitimises the actions taken in its name. However, Foucault insists, it is not merely that a scientific guise is used to cloak a political project that would otherwise be unacceptable. It is rather that, born out of the evolutionist project, the notion of human hierarchy becomes

> really a means of thinking about the colonial relationship, the necessity of war, criminality, the phenomena of madness and mental illness, the history of societies with their different classes etc. In other words, each time that there has been confrontation, killing, conflict or the risk of death, it is in the form of evolutionism that we have been constrained, literally, to consider them.
>
> (ibid.:229)

By the turn of the twentieth century, the focus on the consolidation of the unified 'race nation' is transformed, using the scientific tools of bio-power, for the external fortification of its borders. The introduction of strict controls over the entry of non-nationals into the territory of the nation-state is inextricable from its novel need to quantify and categorise those living under its jurisdiction, in the aim of achieving the efficiency of the 'race'. The rise of demography, as a science of the state, and the concomitant rise of immigration control is not unrelated to the seemingly paradoxical spread of at least the consciousness of the right to universal suffrage within states on the one hand, and more generally on the other, to the demand for self-determination that accompanied this era. As Wagner (1994:90) makes clear:

> Paradoxically, the increased acceptance of the people's right to self-determination at the beginning of the twentieth century, and especially after the First World War, exacerbated the process of imposing nationalised rules on individuals and, furthermore, of excluding groups of other human beings from this right.

Inclusion in the polity becomes conceptualised uniquely in national terms that, by defining themselves racially, and therefore purportedly grounded in scientific principles, directs the focus of state racism towards the protection of the 'race nation' from external contamination.

For Gérard Noiriel (1991), the key period connecting the national-isation of European societies to the racialisation of immigration policy is the end of the nineteenth century, an era of protectionism which marks the end of the laissez-faire, liberal state. His examination of the 1889 French citizenship law reveals its combination of *jus san-guinis* and *jus solis* for the differential treatment of the 'racially' French and those of immigrant origin. This law was based neither upon the traditions of 'the philosophy of human rights' nor the 'republican tradition'. Rather, it represented a compromise between the various social groups for whom the issue of nationality had gained primacy. Despite the support, primarily of industrial leaders, for a more open nationality law that would facilitate incoming for-eign labour, the persistent power of the, albeit significantly reduced, nobility pressed for a racial conception of the French nation.

For Noiriel, the extent to which the 1889 law conceded to this group of 'defenders of the French identity' and their aristocratic supporters has been too often neglected. According to the law, the newly naturalised were denied the right to vote for their first ten years as French residents, so creating a two-tiered system of nation-ality within the population. The introduction of such laws relates to the growing importance of information regarding the population for the functioning of the state according to a logic of bio-power. The classification of populations as divisible into national, natu-ralised and alien by law made information available to the state, its institutions and, importantly, employers and others that would have influence over a newly naturalised worker's life, that facilitated and justified the internal hierarchisation of these groups under the state's jurisdiction. Noiriel demonstrates how the introduction of nationality laws in the French Third Republic enabled the institu-tional discrimination of these various groups on the grounds of their classification as national or other:

> The 1851 law on aid to the poor obliged hospitals to treat the poor and the sick whatever their origins; similarly, the law on the *sociétés de secours mutuels* did not in any case establish a difference between workers on the basis of criteria of nationality. The majority of the

'social' laws of the Third Republic, in contrast, specify that the advantages permitted are reserved for nationals.

Noiriel (1991:89)

This discriminatory practice is replicated in a whole range of fields, most prominently the job market which becomes increasingly restrictive for non-national workers, especially professionals such as doctors certified outside France. Such restriction is made possible due to the shift from localised, non-national understandings of who constituted a 'foreigner' to the abstract principles of belonging that became inscribed with the consolidation of the nation-state. Indeed, national identity becomes imposed by means of its very bureaucratisation. The abstractness of this common identity, which belied the fact that the localised character of most European societies at the time meant that an identification of the individual with the nation was rather intangible, signals the importance of the role played by a discourse of 'race'. The biologisation of the purportedly historically shared traits of national identity turned the intangible into indisputable fact, the state's implementation of laws on these principles concretising this still further.

Such new restrictive nationality laws were not contradictory of democracy. On the contrary, the control of immigration is inherent to the newly democratic nation-state. It was not, for example, until 1880 that the United Kingdom introduced restrictions upon incoming 'aliens' whose arrival in the country until then went completely unregulated. The British 1905 *Aliens Act* marks a marriage between this new conception of national identity and the increasingly coercive state 'which multiplied the measures of regulation, control, restriction and expulsion of the foreign population' (Noiriel 1991:94). Noiriel's examples demonstrate how these newly national societies begin, as Foucault claims, to conceive of the 'social body' (*le corps social*) as binary in nature (Foucault 1997:75). There are either nationals or there are foreigners. And as Gérard Noiriel points out, the problem for national cultures is not only to render perennial their own existence 'but also to expand to the detriment of others, by a means of a process of homogenisation and the subjectivation of neighbouring peoples' (Noiriel 1991:96). This new 'race war' is now the legally legitimated driving force behind nation-state ideology: 'The clash of races, race war via nations and laws' (Foucault 1997:60). This oppositionary construction of human relations is institutionalised in the nation-state by the ever more influential idea, held by Ludwig Gumplowicz (1875), that 'the birth of states was analogous to all other births, subject to biological and social laws pertaining to races' (Hannaford 1996:300–1).

RACISM, ANTISEMITISM AND THE PARADOXES OF EQUALITY

Within the major nation-states of western Europe, the racialisation of national identity by means of the growing restriction of those conceived of as non-members of the 'race nation' is epitomised by the growth of political antisemitism in the years following 1880. In a particularly striking manner because of the Jews' relative integration into bourgeois society, the case of the politicisation of anti-Jewish feeling in the form of the practice of modern antisemitism indicates the seeming contradiction between a modernising nation-state and its imposition of increasingly narrow definitions of belonging. The legacy of antisemitism, although officially refuted in the aftermath of the *Shoah*, informs the racism that persists in the latter half of the twentieth century, displaced onto 'immigrants' or black people. While large-scale immigration is significant of the modernity of the state in which it occurs, in fear of the dilution of national coherence, the immigrant population is excluded from full participation in society or the polity – be it through its assimilation or the direct denial of full rights – a process which continues to stigmatise those generations descended from it. This penultimate section of the chapter, through a closer examination of these processes, discusses the ambivalence at the heart of the modern nation-state which enables racism to emerge under the conditions of a heretofore inexperienced equality.

Antisemitism as modernity

> Modern anti-Semitism was born not from the great difference between groups but rather from the threat of absence of differences, the homogenisation of Western society and the abolition of the ancient social and legal barriers between Jews and Christians.
>
> Patrick Girard (1980; cited in Bauman 1989:58)

Arendt situates the emergence of political antisemitism in France in the aftermath of the Franco-Prussian war, following 1880. The process that resulted in this phenomenon belongs to the political context of the European states since the Enlightenment which gave rise both to the emancipation of the Jews, as part of the general conferral of equal rights, and to the birth of the class society which, in seeming contradiction, divided members of a population according to privilege.[6] Jews had no place within the class system because they were defined, not in relation to other classes, but solely in relation to the state; at the behest of its bestowal of special privileges or edicts of emancipation. Arendt shows how this very process, together with the growth of European expansionism and the rise of 'imperialistically minded businessmen' (Arendt 1966:15) served to undermine western Jewry. The Jews' special relationship with the state – in their historic role as bankers – is interrupted by this process with only some individuals retaining a position of influence. With what Arendt calls the financial organisation of the Jewish communities gone, national Jewish communities in the West all but disappear by the first years of the twentieth century. This process is accompanied, on the one hand, by the deepening of Jewish assimilation in the metropolises of western Europe and, on the other, by the growth in, apparently paradoxical, ideological antisemitism.

Such ideology, developing during the period from 1860 to 1890 after which it remains relatively unchanged to the present day (MacMaster 2001), is based upon a conspiracy theory that 'could always "prove" that any misfortune was the work of the Jews, even in the absence of any evidence' (ibid.:88). It was made up of various components which were mobilised under different circumstances. Jews were targeted as the exploiters of the working class due to their control of world capitalism, which in turn enabled their manipulation of public opinion. This theory in particular linked the Jews' purported power and deviousness to the fears of those 'that were losing out in the crisis of modernisation' (ibid.:90) across social classes. Antisemitism's requirement of myth was fuelled by its underpinning by a religious dimension that drew a connection between new fears arising from the conditions of modernity, and old European hatreds that for centuries had targeted the Jews as the killers of Christ. The crucial difference between ancient Jew hatred and a modern antisemitism capable of becoming a principal tool in the state's suppression of difference, is the removal of the eschatological dimension that remained a feature of the former. Modern antisemitism manipulates elements of the old myth of the Jews as demonic, most prominently the notion of the blood libel, but eliminates the possibility of salvation through conversion preached in premodern Jew hatred. The racialisation of human difference so as to irredeemably fix the members of each 'race' meant that 'the

Jew remained a Jew even after conversion' (ibid.:91). The essentialisation of Jews according to their religion became the primary message
in the contemporary manipulation of religious motifs by modern
antisemites.

Furthermore, antisemitism did not exist outside the development
of the racial notions of degeneration that most strongly characterise
racism's marriage of science and politics. Again this discourse related
the modern 'scientific' pathologisation of the Jews as the carriers of
degenerative and sexual diseases that threatened to contaminate the
European population to the age-old belief in the image of the Jew 'as
a monstrous fungus, a parasitic growth that fed upon the healthy
body of the host society, finally reducing it to an emaciated and
sickly shell' (MacMaster 2001:92). It was the widespread view of the
Jews as spreaders of plagues in the societies of the Middle Ages that
led to their ghettoisation. In the western Europe of the mid to late
nineteenth century in contrast, the Jews' liberty to live among their
Christian conationals heightened societal paranoia of the danger of
the Jew as 'everywhere'. This view of the Jews was further compounded by their portrayal as anti-nationalist. Not only were Jews
physically dangerous, they also posed a political threat because their
essentially alien character contravened the political romanticist view
of members of the *Volk* as carriers of the 'blood line' that determined
membership of the nation. The anti-national character of the Jews
was fed by the popular image of the 'wandering Jew' and the belief
that as a people, in whatever situation, they clung to a shared ances-
try that set them apart. Jews, as a group, were constituted as a nation
rather than a religion, which meant their allegiances were not to the
nation-state in which they lived but rather to their own 'state within
a state'.

Contradictions of emancipation

These diverse elements of ideological modern antisemitism were
couched in racial terms that denied the Jews any means of escape
from their essentialised traits. The modernity of this conspiratorial
ideology, beyond its embedding in a discourse of science, is characterised by the conditions under which it developed, namely the liberatory possibilities of the democratic nation-state. The greatest
effect of the Jews' emancipation was their gradual assimilation into
mainstream society. Although, in all states a sizeable number
remained committed to an Orthodox way of life, many Jews no
longer observed religious customs, intermarried and thought of

themselves primarily as citizens of the nation-state. In this sense, the unified Jewish community as such disappeared in Europe (Arendt 1966). In its stead remained Jewish individuals that, with the rise of antisemitism leading to the *Shoah*, were grouped artificially into an enforced unity that belied the very great socioeconomic and cultural differences that lay between them.

It is the condition of Jewish assimilation that ironically facilitates the success of ideological antisemitism in enjoying public popularity and becoming open to political manipulation. Jews are described as the 'race' present among all 'races' (Foucault 1997). And it is the achievement of assimilation, both enabled by modernity and representative of the highest threat posed by modern living, that lifts Judeophobia onto a new, and as yet unknown plane. As Zygmunt Bauman (1989) makes clear, this shift is brought about by the rupturing of the naturalness with which the premodern separation of the Jews from society at large was perceived. The separate life led by Jews enclosed in ghettos, although mysterious and feared, was not questioned: 'their distinctiveness was not an issue' (ibid.:57). In contrast, with the development of modernity and the nation-state as the configuration in which modern life was to be lived, there is a rationalisation of society which rids the preexistent order of its perceived naturalness. Bauman demonstrates this transformation by means of the metaphor of gardening. Racism's modernity is encapsulated by the passage from a premodern game-keeping mentality to the modernity of gardening. Whereas premodern society could be 'left to its own resources' (ibid.) without the necessity of planning its course, with the advent of modernity, laissez-faire game keeping was replaced by the skill of gardening in order to ensure the achievement of a predetermined outcome. The gardening metaphor serves to illustrate the strategic nature of modern politics, the gardener determined 'to treat as weeds every self-invited plant which interferes with his plan and his vision of order and harmony' (ibid.).

Under the new conditions dictated by racialisation, 'gardening' translates into the increased vigilance that modern European society is necessitated to observe over its population. In the case of the Jews, this is complicated by the fact of assimilation which rendered the Jews 'invisible' or in Foucault's terms, as the disguised 'race', present among all 'races'. The separation of the Jews was now rendered artificial whereas previously, during their physical separation from society, their difference appeared natural, 'a tacitly accepted assumption' (Bauman 1989:57). Restoring the impression of the

Jews' foreignness as a natural state of affairs required construction; where Jews and Christians appeared alike, racial theory, ancient religious myth or conspiratorial rumours had to be manipulated to prove the contrary.

These conditions ensured the ultimate impossibility of the Jews' assimilation (Bauman 1991), despite their almost complete secularism and high levels of achievement (Traverso 1996; MacMaster 2001). For the German Jews Bauman describes, assimilation functioned as a type of trap. On the one hand, the refusal to relinquish a particular communal lifestyle meant 'a life-sentence of strangerhood' (Bauman 1991:112). On the other hand, by choosing to adopt the cultural hierarchy imposed by the state that saw Judaism as inferior to national (Christian) culture, Jews and other outcasts helped to prove both its superiority and its universal validity. The further assimilation progressed, the less equipped was Judaism itself to provide an alternative role model, especially for the Jewish liberal middle classes. On the other hand, the Jews' greater immersion in Germanness was looked upon with suspicion. For Bauman (ibid.:121) the situation was a vicious circle within which 'the assimilating Jews acted under the pressure to prove their Germanhood, yet the very attempt to prove it was held against them as the evidence of their duplicity and, in all probability, also of subversive intentions'.

The double-sidedness with which assimilation presented itself, undeniably in the German case, and gradually with the growth of nationalism in France, is encapsulated by the tension between Judaism and Jewishness (Arendt 1966). What Arendt calls 'the fashionable "vice" of Jewishness' (ibid.:87) was to be the downfall of the western European Jews. While Judaism could be escaped by conversion, the essence of Jewishness, which was said to remain in even the most assimilated Jew, could not be overcome. Modern antisemitism emerges out of a growing fascination with this Janus-faced characterisation of the Jewish figure. For Arendt, this 'philosemitism' developed in France with the Dreyfus Affair, and in Germany and Austria with the First World War. The ideological antisemitism which mobilised a view of the Jews as the orchestrators of such events (directly in the case of Dreyfus and indirectly in that of international conflict), heightened society's fascination with them. The success of political antisemitism would for Arendt have been unthinkable without the construction of the social conditions under which, since the Dreyfus Affair, the Jew was 'everywhere'. This was not only a theory invented by antisemitic movements, but was grounded in 'social factors' so deeply rooted that they were unaccounted for by either political or economic history.

These factors were based upon the condition of assimilated Jews and their image in contemporary European society. Political antisemitism succeeds in mobilising public support because of the preexistent societal construction of 'Judaism as a psychological quality' (Arendt 1966:66). The social antisemitism of the post-emancipatory period that depicted the Jew as either a 'pariah' or a 'parvenu' essentialised the Jews as a group and forced each individual within it to personally grapple with the 'Jewish question'. Society became fascinated with the notion of such individual psychological struggle, while the Jews, because assimilation had perfected their integration of societal norms, became obsessed with the unfair choice between either social rejection or religious betrayal. The roles of pariah and parvenu persisted despite the fact that they neither adequately represented Judaism, from an historical or religious point of view, nor did individual Jews identify with them. They survived, and came to form the popular rationalisation of political antisemitism, precisely because of the ambiguity to which the Jews were held, based upon the artificiality of the choice they nevertheless felt it necessary to make in order to achieve acceptance. The strong social constraint to conform to one of these images would have been better abandoned to the Jewish reality that meant 'to belong either to an overprivileged upper class or to an underprivileged mass which, in Western and Central Europe, one could belong to only through an intellectual and somewhat artificial solidarity' (ibid.:67).

The demand of assimilation attached to Jewish emancipation resulted, following the consolidation of the nation-state, in the incompleteness of this freedom. By applying constant tests of allegiance that, however, gave no clues as to which comportment would favour their inclusion, even the most assimilated Jews in practice were never granted full membership of the nation.

Modern antisemitism developed first as an ideology for antisemitic parties and racial theorists from 1860 on. It was made popular through its use of age-old Judeophobic myths, but gained political weight because of its reaction to an opposite process: the Jews' modern embracing of the dictates of European, Christian society. Assimilation, the process that, in its revolutionary conception, would bring about an end to the Jews' subversiveness, is contradicted by the 'proof', provided by 'race', of the supremacy of genetic essence over social conditioning. In fact, assimilation could never result in such freedom because despite the benefits accorded them by emancipation, the Jews remained the objects rather than the subjects of the emancipatory process. They were not the agents of their own liberty. Indeed, for many Jews, the granting of their rights was experienced as a 'revolution from above' (Traverso 1996:24).

Jewish emancipation was therefore utterly symbolic of the possibilities opened by the Enlightenment. But, according to Arendt, as the Enlightenment is carried forward by the non-Jewish world, so the process of admitting the Jews into society is, in fact, an exclusionary one that involves no consultation with those it targets. Emancipation proceeds – in the different western European states at various times – following criteria for the Jews' societal role set in place by the state. As Bauman (1989:104) notes, these criteria were grounded in the modern state's need for unity which, in turn, 'meant the disempowerment of communal self-management and the dismantling of local or corporative mechanisms of self-perpetuation'.

The Jews' emancipation was deemed necessary as a precautionary measure against their perceived status as a 'nation'. Their cohesiveness had to be deconstructed and the Jew turned into an individual. However, as Traverso points out, this outcome of cosmopolitan universalism contradicts its later embodiment in the nation-state, under which the Jews of Germany were emancipated: the Jews' individuality now conflicts with the demand for unity that could only be achieved through the identity of the nation's members. Emancipation was unable to curb antisemitism not because the rights it afforded Jews were ill-conceived or unwanted by the Jews themselves, but because it contained a 'normative vision of assimilation' (Traverso 1996:32) that, while secularising the majority of Jews, did not render them seamless individuals. By focusing on religious separateness, the assimilatory project could not control the antisemitism which now targeted the Jews as a relatively distinct group, due both to the relative paucity of intermarriage and the narrowness of their area of socioeconomic activity. It is under these conditions of separateness yet equality, fabricated by the assimilatory regime that nonetheless draws out difference by watching for signs of 'imperfect' assimilation, that the Jew becomes what Traverso calls a 'cultural code'. This code embodies in a single word – Jew – everything foreign to the nation; a group that remains apart, and so threatening, despite all efforts made to the contrary.

RACISM, EUROPEANNESS AND THE IDEAL OF HUMANITY

The idea of extermination lies no farther from the heart of humanism than Buchenwald lies from the Goethehaus in Weimar. That insight has been almost completely repressed, even by the Germans, who have been made sole scapegoats for ideas of extermination that are actually a common European heritage.

Sven Lindqvist (1992:9)

The generalised failure to regard modern racism as functioning *within* the logic of an expansionist, modernising and increasingly competitive European nation-state is grounded in a generalised belief in the overriding value of the project of modernity. In other words, its secular, universalist and emancipatory elements, upheld as the foundations of present-day democracy, have been counter-factually taken at face value, often in the absence of a problematisation of the course they have taken in history. On the contrary, both colonial and post-colonial racism became fundamental to the organisation of state power because of their seemingly paradoxical appeal to universalism. The final section of this chapter argues for a view of racism as set inside a Janus-faced universalism that is foundational of European modernity so that, with the advent of nationalism, racism cannot but be seen as a structural condition of the political configuration of western Europe.

The essence of racism's universalism is captured by Balibar's (1991b:61) depiction of racism as a 'supranationalism'. This paradox, which disrupts the logic of the political conception of 'race' as identical to national particularity, is in fact at the core of racism's strength. Far beyond the artificiality of a myriad of individual 'race nations', the power of racism was in its ability to define the 'frontiers of an ideal humanity' (ibid.). These divisions of humanity, constructed on a grander scale than the localised specificities of individual European nations, based themselves on the difference between both the 'civilised' and the 'primitive' world and, within the former, between the superior 'race' and its internal enemies. With the advent of non-European immigration, the closing of the geographical gap between the former colonisers and their colonised leads to the irreconcilability of primitive existence being reconceptualised in terms of the internal 'threat' once 'posed' by the proletariat and the Jews.

Racism sustained the passage into the post-colonial era and the aftermath of the *Shoah* because of the universal appeal of 'racial signifiers' which constructed the European, rather than the individual nation, as the dominant and therefore ideal, human type. This was achieved by means of the emphasis placed on the degrees of difference that separated 'man' from the 'savage', so that 'all nationalisms were defined against the *same* foil, the same "stateless other", and this has been a component of the very idea of Europe as the land of "modern" nation-states or, in other words, civilisation' (Balibar 1991b:62). The sharpness of this divide is epitomised by Lindqvist's (1992:52) comment on the invention of modern weaponry that 'the use of dumdum bullets between "civilised" states was prohibited. They were reserved for big-game hunting and colonial wars.'

The evocation of colonial terror is of the greatest relevance here because, as Gilroy (2000) makes clear, the paradoxical compatibility of Enlightenment ideals of universal equality and the racialisation of an overwhelming segment of humanity is most crucially linked to the demands of imperialist expansion. Commenting on the parallel existence of notions of 'race' and cosmopolitanism in Kant, Gilroy claims that 'modern political theory was being annexed by the imperatives of colonial power even in its emergent phase' (ibid.:59). In other words, the aspirations for a cosmopolitan democracy built upon the nebulous notion of a universal fraternity, 'could not encompass a black humanity' (ibid.:60); black here coming to stand for all those considered primitive or subversive in relation to the ideal-typical European image of 'man'. The inability for an unarguably revolutionary conceptualisation of 'humanity' to practically incorporate such difference was but one step behind the rationalisation of violence. As Gilroy notes, it is following the identification of the racialised 'as a properly philosophical object' (ibid.) that violence against them became legitimated and spoken of in terms of a necessity which gave rise to both the slave plantation and the concentration camp.

Whereas Gilroy writes more in terms of a perversion of Enlightenment ideals that, rather than being abandoned, should be countered by a reinstating of the 'democratic and cosmopolitan traditions that have been all but expunged from today's black political imaginary' (ibid.:356), Balibar (1994) makes a less sharp distinction between Enlightenment intentions and practices. Focusing on the ideal of universalism and, in particular, the 'general idea of man' that it contains, Balibar, while not arguing for the reducibility of universalism to racism, proposes the impossibility of clearly dividing between the two. Rather, 'universalism and racism are indeed (determinate) contraries, and this is why each of them has the other inside itself – or is bound to affect the other *from the inside'* (ibid.:198). Because universalist philosophy is based upon the premise that moral equality is a natural entitlement of the 'brotherhood of man', racism (like sexism) becomes the prism through which we may understand the very possibility of talking about a universalist ideal. In other words, both racism and sexism serve to justify the fact that there are always exemptions to inclusion in universal humanity.

Racism is inseparable from the task of creating a 'general idea of man' because of its implicit invocations of superiority and inferiority. The construction of universally rational man necessitates a definition in relation to an Other that also calls for a hierarchisation of human beings, ranked in relation to the universal ideal. Koselleck (1985) proposes that historically, groups have always demarcated their 'singularity by means of general concepts' (ibid.:160). The claim to universality creates oppositions, or what Koselleck calls 'counter-concepts', 'which discriminate against those who have been defined as "other" ' (ibid.). Such categorisations lead to a definition of humanity, rooted in the European philosophical tradition, that formulates a Eurocentrism that structures the patterns of exclusion and inclusion according to what is claimed to be a universal point of view that, in fact, establishes the European as the norm. It is because of the development of such accepted visions of humanity in tandem with the growth of the European nation-state, that universalism and racism cannot but be seen as conceptually inextricable. Balibar's preference for such an analysis over that of Wallerstein (Balibar and Wallerstein 1991), who rather stresses a *complementarity* between racism or sexism and universalism, is based on his suggestion that 'we do not know how universalism could exist without being affected from the inside by racism' (Balibar 1994:199). While this is not to say that an alternative would be unthinkable, we need to operate within a reconstruction of the history of modernity that recognises the truth of racism's compatibility with the preexistent notion of universalism.

Balibar's proposal that racism and universalism each contain the other within itself leads to a constant questioning of '*who* you are in a certain social world, *why* there are some compulsory places in this world to which you must adapt yourself, imposing upon yourself a certain *univocal* identity' (Balibar 1994:200). Racism provides the answer to the dilemma of a universalism that seeks to homogenise us when, in fact we feel different and strive towards uniqueness. Or as Balibar (ibid.) puts it, racism has successfully been instituted as a mode of thought,

> because we are *different*, and, tautologically because difference is the universal essence of what we are – not singular, individual difference, but collective differences, made of analogies and, ultimately, of similarities. The core of this mode of thought might very well be this common logic: differences among men are differences among sets of similar individuals (which for this reason can be 'identified').

Following such logic, racism creates its own communities which fulfil the need for uniqueness made urgent by the rise of nationalism; a uniqueness made so only by the existence of each 'community' within a universalised system of 'races', to one of which, come the consolidation of the 'race' idea, each superior or inferior individual was compelled to belong. As the notion of 'race' was invented by Europeans and applied to themselves as superior and to others as inferior to various degrees, the violence that accompanies racism is grounded in the concomitant need to preserve the hierarchical order of things. This order was beneficial solely for those who invented the racial classification of humanity: the Europeans.

However, universalism has been said to be Janus-faced because it creates a standard ideal of humanity which results in the oppression of those who do not conform to it. It also, based upon this same standard, contains the possibility of extending that humanity to those whom it does not 'naturally' incorporate in the effort of breaking down the divide between the 'civilised' and the 'primitive'. This was the 'mission of civilisation', or the belief that, through the application of the values of humanism, the 'native' in the colonies or the Jew ripe for assimilation, may become incorporated into the vision of ideal humanity. In other words, within universalism itself was already the possibility – although not the inevitability – of racial exclusivity as compounded by the modern nation-state.

It is in recognition of this that anti-colonial authors such as Fanon and Césaire mobilised an anti-humanist discourse in their analysis of the asymmetrical relationship between the coloniser and the colonised. The racialisation of colonial society was based fundamentally upon the quest to gain access to humanity, a process brought about by the establishment of a functional link between 'race' and bureaucracy as part of the imperial system (Arendt 1966). This system constructed a constant parallel between the colonised and the 'motherland', not least through education, that instilled the former with a sense of inferiority. For Cox (1943:336), the complete compatibility of what he calls 'race' prejudice with a logic of 'production and competition for markets' means that the systemised nature of racial antagonism in the colonial context is rarely recognised. The value placed on whiteness operates as a mechanism of control over the colonial system of exploitation and domination. It becomes an obsession amongst the 'native' population which does all it can to climb a rung up the ladder of whiteness in the hope of gaining greater social acceptability.

The significance of the ideal of humanity for the creation of – a subjugated – 'native' identity that survives well into the post-colonial era (Fanon 1963) is condemned by Césaire as indicative of the dominance of a ' "pseudo-humanism" ' (Gilroy 2000:62). The humanist values preached by the pioneers of the 'civilising mission' were based on a partial interpretation of the 'rights of man' that is 'narrow and fragmentary, incomplete and biased and, all things considered, sordidly racist' (Césaire 1972; cited in Gilroy:ibid.). It is in the colonial context that this becomes apparent because of the complete reduction of all relations, in particular the economic, to the 'fact' of racial difference so that richness is a consequence of whiteness and *vice versa* (Fanon 1963). Despite the obviousness to the 'native' of her inability to attain a status of wealth, she is nevertheless expected to conform to the accepted behaviours of white society in an absurd mimicry that silences local practices.

The obviousness of the disparity between humanist values and 'civilising' practices for Fanon and Césaire, as well as Sartre and Barthes, is what leads to the call for 'anti-humanism' (Young 1992). Fanon's mockery of the 'western values', that at another time he may have assimilated, emerges from the realisation of the repression that they implied, that for many came about only with decolonisation. In the same way as Jewish assimilation was the price paid for an emancipation that never resulted in true liberty, so the instillation of humanist values in the 'native' was always accompanied by the enactment of violence. The epidermilisation of the racialised at the same time as their admission into 'civilisation' indicates the futility of the attempt to adopt such values.

The project of anti-humanism, central to structuralism, sought to make clear the unacceptability of the general refusal to acknowledge the primacy of violence and extermination in western culture (Young 1992). Both Sartre and Barthes advocated not only a philosophical anti-humanism, but one that reacted directly to the injustices of colonialism. The extent of the violence enacted against those considered inferior, yet nevertheless human, pointed out the bitter irony of speaking about the 'family of man' (Barthes 1957). As Young remarks, 'the category of human, however exalted in its conception, was too often invoked only in order to put the male before the female, or to classify other "races" as subhuman, and therefore not subject to the ethical prescriptions applicable to "humanity" at large' (Young 1992:247). Humanism, like universalism is therefore necessarily double-edged because in order for a vision of humanity to be produced, a definition must first be constructed of what humanity is *not*. It has therefore been compatible with racism precisely because by defining the frontiers of humanity, it provides racism with preestablished categories of superiority and inferiority.

Alain Touraine (2000:78) criticises what he interprets as an outright rejection of the values of humanism by these scholars, preferring to characterise it as having 'nothing in common with appeals to natural entities, such as nations, races, the proletariat or colonised nations'. Indeed, a 'universalist consciousness' can be rescued if strictly separated from the 'temptation to base society on reason' (ibid.). This recalls Althusser's and Sartre's recognition of the utility of humanism under specific conditions, such as the Third World struggle. However, Young (1992) asks whether the recourse to humanism or universal values can be neutrally achieved in the knowledge of its historical definition 'against a subhuman other' (ibid.:249). Touraine argues that the rejection of humanism also rejected the Subject and the possibility of her agency, most importantly in the reconciliation of universalism and cultural diversity which, he claims, was already a possibility of the Enlightenment.

In conclusion, it appears that the conflict between Touraine's optimism and the distinct scepticism of the anti-humanists is reflective of the problems confounding a scholarly analysis of the history of modern racism. This may be particularly problematic for anti-racist accounts that normatively seek solutions to racism and which may therefore perceive the critique of humanist 'values' as unhelpful. This is indeed the gist of Touraine's argument against the anti-humanists which deems it possible to recuperate the positive elements of the universalist ideal by consigning its more negative elements to the annals of history. The starkness of the separation made between the world before and after 1945, in rough terms, is mirrored in much anti-racist discourse. This approach, however, is largely unable to overcome the 'strategic blindness and refusal to come to terms with the violence intrinsic to Western culture' (Young 1992:249) most often heard in arguments for consigning the *Shoah* to the realm of the irrational or to the particularity of the German national character (cf. Goldhagen 1996). For even when that violence is acknowledged to have been widespread and state-approved, the apparent 'fact' that, following the *Shoah*, the entire western world rallied to discredit 'race' and eradicate racism seems to be proof, at the very least, of the temporary nature of this historical trend.

Far from being able to resolve this conflict that has fired intellectual arguments for at least the last five decades, the historicisation of the collusion of racism and the state in modernity attempted here builds on Adorno and Horkheimer's (1979) appeal to recognise the 'self-destructiveness' of Enlightenment. Writing before the end of the Second World War, they call for Enlightenment to consider the 'destructive aspect of progress' (ibid.:xiii) lest the task be left to its enemies. This is vital because the explanation of the outdoing of Enlightenment thought by the 'mythology' of nation and 'race' should not be sought within the latter, but in Enlightenment itself 'when paralysed by fear of the truth' (ibid.:xiv). This fear of the truth and the concomitant belief that racism constitutes a perversion of the course of modernity has resulted in the widespread repression of the profound articulation of 'race' and state. The urgency with which the 'values' of universal progress were set back in motion following the *Shoah*, by the leading nations of the international system, was manifest not least in anti-racism in which a language of humanitarian diversity, yet gentle assimilation came to characterise much of the discourse developed in the post-war period. It was this generalised urgency to 'pick up' where humanity 'left off' which made a political historicisation of modern racism and the utility of a discourse of 'race' to expansionist states almost an impossibility until the advent of the anti-colonialist critique, at least a decade after the liberation of the camps.

2

Explaining Racism: Anti-Racist Discourse between Culture and the State

It is frequently taken for granted that we know what we mean when we refer to antiracism. All but the most superficial glance at the literature reveals this not to be the case. What do we know of the workings of antiracist ideas and where these ideas come from? Is antiracism more than simply the straightforward antithesis of racism? At a time when the 'left' and 'progressive' ideas are in crisis, can antiracist organisations maintain successful opposition to racism? What is the relationship between antiracism and modernity?

Cathie Lloyd (1998:1)

Europe, in the aftermath of the *Shoah* and the revelation of the extremities to which a mobilisation of 'race' thinking could lead, required a public and institutional denial of racism. Anti-racism was not a new phenomenon; anti-slavery and self-help movements became established in Europe during the nineteenth century and were complemented, come the 1920s, by the work of anti-racist scientists, determined to prove the unscientific nature of the 'race' concept (Barkan 2003). Anti-racism (re)emerged in the early post-war era, primarily in reaction to the horrors of the Nazi genocide, to construct itself not only in opposition to racism but as 'an alternative interpretation of political discourse' (Lloyd 1998:4). This work of interpretation is concerned above all with the explanation of the phenomenon of racism. Anti-racists, activists and scholars alike set themselves the task of determining the reasons for which an atrocity on the scale of the *Shoah* could have unfolded in the very heart of democratic Europe.

The anti-racist construal of 'race', as a basis for the development of a critique of racism, is inextricable from the construction of the continuum of proximity-to-distance from the public political culture of the nation-state that this research indicates is interpretative of the variety between coexisting anti-racisms. In other words, the intellectual tools used in the development of an ontology of racism and, in particular, their political origins and articulations, are crucial to determining the positioning of a form of anti-racist discourse vis-à-vis the history of the state. The existence of a variety of anti-racisms, differentiated according to the degree to which a national public political culture may be said to be incorporated into their respective discourses, is the outcome of a history of struggle for the political 'ownership' of anti-racism which marks the years from the aftermath of the Second World War to the present day. The concern of this chapter is to demonstrate the evolution of anti-racism's proposed continuum within this period by focusing on the competing interpretations of racism offered by the anti-racism of the various institutions, political movements and self-organised groups organised under that name. Principally, anti-racism may be said to be constructed around a central tension which has the European state as its focus. The extent to which anti-racist discourse identifies a compatibility between the political idea of 'race' and the consolidation of an expansionist and increasingly bureaucratised modern state is vital to the explanation of both the heterogeneity of contemporary anti-racism and of its history of seemingly inherent disunity.

The notion of 'culture', as used both in opposition to 'race' and as an explanation of persistent racism, may be seen as central to an understanding of the heterogeneity of anti-racist discourse. In order to account for this central tension in the conceptualisation of anti-racism, this chapter shall provide an historicisation of the variable development of anti-racist explanations of racism, along either 'culturalist' or 'statist' lines. An early anti-racist discourse, generated by the post-war international institutions, principally UNESCO in cooperation with leading anthropologists, relies upon a discourse of cultural relativism that shaped emergent anti-racist praxis and remains influential to the present day. The cultural relativist approach proposes both an explanation of 'race' and the means to combat racism that emphasises the promotion of the greater knowledge of different cultures through education. By replacing pernicious 'race' with a perennial cultural diversity, the so-called UNESCO tradition (Barker 1983) seeks to explain the differences that exist between human groups without implying the superiority of some over others. The facility of this mechanism of substitution dehistoricises the political relationship between the 'race' idea and the modern European state.

In contrast to this culturalism, a 'statist' account of the origins of racism was developed in the late 1950s and 1960s under the influence of the anti-colonial movement. It came to underpin an alternative conception of anti-racism. Although this was not the first time an analysis of 'race' had been linked to the state, the mobilisation of this state-centred account by anti-racist organisations indicates the importance of international borrowings – mainly of the anti-colonial and US models of black resistance – for the diversification of European anti-racism. The contrast between these two oppositional discourses in anti-racist explanations of racism shall be related to the more recent scholarly theorisation of a new, culturalist racism. The proposal that a so-called neoracism (Balibar 1991a) is made possible by the conditions of widely accepted cultural relativism imposed upon western society by a far left-wing anti-racism (Taguieff 1991b), shall be critiqued by an alternative view, based upon an analysis of the contextual transformation of political processes (Barker 1981). The different implications in these two accounts of the same development in racist thought indicate the extent to which 'race' has been successfully theorised beyond the realm of the state and politics. The critique of this more politicised perspective, which is grounded in resistance to the anti-racism developed by the racialised themselves, attests to the tension between culture- and state-centred anti-racisms that suppresses the development of a coherent anti-racist thesis of the origins of 'race'.

THE CULTURALISM OF THE UNESCO TRADITION

The 'UNESCO tradition' (Barker 1983) encapsulates the attempt to defeat racism as racial science. UNESCO conceded that racism manifested itself in several ways, including individual prejudice borne of a lack of education and the discrimination inherent in the colonial relationship (UNESCO 1968). Despite this, it was felt that racism could only be discredited on its own terms; the terms upon which it sought both popular and academic legitimation, namely as a biological science. UNESCO assembled its first 'world panel of experts' in 1950, resulting in the publication of the UNESCO Statement on Race and Racial Prejudice. The panel consisted of anthropologists, sociologists and psychologists from various world-renowned institutions (Hannaford 1996). The document it produced, updated by subsequent meetings, was backed up by a series of anti-racist publications on the status of racial theories (Barkan 2003). The Statement is epitomised by the assertion that:

> all men belonged to the same species, *Homo Sapiens*, that national, cultural, religious, geographical, and linguistic groups had been falsely termed races; that it would be better to drop the term and use 'ethnic groups' in its place; that the 'race is everything' hypothesis was untrue.
>
> Hannaford (1996:386)

The statement was the subject of significant criticism at the time of its publication. Its revised version in 1951 was submitted to a panel of over one hundred anthropologists and geneticists from all over the world. It was criticised on the grounds that 'the committee was too heavily inclined towards the sociological and had continued to confuse race as a biological "fact" with the idea of race as a social phenomenon' (Hannaford 1996:386). The divisiveness of opinion among the academics consulted by UNESCO, including that which sustained the continued scientific utility of racial divisions, resulted in a largely apolitical declaration that, even in its 1968 version following significant revision, used a rather diluted phraseology. The following, point 3(b), shows how the recourse to 'convention' and 'arbitrariness' naturalises racism and disconnects it from the political processes with which historical analysis reveals it is bound:

> The division of the human species into 'races' is partly conventional and partly arbitrary and does not imply any hierarchy whatsoever. Many anthropologists stress the importance of human variation, but believe that 'racial' divisions have limited scientific interest and may even carry the risk of inviting abusive generalisation.
>
> UNESCO (1968:270)

By concentrating so heavily on the 'race' concept rather than on its idea, both the UNESCO Statement itself and an alternative statement produced by the geneticists and anthropologists (Comas 1961) fail to account for the relationship between 'race' and state. Whereas the UNESCO campaign 'contributed to the discrediting in the public domain of the scientific credentials of racism' (Barkan 2003:15), it did not fully address the political implications of racial theory and racism in recent history. In admitting the role played by 'the conditions of conquest' (UNESCO 1968:270), the UNESCO Statement recognises the racism of colonialism, but proceeds as if such 'conditions' were established in the absence of the deliberate actions of the expansionist state. While admitting that racism is historically rooted and, thus not universal, the Statement does not specify the aspects of this history. Nowhere in the Statement is there a declaration of agency on the part of western states in creating the conditions under which racism is deemed to have emerged. In contrast, it emphasises the progress achieved by the inclusion of many 'formerly dependent countries' (ibid.) in international organisations. The choices made in the Statement's formulation indicate a refusal to recognise the power relations between large and small, and western and 'developing' states that still define the workings of such institutions, as well as of the neocolonial dependency that persists despite the official withdrawal of colonial rule.

A second problem in the UNESCO approach concerns its search for an alternative explanation of human difference. UNESCO sought to replace biological theories of human difference with a culturalist definition of diversity. This tendency, which came to dominate the anti-racist approach promoted in the UNESCO vein and to be widely upheld, was opposed by the geneticists and physical anthropologists who wished to retain 'race' as a useful tool for the explanation of certain phenomena, such as the 'genetic composition of isolated populations' (UNESCO 1951; cited in Comas 1961:304). Against these reservations, the UNESCO tradition gave rise to terms such as 'ethnicity' and 'culture'. The preference for such terms as markers of human difference, over the racial descriptors that had served previously, was based on the belief that the former were stripped of any implication of superiority or inferiority upon which the idea of 'race' was based:

> Current biological knowledge does not permit us to impute cultural achievements to differences in genetic potential. Differences in the achievements of different peoples should be attributed solely to their cultural history. The peoples of the world today appear to possess equal biological potentialities for attaining any level of civilization.
>
> UNESCO (1968:270)

The overwhelming obviousness of human difference, becoming even more so in public perception with the rise in European-bound immigration, was the central dilemma for those seeking to counter the common-sense or gut-feeling qualities of racist sentiment. The problem posed by the popular 'fear' of diversity, played upon by racist politics, is that which the culturalist approach taken by the UNESCO tradition, influenced by the anthropologists it involved, attempted to address. An explanation had to be found, both of the fact of physical differences between individuals and for the perception that 'at certain times and certain places, some cultures "move" while others "stand still" ' (Lévi-Strauss and Eribon 1991:148). What would be sufficient for explaining these differential rates of 'progress' – the ultimate measure of modernity – without invoking the existence of human hierarchies?

UNESCO's response to this dilemma proposed the substitution of the notion of hierarchical 'race' with that of equal but different 'culture'. This stance should be seen in the light of the other main dimensions of the Statement, namely, the negation of the superiority of certain groups of people over others, and its emphasis on racism as prejudice. Both elements circumvent a discussion of the role of the state in the rise of the idea of 'race'. Instead, the formula proposed is based on the proposition that real cultural differences between human groups do exist which in turn are perceived by people who, in reaction, often behave in prejudicial ways. This state of affairs was instrumentalised by a racial science which had been proved false. Therefore, contemporary aversion to human difference could be discredited as prejudicial, rather than being justified by a theorisation of a hierarchy of superior and inferior 'races'.

Cultural relativism: the anti-racism of Claude Lévi-Strauss

> Overall, I was looking for a way to reconcile the notion of progress with cultural relativism. The notion of progress implies the idea that certain cultures, in specific times and places, are superior to others because they have produced works that the others have shown themselves incapable of producing. And cultural relativism ... states that there is no criterion that enables one to make an absolute judgement as to how one culture is superior to another.
>
> Lévi-Strauss and Eribon (1991:147–8)

The cultural solution that founds the UNESCO tradition was influenced by the role of anthropologists in the production of the Statement and subsequent pamphlets, the most prominent of whom was Claude Lévi-Strauss. The anti-racism of individual anthropologists, however, had a longer history. The inter-war years constituted an important time in the development of anti-racist ideas, particularly in the 1930s reaction to Hitler's rise to power and the growth of racism and antisemitism throughout Europe. It was mainly during this time that the work of several anthropologists and anti-racist scientists, such as Boas, Huxley and Klineberg, sought to denounce the scientific credibility of the 'race' concept. It laid the ground for the later approach mobilised in the delegitimation of racial science. The anthropological emphasis of the refutation of 'race' was largely influenced by its concern to rid itself of the appellation, 'the handmaiden of colonialism' (Chaterjee 1987:16).

Lévi-Strauss's contribution to the UNESCO series was probably most well-known, not only because of his status as the 'father of structuralism' and a widely published anthropologist, but also because his essay *Race and History* was published separately in its French version as a book. In France, the short book became 'a classic anti-racist document' (Lévi-Strauss and Eribon 1991:148) which 'is even read in the lycées' (ibid.). The work is based on two main propositions, both of which are constitutive of the culturalist trend in anti-racism attributable to the UNESCO approach. Firstly, Lévi-Strauss proposes the use of ethnicity and culture as alternative explanations for the difference previously covered by 'race'. Secondly, he advocates that racism may be combated by a spread of knowledge of different cultures through the education of a future generation in the importance and richness of global cultural diversity. The cultural relativism upon which both the explanation and the solution to racism proposed by Lévi-Strauss are based underpin the specific approach to anti-racism that dominates the policy of the international institutions. It also had a profound impact on the development of a solidarity model of anti-racism that advocated knowledge of other cultures, in order to combat persistent racism in a post-war climate of growing cultural diversification.

Lévi-Strauss's search for alternative explanations for human difference is necessitated, in his analysis, by the widespread recognition of this difference as a 'fact', and the tendency to equate it with a belief in 'racial' inequality. To merely proclaim the equality of all human beings is of little use because it refutes the common-sense perception of diversity which has been schooled to think 'racially'. In other words Lévi-Strauss, quoting the preamble to the UNESCO Statement notes that 'the thing which convinces the man in the street that there are separate races is "the immediate evidence of his senses when he sees an African, a European, an Asiatic and an American Indian together"' (Lévi-Strauss 1975:102).

The use of culture to explain observable differences is not merely an essentialising means of replacing the explanation of difference offered by 'race'. Lévi-Strauss also celebrates the importance of cultural diversity.

Both cultural diversity and progress are affected by the degree of interaction between groups. The western tendency to see other cultures as primitive is based on the historical 'chance' that led to the industrial revolution taking place in the West, just as the Neolithic revolution erupted in the Middle and Far East rather than in Europe. Just as both revolutions eventually affected and transformed the rest of the globe, the diversity that attributes different processes to a variety of cultural sources is not static. Only seldom do cultures develop in isolation. Nonetheless, the connection and ultimate closeness between societies despite their difference, or what Lévi-Strauss claims is the naturalness of cultural diversity resulting from direct or indirect relations between groups, is not easily accepted in European society. The paradox of cultural relativism is that by discriminating between cultures we become identical to that which we seek to condemn. Seeing others as savages unveils the very savagery of our own society. This is the essence of what Lévi-Strauss calls 'ethnocentrism' which replaces 'racism' as a term to better describe the animosity between cultural groups; the phenomenon that, according to the author, is actually what is meant when the term 'racism' is used.

The solutions Lévi-Strauss offers to the ethnocentrism bred by the western obsession with the idea of progress are the tenets of the cultural relativism central to much anti-racist thought. The notion of cultural relativism originates in the efforts of an anti-racist strain in anthropology of the 1930s and 1940s to critique the biological determinism of that time (Taguieff 1991b). According to Taguieff (ibid.), the impact on post-war anti-racism of this approach centred around three principles: the autonomy of cultural phenomena; the domination by cultural determinism of mental structures and lifestyles; and the equal value of all cultures. Its formulation reveals the ambivalent relationship between the notion of culture and a discourse of anti-racism. This is because Lévi-Strauss's insistence upon the invalidity of 'race' and his substitution for it of cultural diversity, as the real root of discrimination, circumvents the problem that the belief in the superiority of some over others upon which racism is said to be based continues to motivate discriminatory practices. While this poses a fundamental problem for the construction of anti-racist discourse around relativist claims, Lévi-Strauss himself appears to be unconcerned by the practical implications of his theory. A closer look at the principles upon which it was based reveals further problems in the application of Lévi-Strauss's perspective on cultural relativism as a solution to racism.

According to Lévi-Strauss, the central basis for ethnocentrism is the problem that, since at least the mid-nineteenth century, almost all 'civilisations' have recognised the superiority of the West and have sought to become westernised. In contrast, the principle of cultural relativism is based on the individuality of each cultural or 'civilisational' group. This produces a dilemma, because the intercultural cooperation brought about by increased westernisation dilutes such individuality, and therefore the value of each culture in its uniqueness, for humanity as a whole. For Lévi-Strauss, the objective of 'world civilisation' is only worth pursuing if it were to reflect a coalition of original cultures. The more diverse the cultures involved, the more fruitful the intercultural cooperation. Yet, the more interaction takes place, the more there is an inevitable homogenisation of resources, and the weaker the coalition becomes.

Two 'solutions' to the problem of cultural dilution are seen by Lévi-Strauss to have been provided by the conditions of the pre-war world. The first relies on ensuring the internal diversification of individual societies, most efficiently produced by social inequality; the second involves an external diversification, such as that created by colonialism. The gradual improvement of conditions, for both the underprivileged in western societies and for the former colonised, will ultimately lead to the end of diversity. For Lévi-Strauss, international institutions such as UNESCO are faced with an immense task because they must attempt to retain the balance between cultural particularism and inter-group cooperation. The only means he can conceive of for accomplishing this delicate balance is to keep sectors of society in conditions of disadvantage until they themselves emerge from them under the natural conditions of progress.

The validity of cultural relativism

The interpretation of cultural relativism for the purposes of anti-racism, particularly that promoted by the UNESCO project, which had widespread effects on anti-racist thought, focused on the importance of cultural knowledge. The idea that knowledge of the histories and customs of other cultures would engender a greater degree of tolerance among a new generation was promoted by anti-racists in western societies transformed by an unprecedented increase in non-European immigration. It continues to underpin a form of anti-racism that sees racism as a prejudicial behaviour, separate from the political conditions of a given state. This anti-racism makes a link between its activity and the notion of 'identity', seen as embodying the cultural 'essence' of a group or society and to differentiate it from any other. Understanding the differences between purported cultural identities remains a key component of the anti-racist response to what are thought of as intercultural tensions. This was evident in the thinking of the Italian organisation, ARCI:

> One of the elements of the anti-racist struggle is somehow to put questions to oneself about one's own identity. Therefore, a strong identity is better able to enter into dialogue and to accommodate diversity and otherness.
>
> ARCI, Italy

The means of creating the conditions for intercultural dialogue are often construed by a recourse to culture itself. The strategies of several anti-racist organisations, very clearly evident in Italy, involve the organisation of cultural events, in particular music concerts and 'multiethnic' dinners. This activity belongs to a multicultural vision of society as made up of identifiable cultural 'communities' that involves an unavoidable reification of both the group and its members. This assumption of the internal homogeneity of 'minority ethnic' communities and the reduction of their very existence to an essentialised culture, is made regardless of the concomitant recognition of the heterogeneity of the dominant national society, with its various social classes, differential sexualities and political oppositions. In Anthias and Yuval-Davis's (1992:163) description:

> The notion of 'community' assumes an organic wholeness. The community is a 'natural' social unit. It is 'out there' and one can either belong to it or not. Any notion of internal difference within the 'community', therefore, is subsumed to this organic construction.

Lévi-Strauss himself comes to criticise the cultural relativist approach taken by UNESCO. The initial publication of *Race and History* was followed twenty years later by *Race and Culture*.[1] Despite the fact that, by 1988 (Lévi-Strauss and Eribon 1991:152), he had judged there to be no 'racism in the true sense of the word' in France, Lévi-Strauss's 1971 lecture reacted to his belief that 'racial conflicts were only getting worse' (ibid.:148). Moreover, he thought both racism and anti-racism ill-defined and claimed that, 'because of this carelessness, racism was being fuelled instead of weakening' (ibid.). Lévi-Strauss (1983) makes two criticisms of the UNESCO approach. Firstly, that 'revelling in fine words year after year doesn't change people', and secondly that UNESCO shelters itself too readily behind what he now thought of as being contradictory affirmations, such as 'reconciling fidelity to oneself with openness to others'. What had changed in the anthropologist's approach during the twenty-year lapse?

By the time he wrote *Race and Culture*, Lévi-Strauss considered that UNESCO had been unable to maintain the balance between intercultural cooperation and cultural preservation that he claimed was a prerequisite of the principle of cultural relativism. In contrast to his original belief in the ability to increase tolerance through cultural knowledge, he notes that 'perhaps the most shocking thing about "Race and Culture" was the idea that cultures want to be opposed to each other' (Lévi-Strauss and Eribon 1991:149). In *Race and History*, Lévi-Strauss wished to show that the differences between cultures make their meeting beneficial. However, his prediction at the end of *Race and History* that the homogenisation of resources brought about by cultural coalitions would lead to a decrease in cultural diversity had indeed come about in the twenty years between the two works. In other words, difference does not stay constant, and so its utility as a means for increasing human knowledge is diminished.

Lévi-Strauss's pessimism in 1971 as to the probability of an end to racism or ethnocentrism has not been seriously challenged in accounts of cultural relativism. *Race and Culture* does not in fact depart radically from the main position developed in *Race and History*. Where it differs profoundly, however, is in the conclusion. Whereas in 1951, Lévi-Strauss believed that the greater knowledge of other cultures that the discipline of anthropology could bring to society could actively inform the fight against racism, he now casts serious doubts as to whether 'the ethnologist can count on his aptitude to resolve, on his own and armed only with the resources of his discipline, the problems posed by the struggle against racial prejudices' (Lévi-Straus 1983:46). While he believes that ethnology has amply contributed to the anti-racist cause, Lévi-Strauss claims that it would be wrong for the discipline to put its faith in the ability of human communication alone to bring about intercultural harmony and a respect for diversity. There is nothing that anthropologists, anti-racists or the international institutions can do, in Lévi-Strauss's estimation, to halt what he calls the progressive fusion of populations, heretofore separated by geographical, linguistic and cultural barriers, brought about by the world's rapid industrialisation. The fight against racism is seen as paradoxical because despite its necessity,

> the fight against all forms of discrimination participates in the same movement that leads humanity towards a global civilisation that destroys those old particularisms to which we owe the honour of having created the aesthetic and spiritual values that give life its richness ...
>
> (ibid.:47)

Furthermore, Lévi-Strauss condemns as naïve the quest for equality and fraternity, for he has come to realise that these aims are unachievable without inducing the end of diversity: 'One cannot both rejoice in the other, identify with him and remain different' (ibid.). Lévi-Strauss predicts that the situation brought about by the negation of diversity will render a 'regime of intolerance' that will not even require ethnic differences for its justification. The past is irrevocable and the only hope is in a change in the course of history, a change more difficult to imagine than the already doomed hope for progress in the realm of ideas.

In order to fully grasp the nature of Lévi-Strauss's argument for the impossibility of intercultural understanding, it is necessary to relate it to his substantive statement, made in both 1951 and 1971, that the only way in which to derive the benefits from a situation of cultural diversity is to maintain the separation between cultural groups. Because he does not make explicit the political implications of the argument, it is possible to interpret it in two opposite ways. Lévi-Strauss may be said to be arguing for the enforced separation of groups of nationalities or cultures that, in political terms, would be opposed to the process of immigration. Alternatively, he may be seen to propose the complete cultural autonomy of individual groups in whatever country they choose to live; a type of radical multiculturalism. However, the second position does not overcome his problem of the dilution of cultural uniqueness that is said to be brought about by intercultural coexistence. Under Lévi-Strauss's conditions, the balance between cultural preservation and fruitful intercultural contact could not be met by such a radical multiculturalism without cultures being forcibly kept from each other in situations of segregation.

The improbability of this alternative being chosen by Lévi-Strauss is compounded by his reference to Gobineau in his explanation of the ultimate self-destruction of global cultural diversity. Lévi-Strauss makes an analogy between Gobineau's theory of racial degeneration as brought about by racial mixture and the dilution of cultural diversity engendered by cross-cultural contact. By replacing the word 'race' with that of 'culture' he proposes a characterisation of the contemporary debate on cultural diversity in anthropology and anti-racism. Lévi-Strauss legitimises his recourse to the work of Gobineau by claiming that 'one of the most famous racial theoreticians of the nineteenth century' (Mosse 1978:13) did not espouse the inequality of the 'races'. Rather, 'like all his contemporaries, he was influenced by the West's historical success' (Lévi-Strauss and Eribon 1991:161) on which the construction of western racial superiority is based. By taking this opinion, Lévi-Strauss is able to use Gobineau's theorisation of the importance of racial separateness for the ultimate preservation of each in its 'natural' environment for making a contemporary argument for cultural diversity. His use of Gobineau in conjunction with current studies in genetics is shown, against classical racial science and contemporary ethnocentrism, as proof of the biological equality of different cultural groups. Nonetheless, both anti-racism and the field of ethnology may only benefit from the principle of cultural relativism if it remains possible to research the contributions of distinct cultural groups to human history; an endeavour which would be made impossible if the process of cultural intermixture was not curbed.

There are two fundamental problems in Lévi-Strauss's approach, in both texts, which have not been considered in the continued adoption of an unproblematised intercultural approach, particularly in multicultural policy making as well as in some strands of anti-racism. These may be said to define the problematic nature of the UNESCO tradition of anti-racism as a whole. Firstly, Lévi-Strauss and the UNESCO Statement demonstrate an apparent belief in the interchangeability of the notions of 'race' and culture. Because the

Statement defines racism as the belief in the superiority of the West over 'primitive' societies (Barker 1983), by advocating that the notion of competing 'races' be replaced by relative cultures, it presumed that the problem of the hierarchy implied by 'race' had been overcome. Nevertheless, the relativity of different cultures is not unrelated, in Lévi-Strauss's analysis, to the notion of progress. While he claims that the progress of distant cultures cannot be uniquely based upon the history of the West, he does not provide an alternative means of gauging this progress. By assuming that non-western cultures, left to their own devices, will ultimately acquire the level of progress already attained in the West, he cannot overcome a hierarchised view of cultural achievements. This is attested to in his biographer Edmund Leach's remark that there is an element in the anthropologist that 'conceives of primitive peoples as "reduced models" of what is essential in all mankind' (Leach 1970:18).

Secondly, cultural differences are explanatory, as Lévi-Strauss quite explicitly claims at the end of *Race and Culture*, as long as cultural groups are physically separated in geographical terms. He is therefore unable to define in what way the coexistence of different cultural groups in a single national space may promote tolerance. This is made all the more problematic because, when interviewed in 1988, he denies that racism is any longer a problem in France but claims that 'there are and always will be communities inclined to like others whose values and life-styles do not go against their own and who will find others less easy to accept' (Lévi-Strauss and Eribon 1991:152). Beyond the reification of culture that this statement implies, Lévi-Strauss assumes both that 'ethnocentrism' is a matter of personal likes and dislikes and that this is not reflective of a situation of institutionalised discrimination.

CULTURALISM AND THE THEORISATION OF A NEORACISM

The pernicious fiction of separate but equal identities based in discrete homelands was an important marker of a change in which the idea of contending national and ethnic traditions was employed to legitimate and rationalise the move from natural to cultural hierarchies. This shift was not, of course, an absolute change. Nature and culture may have functioned as neatly exclusive poles in the models of early modern thought, but as the organic overtones of the word 'culture' reveal, the boundaries between them have always been porous.

Paul Gilroy (2000:33)

The legacy of the cultural relativism of Lévi-Strauss and the UNESCO tradition has remained vital to a contemporary analysis of the attempts to explain racism which, this chapter argues, is a principal task of anti-racism. Since the 1980s, such explanations of racism have increasingly proposed the replacement of the discourse of biological legitimation that underpinned classical racist thought, with one of cultural incompatibility. The theorisation of a new cultural racism is based on the observation, particularly in the discourse of right-wing anti-immigration parties, of a utilisation of the idea of separate but equal cultures that is not immediately distinguishable from the main proposals made by Lévi-Strauss. My analysis of the nature of this neoracism shall argue that it is confounded by a central theoretical opposition. On the one hand, the new racism has been described as the consequence solely of a culturally relativist anti-racism that has created the conditions for a culturalised view of society. This position, advocated by Taguieff (1991a,b) holds two strands of anti-racism accountable for the advent of neoracism. However, neither of these – left-wing and anti-colonial anti-racism – were responsible for the cultural relativist approach which was mainly influenced by the position taken by a mainstream international institution: UNESCO. By approaching a theorisation of the phenomenon in this way, Taguieff criticises anti-racism, which he sees as dangerously opposing the universal values of secularism and humanism. This singling out of anti-racism fails to perceive the relationship between the shift in racist discourse and concurrent political transformations at the level of the state.

In contrast, Barker (1981) has analysed the development of cultural racism in terms of a theory which, while publicly relying on a discourse of apparently benign cultural incompatibility, is related to scientific developments in the field of sociobiology that attempt to narrow the gap between heredity and culture as explanatory of hierarchies of human progress. The mobilisation of this discourse is contextualised by an analysis of the changing political conditions engendered by the appearance of Conservative neoliberalism in the early 1980s in Britain. The way in which the mutual dependency of science and politics is mobilised by a new racism which presents itself as a novel theorisation of human difference to replace the outdated 'race' idea, indicates the importance of linking the analysis of racism to the political processes at the core of the state. Barker's argument against a 'culturalisation' of the very culturalism proposed by the new racism, which would imply an acceptance of its main argument, provides the link to the final part of this chapter that examines the very different legacy of the state-centred theorisation of racism by anti-colonialism as it was applied by an emergent self-organised anti-racism in Europe.

Cultural relativism and the new racism: anti-racism's culpability

Pierre-André Taguieff bases his analysis of the advent of a neoracism on the success of the *Front national* in France in the early 1990s, and on the proposal that the anti-racist Left was unable to oppose the rise of the far-right party. In all three of the books he wrote on racism between 1990 and 1991, the first chapters treat the subject of anti-racism and its discontents. Taguieff rightly proposes the need for an intellectual discussion of the shortcomings of the anti-racist project. However, there is a serious absence of critique, both in France and abroad, of his preference for developing elaborate attacks on anti-racism in books that claim, on the contrary, to be concerned with racism. As a consequence, Taguieff is not concerned with structural transformations undergone at state or governmental level with an effect on the emergence of new racist rhetoric. On the contrary, he confines his criticism to the fringes of left- and right-wing politics. Secondly, Taguieff does not argue for the theoretical nature of neoracism and so compartmentalises its popular appeal from any form of academic legitimation. In contrast, he does discuss the limitations of theoretical *anti*-racist discourse (Taguieff 1989). For Taguieff, a 'differentialist' racist argument that opposes the notion of multicultural society has entirely replaced biological accounts of racial difference. Culturally relativist anti-racism, according to Taguieff, facilitated the development of a culturally oriented neoracism.

Taguieff attacks the anti-racist movement in France, both for creating the discourse upon which a culturalist racism itself is built and for its proposed failure to account for the Right's new focus on culture. Taguieff's argument is an assault on left-wing political faction-alism that circumvents a theorisation of the role of either political institutions or the academy. Body-Gendrot (1998:850) supports Taguieff's approach and summarises his main argument as

> saying that the anti-racist postures are mirrors of the racist ones. When anti-racists denounce the return of racist regressions into modernity, they hold orthodox dogma, they stigmatise the racist as the Other in

the same way as the racist stigmatises the Other. In France, anti-racist graffiti, for instance, stigmatise Le Pen as such: 'A Breton, not even a Frenchman, deport him.'

The question appears to be not whether it is problematic that anti-racist discourse often comprises overtly patriotic slogans, but whether this can rightfully be termed a type of racism as Taguieff argues.

A central problem for Taguieff is the fact that the definition of racism has been provided by anti-racists whose lack of objectivity is witnessed in the nature of anti-racist mobilisation which demands a preference for 'instruments of struggle rather than tools of knowledge' (Taguieff 1991b:21). He attacks four main trends in the evolution of anti-racist discourse. First, cultural relativism which he attributes to the UNESCO tradition. Second, a teleological, or what I would also term an anti-fascist, position that sees 'everyday racism' as potentially leading to genocide. Third, Taguieff examines the relationship drawn between 'race' and class by what he calls 'the economist vulgate steeped in the Communist tradition' (ibid.:26). Lastly, he critiques the Third World reinterpretation of anti-racism from a perspective of anti-imperialism.

Taguieff proposes that cultural relativism opposes the fundaments of a secular, egalitarian universalism. He sees the evolution of a new, 'differentialist' racism as based upon the idea of culture fixity. This transformation means that neither of the existing notions of racism or anti-racism is able to explain the complex nature of the cultural differentialism proposed by the new racism. However, rather than criticising the emphasis placed on culture as an alternative to 'race' and the associated denial of the relationship of 'race' and state, Taguieff considers that the cultural relativism of anti-racism led directly to the culturalist racism of the New Right. Moreover, anti-racism now finds itself in a situation of ambiguity because advocates of neoracism, such as the *Front national*, make use of the very discourse upon which the anti-racist milieu relied: 'It is necessary in fact to consider ... the incapacity of the organised anti-racist milieus, by means of coherent counter-arguments, to face up to this new ideological situation in which symbolic racism artfully absorbs certain traditionally anti-racist principles' (Taguieff 1991b:54).

While the anthropological cultural relativism that informed the UNESCO project has undoubtedly been central to the development of anti-racist discourse, it is implausible to suggest, as Taguieff does, that neoracist doctrine purposefully borrows this language. Certainly the entrance of categories such as 'ethnicity' and 'culture' and descriptors such as 'ethnocentrism' into common parlance has facilitated the neoracist turn. Yet, Taguieff goes beyond this and implies rather that there is a borrowing from anti-racists by racists of which the former are aware but against which they are unable, or unwilling, to act. In fact, there was little evidence from my research that anti-racists remain ignorant of the proposition that racist discourse has been transformed by the language of culture. One interview revealed an awareness of the rise of a new, cultural racism such as that proposed by Taguieff himself and in the same way stressed the need for anti-racism to 'catch up':

> There is a real cultural racism which has nothing to do that much with 'race' as a biological category … Anti-racism I think to a great extent has to catch up with racism because I think they're becoming better and better at it every day. Racism is transforming constantly. It's very powerful. And you would think that in the western world those forces would be on the margins but they're not. The Conservative party and their ideas – it's coming into mainstream policy. Look what happened in Austria. Look what's happening in Denmark. If it comes through the centre Right onto the political agenda, the problem that happens is that the extreme Right will come in on the scene and say now we have to do it properly.
>
> NCADC, UK

Taguieff proposes the means by which he believes anti-racism may transform itself in the face of racism's new ambiguity. In his opinion, culturalist or differentialist racism enters political discourse in the 1980s for two reasons. Firstly, extreme right-wing organisations such as the *Club de l'Horloge*, concerned with 'the defence of cultural identities', perceive the need for more palatable formulations of their ideas (Taguieff 1991b). Secondly, the issue of immigration is reformulated by these organisations as concerning the preservation of culture and identity, a view in which multiculturalism is seen as indirect genocide. The undesirability of North Africans, as opposed to the more acceptable Polish and Italian immigrants that preceded them, is based on the purported impossibility for them to assimilate into French society. Arguments calling for a stop to immigration into France claim to consider the good of immigrants themselves who, like the French, seek to 'preserve and cultivate their differences' (ibid.:50). Faced with this new culturalist rhetoric, anti-racism whose very language has been borrowed by its adversaries, should concern itself less with stigmatising and condemning those it calls racists. Rather, anti-racism should determine the reasons for which a large immigrant population has remained 'badly integrated' into French society and propose methods for rectifying the problems of 'social exclusion' to which this has led.

Etienne Balibar (1991a, 1994) critiques Taguieff's identification of neoracism as a novel phenomenon by demonstrating how his decontextualised account of its development fails to explain it in relation to the historical growth of the 'race' idea in modernity. Taguieff's explanation of neoracism is recognised by Balibar as emphasising above all the conflict between racism and anti-racism. He refutes Taguieff's argument for the complete replacement of biological explanations of 'racial' difference by culturalist attitudes. Rather, it is more correct to argue that there is no real or significant difference between the various theoretical justifications for discrimination, be they biological or cultural. The problems in anti-racism will not be overcome if, as Taguieff suggests, anti-racists were to realise that racism is now built upon a belief in cultural preservation rather than biological superiority. Balibar does claim that it is important to have shown that differentialist racism presents itself as the 'true anti-racism' by sustaining a cultural relativist stance on the importance of cultural differences. However, by making no difference between the various traditions of anti-racism, Taguieff fails to recognise that more recent reformulations of cultural relativism within multiculturalism do not preclude the possibility of intercultural 'mixing', or that other anti-racisms prioritise a statist, rather than culturalist, analysis of racism within which relativism has little or no place.

What in fact appears to be at the root of Taguieff's condemnation of anti-racists for creating the conditions within which he proposes culturalist racism was able to evolve, is his exasperation at the failure of the politics of assimilation in France. This is upheld by Taguieff's self-avowed republicanism, intransigent secularism and his insistence on the strict division between society and politics on the one hand, and 'community affairs' on the other. In the historical tradition considered in Chapter 1's discussion of the relationship between assimilationism and racism, this approach is grounded in what Balibar thinks of as a specifically French mode of racist thought:

> There is, no doubt, a specifically French brand of the doctrines of Aryanism, anthropometry and biological geneticism, but the true 'French ideology' is not to be found in these: it lies rather in the idea that the culture of the 'land of the Rights of Man' has been entrusted with a universal mission to educate the human race. There corresponds to this mission a practise of assimilating dominated populations and a consequent need to differentiate and rank individuals and groups in terms of their greater or lesser aptitude for – or resistance to – assimilation.
>
> Balibar (1991a:24)

Consequently, culturalist racism is not as new as Taguieff would have it. 'Differentialist' racism, or racism without 'race', existed long before the advent of a neoracism in the phenomenon of modern antisemitism. Antisemitism is a form of differentialist racism *par excellence* which could describe all forms of contemporary neoracism, in particular Islamophobia which is based upon the perception of Islam as a 'world view' that is incompatible with Europeanness (Taguieff 1991b). Taking this into account, neoracism cannot realistically be said to have been brought about by the proposed failures of anti-racism – its insistence upon cultural relativism, its refusal to combat racism on cultural grounds or its operation of a theory of class conflict to explain working-class prejudice. Rather, racism of this type is essentially a function of state, institutional, class-based and individual participation in the legitimation of an established dominant culture. By choosing not to recognise this and to hold anti-racism responsible for the development of neoracism, Taguieff makes clear his opposition to an anti-racism, grounded in the experiences of the racialised in France, to subvert the republican vision of an integrated society which denies the possibility of publicly expressed cultural difference.

Conservative ideology and scientific legitimation

Barker (1981) traces the emergence of the theory of neoracism, from the political context of 1970s and 1980s Britain and through the advent of biological determinism as a scientific means of 'proving' the principles of human nature on which the new racism is said to be based. The construction of a new theory of racism within the

British political arena can be traced back to 1976. The idea however is not new in itself, rather 'its self-conscious renewal at this time has brought forward new elements; and some of its connections are dangerously new' (Barker 1981:24). The self-conscious nature of its construction is vital for Barker as it proves the status of the new racism as a purposefully constructed theory, rather than as either a circumstantial development of events or the unfounded interpretations of certain scholars. This form of racism stems from two sets of ideas that are presented as 'facts'. Firstly, there is what Barker terms the 'argument from genuine fears', one which has been central to the British debate on immigration since the heyday of Enoch Powell in 1968. This is based on the description by politicians and the media of a situation said to be faced by ordinary, British people as a result of the influx of immigrants into their neighbourhoods, schools and workplaces. The fear felt by these people is purportedly based on a 'real' fear of the unknown that understandably results in prejudicial sentiments and behaviours.

Barker cites parliamentary speeches such as Churchill's and newspaper debates on immigration in order to point out that, whether or not the fears they expressed were based on any real experiences, the suggestion that the people believed to be feeling in such a way were ordinary citizens consequently was said to make these fears genuine in the eyes of popular opinion. Barker describes the argument from genuine fears as a bridging mechanism that links 'an apparently innocent description and a theory of race' (Barker 1981:16). By emphasising the concerns of 'everyman', these fears are related to a particular way of life lived by the ordinary citizen which comes to symbolise the unique culture of the British people, whose national, regional, class-based or religious differences are overrun by the perceived spectre of black immigration.

Therefore, genuine fears are linked to a second idea in the construction of the new theory of racism: the defence of a 'way of life', becoming an argument about the unique cultural heritage and traditions of those who have for centuries belonged to the British nation (sic). The defence of a culture is inextricable from the fears deemed to have been expressed by its members because 'the very existence of fears about damage to the unity of the nation is proof that the unity of the nation is being threatened' (Barker 1981:17). Because immigrants are said to threaten national unity by being unable or unwilling to assimilate into the British way of life, the whole meaning of racial prejudice is inverted. Racism now becomes the very refusal of immigrants to adopt the national lifestyle of their host country. According to this unfolding theory, it becomes natural for the ordinary person to want to defend herself by protesting against the rise in immigration. This reformulation of racist discourse strips it of its very racism by purposefully refusing any proposition of racial hierarchy that would characterise immigrants as the members of inferior 'races'. Rather, the argument is that any national group would react similarly to such inflows of immigrants and that the new racist theory is therefore universally resonant. The control of immigration is postulated as a kindness to foreigners themselves who 'too have natural homes' (ibid.:21). In this way, racism becomes a common-sense argument based on the natural tendency of human beings all over the world to form exclusive groups. The new racism is, thus, a theory of

> pseudo-biological culturalism. Nations on this view are not built out of politics and economics, but out of human nature. It is in our biology, our instincts, to defend our way of life, traditions and customs against outsiders – not because they are inferior, but because they are part of different cultures. This is a non-rational process; and none the worse for it. For we are soaked in, made up out of, our traditions and our culture.
>
> (ibid.:23–4)

This type of argument is largely recognisable in the current anti-immigration climate of western Europe and became widespread in the early 1990s. However, Barker locates the emergence of the new racism at least one decade previously, in the rise of the British Conservative party and Thatcherism. Firstly, the rise in Thatcherite Conservatism would not have enjoyed as much success in the absence of the crucial role played by the British media. Despite Enoch Powell's relative success in the late 1960s on an anti-immigration ticket, the real force of the movement he triggered was created by the 'increasingly conscious bid to organise people's experiences and prejudice' (Barker 1981:24). This was mainly played out in the newspapers, but was orchestrated by 'the Tories, led by their Right' (ibid.:25) who actively pushed for a new theorisation of 'race'. The old, biological racism that claimed the superiority of some 'races' over others smacked too much of Nazism which, due to the British experience of the Second World War was opposed almost universally. The new racism was thus, for Barker, a 'struggle to create a new commonsense' (ibid.) to which 'race' and immigration as problems to be solved were central prisms through which the future of nation, culture and community could be envisaged.

Barker demonstrates, firstly, how 'race', even when reconstructed as cultural difference, continues to be 'a major means of differentiation and division' (Gilroy 2000:56), and so a key tool of politics. Secondly, by portraying the extent to which the new racism shapes the (re)definition of the national 'we', Barker squarely relates 'race' to the establishment of the political conditions of the modern nation-state and embeds it in the structures of contemporary politics. Thirdly, Barker shows how the new racist thesis does not completely depart from an appeal to science. It is not the case, as Taguieff presumes, that biological arguments for racial superiority have been stripped of all validity by the advocates of the new racism (Taguieff 1991b; Stolcke 1995). On the contrary, the existence of insurmountable cultural differences, according to neoracist theory, mirrors the perennial and universal characteristics applied to human nature by the racial science of the past. Barker shows how the neo-Darwinist schools of ethology and sociobiology become fundamental to the 'Tory ideology [which] claims that it is biologically fixed that humans form exclusive groups, and that these groups succeed internally in so far as they close up against outsiders' (Barker 1981:78).

The reliance of the neoracist thesis on parallel developments in sociobiology is significant on two counts. Firstly, it points out the persistent attraction of scientific theories of human difference, well after the end of the Second World War and the official rejection of 'race'. This is true whether they theorise the superiority of some groups over others or, more acceptably, that genetic relatedness proves the naturalness of the cultural community. The new racism relies on the appeal to human nature and 'common sense' for its success. Nevertheless, this appeal is not completely justifiable without recourse to scientific validation. The explanation of cultural differences in genetic terms is as central as it once was to the explanation of racial superiority. However, the contrast is made between the 'superiority' of 'race' on the one hand, and the more benign 'difference' of culture on the other. Secondly, Barker points out that sociobiological theories are used to illustrate, not only the purported naturalness of cultural protection, but also that of racial prejudice. Most importantly, this argument has been used in explanations of racism written from an apparently anti-racist stand-point, for example the work of Pierre Van den Berghe.

Van den Berghe's *Race and Racism* (1967) is described by Hannaford (1996:392) as an important work which critiqued the tendency of the American study of race relations 'to perceive the world as being divided into races and ethnic groupings and in no other way'. By 1978 however, the 'former liberal sociologist of race relations' (Barker 1981:97) published an article tracing racism, ethnocentrism and nationalism back to the notion of kin altruism. Genetic rea-soning is mobilised in a new 'non-racial' explanation of racism, and therefore offered as an anti-racist explanation of human difference and intercultural animosity. The novelty of the new racist thesis according to Gilroy was precisely its ability to articulate apparent opposites, most notably racism and anti-racism. For Gilroy,

> what seems new about the New Racism, twenty years after this insight was first employed, is not so much the tell-tale emphasis on culture that was its intellectual hallmark but the way its ideologues refined the old opposites – nature and culture, biology and history – into a new synthesis: a bioculturalism that, as Barker had pointed out, drew its deter-ministic energy from the intellectual resources supplied by sociobiology.
>
> Gilroy (2000:33)

The theorisation of the existence of a neoracism has been funda-mental for the development of new modes of thinking about 'race' and racism. It was developed in response to the perception, on the one hand, that due to the growing diversification of European soci-eties, the issues of 'race' and racism were losing relevance and, on the other, to the observation that the far Right was gaining ground on the back of such complacency. Despite the importance of this recognition it has not led to an overcoming of the original problem in the UNESCO project which, by directly substituting 'culture' for 'race' failed to deal with the persistence of *racism*. A culturalist ten-dency in both racism and anti-racism results in turning ' "race" into a synonym for ethnicity and a sign for the sense of separateness which endows groups with an exclusive, collective identity' (Gilroy 1987:16). The development of understandings about the nature of neoracism, as Balibar makes clear, needs to be more strongly related to the theoretical and epistemological shifts of European modernity and so to the history of the European nation-state in which the construction of difference equally fits both its biological and cultural variants.

ANTI-COLONIALISM, 'RACE' AND CLASS

The development of the culturalist explanations of 'race' central to the UNESCO tradition was countered by the development of a state-centred perspective, inspired by the anti-colonialist movement that emerged in Europe by the late 1950s. This was based on an analysis of 'race' and racism as shaped by the demands of class and capitalism. The exploitation of the colonised could be contrasted with that of immigrant workers in the metropolises, and the system of colonisation with that of the capitalist means of production (Fanon 1963; Sivanandan 1982; Mullard 1985; Gilroy 1987). The discussion of the main elements of the anti-colonialist critique shall be transposed to the European context by contrasting two versions of the so-called 'race and class' approach that prepare the development of a model of anti-racism grounded in the experiences of the racialised. A state-centred account of racism was developed by the proponents of a left-wing and trade union-based anti-racism that was based on the belief in the natural alliance between immigrants and the indigenous working class. This overlapped with a self-organised anti-racism that built upon the anti-colonialist and American experiences of black resistance.

If we are to seriously consider Gilroy's suggestion that 'anti-racism is not and probably has never been an adequate heading under which the content, scope and direction of black protest and self-organisation can be assessed' (Gilroy 1987:24), it is necessary to evaluate how the impact that anti-colonialism has had on black collective action in the West in turn affected the development of left-wing anti-racism. The complexity of leftist anti-racism's romanticisation of the mythical heroic figure of anti-colonialism is well-described in Etienne Balibar's (1992) discussion of the effect of the anti-colonial movement on the French Communist party. Gilroy proposes that black collective action differs fundamentally from anti-racism because it relies on a 'utopian political language' (1987:25) that baffles Eurocentric critics. But Gilroy makes too sharp a distinction between the two forms that certainly does not take into account a European perspective on anti-racism beyond the

British context. In contrast, I propose a wider definition of anti-racism in which black and 'minority'-led organisations, whose discourse differs considerably from that of mainstream anti-racist organisations, are nonetheless seen as important for a consideration of the full scope of the phenomenon. The impact of negritude, self-determination and emancipation, as exemplified by the Third World movement against colonialism and its shaping of the struggles of black people in Europe and the US, is integral to the historicisation of these anti-racist forms.

According to Mullard (1985), the black liberation movements of the 1950s and 1960s constituted both a revolt against western values, epitomised by Fanon's (1963:43) remark that 'every time Western values are mentioned they produce in the native a sort of stiffening or muscular lockjaw', and 'an articulate ideological expression of that revolt' (Mullard 1985:30). Grounded primarily in the African experience, the call for self-determination not only expressed frustration with colonial oppression, but also developed programmatic methods for bringing it to an end. Mullard lists four main elements of African resistance which later informed the western experience of black resistance. These are:

(1) The total rejection of the dominant social, political and economic order; (2) Total rejection of the beliefs, values and institutions which underpinned the dominant order; (3) The possession of an alternative conception of a social, political and economic order; (4) The possession of an alternative institutional value and belief system.

Mullard (1985:31)

Mullard identifies this programme in the negritude movement, and later in that of US-based Black Power. Adhesion to tenets of black resistance involved an identification with 'a politically based black consciousness' (Mullard 1985:32) grounded in the experience of colonialism. This meant building empathy with those with whom one shared similar experiences of racism and who, together, could develop a shared consciousness of the course of action to be taken. The emphasis on resistance that emerges from the anti-colonialist struggle informs a new type of anti-racist activism that differs radically from that typified by the US Civil Rights Movement. The movement remained within the institutional boundaries of the state and so did not challenge the legitimacy of its inegalitarian constitution. Resistance takes both a negative and a positive approach according to Mullard. Negatively, it directs itself against the control, values and institutions of society. Positively, it aims to replace the ideologies and control systems of the dominant group with those 'consistent with a utopian, alternative and consciously avowed set of beliefs, values and institutions' (ibid.:35). In other words, it proposes the means of throwing off oppression and, in so doing, creates a basis for collective action which defines resistance as positive and proactive.

Anti-colonial movements in the Third World provided the inspiration for the definition of a colour-based consciousness that liberated many European 'immigrants' and American blacks from the perceived need to assimilate. However, the internal intellectual critique of colonialism also strongly emphasised the relationship with capitalism. Black resistance and self-organisation in the metropolis did not develop independently of a critique of the fact that blacks and ethnic 'minorities' were 'faring consistently badly in the markets for jobs, housing and education' (Gilroy 1987:21). The contribution of anti-colonialism was in identifying colonialism's logic in that of capitalism (Cox 2000). This was not only true in the obvious terms of western capitalism's exploitation of colonial resources, but also in the ability to draw direct comparisons between the treatment of the 'natives' in the colonies and of the underprivileged in western societies (Fanon 1963). The most significant aspect of the contribution of anti-colonialism was that it directly informed metropolitan anti-racist positions and emerging studies in the Anglo-American field of 'race relations'. Not only did the events of decolonisation, fundamental to the transformation of world history and geopolitics in the post-war era, inspire anti-racist activity in the West, their protagonists handed down a set of principles to a new generation of activists: 'New World blacks' (Gilroy 2000:130) with workers in the front lines.

For the study of 'race relations' it was crucial that this point be understood. Much early scholarship in the field, particularly that of sociologists, opted for socioeconomic readings of racial discrimination that shared little with the culturalist approaches of their anthropologist colleagues (Rex 1975). The issue of organising as immigrant workers is cognisant of the contrasted relations to labour between the colonial context and the European metropolis. The former was a pure relation of exploitation, while the latter mobilised a discourse of rights enabled by the historical struggle of the European workers' movements. The theme of immigrant workers' rights, shaped in some cases by ongoing colonial experiences such as that of Algeria, was developed in two stages; firstly, by preexisting anti-racist movements, trade unions and left-wing political parties (Lloyd 1998); and secondly, by blacks and 'ethnic minorities' themselves as an expression of the necessity of self-organisation. Both of these trends were directly influenced by the anti-colonialist movement, its writers (Césaire, Senghor, Fanon, Memmi ...) and by the movements built subsequently in the US context (from civil rights to Black Power).

Black and white worker solidarity

Cathie Lloyd (1998), in her analysis of the development of French anti-racist discourse, describes the process of transformation undergone by the *Mouvement contre le racisme et pour l'amitié entre les peuples* (MRAP), an anti-racist organisation set up after the Second World War in France, under the influence of the intellectual productions of anti-colonialism. In France, the war with Algeria and the parallel and subsequent discriminatory policing of Algerian immigrants, targeted as potential members of the FLN, is a theme central to both anti-racism and the political discourse on immigration, as is testified to by the following statements:

France has a problem with its Algeria.

La lettre pour la citoyenneté, France

You should know that in France immigration is strongly conditioned by colonial history: this is clear. Islam is not neutral in France. Islam is the religion of the formerly colonised people. Algeria has marked the way of thinking for a long time as well as the French state in its practices with regard to the Muslim community in France.

ADRI, France

It is also the link made with Algeria that bridges the themes of 'race' and 'class', the Algerian becoming symbolic for many in France of the negative outcome of decolonisation – the perception that racial problems were being brought to the mother country – and the image of the Algerian (symbolic of all black and North African migrants) as migrant workers who would eventually return home. This is echoed in much of the British anti-immigration rhetoric of the 1960s in which black people are pictured as both racially incompatible with British society and as an economic threat to the indigenous working class (Dummett 1973; Barker 1981).

Lloyd shows how French anti-racists allied themselves closely with the trade union movement, particularly the *Confédération générale des travailleurs* (CGT), over the Algerian question. The involvement of the trade union movement alongside the anti-racists was indicative of the belief, generalised on the Left, that the working class was the natural ally of the colonised and of immigrants. Despite recognising the perceived competition posed by immigrants, willing to work for lesser pay and in poorer conditions than French workers, it was thought that 'once French workers understood the iniquities of the colonial system they would unite with immigrants against the real exploiters: the capitalist employers' (Lloyd 1998:134). However, the involvement of the left-wing trade unions, who in the 1950s and 1960s played a major role in anti-racism by seeking to protect black workers' rights, inevitably led to a questioning of the purported anti-racism of the working class. The assumption of the 'organic' anti-racism of the working class was an integral part of the Left's interpretation of anti-colonialism as a critique of capitalism. The mobilisation of this idea, which facilitated gaining the support of the new immigrant public, was instrumentalised in the furthering of the political objectives of the left wing. The Left could not concede that the idea was problematic because 'if it was recognised that the working class was divided by racism, it would have been difficult to sustain an uncomplicated universalist analysis of the impact of capitalism' (Lloyd 1998:135–6).

Developing a stance on the situation in the colonies was seen by the Left as vital for building alliances of solidarity with immigrant workers in France. French anti-racists in the 1960s sought to universalise their discourse by connecting their objectives to those of decolonisation in Africa and civil rights in the US. This was principally achieved by the use of the American notion of internal colony, developed by civil rights activists to link their domestic struggle against Jim Crow to that against colonialism in Africa (Lloyd 1998). By making such international links, French anti-racists aimed to concretise their emphasis on solidarity and win over their ultimate target group: the immigrant workers.

The attitude of the political left wing to the struggles of racialised groups in France, over the last three decades, has entailed an unofficial competition for winning the votes of the anti-racist public. This has been played out between the Communist, the Socialist and increasingly the Green parties. In the 1960s, the French Communist party (PCF) aligned itself with the anti-colonialist cause while the Socialists are largely held to be behind the emergence of *SOS Racisme* in the 1980s and the *Verts* in recent years have supported causes such as that of the *sans-papiers*. Etienne Balibar's (1992) analysis of the PCF's engagement with the anti-colonial movement goes towards explaining the difficulties raised by the dominance of the left wing in the politics of anti-racism and its consequent detachment from the concerns of the actual or potential victims of racism. Balibar questions the role of the Communist party in the campaign to end Algerian colonialism. Specifically, in Charonne in 1962, the killing of eight people, seven of whom were communists, at a demonstration for peace was marked by a march attended by 800,000 at the event of their burial a week later. The anti-colonialist cause clearly resonated loudly for the Communist party of the time, but the nature of this support has never been fully clarified by the party, according to Balibar. On the contrary, the anti-colonialism of the PCF is 'today repressed and covered over with myths' (Balibar 1992:21).

Balibar claims that the PCF's anti-colonialism has always had recourse to the events of Charonne as proof of its commitment. However, the party failed to connect these events to those of the previous year when hundreds of Algerians who marched through Paris calling for liberation from French colonial rule were killed and deposited in the River Seine by the French Special Brigades. Balibar asserts that the PCF's failure to explicitly link its protest to the Algerian deaths (which remained covered up in France until the 1980s) must be seen in light of both the general effects of belonging to an imperialist nation and the party's establishment in Algeria as part of France's 'civilising mission'; testimony to the ultimate nationalism of the French Communist party. For Balibar, its nationalism stopped the PCF from becoming the party of the whole of the working class and from practising a true internationalism. The party continues to evoke its anti-colonial history, exemplified by the deaths at Charonne and its presence in Algeria, and labels itself the defender of immigrants, while today it also calls for an immediate halt to immigration. The paradox of this duplicity is enabled by the adequate mobilisation of the PCF's mythical anti-colonialism that disconnects the romanticism of that past from the 'realities' of contemporary immigration.

In addition to the dominance of the PCF and the CGT in the 'defence' of immigrant workers, the fact that anti-colonialism in France resulted in a solidarity-based anti-racism rather than an impetus to self-organisation may be explained by a further two factors. Firstly, male immigrant workers initially arrived alone, in small numbers and were largely kept separated from society in hostels or shanty towns, known as *bidonvilles* (Lloyd 1998). This contrasts with the British situation, in which significant numbers of people from the Commonwealth came to Britain as workers like in France, but whose citizenship status meant that they could not be confined to as great an extent and where black-led organisations had existed since the 1920s (Bush 1999; Hesse 2000). Secondly and more generally, anti-racism in France is today still perceived as a specific form of activism that does not necessarily mould itself around what are considered to be the particularist concerns of racialised ('immigrant') communities. The associations that were eventually created by what have come to be known as *résidents étrangers* in France set themselves the practical tasks of assisting newly arrived immigrants and integrating them into the community and French society. Moreover, in the 1960s, the Algerian community in France – in that Algeria was the main focus of French left-wing anti-colonialism – saw its concerns as more aligned with events in Algeria than with racism in France which was experienced as a side-effect of the ongoing war of independence.

Anti-colonialism and self-organisation

The influence of anti-colonialism on anti-racism was equally significant in the British context. Anti-racism was not new to Britain. The Pan-African Congress held the majority of its five meetings between 1900 and 1930 in Britain, 'the main locus of pan-Africanist discourses (in the English-speaking world)' (Hesse 2000:104). Some of the precursors of anti-racist organisations in Britain, like the Jewish self-help organisations in France, include those set up by early African immigrants to Britain such as the West African Students Union (1925) and the League of Coloured People (1931). According to Hesse, the existence of such organisations in Britain was fundamental for the development of pan-Africanism. The 1945 congress, held in Manchester, discussed both the aims of anti-colonialism and the concerns of African countries, but also 'race' in Britain, indicating an early foregoer of the later connections made between metropolitan racism and the anti-colonial struggle.

The history of the Pan-African Conference reveals how anti-racism has always been heterogeneous, with certain strands enjoying more prominence than others at different times. The first Pan-African

Conference was held in London in 1900. A look at the anti-imperialist movement in the UK at the turn of the century reveals how a nascent movement against colonialism coexisted with a paternalistic approach to those it sought to defend, much like the later solidarity-based anti-racism of the 1950s and 1960s in both Britain and France. Schneer (1999) comments on the variety of contradictory versions of anti-imperialism that existed at the time and proposes that 'if London in 1900 was the great imperial metropolis, it was also a nexus of anti-imperialisms' (Schneer 1999:254). Unsurprisingly, a central variant of the anti-imperialism that he describes coexisted comfortably with a scientific racism, particularly amongst British-born activists and Irish nationalists. Groups such as the Anti-Slavery Society, made up mainly of the former, offered the third group – black anti-imperialists – what Schneer calls 'condescending support' (ibid.:257). This group was mainly composed of black clergy in Britain, inspired by the links between African Americans and British radicals that followed the American Civil War.

The parallel activism of black and white anti-imperialists led to the establishment of the African Association (1897), organisers of the first Pan-African Conference. The African Association went further than its precedents, such as the Society for the Recognition of the Brotherhood of Man, because it 'represented the *organised* expression of African-British and African-Caribbean sentiment regarding the British empire' (Schneer 1999:261; emphasis in original). The Pan-African Conference held in July 1900 was attended by 32 delegates from Africa, North America, the West Indies and Britain including W.E.B. Du Bois whose words – 'the problem of the twentieth century is the problem of the colour line' – were used to introduce the document produced by the Conference. As Schneer points out, the Conference did not seek the abolition of the Empire – a future that at the time appeared impossible to envisage – but wished to improve the conditions of those living under its rule. This was in itself a radical project to embark on 'in an era characterised by racism, intimidation and slaughter' (ibid.:264) and, in many ways, was a precursor to the later anti-colonialism of the second half of the new century.

With the advent of post-war immigration and particularly after the achievement of Indian independence, anti-colonialism in Britain, like in France and the US, had particular resonance for the left wing, the trade union movement and for intellectuals developing the field of 'race relations' (e.g. John Rex 1975). The 1960s and 1970s also spawned a departure from the traditional bases of anti-racism on the Left and in anti-fascist circles and saw the emergence of black self-organisation founded upon the concept of resistance (Mullard 1985). However, the attempt to ensure 'that immigrants, West Indians, Pakistanis, Indians and Africans could themselves decide on their own priorities, build their own organisation, and in so doing those things break the circle of dependency' (Glean 1973:13) was not always smooth-running.

CARD (Campaign Against Racial Discrimination), which was founded following Martin Luther King's meeting with British immigrants in 1964 (Glean 1973) folded over a power struggle between an intellectual approach that failed to concede to the impetus, coming from among its member organisations, to root it in Britain's diverse black and 'minority ethnic' communities, and the perception that Indian and white groups were conspiring to deny access to West Indians (Dummett 1973). However more importantly, according to Dummett, CARD failed to make opposition to racism the focus of its concerns, leading to the alienation of many of the communities who initially supported it. The outcome is emblematic of this period that marks the beginning of self-organisation, based in part on an anti-colonialist or resistance-based model. On the one hand, there was the initial realisation – mainly of intellectuals – that racism needed to be fought against on a united front. On the other, the need felt within black communities to represent and prioritise their own interests in the anti-racist fight before entering into coalition was growing.

The rise of the notion of self-organisation and its specific connection to the fight against racism in Britain did not only result from the influence of developments in the US and the former colonies. It was obviously interpreted for the particular struggles by black and 'ethnic minority' groups to resist both racist discrimination (in employment, housing, education, policing etc.) and the perceived paternalism of the liberal and left-wing approaches. This is mirrored in the France of the 1980s with the growth of the *Mouvement beur* in which young people of North African origin sought, against the dominant solidarity-based approach, to take responsibility for the anti-racist agenda. In Britain, one of the principal phenomena shaping the emergence of self-organisation in the early 1970s was the takeover of the Institute of Race Relations by members of its staff under the leadership of black librarian, A. Sivanandan (Mullard 1985).

The 'Commonwealth Institute of Race Relations' was set up in 1958 to research 'the problems of the end of Empire' (Mason, cited in Mullard 1985:17) and in order to prepare 'our civilisation' for the conjoined problems of Communism and race relations (ibid.). The takeover took 'the white, prestigious body and turned it into a research and political centre of and for the victims of racism' (ibid.:1; emphasis in original), and so was an important part of the overall shift to a politics of anti-racism that was grounded in the concerns of racialised groups. The new IRR published a bulletin entitled *Race Today* that reported on a wide range of issues facing blacks and 'ethnic minorities' in Britain and internationally, and especially the activism of black workers against discrimination. The IRR's perspective, undeniably heavily influenced by the writings of Sivanandan, emphasises the structural link between 'race' and class, or more specifically the relations of production and markets (Gilroy 1987). However, unlike the treatment of 'race' in the more general Marxian approach, *Race Today* also dealt with the specific concerns of black women (*Race Today*, August 1974), adding gender as a third factor to the 'race'/class dichotomy.

A central theme of the editorials written by the *Race Today* collective is that of the self-organisation by blacks in Britain. The IRR is in fact both an outcome of such politics of anti-racism as well as a witness to their further development. In March 1976, the editorial refers specifically to the differences between the 'self-organised activity of a black community' (Race Today Collective 1976:51) and the period of the 1960s when the predominantly white left wing took the responsibility to 'organise' it from outside. The self-organisation of black workers within the overall system of labour is stressed as against, for example, the principle of black self-help adopted from the American Black Power model of the 1960s. This model urged blacks to take responsibility for their own welfare through participation in a programme of black capitalism (Gilroy 1987). It was strongly criticised by *Race Today* and contrasted with self-organisation:

> *Race Today* has never been, nor intends to be, a crutch for serving a community, whom we do not see as crippled. We are not in business to patch up the derelict property of the various councils, or to gather and redistribute meagre welfare benefits to the jobless, the wageless or the homeless. The responsibility of the functioning Welfare State must remain with the Welfare State ...
>
> Race Today Collective (1976:51)

The state-centred analysis of racism crucial to the development of a self-organised anti-racism coexists in constant tension with the culturalist tendency which defined a hegemonic approach to anti-racism from the inter-war years on. The recognition of this is important for an understanding of how the heterogeneity of contemporary anti-racism is rooted in antecedents that mirror wider trends in the interpretation of political processes. Bush (1999) demonstrates how the influence of the Trotskyist Trinidadian C.L.R. James and other black intellectuals in the Anglo-American context of the 1930s already introduced a statist account of racism and an internationalist vision of the struggle against it. For example, James, but also W.E.B. Du Bois saw the black nationalism of a Marcus Garvey as irrational in comparison with a developing pan-Africanism that made the explicit link between 'race' and class and incorporated a Marxist analysis of imperialism. Garvey's promotion of the US system of democratic government and black capitalism was seen as eccentric. It fundamentally failed to observe the interrelationships of 'race', capital and Empire that black intellectuals' engagement with Marxism – but also their first-hand experience of racism in both the colonies and the metropolis – revealed. This structural account of racism and its channelling into the Pan-Africanist project is a constant reminder of how anti-racism has long been considered central to general political and social preoccupations, while others wished to isolate it from politics, not least by means of a mobilisation of the notions of 'culture' and 'identity'.

CONCLUSION: THE RETURN OF CULTURE

> At the end of the day, an absolute commitment to cultural insiderism is as bad as an absolute commitment to biological insiderism.
>
> Paul Gilroy (1992:57)

The discussion of some of the formative ideas of an anti-colonial approach, based upon a model of black resistance and an analysis of the interrelationship of racism and capitalism, contrasts strongly with the earlier definition of racism as prejudicial, and of difference as purely cultural. In Europe, self-organised anti-racism has generally been based on a state-centred analysis of the origins of racism and the mobilisation of a discourse of 'race' and, for an important period in the 1960s and 1970s, on a perspective that linked racial discrimination to socioeconomic domination. The importance of this critique, particularly in the impact it had on later formulations of notions of institutionalised or 'everyday' racism, has been overlooked in the widespread equation of a self-organised anti-racism with the new culturalisation of politics attested to by several authors since the 1980s (cf. Taylor 1994). In conclusion, I argue that, in marked contrast to the relationship drawn between the appearance of a new, cultural racism and an anti-racism grounded in the anti-colonial tradition (Taguieff 1991b), the culturalisation of anti-racism has its roots in the institutionalised anti-racism of the UNESCO tradition. Drawing on that legacy, culturalism has been much more a factor of a state-sponsored anti-racism, that forces self-organised anti-racists to conform to its vision of reified cultural groups than it has been the tool of a purportedly 'identititarian' movement.

While 'identity politics' have flourished over the last three decades, beginning with the women's movement and spreading to 'minority' groups of various kinds on a global scale, they have been mistakenly associated with anti-racism (cf. Wallerstein 1989; Taylor 1994). The failure to distinguish between racialised groups organised against racism along political lines and the struggles of marginalised communities for the equal recognition of their cultural, national or religious identity has led to confusion and the attribution of the process of culturalisation to self-organised anti-racism. This flawed proposal is undoubtedly based upon the observation of the situation with which anti-racist organisations and those of black resistance were faced in the 1980s. In France, specifically anti-racist organisations based on the concerns of the racialised in society did not emerge until the mid 1980s with the *Mouvement beur*, led by a second generation of North Africans. Their parents, as foreigners, were not permitted to lead political organisations until the change in the law in 1981. The associations that did exist until that time were mainly established to serve the internal needs of the community. However, the short-lived existence of the *Mouvement beur* led to the retreat of its main protagonists into a localised community politics that, in the French context of large, national and secular organisations, was not considered to belong to the political domain of anti-racism. In Britain, the multicultural policy of local government, apparently derived from the UNESCO tradition's stress on the importance of cultural education, led to a depoliticisation of anti-racism. Many of the self-organised black groups of the 1970s that had relied on the support of local government disappeared due to their unwillingness to submit to the culturalist perspective imposed by a new set of funding priorities.

The multicultural approach to anti-racism established links with the representatives of 'minority ethnic' or religious communities rather than with the protagonists of a political anti-racism. Vertovec (1996) notes the establishment of special liaison committees between local government and the 'community' in the 1960s in Britain for dealing with the arrival of new immigrants and their 'integration' into the local area. Their establishment enabled a separation between what were considered to be the specialised concerns of 'ethnic minorities' and general politics at both the local and national levels. These communities were considered both to be internally homogeneous and to be unconcerned with political processes that, it was presumed, had no effect on the daily life of their members which was seen to be entirely structured by culture and tradition. This allowed for an undemocratic system of representation that belied the greater cultural and political diversity of such communities and the fact that 'ethnic minorities' were involved, mainly through the workplace, in a range of political and societal discussions. Nevertheless, according to Ellis (1991; cited in Vertovec 1996:53):

> [T]he representatives (here 'of the Asian community') had little democratic foundation. Yet their central roles of interaction between local government and minority citizens virtually made them 'the sole rulers of the Asian community – not because they were influential in the community, but because the authorities gave them that role'.

The combination of a multicultural perspective in which 'the definitions of "community" became increasingly dependent on notions of "culture" at the expense of much else' (Vertovec 1996:55) and the official installation of a leadership that did little to counteract these images led to the creation of a relation of dependency between these communities and the local state. In practice, religion and activities promoting 'ethnic' dance, music and cuisine were easier to promote than the more pressing issues of racism against 'minority' groups in European societies: 'Asian religious groups or a scheme set up to promote, for example, African drumming would have a stronger chance of survival than, say, a group concerned with the treatment of young West Indians in police detention' (Anthias and Yuval-Davis 1992:182).

The culturalisation of the concerns of 'minority ethnic' groups, be it through the active promotion of a politics of multiculturalism in the British context or the devalorisation of the activities of 'minorities' in France as non-political, is to a large extent an imposition rather than a political choice. It continues to be a central factor in the contemporary anti-racism of solidaristic groups, concerned by the conditions faced by both new immigrants into western European societies and the 'minority ethnic' communities. For example, *SOS Racisme* builds its vision of a mestizo society on a belief in the success with which French culture has integrated diversity:

> French society is a society which, culturally, has completely integrated minority cultures, much more than the countries that accuse France of being an assimilationist country ... The French culture is a culture which has integrated massively, in terms of language, style, lifestyles, music, sport etc. The valorisation of immigration and the enrichment of immigration is a pedagogical process which we have been responsible for.
>
> *SOS Racisme*, France

The organisation advocates the teaching of cultural diversity, in the UNESCO tradition, as the means both of valorising the various cultures that coexist in French society and, in so doing, of creating a unified France with one global culture made up of borrowings from all of these.

> We have modified the teaching of French history etc. with our own 'teachers', with our own speakers, to remind us both of the dark periods of our history and at the same time of immigration and the fight against racism. A small contribution to the fact that the Ministry of Education and the public authorities recognise that immigrants have brought a culture to this country and that they should not simply integrate a Gaullist culture but that the Gaullist culture should recognise that it is always enriched by immigrant cultures. I think it's much more interesting that there should be a common culture for all the French, whatever their origins, that says France has welcomed Polish, Italian immigration and then Portugese, Spanish immigration, and then Algerian, African immigration etc. It has been enriched by all those cultures. It therefore has a part of its culture that comes out of immigration.
>
> *SOS Racisme*, France

Organisations with a state-centred analysis of racism note the difficulty of financing activities that do not conform to the depoliticised emphasis on culture promoted, in particular by the European Union since its 1997 Year Against Racism.

Certainly from our perspective – I don't think we got any money from the European Union at all – is that I think what was funded was not anti-racist work. It was cultural work, multicultural work. The best way to get funding was multicultural work not stuff that was going to be critical of state institutions.

CARF, UK

The emphasis on intercultural understanding as the primary means of dealing with racial discrimination has been handed down directly from the UNESCO tradition, through the decades from 1950 to the late 1990s without accounting for the profound transformations in anti-racist discourse that took place in the interim. The dominance of a culturalist discourse as the principal means of voicing the racism against new migrants, refugees and asylum seekers to Europe today is undeniable. Nascent migrants' organisations do at times form around linguistic, religious or national ties for practical reasons. This is often complicated by internal conflicts that are not immediately apparent to observers in the country of immigration:

If you take the Bosnian community for instance, you don't know if they're Bosnian Muslims or Bosnian Serbs or Bosnian Croats. For any of these three it would be difficult if they don't have personal links to now forge partnerships just because of deportation. They are in a very vulnerable position.

NCADC, UK

When it does occur, it is often interpreted by their supporters among the 'white left wing' as a fixed condition that indicates the preference of such new 'minority ethnic' communities for remaining beyond the domain of politics. The cultural diversity that this breeds is also seen as beneficial. For example, ARCI describes its inclusion of a variety of communal organisations within its membership as adding to the richness of the association itself:

> We, on the other hand, saw that we needed multiethnicity. Therefore, in our association from the beginning, there were hundreds and thousands of immigrant members ... there are cities in which both immigrant communities and immigrant associations that do not have their own premises know that, at the ARCI club, they can use – they can have meetings, organise a dinner, a forum or a multiethnic concert.
>
> ARCI, Italy

The cultural format described by ARCI is based on the belief that discrimination may be countered by greater cultural understanding and is filtered down to the communal organisations themselves. For example, the Roma community of Florence regularly organises concerts and dinners at local Social Centres in order to introduce Italians to a community that is largely stigmatised in the city, not least due to its segregation in designated camps on its outskirts.[2] These events are held in order to overturn widely held stereotypes and engender an appreciation of Roma culture:

> Explaining or trying to understand the Roma culture which is not based on equating the Gypsy with thief, dirty, liar or I don't know what. The Gypsy in the old sense of the word is something that we are not. The nomads probably moved around in the old days. Unfortunately, we stay in one place. The Roma lived with other people which was always the case because the Roma were migrants to the city.
>
> Associazione Rom, Italy

The emphasis on an explanation of culture, tradition and history is seen to be more effective than the mobilisation of a political discourse, for example of rights. However, this is ultimately countered in the association's own discourse by an admittance of the racist nature of the discrimination faced by the Roma community and a realisation of the futility of cultural work in the absence of significant structural change:

> There is still injustice towards Roma today and we fight it every day. During these last ten years, we lost ten of our children in the nomadic camps. So, for us that is real racism ... For me, racism exists in that we were left in the camps for ten years – based on the thinking that all the Roma were like that and nothing else.
>
> Associazione Rom, Italy

The lack of empirical and historicised studies of anti-racist discourse and praxis leads to a confusion of repertoires that equates cultural and identity politics with the domain of anti-racist activism writ large. This reduction of the fight against racism to the demands of cultural 'minorities' is also derived from the legacy of the UNESCO tradition; the institutionally legitimised project to replace 'race' with culture as the means for explaining human differences and overcoming racism, repackaged as the less harmful 'ethnocentrism'. The directness of this successful process of substitution, which has had a profound impact even on everyday discourse, masks the historical relationship of 'race' and state. Furthermore, by advocating a culturalist approach to anti-racism, it also serves to disguise attempts to make this link and to theorise the existence of a state-based, institutionalised racism rooted in the history of the modern European nation-state. The persistence of culturalist explanations of racism, now mobilised by the New Right itself in its mobilisation of a racism of cultural differences, is testimony to the reluctance to relinquish the anti-racist struggle to the proponents of a state-centred account of racism which fundamentally opposes the humanist foundations of European public political culture.

3
Anti-Racist Orientations: France, Britain, Ireland, Italy

> SOS Racisme was created in 1984 following the Marche des Beurs which left from the problem neighbourhoods of Lyon to claim the rights of the minority originating in the Maghreb.
>
> *SOS Racisme*, France
>
> And, basically the Anti Nazi League came out of that and grew out of that, out of people opposing the Nazis, confronting them on the streets.
>
> ANL, UK
>
> You want to know how RAR happened, how it came about? Well, it was started as a group in support of a Congolese man, Belmondo Wantete, who was treated appallingly badly in this country.
>
> RAR, Ireland
>
> I think the birth of the Italian anti-racist movement, and therefore the presence, the work of ARCI, was in 1989. In 1989, in the southern countryside, a South African immigrant was killed by a gang of criminals who were at Villa Literno for the tomato harvest.
>
> ARCI, Italy

By developing a political sociological account of anti-racism in France, Britain, Ireland and Italy, this study seeks to illustrate the nature of anti-racism in the political space of western Europe as a whole. This is based on the suggestion that a more nuanced vision of the various anti-racisms in this arena may be benefited by a work of multi-levelled comparison that takes the differences between organisations and discourses both within and across individual countries into account, rather than relying solely on the comparison of processes across national societies. Such work recognises the internal heterogeneity of anti-racism within individual state

113

societies, and more generally, the problems involved in considering them as unitary elements that may be engaged in direct comparison. This chapter sets out to offer an insight into anti-racist discourse and practice as it has evolved over time in each of the study's four countries. It does not, however, do so in order to establish a basis for submitting all further analysis carried out to a country-based comparative research. Neither does it propose to provide the reader with a comprehensive history of anti-racism in France, Britain, Ireland and Italy. Rather, the chapter's purpose is to further historicise the general object of this research, that of anti-racist movement forms and the construction of anti-racist discourse in western Europe. Following the principal argument of this book, the material in this chapter is examined to give further weight to the notion that, in order to establish the reasons for which anti-racism represents a heterogeneity of discourses and practices, it is necessary to anchor its contemporary perception in an historicisation of its development. The emergence of anti-racism cannot be adequately explained without an understanding of how it constructs the object of its opposition: racism. Moreover, this would be further hindered by a failure to recognise that such construction occurs differently at different times, due to a variety of structural-political determinants, due to variations in political principles and – but not solely – as a function of the specificity of racism in a given society.

Taking this into account, each of the chapter's four sections shall attempt to determine, by means of an analysis of the emergence of anti-racist discourse and practice in each setting, how anti-racisms variously define the racism they oppose. The means for doing this shall differ from section to section in recognition of the highly diverse factors contributing to understandings of racism and the political possibilities for anti-racism in each country. In general, I propose to 'set the scene' in order to provide the reader with a more tangible sense of what could be thought of as the political, social and cultural 'opportunity structure', to rather loosely evoke Tarrow's (1994) theory, in which anti-racism intervenes. What are the prevailing discourses regarding immigration, colonial history and indeed, democracy and equality that shape the choices made by anti-racism? How are such discourses differently perceived and interpreted by the various groups collectively organised under a given version of anti-racism? How, differentially, do notions, such as community, Republic, minority, victimhood, responsibility, solidarity, blackness, emancipation, memory … come to be the organisational principles of varieties of anti-racism? Finally, how do the polarities between these varying notions come to create significant disunities between anti-racisms, both within a single society and across them? The discussion develops an historicised framework within which the remainder of the book, a more contemporary analysis of the qualitative research upon which this work is based, may be interpreted. The division by national setting – presently a useful tool of presentation – is blurred, in Chapters 4 and 5, by the increasing emphasis on dichotomous discourses and organisational themes as the most analytically interesting means of debating the contemporary sociological relevance of a study of European anti-racism.

TOUCHE PAS À MON POTE!:[1] THE EMERGENCE OF ANTI-RACISM IN FRANCE

French conceptualisations of anti-racism are to a great extent tied to the republican ideologies that are central to the public political culture of that country. Anti-racism has been a discourse employed by mainstream political parties, intellectuals and celebrities as well as social movements since the end of the Second World War. The importance periodically placed on anti-racism in French post-war politics reflects the extent to which, rather than being the preserve of groups of the racially marginalised, it has been constructed as inherently French, and therefore hegemonic. The ideals of anti-racism have been construed as universally applicable through their connection with the republican principles of liberty, equality and fraternity, strongly emphasised by the large established anti-racist organisations: the LICRA, LDH, MRAP and, more recently, *SOS Racisme*. Ownership of anti-racism has been estimated according to the capacity of the discourse promoted by the various organisations to effectively sustain these tenets of republicanism.

The struggle between organisations upholding a generalist, colour-blind or universalist vision of anti-racism and those grounded in the particularist experiences of racialised communities indicates the extent to which anti-racism has been conceptualised in the absence of a problematisation of the process of racialisation in French society. Therefore, an examination of the emergence of French anti-racism must include an understanding of the way in which it has been naturalised, almost as a mode of behaviour, within French public political culture: being anti-racist is deemed to be an inherent aspect of French socialisation. In much anti-racist thinking therefore, racism is deracinated from its roots as a political idea with an historical function in the modern French state. While anti-colonial writers in the French language, such as Fanon and Césaire, had an enormous impact upon the development of 1960s American thinking on black liberation, negritude received little attention from the generally white, left-wing French anti-racists and anti-colonial activists of the time.

Racism in France, as an attitude or behaviour (rather than a political idea), has been abstracted and extended to include a myriad of discriminations, against the young, the old, women or the workers (Wieviorka 1994). This has been possible in French political rhetoric because of the profound discomfort with the notion of difference that conditions both official policy towards black and 'minority ethnic' groups and the construction of much anti-racist discourse in terms that avoid direct confrontation with the fact of the racialisation of large sectors of the population in France. French anti-racism's unease as regards the idea of 'race' undoubtedly, as Varikas (1998) rightly points out, stems from the wish to delegitimise its biological and hierarchical connotations. However, the forcefulness with which the egalitarianism of French republican culture is upheld as a panacea for all forms of discrimination means that there is a failure to conceive of racism differently from other discriminations. Racialisation is therefore stripped of its continual power to exclude and violate. While challenges have been posed to this dominant anti-racist discourse, notably by the young North Africans whose racialisation continues to jar the construction of anti-racist strategy, the struggle for the recognition of their activism as anti-racist, rather than as the particularist politics of community, is largely overshadowed by the generalising tendency of the established anti-racist movement.

An understanding of the lack of ease with which 'race' and racialisation are approached by mainstream anti-racist discourses must take into account the relationship to otherness that takes hold in France following the Second World War with the onset of large-scale immigration from the colonies, the subsequent process of decolonisation and, in particular, the Algerian war. In the aftermath of the *Shoah* and despite the force of French antisemitism during the first half of the twentieth century, difference is associated almost completely with the new black and brown immigrants and dissociated from the preexistence of 'minority ethnic' groups, including Jewish immigrants from the East, in France for many years (Vinen 1994).

Understandings of difference were increasingly related to the novelty of colonial immigration. The societal heterogeneity it generated
led to immigration being posed as a problem for French unity
(Baillet 1997). This had an undeniable effect on the evolution of an
anti-racist discourse that attacked discrimination on the grounds of
difference on the one hand, and advocated assimilation (and later
integration) as the solution to racial unrest on the other.

   Anti-racism was therefore shaped from the outset by the republican underpinnings of public political culture in France. It is constantly required to reconcile its opposition to discrimination on the
grounds of difference with the republican principle that preaches a
colour-blind attitude. This is strikingly apparent in the separation
made between the public and private domains:

> In France, there is a law that says that everyone is equal, and so you
> do not have the right to ask someone what her nationality or her
> religion is etc ... Those whom we in France call Republicans are
> violently against that, which is not the case for Americans: every-
> one says what they are: if they're Jewish, Arab, Sikh ... In France, it
> is practically forbidden to say that you belong to a community.
> That is the private domain.
>
> *La Lettre pour la cityonneté*

For many anti-racists, the public level at which racism is often
enacted and at which racialisation is often (although not always)
visible is irreconcilable with their belief in the necessity of keeping
difference a matter of individual practice. Mainstream French anti-
racism organisations, rooted in the legacies of universalist values,
human rights and the *Résistance*, have felt threatened by any project which seeks to blur the boundaries between public and private
inscribed in republican political culture. What are the implications
of these public–private divides for a comprehension of the evolution
of French anti-racism?

   The strong separation of the domains of the public and that of the
private in French republican tradition stems from the emphasis placed
on secularism and anti-clericalism. The overwhelming association of
the identity of 'minority ethnic' groups in France with the Islam of
the North African immigrants and their descendants results in a

reluctance to view 'immigrants' as fully French (Boutih 2001). Preceding the present concern with the 'illegal' immigration of migrants and asylum seekers, this led to the construction of the prevalent view in French society of racialised groups through the sole prism of immigration. The use of the term 'immigrant' to describe the second and third generations is confined to those of non-European origin, most commonly Maghrebi, and is not generally used to describe those of Italian, Portuguese or Polish descent, amongst the other big immigrant groups in France (Fysh and Wolfreys 1998; Spire 1999):

[The] French of foreign origin: to be clear, they are Maghrebi, because the problem here is a Maghrebi problem. When one speaks of foreigners it means Maghrebis, when one speaks of Maghrebis it means Algerians because France has a problem with its Algeria.

La lettre pour la cityonneté

There are two interesting dimensions to this comment. The first is the interchangeable use of the words 'immigrant' and 'foreigner', important because many of those living in France with origins in the former colonies do not have French citizenship. This is particularly the case for Algerians residing in France who, following the Franco-Algerian war were required to choose between French and Algerian citizenship. Many chose Algerian citizenship, out of allegiance to the FLN or because they believed that their stay in France was to be temporary. Secondly, the use of the word 'foreigner' – which may have pejorative connotations in other linguistic contexts – rather than 'immigrant' is an attempt by French anti-racists to close the gap between the descendants of European and non-European immigrants. Spire (1999:50) proposes that the reference to 'foreigner' rather than 'immigrant' seeks to narrow the gap between the descendants of European immigrants and those of North African origin, perceived to have integrated less 'well':

The foreigner is most often Italian, Spanish or Portugese, while the immigrant is rather Maghrebi and, more than anything else, Algerian. Systematically suspected of wanting to establish himself indefinitely in the country, the immigrant is contrasted to the foreigner who is associated with the image of a temporary visitor, and whose presence is rarely perceived as a threat to national cohesion.

The representative of *La lettre pour la cityonneté* also identifies the special relationship between France and Algeria that refers to the history of the Algerian revolution and the violent sentiments evoked by the association, made by many French people, of Algeria and Algerians with a rejection of France and the French. In racist rhetoric, 'Algerian' comes to symbolise all that is dangerous about immigration; the refusal to assimilate and the ultimate rebuttal of France's generosity towards its colonised peoples.

The association made in dominant French discourse between racialisation and immigration and the problem posed by this standpoint of 'difference' for the full inclusion of those of non-French origin into the society is also related to the importance of locality or 'territory'. The reference to 'peripheral neighbourhoods' (*quartiers periphériques*), made for example by the ATMF, or to 'underprivileged neighbourhoods' (*quartiers défavorisés*) or the 'suburbs' (*les banlieues*), is often used to describe the territory in which the politics of racism are acted out. These are generally the large complexes of rent-controlled housing estates (HLM) on the outskirts of big cities where many families of North African, African and Middle Eastern origin have been housed, often together with poor French families (Jazouli 1986; Fysh and Wolfreys 1998). These territorial bases often act as frontiers between anti-racisms. Mainstream anti-racism is centralised in the large cities, while that of the *Mouvement beur* for example was rooted in the suburbs.

According to Lloyd (1996a), the emergence and development of French anti-racist organisations should be understood in terms of the interaction between 'traditional' associations and newer ones. French anti-racism may be seen as falling into four categories: traditional human rights organisations, anti-racist/anti-fascist organisations, immigrant and solidarity groups and the new associations of the 1980s. The first category is typified by organisations such as the *Ligue des Droits de l'Homme* (LDH), established at the time of the Dreyfus Affair and strongly committed to republican principles. This nationwide association espoused the teaching of the 'Declaration of the Rights of Man and Citizen', the separation of church and state and the provision of free education. It was a strong critic of France's colonisation of Algeria and linked its primary message of human rights to racism, colonialism and antisemitism.

Lloyd's second type is epitomised by the *Mouvement contre le racisme et pour l'amitié entre les peuples* (MRAP) and the *Ligue contre le racisme et l'antisémitisme* (LICRA). The MRAP was established in 1949 by Jewish and resistance groups in response to the climate of the aftermath of the Second World War and the *Shoah*. Its focus was largely on the inadequacy of denazification in Europe and the reemergence of fascist groups on the French political scene. Later police raids on Algerians were compared to the *rafles* of Jews during the war. The direct relation of racism to fascism and its situation within the wider context of the colonial system meant that the MRAP 'represented a realisation of the need for particularistic struggles within the universalistic framework of French life' (Lloyd 1996a:37). The LICRA, primarily an organisation established against antisemitism with a focus on the legal means for tackling racism and antisemitism, can be seen in a similar light. The organisation's principle focus to this day is against the rise in far-right or fascist activity and Holocaust denial. For this reason, one of its principal activists claims that many identify the LICRA as a Jewish organisation, although in fact it is based on strong secular principles.[2] This does not deny the fact that a large number of its activists are Jewish and that, although efforts are made to intervene in cases of racism against black and Arab people, the organisation's roots mean that it is constantly identified as Jewish in orientation. The position of the LICRA is emblematic of the premium placed on the history of the Jewish experience of the *Shoah* in contemporary anti-racism. Vinen (1994) makes clear that dominant French opinion after the war did not identify the atrocities enacted by the Nazis to have exclusively, if at all, affected the Jews. However, the growth in the public perception of the Jews as the main victims of Nazism by the 1970s was already actively promoted within anti-racist circles two decades previously due to the significant numbers of Jews and ex-Resistance fighters active within them. The central role played by organisations such as the LDH, the MRAP and the LICRA has led to the strong focus in French anti-racism on education for the memory of the *Shoah*.

The third category of anti-racist organisations, in Lloyd's analysis, is that of immigrant and solidarity associations. Immigrants began to organise politically for the first time by joining the protests and rent strikes over public housing in the years between 1975 and 1980. Groups of self-organised immigrants used hunger strikes to demonstrate against housing conditions and rent rates at the hostels in which they were housed, generally close to the factories or building sites at which they worked. This directly contravened the law that did not permit foreigners to head political organisations that was repealed only in 1981:

> In France, the right of foreigners to form organisations was extended in 1981 with the arrival of the Socialists to power and with François Mitterrand who enlarged, or rather rectified, a social and political discrimination, that of not being able to create an association when you originate from ... when you are a foreign resident.
>
> ATMF

They were met with hostility, not only by the authorities, but also by the CGT and CFDT unions, who saw the autonomy being displayed by immigrant associations as a danger to the unity of the working class. These experiences served to politicise traditional immigrant organisations, such as the ATMF, originally set up to look after the welfare of guest workers. The changing nature of immigration politics that led to the halting of immigration and the policy of *regroupement familiale* in the 1970s, involved important transformations for the association:

> Since '74, immigration policy in France completely changed, that is to say that it was officially decided in bilateral agreements to allow families to come within the framework of family regrouping. The immigration trajectory also changed and with it its demographic and socioprofessional nature. It changed because the immigrants that came at the beginning often left their families over there, in their countries of origin, in the countries of the Maghreb for example. They came alone to work in the aim of going back home one day. So, that myth of returning home became blurred while immigration continued here in France. And with the family regrouping the nature changed, so there were children who came, who had to be educated, women etc.
>
> ATMF

The opening up of the association also led to its politicisation and to the consciousness of racism and the discrimination faced by 'immigrants' and their children:

> On the political level, there is the struggle for equal rights especially against the rise in xenophobia and racism, racism in all its forms. We have always also denounced all forms of discrimination, discrimination in hiring, at work, discrimination in training, discrimination in the orientation of schools etc. All forms of political discrimination.
>
> ATMF

The politicisation of immigrant associations in the protests over housing, hastily erected in transit *cités* to replace the crumbling *bidonvilles*, founded a new placing of anti-racism in the suburbs, where a second generation of 'immigrants' were beginning to become politically aware. However, despite the open disregard for the law of some groups such as the immigrant worker residents of the *'foyers SONACOTRA'*, until 1981 immigrant associations did not generally enjoy much autonomy. Rather, they were often steered by French solidarity organisations, trade unions and parties on the extreme Left on the one hand, and by associations controlled by their countries of origin (particularly Algeria) on the other (Blatt 1995).

A fourth type of anti-racism, led by the sons and daughters of immigrants, is both continuous and reactive to the collective action of immigrant associations in the period up to 1981. This action by young people of North African origin is clearly located in the housing estates on the outskirts of large cities and towns where many of the young *Beurs* grew up. Jazouli (1986), in his study of collective action among young Maghrebis in France, links the emergence of these movements to the rage felt by these young people at the situation in which they lived, the lack of opportunities they faced and the, often violent, racism they experienced. This rage was often expressed in drug abuse, crime and suicide. Yet, an element amongst young *Beurs* turned their rage into social, cultural and political collective action that led to the *Mouvement beur*'s outburst onto the French political scene. The rise of the *Mouvement beur*'s responded to several events of extreme racist violence against North Africans in the early 1980s and to the growth in popularity of the *Front national.* In these years, 'murderous crimes perpetrated against Arabs, Turks or West Indians', rendered banal in public memory (Malik 1990:21), deeply disrupted the lives of young *Beurs*.

There is a sizeable body of sociological research carried out on the *Mouvement beur* (Jazouli 1986; Lapeyronnie 1987; Poinsot 1993). It became the object of scholarly attention due to the national prominence it achieved after the *Marche pour l'égalité et contre le racisme* which took place in 1983, organised by young people from the *banlieues* of Lyon. The interest of sociologists in the various phenomena that the movement comprised is due to the marked contrast between this contestatory group of organisations and the perception that 'immigrant' groups until then did not directly challenge the racism of French society and of its institutions, due to their general 'invisibility' in the French political arena. The 1983 march was organised by a group around Toumi Djaidja, the president of the local Lyon-based organisation *SOS Avenir Minguettes* who had been 'seriously injured with a bullet, by a policeman on June 21, 1983' (MIB: http://mibmib.free.fr). This march which ended, after three months, with the arrival of thousands of young people in Paris on 3 December 1983, was dubbed the *Mouvement beur* (ibid.).

As Blatt (1995) points out, the tendency to refer to the *Mouvement beur* as a unitary phenomenon belies the divisions between the different associations that comprised it. For example, the *Association de la nouvelle génération immigrante* (ANGI) represented an attempt to unite the Franco-Maghrebi community around a common culture. On the other hand, *Zaama d'Banlieues*[3] and Rock Against Police focused on the racism, unemployment and substandard housing conditions of the *cités* and downplayed culture. This strain was often most critical of the traditional immigrant organisations who 'appeared to them, often with reason, to be like simple transmission cables of rival political tendencies drawing their legitimatory sources from political orientations related to the situation in their countries of origin' (Jazouli 1986:58). Other tendencies involved alignment with French political parties on the far Left, trade unions and anti-racist organisations on the one hand, and Islamic groups or subcommunities such as the Berbers or Harkis on the other (Jazouli 1986; Blatt 1995).

All of these different tendencies within the *Mouvement beur* represent an important turning point in French anti-racism which now developed a language of civil rights (Poinsot 1993), based on the experience of racist discrimination by a new generation of French citizens of immigrant origin. However, the movement such as it existed was beset by deep divisions. The website of the *Mouvement de l'immigration et des banlieues* notes that the attempt to create a unitary movement a year after the march resulted in failure due to the attempt, made by Parisian organisations such as the nascent *SOS Racisme*, to impose a traditional structure upon it. A similar attempt was made through *Convergences 84*, a march organised by Paris-based 'anti-communitarians' (Blatt 1995; MIB) within the *Mouvement beur* in the hope of reunifying the movement. These divisions were largely due to the battles fought between the march's organisers and their allies on the political Left and amongst the traditional soli-daristic and anti-racist movements. It was this inability of a move-ment led by and for racialised youth to succeed on these grounds alone in the French context that led to the emergence of two organ-isations – *France Plus* and *SOS Racisme* – as the forerunners in the new, youth-led anti-racism. Both organisations focused on the inclusion of young Maghrebis into mainstream French society and increasingly alienated the local groups who had been at the origins of the *Mouvement beur* by creating centralised structures.

> For local groups of young Maghrebians, the desire of both national organisations to impose a hegemonic identity on what the second generation is or should be, rapidly became oppressive. They rejected SOS Racisme's moral crusade against racism which dented the impact of their local struggles. They did not accept either France Plus's pro-motion of a *beurgoisie* based on the ideology of personal merit which established a strict separation between the first and second genera-tions of the North African community.
>
> Poinsot (1993:83)

The organisations that made up the *Mouvement beur* were divided internally between those who were seen as having no link to the daily life of the *banlieues* and who spoke in terms of 'integration' and 'citizenship', and those who sought to promote a locally grounded anti-racism that targeted the racism of *'Police-Justice'* (MIB: http://mibmib.free.fr). Activists of organisations such as *Jeunes arabes de Lyon et banlieue* (JALB) in particular attacked the centralising 'Jacobin' tendency of French politics (ibid.), mirrored by members of a new generation of the anti-racist *beurgeoisie* who attempted to reappropriate the struggles of the local groups. The

clash between these two tendencies, the latter increasingly represented by the officially endorsed *SOS Racisme*, is summed up by the
words that appeared on a banner in Lyon in 1981: 'Against the
police, against the legal system, against the press, we count on no
one but ourselves.' The claim to self-organisation was rooted in a
longer tradition among immigrants to France that, nevertheless, has
become all but completely covered over in accounts of the trajectory of French anti-racism. The organisations that for a time were
known collectively as the *Mouvement beur* have long since retreated
from their brief appearance at national level to the localised politics
from which they emerged. Organisations, such as MIB or JALB that
see their action as inscribed in the actions of the former generation,
reveal an awareness of the extent to which the history of what are
described as 'the struggles of immigration' – 'too often distorted
by selective readings that alter the historical meaning and the
quality of its own actors' (ibid.) – must be written by the activists
themselves.

The arrival of *SOS Racisme* on the anti-racist scene in the mid
1980s is often interpreted as having brought about the depoliticisation of anti-racism, in particular due to its unique targeting of the
youth and its courting of the media. Its success in overturning the
serious challenge posed by the *Mouvement beur* in favour of a republican project of anti-racism, based on the teachings of collective
memory inherited from established organisations such as the MRAP
and a rejection of 'difference' in favour of a vision of a unified youth
unhindered by particularist attachments, is highly revealing of the
history of French anti-racism as a whole. Despite the attempts by
groups of racialised youth or migrants to gain ownership of anti-
racism, it remains dominated by a restricted group of progressive
organisations whose secular republicanism is in constant conflict
with an openly multicultural vision of French society. Where may
the sources of this dominant perspective on anti-racist principles be
identified?

Lloyd (1999:260) has noted that in France 'much anti-racist
discourse still resounds to the great names of the Enlightenment,
and that the first anti-racists were some of the philosophes and
revolutionaries of the eighteenth century (in particular Abbé
Gregoire).' In her analysis of publications by the MRAP from its
beginnings in the early post-war years to the present day, Lloyd, citing the organisation's founding statement[4] shows how it bases itself
to a large extent on the belief that 'France is essentially democratic

and antiracist, "wealthy enough to take in new children", and with a "millenarian civilisation" destined to bring light to the world' (Lloyd 1996b:127).

By going back to the writings of the 'founding fathers' of modern France, among them Voltaire and Rousseau, Lloyd claims that the MRAP sought to use republican myth in order to 'hegemonise and root antiracism in France' (1996a:130). This message becomes somewhat weakened with the realisation in the 1950s and 1960s that racism and fascism had not diminished as problems. Nonetheless, many believe that the 'real' France is anti-racist. This belief is filtered through the notion of fraternity which 'conjures up images of human unity against oppression, linking to the founding of a national myth' (ibid.) and the principle of tolerance. Anti-racism is grounded, by groups such as *SOS Racisme*, LICRA and MRAP, in a national tradition that uses the myths and symbols generally associated with patriotism to attack racism. This form of mainstream anti-racism intervenes in public debates to a much greater extent than in other European countries. The belief, promoted by organisations which refer to themselves as 'majoritarian' or 'generalist' in orientation, that French people are predisposed to be anti-racist is employed in order to position anti-racism at the centre of public debates, not only on racism itself but also on the wider issue of multiculturalism.

The hegemony of an anti-racism framed by public political culture conditions the activity of supposedly 'particularist' groups such as the ATMF, whose main demand is for equal rights of citizenship. These republican ideals are called into question by such groups at

It isn't normal that in Holland the right to vote was given to foreign residents over ten years ago and that in France we are lagging behind. France that calls itself the country of human rights, of the French Revolution etc. There were always government promises, starting with Mitterrand. When he organised his campaign before the presidential elections, he said yes, I promise you that if I am elected President I will grant the right to vote to foreigners and afterwards he said, now French public opinion is not yet ready, so it would be better to delay; it would lead to the rise of the extreme right, of racism etc.

ATMF

the same time as they themselves are forced to work within an understanding of anti-racism based on equal rights, handed down by the Republic.

In this, the complexity of the task facing organisations such as the ATMF becomes clear. Two important points are made that relate to the discussion of the predominance of national traditions in the construction of a French anti-racism. Firstly, the ATMF representative recognises the paradox in France's self-construction as the 'country of liberty and human fraternity' (Lloyd 1996a:126). The fact that the French state has not yet granted equal citizenship rights to 'immigrants' is seen as incompatible with the republican social contract through which 'Jews, Protestants, black slaves in the colonies enter the community of citizens in the name of the universal principles of Reason and Rights' (Amalvi 1984; cited in Lloyd 1996a:129). Secondly, the reasoning behind the unkept promises of successive governments is related to the belief, often expressed by politicians and the media, that granting leeway to 'minorities' itself brings about racism and justifies the activity of the far Right.

Therefore, by appropriating the discourses of human rights, equality and liberty, non-'majoritarian' groups in the French antiracist movement can gain access to mainstream debates and question their legitimacy. An example is given by the spokesperson for the *Maison des ensembles*, an autonomous collective of *sans-papiers* made up of 300 men who, when I met them in 2000, had occupied a building in the Gare de Lyon area of Paris in protest against their illegal status. He prioritises a language of human rights as a means of making the *sans-papiers'* message heard. At the same time, however, he recognises the more complex nature of France's current attitude to immigration and the contradictions within the Declaration of Human Rights, to which he has recourse. The problem of nationalism is also raised as a barrier to openness, leading to suspicion of foreigners, seen as undesirable. Although human rights are evoked as a means of combating the discrimination faced by illegal immigrants to France, when questioned further on their utility, the interviewee places greater emphasis on economic questions. Human rights are important, but the socioeconomic inequality bred by capitalism and globalisation is ultimately considered the real problem to be overcome.

The tension in French anti-racism relates to the strong separation made between the public and private domains that is applied to culture and religion and therefore impacts upon the discussion of

I am for a world without borders. This idea of Europe or Africa, it doesn't have any sense. The human being, the human species, the human race, that's the thing ... As long as we don't manage to try and suppress this atmosphere of nationalism – from one country or from a continent – there will always be suspicion. There will always be undesirables. We have to manage – I know it's a very difficult struggle, it's a struggle of many years – to have the universal Declaration of Human Rights respected, for example in all the countries that have signed and that nobody today, there is no country that respects it.

AL: Is it really a question of human rights?

There is a question of human rights but it is more an economic question in fact. I myself was a victim of injustice in my own country ... So, if we manage to have that respected, it's hard, but if we manage to have that respected it's already not bad. We know that we are in a world in which globalisation is increasing and, above all, we are in a capitalistic world where the interest ... the life even of the human being no longer has any value.

MDE

racism. In public, anti-racism is supposed to educate against the racism of the fascist past and towards an integrated, egalitarian society. In private, groups organised according to 'culture' were free to practice their traditions so long as they had no influence over the public world of politics. This separation was challenged by the rise of the *Mouvement beur* in the 1980s and the stand of a disenfranchised generation of North African youth against the institutionalised racism they faced. However, the rage expressed by these organisations was dampened by the *beurgoisie* element within the movement whose belief in a system of meritocracy replaced a movement for communal empowerment, based on the principles of civil rights originating in the US, with a home-grown push towards the mainstream.

Today, French anti-racism, largely due to the crisis-level discrimination against asylum seekers, migrants and refugees as in other national contexts, is more openly heterogeneous. Nevertheless, mainstream French anti-racist organisations, who practice a secularised and colour-blind approach to anti-racism, continue to refuse organisations that originate in the concerns of a particular community as part of a movement against racism. On the other hand, the latter often identify the main anti-racist organisations as political, in the sense of being partisan, and refuse to identify themselves as anti-racist. This is as much the case for the *sans-papiers* movement as it is for organisations, such as the ATMF originating in the long-standing struggles of *résidents étrangers* for equal status in the Republic. Instead, these organisations and others, including the direct descendants of the protagonists of the *Mouvement beur* in the *banlieues*, continue to organise outside what is considered the official arena of anti-racism. Such groups today are concerned primarily with the issue of racist murders including those committed by the police, the mobilisation of a public discourse of security to target non-white youth and the use of the law of *la double peine*[5] in the taking of a 'strong stand' against immigration. This contrasts markedly with the continuing stress on 'equal rights', 'citizenship' and 'anti-discrimination' which characterises the discourse of mainstream French anti-racism.

BLACK AND WHITE, UNITE AND FIGHT: THE EMERGENCE OF ANTI-RACISM IN BRITAIN

Anti-racism is possibly more developed in Britain than in any of the other countries of this study. It is perhaps for this reason that defining its character and narrating its history are tasks complexified by the multiple traditions of activism that may collectively be known as anti-racism. The label of anti-racism has, often simultaneously, been rejected and claimed by the 'black' activists with which the struggle against racism in Britain is most clearly associated. The coexistence of both the local activism of groups grounded in the concerns of 'black communities' and of the institutional efforts to combat racism, through the introduction of multicultural and anti-racist policy making, make it difficult to assume a common sense of identification with the term 'anti-racism'.

The tensions between activists and state structures have led key figures in black activism to reject anti-racism in favour of black liberation which was seen by those such as the radical head of the Institute of Race Relations, A. Sivanandan, as a richer and more long-term project of emancipation than that offered by what was often perceived as the narrow confines of anti-racism (Gilroy 1987). On the other hand, many organisations rooted in the legacies of the self-organised black groups of the 1970s, stake their claim to the leadership of anti-racism and direct their activity towards the exposure of racism in the institutions of British society. This work of 'self-defence' constitutes itself as both overtly political and as emancipatory; a black-led anti-racism that insists on taking direct responsibility for the fight against racism as part of the lived experience of non-whites in British society. For my purposes, anti-racism will include the experiences of black liberation, beginning in the 1970s, which were formative of the coming to political consciousness of large sectors of the racialised in British society. Anti-racism, as it exists today in both the large national associations and networks, the local monitoring groups and the campaigns against the racist treatment of asylum seekers and refugees, is undeniably shaped by these evolutions, and so cannot be interpreted in their exclusion.

Three main forms can be said to be formative of the British anti-racist experience. They have in turn been responsible for the formulation of the key terms of the discourse, not only of anti-racism itself, but also of the more general 'race relations industry', with its emphasis on culturalist and psychologised interpretations of the reasons for continued racial 'disadvantage'. Firstly, as we saw in the previous chapter, a solidaristic anti-racism emerges in the 1960s, mainly promoted by the left wing and the trade unions. This form, often focused on the activities of far-right groups, can be thought of as the direct antecedent of the mass anti-racism of the late 1970s, epitomised by Rock Against Racism, and later the Anti Nazi League.

The second form evolves in the 1970s, influenced to a great extent by the call to Black Power, and is grounded in the self-organisation of black people and 'ethnic minorities'. It is through this movement that the interrelated ideas of political 'blackness' and 'community' are evolved as key discourses of an anti-racist vocabulary rooted in the experiences of the racialised in British society. This form of anti-racism is at the core of the development of the notion of institutionalised racism as a framework for making sense of racist practices in contemporary Britain. This state-centred interpretation of racism as inherent in the 'apparatuses of the state and the structures of society' (Bourne 2001:9) shall be shown to be crucial to a general understanding of the construction of British anti-racism writ large.

Thirdly, anti-racist initiatives were developed by the mainly Labour-dominated local state in the 1980s in reaction to the Conservative neoliberalism of the government and the Thatcherist denial of the

importance of the social. Beyond the culturalist policies which reified 'minority ethnic' groups in rejection of the political definition
of 'black community' (Gilroy 1987,1992), so-called municipal anti-
racism developed its own methods of anti-racist praxis. The influence of psychological explanations of racism upon these methods
had the effect of reducing racism to individual prejudice, and the
solution to racism to the creation of a black middle class.

What are the principal tensions characteristic of the often
ambiguous relationship to anti-racism displayed among British
activists? Beyond the clear differences between localised and
national initiatives, and between large urban centres and small
towns, British anti-racism can be said to be shaped by the split
between the oppositional interpretations of racism as either institutionally engendered or as a set of behavioural attitudes. Unlike the
contemporary French context, the discourse of anti-racism in
Britain and the understandings of racism they entail is much less
polarised among the various anti-racist organisations than it is
between the state on the one hand, and social movements on the
other. Anti-racism in Britain is moulded around the struggle for
the recognition of the salience of institutional racism on the part of
the locally grounded anti-racist organisations and monitoring
groups on the one hand, and either its rebuttal by the state's authorities or its reinterpretation by specially constituted bodies for
formulating institutional responses to racism, on the other.

The institutionalisation of racism therefore centrally shapes
British anti-racist interpretations of the sustained discrimination
against the racialised in post-colonial metropolitan societies. The
recognition of the state's appropriation of racism, notably by the
introduction of increasingly severe immigration acts between 1962
and 1971 (Sivanandan 1976), was squared against official discourses
of 'tolerance' to 'cultural diversity'. It also challenged white-left
interpretations of racism as personal prejudice, instead seeking to
show how education, the criminal justice system and immigration
laws consistently excluded, and even pathologised black people and
'ethnic minorities' (Bourne 2001). The publication of MacPherson's
inquiry into the murder of black teenager, Stephen Lawrence in
1999 was perceived as a watershed by anti-racist organisations and
the wider British public alike. MacPherson's overturning of the previous conclusion drawn by Lord Scarman into the Brixton 'riots' of
1981 that 'institutional racism does not exist in Britain' (ibid.:11),
and his finding that the investigation into the Lawrence murder was

marred by institutional racism was received by black 'community workers' as a personal triumph. By defining institutional racism as 'the collective failure of an organisation to provide an appropriate and professional service to people because of their colour, culture or ethnic origin' (The Stephen Lawrence Inquiry 1999: point 6.34), the report appeared to admit the rootedness of racist practices in British public institutions, primarily the police.

The vocabulary of institutional racism is developed by the 'black communities'[6] that constitute self-organised anti-racism from the 1970s on. Although it is widely perceived as being a recently developed interpretation of racism, or even to have been generated by the institutions themselves, the struggle for the public acceptance of the connotations of institutional racism has underpinned the anti-racism of the 'black communities' for at least two decades, since the Brixton uprisings. The general acceptance of the reality of institutionalised racism, as formative of much of the lived experience of non-whites in Britain, among anti-racists and the Left is explanatory of the polarity of British anti-racisms between the state and social movements.

The 'municipal anti-racism' (Gilroy 1987) of the 1980s sought to underplay institutional racism and instead to counter the 'racial disadvantage' that Scarman concluded existed in British society. It did so by promoting an 'ethnic' middle class of 'race managers' (Bourne 2001:12) based on the belief that by including the racialised in the institutions and improving their personal lot, rather than that of 'whole black communities, mired in poverty and racism' (ibid.), that racist attitudes would be overcome. Under this state-sanctioned anti-racist structure, the localised anti-racist groups which remain central to British anti-racist organising were marginalised. The local government authorities preferred dealings with individual 'race relations officers' or the 'ethnic entrepreneurs' of religious or 'ethnic minority' communities over those with the state-centred anti-racists of the 'black communities'. This conflict provides the background to the acceptance of the interpretative importance of institutional racism. The history of its formulation and eventual recognition is also to a certain extent that of the British anti-racist 'movement'.

What was the context in which this interpretation of racism was theorised within the specific context of British anti-racism? The understandings of 'race' and racism developed in the British context are strongly influenced by reinterpretations of the imperial-colonial relationship, transposed to post-colonial Britain; now an immigration society. Britain's history as a colonial power meant that the majority of its incoming migrants were recruited, following the war and until the 1971 Immigration Act ended primary immigration, from its former colonies in South Asia and the West Indies. Emphasis is often placed on the arrival of the *Empire Windrush* in 1948 as symbolic of the beginning of large-scale immigration to Britain. The ship that brought immigrants from the Caribbean, and mainly Jamaica, is tied to a public memory of the reshaping of British 'identity' and the transformation of homogeneous white society that this entailed. However, the identification of the beginning of multiculturalism with the docking of the *Windrush* belies the presence of non-whites in Britain for several centuries (Hesse 2000; Goldberg 2002).

Alongside black communities, the consistent presence of Irish immigrants in Britain since the Irish famine of the late 1800s also meant that, by the 1960s, the urban centres of Britain had become multiethnic societies. The reaction of the local population to the mix of black, Asian and Irish migrants – mostly young men – who began to populate particular areas of British towns and cities at this time is typified by the sign commonly seen outside rental accommodation: 'No dogs, no blacks, no Irish'. For my interviewees, the diverse makeup of the British urban landscape is both enriching and fundamental to politics and policy making as a whole:

'Liverpool: the healing city', because it's got such a melting pot of different cultures. You know, it's the oldest Chinatown in Europe, big Chinese community, big West African community, you know going back generations to the slave trade – a slave city. You had Irish – 30 per cent of the population has Irish background, Welsh, there's very few English in Liverpool, it's like an independent republic.
SARI, Ireland

In London there are 33–34 per cent black and ethnic minority people and our point is not that this is small, it's big. And therefore, London and government and London government have to change to reflect the reality of London not to try to push it into a corner.
NAAR

The settlement of these migrants, generally joined later by their families, in particular areas of Britain's towns and cities, their employment in certain sectors and their establishment of shops, restaurants and community centres led to the perception of the wider population that these groups were different, yet internally identical. Afro-Caribbeans, Africans and South Asians (Indians, Pakistanis, Bangladeshis etc.), the biggest and most visible groups of immigrants, were compared to each other and each assigned fundamental characteristics. Gilroy and Lawrence (1988) show how this becomes important in reaction to the Brixton uprisings of 1981. The association of the uprisings with Afro-Caribbean youth led to Asians being seen as having integrated better into British society for the apparently paradoxical reason that they had remained different, spoke their own languages and practised different religions. Despite the fact that Afro-Caribbeans spoke English and practised Christianity, they were seen as having failed to become a seamless part of the society because they did not possess a 'whole', separate culture.

These characterisations of black and 'minority ethnic' people in Britain has been central to the explanation of racism by both the Right and the Left. These groups, seen as internally homogeneous by those around them, became racialised in that the characteristics said to typify them were seen as reasons for inadequate 'race relations' in British society. Racism was constructed as a 'black people's problem' by the conservative and far right wing, whose extreme fringes call for immigrants' repatriation as a solution to Britain's 'race' problem (Gilroy and Lawrence 1988).[7] Elements on the Left also found acceptance of difference difficult and, like in France, many lamented the apparent unwillingness of the majority of the black population to join the 'class struggle'.

These perceptions of black and 'minority ethnic' people in Britain are based upon their very quickly being seen as belonging to 'communities', living in clearly demarcated areas. Public and political reaction is not so much one of indignation at the refusal of 'immigrants' to assimilate, as was the case in France. It is rather aimed against the demands of black and 'ethnic minorities' for equal opportunities in British society and the choice of many to adopt a hyphenated British identity. The right to such claims is central to the emergence of black-led anti-racism in Britain (see box).

The media in Britain also plays a significant role in compounding racist images (Mac an Ghaill 1999). This was evident in the association of black youth with criminality in the right-wing press, a theme taken up by the National Front in its 1975 'March against Mugging'. Gilroy and Lawrence (1988:126) also show how social

> We do not for example say that the Bangladeshi community is an immigrant community because most of them now have British passports and they're a black-British ethnic minority community of Bangladeshi origin and to talk about them as immigrants sets the wrong framework.
>
> NAAR

scientific research contributes to the racialisation, of black people in particular, by extending the involvement of some blacks with drug dealing or prostitution to 'the whole group, in particular the nature of the "sending society" and the customs and mores of "immigrants" '.

Against the process of racialisation that developed a uniquely British analysis of the place of non-whites in the society, a variety of anti-racist forms may be seen to develop. Anti-racism in Britain is as much shaped by the reification of racialisation and the mental division of non-white societies into individual 'communities' as is much of popular opinion. The narration of the three major forms that compose British anti-racism reveal how each rejects or upholds the reification of 'community', upon which much of the discourse on 'difference' in Britain is based, in different ways. Each of the three can be shown to correspond to elements of anti-racism that emerge and reemerge at different times in the post-war period and to the present day. They may be thought of as trends within which various key discourses of anti-racism have been developed.

The first efforts to construct national anti-racist movements in the 1960s were quickly thwarted due both to the predominance of a solidaristic model imposed by white 'supporters' of immigrants' rights and to the infighting between factions within the groups themselves. The quick decline of organisations such as CARD and the Coordinating Committee against Racial Discrimination (CCARD) anticipated the breakup of British anti-racism by the early 1970s into various locally based 'solidarity' and black self-organised groups. It is important to note that:

the failure of the Campaign Against Racial Discrimination (CARD) in the 1960s illustrates the general difficulties of establishing a broad anti-racist movement in the UK. There were problems of a fundamental clash between reformists and radicals; the paternalism of white social democrats; and divisions between 'immigrant' groupings, in an attempt to establish an overambitious campaign with ill-defined goals.

Lloyd (1999:261)

However, these organisations were the precursors to the mass-based anti-racisms that emerged in Britain by the mid 1970s and which appealed to a wide audience amongst the youth and the left wing. Rock Against Racism, later followed by the Anti Nazi League, were expressions of the revolt of young, left-wing activists against the popularity of the far-right National Front in 1970s Britain (Gilroy 1987). However, as Gilroy is careful to show, the unifying factor that led to the aggregation of the preexisting local anti-racist/anti-fascist groups into a national movement was one, not of politics, but of culture. For Gilroy (ibid.) and Gilroy and Lawrence (1988) the success of RAR, in particular, was grounded in the ability of new musical and cultural forms to create alliances between black and white youths that led symptomatically to the development of an anti-racist consciousness to which the movements could tap in. This solidarity which was also based on shared working-class experience, contributed to the 'local campaigns in support of Rastafarian youths refused entry to school until they had cut off their locks' (ibid.:137). It was this interrelationship of music and a concern for justice that led to the success of Rock Against Racism (RAR) in the 1970s. This organisation, which organised 200 concerts in the first year of its existence, was formed by activists close to the Socialist Workers Party (SWP). RAR's slogan, now almost monolithic in British anti-racism, 'Black and White, Unite and Fight', played upon the habitual leftist identification of 'race' with class. However, Gilroy points out a fundamental difference which later was to demarcate RAR from its successor, the ANL: 'It deviated sharply from this traditional leftism in its insistence on the autonomous value of youth cultures and on the radical potential of "rock" and its offshoots' (Gilroy 1987:121). The arrival of punk on the scene was central due to its radical critique of 'racist nationalism and nationalist racism' (ibid.:125).

RAR has been criticised for depoliticising the issue of racism by locating it in the binary oppositional relationship embodied by its slogan, 'Love Music, Hate Racism'. Criticism was mostly heard from the radical Left who opposed the youthful, colourful anti-racism of the RAR 'carnivals' and called instead for 'workers' self-defence'

(Gilroy and Lawrence 1988). Gilroy argues that, contrary to its critics' condemnation of RAR's campaign as simplistic, the organisation's conceptualisation of racism was more complex. Its critique equated racism with national institutional practices while recognising the limitations of its own actions.

RAR can be contrasted with the launching of the Anti Nazi League (ANL) in 1977 (Gilroy 1987; Bonnett 1993; Lloyd 1999). Although the ANL emerged on the back of RAR's success, it sought to redirect the heterogeneity of the concerns raised by Rock Against Racism into a single-issue campaign, against the growth of the British far Right. By equating the contemporary racism of the far Right in Britain with Nazism, the ANL chose the most direct route to achieving its aims. Despite the problems that this reductive vision of anti-racist strategy poses, particularly in light of the traditionally divisive nature of British anti-racism, the ANL enjoyed massive success, witnessed in its ability to mobilise large numbers in the protest against racism. Its organisation of demonstrations and media campaigns in response to far-right activity attracted large sectors of the general public. This had the effect of taking mass-based anti-racism out of the domain of youth and popular music, instead attracting an older audience and returning anti-racism/anti-fascism to the 'class struggle'. For Gilroy (1987), the unifying message developed by RAR was fragmented by the very success of the ANL. Renton (www.dkrenton.co.uk/anl.html) criticises Gilroy's claim that RAR's politics were more radical than those of its successor. In his analysis, the ANL was the logical continuation of a campaign to popularise anti-racism begun by RAR: 'his [Gilroy's] distinction between RAR and the League would make no sense to David Widgery and Roger Huddle, the most prominent members of RAR, who went directly to working for the League' (ibid.). Rather than being radically different, both RAR and the ANL are both presented as making anti-racism work.

Authors who have commented on the emergence of British anti-racism (Gilroy 1987, 1992; Mac an Ghaill 1999; Lloyd 1999; Bonnett 1993, 2000) have noted that in the 1970s, 'anti-racism provided a strategically important critique of the liberal race-relations problematic that underplayed the importance of racialised structures of power at the level of economy, state and civil society' (Mac an Ghaill 1999: 104). This was brought about, as the history of black self-organisation as well as the mass-based RAR and ANL mobilisations show, in a spirit of autonomy, particularly from a Labour government seen as hypocritical in its stance on 'race'. Nevertheless, Gilroy's contrast of

RAR and the ANL demonstrates the way in which the latter moved popular, mass-based anti-racism away from the spontaneous alliances based on common interests and shared lived experiences that RAR reflected. The ANL's discourse of 'class struggle' inspired by its roots in the SWP created a rupture with the local, self-organised anti-racism that first emerged in the first half of the 1970s.

The discourse of black self-defence that was developed in the early 1970s in Britain, under the influence of parallel movements in the US, differs fundamentally from the anti-racisms of both RAR and the ANL and from the later move towards the institutionalisation of anti-racist practice in the 1980s. While theorists such as Gilroy (1987) and Sivanandan (1976) in particular argue that reducing these forms of black activism to anti-racism is to obscure the richness of the former and the full extent of its emancipatory capacities, excluding them from an analysis of anti-racism would be to neglect the significance of self-organisation for the development of the uniquely British focus on institutional racism. Many of these organisations were established in self-defence against the rise of far-right extremism in the local areas where immigrant populations lived among the indigenous white working class. The 1970s saw the most active mobilisation and electoral success of the National Front whose tactics of extreme violence included marching through these areas. The Campaign Against Racism and Fascism (CARF), 'an independent newspaper/magazine servicing the anti-racist movement' was founded against this background (interview with CARF):

When CARF was launched in the '70s it was a time where Britain was experiencing extreme levels of racial violence. Although you know things are bad now, they were a lot worse then. At that time it was the beginning really of a very important self-defence movement in so-called immigrant communities but actually these were black settler communities, they weren't immigrants because they were second generation who had citizenship rights. So, the very raison d'être of CARF was actually to reflect and work with the movement of those black organisations; I mean there were things like the first police monitoring groups that were set up in Southall and Newham in London by Asian and Afro-Caribbean youth. CARF was then instrumental in those campaigns.

CARF

These locally based anti-racist/anti-fascist committees, established between 1973 and 1976, were mostly concerned with the struggle between black people and the police over racist policing and the racial harassment of blacks and 'ethnic minorities' in custody and other issues of social concern such as housing and education. External references were important in the construction of these British visions of self-organised anti-racism. They have included the American civil rights movement, Black Power and the African National Congress (Mac an Ghaill 1999). Black Power influenced organisations such as the Black People's Alliance and, as we have seen, the radicalisation of the Institute of Race Relations. It also played a significant role in organising against Enoch Powell and against the 1968 Commonwealth Immigrants Act which refused to recognise the British passports of Asians in Kenya (CARF 1998). The organisations that organised around these concerns gave rise to monitoring groups, such as the Newham Monitoring Project which was established in 1980, based on the experiences of racism of black people and 'ethnic minorities'. Organisations such as the NMP illustrate well the marriage of a discourse of black self-defence with a wider interpretation of the effects of racism on the racialised in British society:

> We came out of a movement whereby black organisations came together, communities came together because of the high incidences of racism in this area. Our work is very specific to this area.
>
> NMP

NMP's self-description demonstrates the centrality of the vocabulary of blackness which defines the approach to anti-racism developed in Britain during the 1970s and 1980s. While blackness was theorised by Sivanandan (1982) as a political term which could be applied to all those facing racially based discrimination, regardless of their actual colour, in its original conception it was linked rather with the notion of 'community'. The term community is taken to refer to the local area and its inhabitants rather than to a shared culture, religion or national origin as in the French formulation of 'communitarianism'. The term 'black community' in the anti-racist language developed by these local organisations is taken to extend to the racialised in general and not confined to Africans or Afro-Caribbeans and, above all, to refer specifically to the populations living in a particular locality. The concept has remained central to British anti-racist discourse. There is a feeling that retaining the term 'black' avoids a blurring of the anti-racist message:

AL: Your definition of black, has that ever been problematic in terms of the definition between African-Caribbean people and Asian people?

No, not at all. I'm a black man myself. People may say why do you identify yourself as black? You're Asian. At the end of the day, it's the political term black in terms of not having power, the definition of power. I mean at the moment there's all kinds of words and semantics being thrown out but this is a problem which I see in that no one has to tell me what colour I am, I know but ... when you have to use semantics to explain to other people, you know, visible ethnic minorities is the word now. So, it keeps on changing so it confuses a lot of people.

The 1990 Trust

The importance of locality and shared working-class identities has also been shown by Gilroy and Lawrence (1988) and Back (1996) to contribute to an anti-racist consciousness that mixes political blackness with a wider sense of common lived experience. Back has shown how local solidarity is created between white and black working-class youths in London's Southgate. Gilroy and Lawrence also emphasise the importance of black–white alliance amongst young people in their analysis of the mirroring of experience reflected in the 1981 uprisings where, despite their racialisation, both white and black youths were at the forefront of events throughout the country. Back shows how the shared experiences of black and white young people shape an anti-racist consciousness, often in reaction to the extreme right-wing organisations that have traditionally used these inner-city areas as recruiting grounds. White young people's knowledge of black culture through their friendship with young blacks is counterposed to a national (English) identity which is seen as exclusionary of such experience:

[T]he aesthetic of Englishness is totally unattractive to young whites in Southgate. For them, the Union Flag is not associated with national unity and pride; rather it connotes neo-fascist politics and an image of skinhead youth who champion the bigotries of racism and national chauvinism.

Back (1996:135)

The emphasis placed both on 'blackness' as a common term of reference and the potential working-class alliances that have at various times formed important aspects of anti-racism has been subject to criticism. According to Modood (1997, 1998), the emphasis placed on 'blackness' in much of British anti-racism has led to both racism against Asians in Britain and religious discrimination being neglected:

> I do, however, have some reservations about the 'new blackness' line of Stuart Hall and Paul Gilroy. My three inter-related criticisms are that, firstly, these socio-cultural theorists invariably focus on Afro-Caribbeans; secondly, that they speak of a plural 'blackness' which they expect Asians to fit into but which most Asians are not interested in; thirdly, they are guilty of a woeful neglect of religion.
>
> Modood (1998:34)

The growth in Islamophobia (Runnymede Trust 1997), particularly in the aftermath of the Rushdie affair in the early 1990s, and again since the attacks of 11 September 2001, is testament to the proposition that 'the anti-racist mode of representation constructs a monolithic black subject' (Bonnett 1993:52). Whereas Afro-Caribbean cultural forms (Rastafari and reggae) as well as the borrowing of black American styles build commonalties between potentially anti-racist youth, the same was not always the case for Asians. This points to the ambivalent position of religion (particularly Islam) against the overarching tendency of much of British anti-racism to equate its goal with black liberation writ large. According to Modood, 'authentic "antiracism" for Muslims ... will inevitably have a religious dimension and take a form in which it is integrated to the rest of Muslim concerns' (Modood 1992:272–3).

However, Modood's objections must be met with care in order not to essentialise the Asian and Muslim identities he proposes differ so widely from those of the wider black community in Britain. Whereas cultural forms imported by the African and Afro-Caribbean communities in the 1970s and 1980s created the potential links between black and white youth and a general identification with black styles, today Asian forms are more likely to constitute that bridging device.

The 'Asian underground' scene, epitomised by the proactive anti-racism of bands such as the Asian Dub Foundation, is radically transforming the images of blackness that are channelled through culture.[8] Politically, Asians have always been involved in the struggles of the local communities and were at the forefront of the establishment of the monitoring groups. The Newham Monitoring Project was established following the racist murder of Akhtar Ali Baig in 1980:

> Horror and outrage – and above all the feeling that no such murder should ever again be tolerated on the streets of Newham – led to a spontaneous eruption of anger, particularly among young Asians who formed the Newham Youth Movement ... From out of the Akhtar Ali Baig Committee and the Newham Youth Movement came the Newham Monitoring Project – a concrete and durable expression of black self-organisation.
>
> NMP (1989:3)

Despite this, it is necessary to draw a divide between the anti-racist activism of Asians living in large black communities in urban centres such as London and the very different situation facing young Asians in more isolated areas of the country today. The eruption of Oldham and Bradford into rioting in the summer of 2001 was not the expression of a suppressed religious identity. In that sense it was not a continuation of the anger of Muslim groups at the publication of Salman Rushdie's *Satanic Verses* in 1988. The interpretation of the riots by much of the press as an expression of Islam as a unifying identity for Asian youth is belied by the various religious backgrounds of the rioters and by the overwhelming evidence that the riots were spurred, not by an identitarian fervour, but by anger against impoverished socioeconomic conditions. Comparing the 2001 riots to those of the 1980s, Kundnani remarks,

> [W]hereas the 1981 and 1985 uprisings against the police in Brixton, Handsworth, Tottenham and Toxteth had been the violence of a community united – black and white – in their anger at the 'heavy manners' of the police, the fires this time were lit by the youths of communities falling apart from within, as well as from without; youths whose violence was, therefore, all the more desperate. It was the violence of communities fragmented by colour lines, class lines and police lines. It was the violence of hopelessness. It was the violence of the violated.
>
> Kundnani (2001:105)

Above all, the 2001 riots were born of the segregation between white and Asian populations in the towns, a policy of the authorities responsible for public housing which has led to the perception, promoted by the right-wing press in Britain, that racism in Bradford and Oldham was black on white, with gangs of Asian youths attacking their white counterparts. In fact, violence was the case on both sides, engendered by the mistrust between whites and Asians whose only contact with each other, due to segregation in both housing and education, 'was through uncertain glances on the street or through the pages of the local newspapers' (Kundnani:ibid.:107). Kundnani relates this context to the legacy of collusion between local authorities and 'minority ethnic' community leaders. The emphasis on community in British anti-racism, meaning the localities in which racialised and white groups coexist and often act together, is translated, in the northern British context, to refer uniquely to a reified concept of ethnicity with its roots in the colonial system. Young Asians are therefore marginalised from the community in both its senses. In Kundnani's analysis (ibid.:108):

> a colonial arrangement which prevented community leaders from making criticisms [meant that] black communities became fragmented, horizontally by ethnicity, vertically by class ... Worst of all, the problem of racism came to be defined in terms of ethnic recognition so that to tackle racism was to fund an ethnic project, any ethnic project, no matter how dubious.

Perhaps it is not, as Modood suggests, that black analysts of racism and anti-racism have concentrated too heavily on the existence of a unifying black identity in neglect of the centrality of religious identities, in particular those of Muslims. Rather, the wide rifts between the British North and South, between the large cities and the small towns and between a legacy of political involvement as against arrangements of hierarchically determined 'ethnic' representation, seem to play a more important role in determining the qualitative differences between understandings of 'race', the enactment of racism and the possibilities for anti-racism across 'communities'.

The transposition of anti-racist initiatives independently organised by communities threatened by racism to an institutionalised response, coordinated by British local government, is seen as responsible for the reduction of racism to an individual problem of prejudice. 'Municipal' anti-racism had the effect of diluting the state-centred analyses of racism offered by the local organisations and leading to the dichotomising of anti-racism on the one hand, now seen to be the preserve of the state, and black resistance on the other. The anti-racist strategy of the local Labour administrations, elected during the spring of 1981, was a dual attack against the hegemony of Conservative-dominated central government and the inadequate responses to racism made by the institutions it established, in particular the Scarman Inquiry:

> The Scarman report tried to play down the influence of racism and tried to put it down to poverty, being underprivileged, and did not make the link between that and racism.
>
> NAAR

However, the local government response did not adopt the definition of institutional racism developed by the local black organisations. Instead it developed its own analysis of racism that was to shape anti-racist possibilities for at least a decade.

Gilroy's study of so-called municipal anti-racism demonstrates the 'narrow definitions of anti-racism being pursued' (Gilroy 1987:137) in the local government approach to anti-racism. This was most evident in the equation of racism to 'power + prejudice'. This view construed racial groups as fixed and assumed that 'race' defines people in the same way as nationality. Racism therefore has no influence on the construction of 'race(s)' (ibid.). By adding the dimension of power to individual prejudice, the municipal approach saw the solution to racism as defined by the capacity of an institution to change the opinions of the individuals within it who used their power, as members of the state's structures, to vent their personal racism. The means of bringing this about was Racism Awareness Training (RAT), described by Bourne (2001:11) as 'classes, based on pseudo-therapeutic techniques [which] played on white guilt and even introduced quasi-genetic reasoning to explain racism'.

The municipal anti-racist strategy with regards to institutionalised racism saw it as existing alongside personal prejudice rather than in a causal relationship with 'everyday racism'. Secondly, it sent out a contradictory message by retaining the management of anti-racism itself, deciding on funding allocations to local groups, embarking on a widespread public awareness campaign and introducing anti-racist education:

> The council becomes the primary site of anti-racist struggle whether the racist object being kicked out of town is made up of the racist institutions which the council manages or the racist opinions of the public which only the council is equipped to challenge.
>
> Gilroy (1987:144)

The objective of the local councils, based on the view of racism as prejudicial, was to shift the focus developed by the anti-racism of the 1970s from the institutional racism of the state to the attitudes of institutional personnel, and more widely the public in general. The result was the return to a culturalist interpretation of the objection to human difference which could be overcome by greater cultural knowledge. Political initiatives were overshadowed by those that stressed the cultural dimensions of communities, now no longer construed in terms of locality, but in ethnic, national or religious terms alone. As funding was redirected to cultural or religious projects,

> the black political unity, which had hitherto held together the immigrants from the Caribbean and the Indian subcontinent and propelled the struggles against state racism over three decades, now began to break down. The anti-racist struggle moved from the streets to the town halls where it became detached from the larger struggle for social justice and, under the heavy hand of management, froze into a series of techniques to achieve 'equal opportunity'.
>
> Bourne (2001:12)

This process was not sudden; organisations based in the black community, such as the monitoring groups, continued to organise in the 1980s. In parallel, there was also a move towards the professionalisation of black activism which took it out of the direct reality of anti-racism. This was evident in the increasingly formalised involvement of black groups in the trade union movement:

> Black organisation in the trade unions really developed in the 1980s so that by the end of the 1980s, most trade unions had race relations committees – but not just race relations committees, these were mainly composed of black trade unionists and accompanying

> them were a movement towards holding black trade unionists'
> conferences. So you have the TUC Black Workers Conference,
> which is the national black workers conference in the whole TUC,
> but most of the individual unions – some of them not till the '90s –
> but now hold black conferences in the way that they hold women's
> conferences, lesbian and gay conferences and developing now dis-
> abled people's conferences.
>
> NAAR

The increase in black people's participation in parliamentary politics around this time is also considered by NAAR to have been an
important process:

> Secondly, you had the whole Black organisation in the Labour party
> and the election of the first five Black MPs, would have been '87 I
> guess … So I think that you have the laying of the basis of a more
> politically interventionist mainstream – oriented to the mainstream –
> black politics, not unified, not homogeneous but homogeneous in
> the sense that it's part of the same process already by the early
> 1990s … I think that there were … that those black organisations
> were insisting … they were saying we don't recognise an anti-racist
> movement that we don't play a leading role in.
>
> NAAR

The emphasis placed on these evolutions by NAAR indicates the
importance, since the 1990s, of national anti-racist organisations
such as NAAR itself, and of a professionalised black NGO sector quite
removed from the local anti-racisms of, for example the monitoring
groups. Organisations such as The 1990 Trust concentrate on advocacy on behalf of black communities in a professionalisation of the
concerns about institutional racism originally raised by the local
anti-racist groups. For example, the Trust organised the mobilisation
of black votes in a highly mediatised campaign to emphasise the

weight of the black British electorate:

> We try to highlight campaigns and causes such as helping to set up Operation Black Vote, a black voter registration drive which has never been done in this country before.
>
> The 1990 Trust

The organisation integrates the specific concerns of a black community with the techniques implemented by the municipal approach to anti-racism. Its response to institutional racism is based upon the transformation of institutions through the inclusion of the racialised, a practice critiqued for being unable, on its own, to transform the daily realities of racism's victims (Bourne 2001):

> The only way you can educate people is for organisations to have say black people within those organisations where they can come in contact with these people and understand their culture. But when you have organisations or institutions that do not have black people involved in the decision making of the organisation itself they're perpetuating racism through institutional racism where they choose to ignore which is just as bad, you know, they choose to ignore that racism is going on in the work place.
>
> The 1990 Trust

The implication of such an approach is critiqued by the NMP with regard to the housing authority. The employment of greater numbers of black housing officers cannot, according to the organisation, bring about a change in the policy regarding segregated housing which is required to alleviate racism. In particular, the report produced by the Commission for Racial Equality and the Federation of Black Housing Officers is criticised because:

> One of their suggestions was a big drive to employ black social housing landlords, black-led community housing associations etc.

> which isn't the solution. That's about equal opps. employment, it's not the solution to the problem. Just employing black police officers doesn't change the fact that the police is a racist institution.
>
> NMP

The differences in approach that delineate national anti-racist organisations and black advocacy groups from the local anti-racisms that continue to exist in Britain shape the ongoing conflicts in British anti-racism as a whole. The large national anti-racist organisations are suspected by local groups of being incapable of effectively dealing with racism.

> Obviously we are part of the British anti-racist movement but as an organisation ... I don't know, because I just don't really like the idea of clumping all anti-racist organisations into one area and saying this is the anti-racist movement in Britain and we're part of that. Yes, we're part of that but the work we do is very, very specific. NMP is an anti-racist organisation who does case work, we work around racism, we work around police harassment in the East London area, more specifically Newham.
>
> NMP

British anti-racism is increasingly defined by the growing concern with the rights of asylum seekers and refugees across Europe. The application of an interpretation of institutional racism to this new context is indicative of the importance of this discourse as a major tool in the interpretation of racism. Its application beyond the concerns of the indigenous black and 'minority ethnic' communities is testament to the relative success of the extension of solidarity to this new focus in anti-racism. Despite the agreement among both national-level, professionalised and localised organisations of various dimensions about the need to reorient anti-racist concerns, the divides between these various approaches continue to define British anti-racism. The success with which institutional racism has been universally adopted and employed in a diverse series of anti-racist campaigns has not at the same time enabled a breaking down of the divisions which characterise the British arena. The overlapping legacies of solidarity, mass-based left-wing anti-fascism, municipal strategies and self-organised black resistance leave traces, the disparate nature of which may only be overcome with difficulty.

ALL DIFFERENT ALL EQUAL ALL EXPLOITED:[9]
THE EMERGENCE OF ANTI-RACISM IN IRELAND

Conceptualising nascent discourses and practices of anti-racism in Ireland requires firstly examining the history of anti-Irish racism, bound to the Irish people's history of colonial domination and enforced emigration (McVeigh 1992, 1998, 2002a; Ní Shúinéar 2002). Irish people's experience of immigration and its centrality to collective Irish memory is used as an argument both for and against anti-racism. Anti-racism in Ireland has become a significant basis for collective action only in recent years, due to the arrival of asylum seekers, refugees and migrants. The history of Irish emigration is central to the discourse of contemporary anti-racism. The current 'atmosphere of fear' (Watt 1998:29, cited in King 1998:49) reacting to the arrival of immigrants to Ireland, mainly from Africa and eastern Europe, is contrasted to the Irish people's own history as migrants, driven out of their country due to starvation or economic necessity. However, the similarities between Irish emigration and immigration to Ireland are not readily accepted by an indigenous public whose own emigration – both the 'Famine tide' of 1847 (King 1998) and the large-scale economic migration to Britain in the 1940s and 1950s – is perceived to be born strictly of necessity and to have been beneficial to the societies in which they settled. On the contrary, contemporary immigrants to Ireland are portrayed in much popular discourse as 'bogus' refugees, economic migrants whose primary purpose is to benefit from Ireland's recent economic success:

> The way that's achieved in my view is by presenting negative images of how much it's costing the state, that they're on the dole, they're spongers in effect, and allowing all sorts of myths to emerge about how much more they're getting than say, our socially deprived, indigenous Irish groups.
>
> NFARC

Related to Irish emigration, the experience of anti-Irish racism has been formative of a uniquely Irish conceptualisation of belonging-ness, of in and out groupings, that now informs both racist and anti-racist discourse. On the one hand, current hostility towards immigrants is explained by the Irish people's own victimisation as a colonised people. After decades of economic hardship that followed the foundation of the Republic, the economic boom of the 1990s is not eagerly shared with non-Irish, non-Catholic and non-white others. On the other hand, the very fact of Irish emigration should, according to Irish anti-racists, mean a greater benevolence in Ireland towards today's immigrants. However, according to Amnesty International's Campaign for Leadership against Racism in Ireland, 'there exists no sense that the Irish, of all people, should welcome migrants in search of a fresh start in the way that they themselves were welcomed across the world throughout the nineteenth and twentieth centuries' (*Time Out Dublin Guide* 1999, cited in Amnesty International 2001).

Ní Shúinéar (2002:177) argues that contemporary Irish racism can be traced back to the Irish experience of colonial domination that produced a 'self-loathing and scapegoating' among the Irish. Similarly, McVeigh (2002a) explains how the Irish have been racialised and simianised in the anti-Irish racist discourse of Britain and the US. The Irish were both the objects of mockery, through jokes and caricatures, and a part of the White Man's Burden, 'a uni-versal of imperialist ideology, evoked from the genocide of the indigenous peoples of the Americas and Australia to the direct rule of Africa and India' (Ní Shúinéar 2002:178). The identification of this as anti-Irish racism came about much more recently, in con-texts of emigration, particularly of the large Irish communities in Britain. In particular, it was what McVeigh (2002a) rightly describes as the 'ethnicisation' of British politics in the early 1980s that enabled the Irish in Britain to be identified as an ethnic group along the same lines as other racialised communities. He also links the currency of the notion of anti-Irish racism to events in Northern Ireland at the time, namely the Hunger Strikes, which helped breed solidarity between 'ethnic groups'. These new links led to the iden-tification of the Irish as politically black (Sivanandan 1983) and to the ensuing presumption, generated by the British Left, that anti-Irish racism precluded the Irish people's inability to be racist: ' "Irish racism" has been theorised out of existence by the disingenuous use of the "racism = prejudice + power" equation to argue that Irish people, like Black people, have no power to be racist' (McVeigh 1992:31).

McVeigh (1992) has drawn a connection between Irish experiences of racism and colonialism and what he terms the 'specificities of Irish racism'. Beyond the experiences of the Irish émigré in the multicultural urban settings of the US and Britain (O'Toole 2000), in Ireland itself until recently the homogeneity of the Irish population was a well-preserved popular myth. The proposition that Ireland did not have a 'problem' of racism because no black people lived there (made by both 'racists' and 'anti-racists'), denies the fact that a perceived lack of racialised people in a given society does not mean an absence of racism (McVeigh 1992).

Contrary to the myth of the homogeneity of the Irish population prior to recent immigration, the country has, since the turn of the twentieth century, been home to a small Jewish community, whose members generally originate in the Baltic states. Other non-Catholic 'minorities' (apart from Protestants) were made up of small numbers of Muslims, mostly of British citizenship. Until recently, non-white people in Ireland were largely invisible due to their small numbers, which makes their heightened visibility today important for understanding the transformation of contemporary Irish racism.[10] Other than small numbers of Vietnamese, and later Bosnian, refugees, 'invited' into Ireland on a humanitarian basis, the most significant group of racialised people is that of the Irish Travellers who number roughly 27,000 (O'Connell 2002). The Traveller movement has been integral to establishing Irish anti-racism. However, to a certain extent it has been the increasing activity of non-Irish, non-white people in recent years in response to institutional discrimination and the growing number of racist incidences against them that has highlighted anti-Traveller racism and made it possible to speak of them as a racialised, 'minority ethnic' group.

The specificity of Irish racism is proposed as involving five interacting processes: the diffusion of British racism; Irish involvement in colonialism; the experiences of the Irish diaspora; the links between racism and sectarianism/nationalism; and endogenous anti-Traveller racism (McVeigh 1992). These factors, especially the 'importation' of British racism, the link between racism and sectarianism and anti-Traveller racism are central to an exploration of the emergence of Irish anti-racism. The position of Britain as a reference point throughout Ireland's history has led, as McVeigh shows, to the reproduction in Irish discourse of post-war British racism against black and 'minority ethnic' people. Therefore, official and popular Irish reasoning against immigration often cites the problems of 'race relations' experienced in the UK. But the British experience also resonated with left-wing political actors: early anti-racism in Ireland consisted of 'branches' of UK-based organisations. For example, Rock Against Racism had an Irish group (Gilroy 1987). This was clearly linked to the activity of the Irish branch of the Socialist Workers Party (SWP) who have, more recently, set up an Anti Nazi League and were active in demonstrations against racism and antisemitism before the later establishment of specifically anti-racist organisations. Whereas the SWP in Britain is seen by many in the anti-racist movement to use the anti-racist platform to further their own agenda, in Ireland the party sometimes acts as the impetus for organisations that later act autonomously. An example is Residents Against Racism (RAR):

> It was actually started by the Socialist Workers Party, none of whom are in the group anymore. They have this campaign ... I was once a member of that party. Suffice to say, they started the group and some of us heard about it. I heard about it and went along to the courts and met Belmondo and his wife. And Belmondo asked me if I would join the group, his support group. The group more or less fell apart because it was going on so long – see, this is two and a half years ago – and it kind of dissolved itself and a couple of us decided that either it was going to go completely or we were going to renew it out of the ashes. And it's now not just Residents of Drimnagh, it's actually people from all over Ireland. So, we have members in Derry, in Kerry, all over the place.
>
> RAR

Particular to Ireland, the relationship between racism and sectarian politics is a central factor of the specificities of Irish anti-racism. McVeigh (1992) refers particularly to the close links between some Northern Irish loyalists and European right-wing groups and the importance of the 'Ulster question' to the British far Right. More recently, this association has ventured beyond Britain with extremist mercenaries in the Ulster Unionist camp fighting on the side of the Croats during the Bosnian war. On the other hand, little has been written about Irish nationalist racism, the assumption being made that Irish Catholic nationalists are opposed only to Protestants, a relation of antagonism construed in religious sectarian terms as well as in terms of a relationship of imperialism. This is complicated by the fact that Sinn Féin has supported the anti-racist cause in the Irish Republic and several anti-racist activists are or have been members of the Irish Republican movement. For the Northern Irish context, McVeigh (1998) draws similarities between the treatment of blacks and Catholics, although he admits that the quality of the discrimination differs. However, the resonance of Northern Irish Catholic nationalism in the Republic complicates the relationship between nationalism and racism generally found in other European settings. The transposition of the legacy of anti-Irish racism to the national context, based on the experience of Irish emigrants abroad, as well as the aforementioned associations made between black liberation and the Irish nationalist struggle contribute to a neglect of the possible connection between racism and Irish nationalism. This, in turn, has shaped the emergence of anti-racist practices in Ireland.

On the other hand, the relationship between anti-sectarianism and anti-racism has, in some cases, paved the way for anti-racist organisations in Ireland. North–South dialogues or meetings between Protestant and Catholic youth, organised by groups such as Co-operation North in the 1980s and 1990s, ran along similar principles to much anti-racist youth work. Ken McCue, of Sport Against Racism in Ireland (SARI), locates his commitment to anti-racism as building directly upon his work in the domain of anti-sectarianism which, in turn, was influenced by anti-racism practices employed in the UK. His current focus on the use of football (soccer) in anti-racism also has roots in these experiences:

So, I looked at the situation in Northern Ireland by conflict resolution and how models that were developed in Liverpool in terms of anti-racism could be applied to the Irish anti-sectarian pattern. And, I found that really interesting because as a kid I used to travel over to watch Liverpool. And I'd be standing in the cockpit by the goal and the guy next to me would have a big King Billy tattoo on his arm and would be shouting for the same team as me. It just didn't make sense that, you know, here we were from the Shankhill Road in Belfast and I was from the inner city in Dublin,

> coming from those completely different backgrounds, but the
> same class background, and we had this in common.
>
> SARI

However, there is also a sense in which the translatability of
practices and symbols may obscure the specificity of the Northern
Irish conflict and its difference from racism. In distinguishing
between the different forms of discrimination that 'structure multiethnicity in Ireland' (McVeigh 1998:16), McVeigh comments that
'anti-Irish racism characterises relationships between British and
Irish people, an anti-Black racism in Ireland characterises relationships between "People of Colour" and "White" people, while sectarianism characterises the relationships between Catholic and
Protestant Irish people' (ibid.:18). The connection between racism
and the sectarianism brought about by colonialist legacies has contributed to a specifically Irish understanding of the interrelation
between various types of discrimination. It has also helped to shape
an Irish approach to anti-racism which comes into play in the interaction with other associations in European networks, such as that
created to combat racism in football, Football Against Racism in
Europe (FARE). As opposed to the British and French situations, the
experience of racism against Irish emigrants abroad enables Irish
anti-racists to intervene on issues of anti-Irish racism, particularly in
the British context. These anti-racist activists display an ability to consider racism as operating on several levels that affect different groups
in different contexts and where the oppressor may become the victim
outside of his/her country. Such a multidimensional approach is
not perceived to be appreciated to as great an extent by British
activists who are said to consider racism mainly in terms of the
so-called colour line:

> Some of our colleagues in the likes of [the campaigns against
> racism in football] Kick it Out and to a lesser extent the Show
> Racism the Red Card which is a sort of – all the teams sign up to it,
> you know. They would have a problem with that. When we raise
> the issue of sectarianism, for example, and the anti-Irish stuff, like

the likes of Paul McGrath being called a black Irish bastard or something like that, and they're saying no. No, for them it's not. It's black and white purely. Purely black and white, that's the issue. … We tried to get sectarianism on the agenda because again it's the situation that in Ireland at the time was a major issue.

SARI

The most important precursor to contemporary anti-racism in Ireland has been the action by and on behalf of Travellers. The Traveller support movement, made up of various groups of Travellers and non-Travellers, known as 'settled people', was responsible for introducing the term 'racism' into Irish political discourse. Racism against Roma, Gypsies and Travellers is an issue which has been almost universally ignored by mainstream anti-racism in most countries. In Ireland, on the contrary, the anti-racist movement can be said to be grounded in Travellers' experiences of racism and their struggle against ongoing discrimination.

Organisations such as Pavee Point were established by settled people with expertise in the areas of human rights and community development (Tannam 2002). As Fay (1992) notes, whereas the debate on Travellers' rights was formerly based on issues of settlement, the late 1980s and early 1990s saw a shift towards a more open discussion of racism and ethnicity. There was a concomitant willingness to more readily accept that Irish Travellers are construed racially in ways similar to the racialisation of black people (McVeigh 1992). McVeigh cites Court (1985):

The terms *dirty* and *clean* and alternatively *black* and *white* have been used in many social contexts, including this Irish one, to designate outsiders and insiders. Tinkers, for example, have frequently been called black by Gypsies as well as by settled Irish, two peoples who were themselves named *black* and *dirty* by the English.

Court (1985, cited in McVeigh 1992:40)

This relates to an awareness by activists, such as those at Pavee Point, of the limitations of existing voluntary work on behalf of Travellers and, specifically, the absence of an anti-racist dimension (Tannam unpublished). The acceptance of the fact that Travellers in Irish society are racialised was built upon an approach to anti-Traveller discrimination that linked it to racism. This, in turn, stemmed from Travellers' own self-identification as a distinct 'ethnic group', 'identifiable by their distinctive lifestyle, values, customs and traditions which set them apart from the majority population' (Collins 1992:82), yet the refusal by Irish institutions and the dominant public to recognise them as such. For Traveller groups, the claim made by local and national government, other public institutions, the media and in popular discourse that their Irishness makes it impossible either to refer to them as an 'ethnic minority' group or admit that they are victims of racism (rather than of discrimination or 'social exclusion'), is contradicted by experience:

> Racism is an everyday experience for Travellers, for most Travellers and someone said earlier on, how would you recognise Travellers? I think settled people has a good way of recognising Travellers particularly if you own a hotel or a pub or a hairdressers or, you know, whether it's the police coming down and informing you which is recently ... I'm just using I suppose as a kind of an example of a hotel in Galway when they find out about a Travellers' wedding[11] but that's quite a common experience across the country.
>
> Irish Travellers' Movement

The positive advances made by Travellers, and by those working on their behalf, towards an organisation of their political demands has laid the foundations for Irish approaches to anti-racism. They are mainly grounded in the 'community development' approach, from which many Traveller groups have benefited. The traditions constructed within this approach have strongly influenced the possibilities open to groups formed to counter discrimination. The lack of a longer anti-racist history in Ireland has contributed to creating a greater dependency of anti-racist groups upon a 'community development' logic. One of its main principles is the notion of 'partnership', or the establishment of widely representative bodies comprised of 'different sectors, such as statutory, voluntary, trade union, community groups, media etc.' (Tannam unpublished). Many of these initiatives are established by governmental bodies, in consultation with voluntary groups, including – but not exclusively – specifically anti-racist organisations. There is a sense in which 'partnerships' can bring about participation and generate an anti-racist impetus where none existed before.

While the community development approach is accredited with giving impetus to initiatives to combat anti-Traveller racism, it is also recognised that the structure created by 'partnership' creates a dependency of Traveller groups on settled organisations. The widespread use of partnerships in a wide range of situations in anti-racism in Ireland is one of the elements constraining the possibilities open to racialised groups to speak for themselves, an important factor in the analysis of anti-racism. Most Traveller organisations in Ireland are still not run by Travellers themselves:

> Here in Pavee Point we do try to have a partnership arrangement but we also would acknowledge that it is a very difficult thing to manage and to achieve and … we are constantly working at ways of improving that because having four Travellers at a table and having four settled people, it's dangerous to suggest that partnership is taking place there because there can be a huge power imbalance in terms of settled people having had all the opportunities re education, training – they have a far superior vocabulary.
>
> Martin Collins, Pavee Point (cited in Tannam unpublished:6)

McVeigh (2002b), looking back upon the history of the Irish Traveller Support Movement, argues that the logic of the 'partnership' model is to enable the participation of disproportionate numbers of settled, or what he calls 'ethnic majority' people, in Irish anti-racism. He compares the Irish situation to that in other countries in which white people have been overrepresented in anti-racism. Whereas this has been challenged elsewhere, in the Irish case the partnership model is used to justify the role of white, settled Irish people, construed as one of support but, in fact, often one of leadership:

> In Ireland, however, the partnership model allowed this situation not only to obtain but also to be regarded as a positive part of anti-racism. The failure to transfer power and resources to minority ethnic people was itself the symbol of 'partnership'. This model became even more dangerous when it began to inform work with refugees and other minority ethnic groups. These groups could be brought into partnership

and here too their non-involvement at a leadership level could be excused as an example of partnership.

McVeigh (2002b:221)

Apart from the initiatives to tackle anti-Traveller racism, contemporary anti-racism in Ireland has other predecessors. For example, Harmony was established following the coming together of a group of parents of black children. Its main aim was to campaign for anti-racist legislation in Ireland. The size of Irish society and the then very small numbers of black people or 'ethnic minorities' must be taken into account as an important factor in the early beginnings of anti-racism beyond the sole concerns of Travellers. As Tannam et al. (1998:28) comment, 'one of its [Harmony's] strengths was the informal network of support that built up between members over the years', primarily grounded in their common experience as members of what Tannam et al. call 'intercultural families'. The relative ease with which families such as these came into contact to eventually form an anti-racism organisation marks Ireland out from the other countries in the present study in which the construction of national movements involves a much less personalised process. The familiarity bred within and across Irish anti-racist organisations does not arise solely from the small numbers making up the Irish population, but also from the country's political culture of familiarity and provincialism.

Another example of early Irish anti-racism, still in existence today, is *Comhladh*, initiated by returning Irish development workers from the Third World. Such external references, other than that of Britain, have been important in framing Irish anti-racist responses and are related to the Irish experience, mainly through the Catholic Church, in development and humanitarian work. However, it is also linked to the affinity of 'freedom fighters' in Third World countries with the Irish Republican 'struggle' and the resonance of such for many in the anti-racism movement. For example, the anti-Apartheid movement constituted an important reference point for Irish anti-racists:

> I made very good connections with the African National Congress, the youth department ... They had, one thing they had was a very good football team. Soccer was always popular among the black population in South Africa. And these were kids who were in school

in Tanzania and they had a football team. So we decided to do some fundraising for them and we approached, at the time the European championships were on and our team – the Irish Republic team – had qualified. And Chris Houghton[12] was one of the players and he was – now coaches Spurs – and he was very active in the anti-Apartheid movement and he was also on the sports panel of the African National Congress. And he gave us his football jersey and we raffled it and we bought a full kit for the ANC team in Tanzania ... And I got involved then in the South African Students Association as well and the anti-Apartheid movement here.

SARI

More recently founded groups can be divided into those initiated by Irish people in response to growing racism, those created by refugees and asylum seekers coming into Ireland, institutional bodies (national and European) and community projects. Many of these groups regularly meet through shared platforms due to both the relatively small numbers of people involved and the emphasis placed on working in partnership. The Platform Against Racism, for example, groups together non-governmental organisations working in the field of anti-racism. The National Consultative Committee on Racism and Interculturalism (NCCRI) is a governmental initiative which lists in its aims the promotion of government–NGO dialogue (Tannam 2002). The movement's size dictates the inability to draw a distinct line, as is possible in other countries, between organisations acting in complete (political and financial) independence from institutional bodies and those which receive the majority of their funds from governmental or European Union sources. Meetings organised by the NCCRI generally involve individuals and organisations from across the spectrum of anti-racist, human rights and Travellers', asylum-seekers', refugees' and migrants' groups active in Ireland. This is despite the fact that the NCCRI, which now has NGO status, was originated under the auspices of the government Department of Justice, the same department responsible for immigration control.

As in the other countries considered in this study, a major concern for contemporary anti-racism in Ireland is the campaign against the detention and deportation of 'illegal' immigrants. To a great extent, as in Italy, groups established with the express purpose of campaigning for a more just system of immigration constitute a new anti-racism that bypasses the various stages of development passed through by the French and British movements. Organisations such as the Anti Racism Campaign (ARC) or Residents Against Racism (RAR) were set up in direct reaction against the treatment of incoming non-Europeans. The contemporary anti-racist movement in Ireland moves anti-racism in a new direction. Whereas the anti-racism of the *Sans-papiers* movement in France competes with the claims of more established organisations of second and third generation 'immigrants' for limited resources, in Ireland it is the agenda set by today's new migrants that shall dictate the future of anti-racist discourse in that country. Lastly, the relationship increasingly drawn between the campaign against restrictions on immigration and for the rights of migrants and the Global Justice Movement, may have the effect of creating firmer links between anti-racism and other movements for social justice. An example of the ways in which the discourses of the Global Justice Movement and contemporary anti-racism in Ireland are connected is evident in the stated aims of the National Federation of Anti-Racist Campaigns:

> We take quite a radical position on immigration controls, i.e. we argue for their complete abolition. Now we haven't argued for their abolition unilaterally or that Ireland must do it in advance of everybody else. But our argument being really that in a world where it's becoming increasingly easier for capital and money, goods, services etc. to move in a virtually borderless world and at the same time becoming more and more difficult for people to actually cross frontiers.
>
> NFARC

How do these novel forms of collective action and the emergent discourses of anti-racism in Ireland bear upon common understandings of the elements of public political culture that may be said to intersect with such discourses and practices? The discussions of France and Britain illustrate the ways in which understandings of anti-racist themes, differing widely between the two countries, have been shaped over a significant length of time and are founded upon the specific perception of the positioning of difference within the history of each country. In other words, neither 'race' and racism nor anti-racism may be conceived of independently of the unique nature of colonial history and that of the increased presence and participation of non-Europeans in these societies. The case of Ireland has demonstrated a wholly different – and much shorter – trajectory of anti-racism.

Irish anti-racism can be understood to occupy a unique space, intervening in a national arena that resembles neither the traditional, ex-colonialist 'host' society nor the 'sending' country of old. Nor did it have its own experience of fascism or Nazism, and therefore of partisan resistance. Ireland's construction as a 'community', bridging the physical space between the territory upon which it has established a republic and its extensive diaspora, has an important influence upon anti-racist possibilities. The predominance of institutional initiatives for combating racism is not based solely on the practical consideration of funding. It also represents an Irish 'way of doing things' which insists on what McVeigh (1992:41) calls the ' "warmth" of the community'. McVeigh employs this concept to describe Irish attitudes to outsiders. It is the opposition of the hegemonic and singularly legitimate 'community' of Irish Catholics (at home or abroad) to the multiple communities seen to be shooting up with the arrival of non-white immigrants, alongside the continued presence of the Travellers, that characterises contemporary Irish racism.

McVeigh, contrasting English and Irish racisms, notes that while the former is steeped in 'colonial domination and imperial justification' (McVeigh 1992:41), the latter is related to Irish 'sedentarism'. The settled nature of the Irish and the connection with the land is contrasted with the nomadism of the Travellers who 'came to occupy a central position within sedentary Irish culture as a symbolic "other" ' (ibid.). Today's racism towards non-Irish migrants, refugees and asylum seekers, beyond similarities to anti-immigrant sentiment across Europe, is an extension of the uniquely Irish conceptualisation of community: generosity is displayed in the extension of Irish identity to millions of descendants of Irish émigrés throughout the western world, so almost completely disconnecting national belonging from the duties of citizenship. Yet, inclusion in the national community is extended with difficulty to those newcomers whose inability to trace their lineage back to even a distant great grandparent sets them apart from community members, perhaps indefinitely.

For McVeigh (1992), the Irish pathologisation of out groups, because of their own experience of colonial and racist oppression, makes impossible an internal problematisation of gender, class or sexuality in Irish society. Irish anti-racism is therefore a means for tackling these issues that have no place in the internal construction of Irish 'community'. Anti-racism, by displacing the oppression of the Irish themselves, takes the place of a discussion of inequalities in gender, class and sexuality, unique to the Irish situation but that, until recently, have had little to do with the presence of non-Irish others in the society itself. McVeigh's point is a valid one: progressive politics of various types do have a general tendency to overlap and, in the Irish case, due to the particularly pressing nature of some issues, such as the campaign to legalise abortion, by necessity lead to the blurring of the boundaries between various social movements. However, by narrowly defining this role of anti-racism, he fails to account for the diversification of its discourse in the Irish context.

Irish anti-racism, particularly that based on the community development perspective with its prioritisation of 'partnerships', seeks to recreate the sense of uniqueness of the Irish community. The 'warmth of community' that McVeigh proposes excludes non-Irish Others, is also applied in the creation of a uniquely Irish anti-racism. The emphasis on partnerships constructs a dependency on the (anti-racist) community that appears to mirror the national Irish need for communal 'warmth' as a major structuring idea. In practical terms, the community development approach breaks the anti-racist target group (Travellers, asylum seekers, immigrants and so on) into individual communities that as a whole make up the general 'warm community' of progressive Ireland. The ability of each to take political action is shaped by the possibilities to build partnerships within the general anti-racist community; and especially with the white, Irish advocates of the community development approach who agree to assist them in promoting their concerns.

The current dominance of the community development approach is being challenged by the purposefully anti-institutional organisations campaigning for free immigration and an end to the detention and deportation of immigrants, such as the Anti Racist Campaign or Residents against Racism. Their mainly Irish membership in the past has more recently been transformed by the addition of many more asylum seekers as active members. These organisations develop a critique of the 'cosiness' of Irish community by attacking the public political culture that extends Irish membership of the nation to the international Irish Diaspora and judges Irishness according to a measure of nationalist values exclusive of non-Catholic, non-white, non-anti-British identities. Such a critique, by attacking received notions at the core of the nationalist notion of community may also be able to inadvertently challenge the hegemony of reified 'community' central to the anti-racist/community development approach. By bringing together increased numbers of Irish and immigrant people to question what such organisations perceive as being the hypocrisy of the state racism of the Irish (as former immigrants), it may be possible to deconstruct the anti-racist vision of community which recreates, in Ireland itself, the diasporic situation into which the Irish were forced as emigrants abroad.

'LAVORATORI IMMIGRATI, ROMPERE LA CATENA DEI RICATTI DI PADRONI E GOVERNO ITALIANI':[13] THE EMERGENCE OF ANTI-RACISM IN ITALY

Anti-racism in Italy cannot be said to constitute a recognisable movement form. In contrast, Italian anti-racists have come together periodically in response to specific instances of racism, from racist murders to discriminatory legislation and detention centres. They constitute a wide range of social actors from a variety of political origins, including the far left wing, trade unions, charitable organisations and, increasingly, the opponents of economic globalisation; the protagonists of the so-called 'movement of movements'. How is the notion of racism constructed and interpreted by anti-racists in the Italian context? What are the specificities of the circumstances in which anti-racism, as a form of collective action, intervenes? Such a contextual examination should go towards revealing the reasons for which it is difficult to speak of the existence of an Italian anti-racist movement.

Unlike Britain, France and even Ireland with its nascent anti-racism, very few studies of either racism or anti-racism have been conducted in Italy. This is because, to a much wider degree than even in France, the problematic of racism in the Italian context is almost universally understood to be one of immigration which, in turn is seen as being the local translation of a global-level object of study: migration (Dal Lago 1999; Mezzadra 2001). Therefore, the study of anti-racism is of interest only in that it constitutes a localised struggle against the much more wide-reaching processes of migration, resultant it is said of globalisation, that will ultimately continue despite the localised efforts to raise awareness of the inequalities they produce. This is supported by my observation of the types of groups and organisations active against racism and of the discourse that is produced and which becomes representative of the Italian anti-racism visible in the public sphere. Organisations are often composed of groups of left-wing activists, adjoined to the more generalised movement for a 'globalisation from below' that has gained strength in Italy over recent years. Groups composed of black and 'minority ethnic' people often have a culturalist orientation, determined by the felt need of the wider Italian left wing to 'deal with' the problems faced by immigrants and, in its own words, to embrace cultural diversity. COSPE, a development organisation that also organises anti-racism training and from which the Italian delegation to the European Network Against Racism (ENAR) is coordinated, claims that the focus on culture serves to marginalise the critique implied by an anti-racist approach:

> Initially in 1990 there were very few organisations ready to pay for anti-racism training in this country and besides they weren't ready to pay for it if you called it by its name ... You didn't call it anti-racism otherwise ... the contents remained the same, we said exactly the same thing. We had a critical analysis, we had the same analysis when you called it anti-racism, we called it multiculturalità obviously.
>
> COSPE

The focus on interculturalism as a major tool in the fight against discrimination emphasises cooperation between different cultural collectivities. The association of both migrants' needs and the preparation of Italian society for diversity with cultural knowledge has served to dissociate the domain of immigrants' rights from the purportedly more political orientation of the Italian social movements.

In addition to this focus on (im)migration as the main process through which to generate understandings of contemporary racism, another dimension of the Italian anti-racism of left-wing organisations is its focus on the history of fascism in Italy. While Irish anti-racists have developed an interpretation of racism based on external factors such as colonialism, emigration and anti-Irish racism, Italian anti-racism tends to focus more on the domestic, internal histories of fascism and partisanship, as shall be shown in the following chapter. The anti-racist endeavours of left-wing organisations, social centres and trade unions are presented as rooted either in the historical struggle of the Partisans against fascism and Nazi anti-semitism or in the effort to admit the wrongs of Italy's fascist and colonialist past. As the following statements from an interview carried out with ARCI[14] point out, the description of such commitment significantly combines an admittance of past wrongdoing with pride in the Italian left wing's tradition of anti-fascism:

> Luckily, the consciousness of the partisan fight against fascism was strong, on the other hand. So, that beautiful struggle of the people was strong, one of the most beautiful stories of Italian history: the anti-fascist resistance.
>
> We have always denied the demagogy of those years of the Italians as great people, the Italians that always stood up against racism. We said no. The Italians, in the past of our history, there are some significant black marks.
>
> ARCI

The mainstream Italian anti-racism of the large left-wing organisations seeks to place its activism on a par with that of Europe's other 'big' countries, in particular France with its purportedly shared history of anti-fascist resistance. In contrast, the conceptualisation of racism in Italian anti-racist discourse does not tend to focus either on the Italian history of economic migration or on that of the internal 'racism' brought about by Italy's 'Southern Question' (Schneider 1998). Italian anti-racists' construction of the problem of racism externalises it so completely that a more intimate narration of racism becomes almost impossible. Racism is construed as entirely new and to uniquely affect non-Italians. The racism experienced by southern Italian migrants to the North or emigrants across the world is not considered worth mobilising in the campaign against racism. Only one reference was made to Italian emigration as a legitimation of contemporary anti-racism during the research, by ARCI:

> Immediately after the war, we, like other countries, experienced emigration. So, we have about 20,000 Italians who have gone around the world, and presently there are 5 million Italians with Italian citizenship who are resident abroad. Ultimately, there are more than 20 million that are Italian immigrants. So that is the historical experience that we somehow wanted to relaunch by saying that the fight against racism is anchored in history, in a part of history that we want to initiate. That is to say also that when we were poorer we were immigrants. Now we can not reject those who come to our country from the poorest countries.
>
> ARCI

This statement is inscribed in the general idea that racialisation is not a process that has taken hold in Italy. Balbo and Manconi (1990) remark that Italy has not yet developed a racial 'social formation', implying that racism is a new problem that has existed only since the arrival of non-European migrants in significant numbers since the 1980s.

No reference was made to what has been referred to as Italian 'neo-Orientalism' (Schneider 1998). The internal racism, operating along the country's North–South divide, receives little mention from anti-racist activists. Schneider (1998) locates the emergence of Italy's 'Southern Question' in the latter half of the nineteenth century, following Italy's unification. She notes that the South, in the conceptualisation of politicians, artists and writers, was both essentialised and racialised. The othering of Italy's South by both northern leaders, and significantly, southern intellectuals, may therefore be thought as a form of 'neo-Orientalist discourse within Italy itself' (Schneider 1998:8). Such a discourse has been used by elites in order to displace Italian feelings of inadequacy in relation to its European neighbours. As Schneider remarks, 'these processes – displacement and complicity – illuminate how Orientalism can work within a country to reinforce the wider geopolitical and geo-cultural ambitions of the great powers ...' (ibid.). In the domestic context, Urbinati (1998), in her discussion of Gramsci's relationship to the Italian South, demonstrates how his denunciation of the racism of the

Italian North reveals parallels with contemporary racisms against immigrants. Gramsci's emphasis on southern workers as the object of northern derision mirrors the widespread image of the (male) immigrant in contemporary Italy as a worker. Rather than northern racism emerging from an attachment to Europe, against which the South presented an obstacle to progress, Gramsci saw the northern attitude as a provincial one which could only be countered by focusing on the importance of national unity:

> Northerners – both intellectuals and common people – never felt 'solidarity' with the South because of their colonising ideology, their total 'ignorance' of southern society, and their prejudices. No less than the Sardinians, the Northerners had to submerge their localism in a unitarian (or national) outlook.
>
> Urbinati (1998:149–50)

The apparent centrality of the North–South divide in Italian political consciousness makes it surprising to realise that it is almost not mobilised at all in anti-racist discourse. Despite this, a closer look at the trajectories of several Italians involved in anti-racist or intercultural work reveals the extent to which it may be a consistently 'silent' presence that motivates individual actions. For example, the director of *Almateatro*, a theatre group initiated by the intercultural women's association *Alma Terra* in Turin said that her involvement was motivated by her family's experiences 30 years previously as southern migrants to the northern city. The area in which the intercultural women's centre *Alma Mater* is situated (which houses *Alma Terra*), was previously populated by a majority of southerners who have now moved, making way for the increased numbers of Somalis, Moroccans, East Europeans and others. A similar background was uncovered during an interview with a lawyer volunteering at the Turin-based *Rete d'urgenza contro il razzismo*, an advocacy group for immigrants experiencing discrimination. Nonetheless, there is the feeling that the question of whether the preceding existence of anti-southern racism in both the personal histories of anti-racist activists or in those of a northern city, such as Turin, was of relevance to contemporary anti-racism had not previously been given much attention. The fact that today's anti-racist activists of southern Italian origin do not directly experience discrimination is felt to delegitimise placing too great an emphasis on the importance of this past in the construction of contemporary anti-racist strategies. This is evident in the following dialogue:

AL: For example, the situation of the Italian Southerners ...

Exactly, exactly.When the Southerners came to Turin there was exactly the same problem.

AL: And is there the memory of that in today's anti-racism work?

Well ... In the sense that it is known that that happened. Maybe ... for example, we are almost all of us very young, those of us who work here, so we have never worked on that other aspect. Maybe Francesco Cefaloni who is from the IRES and who works with us too has worked also on this. He brings all of his experience on this theme also to the work that is done with immigrants. He is possibly the only one who has experience of that nature. And so when we talk we say, yes but that happened also when there were I don't know ... there are things that are known but that none of us has ever experienced. The fact that there were notices – 'We don't rent to Southerners' – is known, I know that my parents when they came had some difficulties even though they were professionals and everything, but I never experienced it myself. And so it is not a direct experience. Maybe it's something that is ancestral in some way. And that doesn't mean on the other hand that people who found themselves in difficulty before because they emigrated to Turin are not racist themselves towards those who arrive today, that isn't the case at all.

Rete d'urgenza contro il razzismo

The failure in contemporary Italian anti-racist discourse to evoke the experiences of anti-Italian racism may be characterised as part of the general tendency to externalise the object of racism in both the general society and the anti-racist Left. If the anti-racisms mobilised in a given country may be explained by focusing on the way in which they interpret racism, the neglect of both the 'Southern Question' and the history of Italian emigration is significant. Unlike the proximity – in both time and space – of the history of fascism and Nazism, what happened to Italian emigrants abroad or southern migrants to the North is perceived as distant, and is therefore externalised. A view of the emergence of anti-racism in the Italian context reveals the positing of the problem of racism by many anti-racist activists, as a phenomenon that is experienced by others. This is undoubtedly tautological in the case of organisations made up mainly of white Italians. However, the relative lack of political organisations composed both of Italians and of immigrants – to employ the sharp dichotomy that characterises normal usage – points to the importance of this point. There are migrants' organisations, acting in the interests of particular communities or intercultural groups, such as those of migrant women, whose remit is clearly anti-racist. Trade unions, *centri sociali*, advocacy organisations and ARCI are committed to anti-racism. In the promotion of anti-racism, these types of organisation often call upon a representative of any one of the former groups to relate their experiences of racism, to discuss the role of their organisation or to assist in the planning of a demonstration. It is in this sense that racism is externalised, as a problem facing an Other – *straniero, extracomunitario*[15] – who, when she leaves the anti-racist rally, takes racism away with her.

The completeness with which racism and otherness seem to be synonymous in Italian left-wing anti-racism clarifies the reasons for which a more encompassing reflexivity seems to be absent from anti-racist discourse. The fact that Italian organisations of blacks and 'ethnic minorities' do not make reference to Italian experiences of racism in a similar way is indicative of the rarity with which it is mobilised by the Italian Left. This in turn demonstrates the overwhelming emphasis placed, instead, on two alternative discourses. The first prioritises the history of Italian fascism and the historic struggle of the Left against it. The second relates directly to the contemporary political situation since the election of a right-wing coalition to power in 2000, and is characterised by the direct connection of anti-racism to the politics of immigration. This is conceptualised using the language of globalisation and neoimperialism, representing a further externalisation and abstraction of racism from its localised realities.

Anti-racism in Italy may be traced back to the increase in immigration to the country, witnessed since the late 1980s, and the mobilisation by politicians and the media of opinion against migrants and asylum seekers. By following the evolution of anti-racist discourse and practice since its emergence at the end of the 1980s, it is possible to see the extent to which it is shaped almost uniquely by concerns about political and public reactions to immigration. The disconnection of the problem of contemporary racism from past discriminations, especially those against meridian migrants, means that Italian anti-racism has constituted the object of its concern as determined solely by migration flows and the attitudes of successive governments towards them. Even the history of antisemitism, evoked by ARCI as a main motivation for the participation of its members in the struggle against racism, is rarely evoked publicly in the way it is for example in France.

Italian approaches to anti-racism, be they reflective of the concern for equality of rights at the core of left-wing trade union ideals or of the struggles of migrants themselves, often purely for survival, focus exclusively on the processes and conditions of immigration. Balsamo (2002) explains that the preference in Italy for the term 'immigrants' rather than, for example 'ethnic minorities' is born of a concern not to mobilise a language of 'ethnicisation that we felt was a risk' (ibid.:17). Furthermore, the term 'immigrants' is supposed more descriptive because the recentness of their arrival in Italy has not yet allowed for the establishment of 'ethnic minority communities' (ibid.). While the concern not to map 'ethnic identities' on to the very diverse groups that have emigrated to Italy over the previous 20 years is of great importance, anti-racism's continual reliance on a discourse of immigration works against the anti-racist argument that racism is not dependent on numbers of immigrants. Aimiuwu and Balsamo (2002), in their research into the experiences of young African women, noted that for some of their respondents, the non-essentalised use of the term 'ethnic minority' was considered a step further towards their recognition in Italian society from which that of 'immigrant' excluded them completely. They recognise that, in political terms, the term 'immigrant' is associated with discrimination which may be overcome by adopting a self-description that implies 'greater recognition in terms of rights' (ibid.:19).

Beyond the self-organisation of 'migrants', in a wide range of community organisations and intercultural projects, political anti-racism in Italy was initiated in the late 1980s by what are thought of as the 'big' progressive organisations: ARCI, the trade unions and charities, most notably the *Caritas*. It is their shared conceptualisation of the Italian immigration problem and the attitude of successive governments since the late 1980s to the arrival of significant numbers of non-Italians in search of work or asylum, that has shaped the development of an anti-racist activism. The strategies promoted to combat racism also reflect the close involvement of the extraparliamentary left wing with the alternative critique or support of national governments of either the Left or the Right. This hinders the possibilities for racialised groups to act politically independently of the Left, according to an autonomously developed anti-racist agenda. As racism is connected at all times to the conditions of immigration, so the force of anti-racism is often determined by the parallel force of opposition to a government seen as proactively promoting anti-immigration policies.

Although opposition to the policies of the centre-left government on immigration could be heard, it was almost exclusively the preserve of the extreme Left and migrants' organisations. The 'big' social movements with a base of support in the centre Left do not accept the suggestion that there are few practical differences between left- and right-wing governments on the issue of immigration. The result of such is that protests against governmental politics of anti-immigration have been stepped up and are enjoying renewed energy since the election of the centre Right, particularly in the aftermath of the protests against the G8 Summit in Genoa in July 2001. The differences between centre-left and centre-right governments are insisted upon by ARCI in its contrast of the policies of the successive governments on immigration. The primary suggestion is that, while the Left may not have taken a strong enough stance against racism, in contrast, the government of today is based upon a xenophobic and racist culture that is slowly filtering down into Italian society:

> There is this culture, which has become inserted into Italian culture, of negation, of intolerance accompanied by another serious element that for the first time in Italy in recent years there are political entrepreneurs of racism. Today they are in government. In Italy today we have several forces, in particular the Lega and some constituent parts of Alleanza Nazionale that in recent years have sized each other up compete between themselves over the occupation of the spaces of racism and intolerance. I know that there are those in the associations that think that there is no difference. But I hold it against the left-wing coalition government for perhaps having too little courage... perhaps too little courage in the face of the general status quo. The specifically racist culture that today is part of the experience of the Lega and of AN is a different thing. In these days, the proposals in the newspapers – because there isn't yet any

articulated proposal – but the proposals of the government are really racist: work contracts between Italians and foreigners, a limit to clandestine entrance, the abolition of the guarantees existing for immigrants. The orientation of the government in Italy is xenophobic and racist. It would be a serious error if one was to think that the governments of the centre Left and that of the Right were the same. In one part of the movement, but I think that these days have shown us that there is a difference. From no minister of the centre Left did we hear worrying things about the need to redirect Italian identity. I think that even those who will throw at you all the things that the centre Left government did think that there is a difference nevertheless.

ARCI

Following the unfolding of Italian anti-racism from the late 1980s to the present day, therefore, requires perceiving the particular status of the issue of immigration within the ongoing battle between Left and Right. It is insufficient to note the Italian non-parliamentary Left's undeniable commitment to bringing about improved rights for immigrants to Italy without, at the same time, setting this within the wider context of left-wing collective action and the traditional relationships between the social movements and the various left-wing political parties.

Italian anti-racism develops on three levels. Firstly, there are the large protest-based actions of coordinations of left-wing organisations. Such coordinations, culminating in periodical demonstrations held across Italy, are usually initiated by a wide alliance of organisations including ARCI, the trade unions, migrants' associations and, increasingly the various city-based social forums. Secondly, anti-racism takes the form of migrants' self-organisation in communities or intercultural organisations. Such associations generally provide practical assistance to other immigrants and work to promote the empowerment of their members, for example by means of language classes or training in a variety of skills. The informal relations often formed between their representatives and the members of left-wing social movements, trade unions and the local social forums may facilitate their participation in the planning of demonstrations and, in some cities, to their growing involvement in the coordination of more long-term strategy against racism and the anti-immigration policies of the government.

Lastly, anti-racism is promoted through advocacy and training activities that focus, more particularly, on the effects of everyday racism in the Italian context. Such work involves the training of cultural mediators for work with immigrants in the social services and relies on a large level of involvement with municipalities and regional authorities. It also looks towards initiatives at European Union level, such as the European Network against Racism (ENAR), as a means to promote anti-racist initiatives in Italy. Behind this connection of localised anti-racist initiatives and the Europe-wide activities of the ENAR is a single Italian organisation, *Comitato per lo sviluppo dei paesi emergenti* (COSPE). It is primarily a non-governmental organisation, working in the field of development within which an anti-racism programme has been developed that has become the focal point for many of the highly dispersed activities of the various organisations of migrants, black people and 'ethnic minorities' in Italy. I shall focus upon the development of relations between the Italian Left and increasingly coordinated organisations of 'immigrants' in an attempt to characterise anti-racism as it emerges in Italy from the early 1990s to the present day. The novelty of this form of collective action, the specificities of Italian left-wing politics and the diversity of situations – in terms of both racism and the possibility to participate in anti-racism – facing immigrants in different cities and regions all contribute to the complexity of Italian anti-racism.

The anti-racism of the large left-wing social movements, initiated in the late 1980s, concentrated on the mobilisation of widely based alliances in the campaign for fair legislation on immigration and against racist discrimination. This was mainly organised along the traditional lines of mass demonstrations that are characteristic of Italian left-wing politics. For ARCI, the ability to mobilise large numbers against the racist murders of immigrants in the late 1980s and the call thereafter for legislation was indicative of the birth of a real movement against racism, adhered to by a range of large and small organisations. The specificity of this Italian movement against racism, in comparison to the existence of particular anti-racist organisations in other European countries, is deemed to be due to the preexistence of an extensive network of progressive organisations in the Italian political sphere:

> We, in the 1990s were part of a large anti-racist movement... In the phase between '89 and '96 there was a large anti-racist movement, different from European anti-racist movements. One of the reasons is that the Italian anti-racist movement relied on the activism of some large associations – ARCI, ACLI and CGIL. Maybe the difference with respect to other European countries in which there are strong anti-racist organisations of immigrants is that somehow, like in France with *SOS Racisme*, they were protagonists themselves. In Italy on the other hand, the anti-racist movement until '96, in comparison to other countries, was run by the large associations. After that – this doesn't mean that there were only the large associations and the trade unions – because then in those years in Italy there were hundreds and thousands of small local associations that, based on the political culture of volunteering, had built up a very sophisticated base. The national representation was indebted to the activism of the large mass-based organisations in Italy.
>
> ARCI

Despite the wide-ranging support demonstrated by the spectrum of progressive organisations for the anti-racist cause, the Italian 'movement' suffered a crisis that, paradoxically according to ARCI, was due to its initial success. The concentration of the anti-racist alliance of trade unions and large and small associations on pressurising the government to provide a law on immigration led to the dissolution of the momentum created during the campaign once the legislation had been achieved. It is here that the inability to establish continuity in anti-racist activism and to separate these aims from the general stated objectives of the Italian extra-parliamentary Left becomes apparent:

> Then something happened – we got the law passed in '89. Maybe the crisis of the movement began then in a way because we didn't succeed. It was a line taken by all the associations, the

demonstrations, the demand for an organic law was taken on by an archipelago of small and large associations, the unions. In '96 we also got through another regularisation of clandestine immigrants and another in '98. In those years, the movement succeeded in holding together in the political sense with regard to the government and the parliament and the experiences of integration of many local organisations etc. There was a problem, in that after the law in '98, perhaps we weren't able to organise... Somehow perhaps we were incapable of building the movement for integration, the movement for the application of the law... Since then we have been unable to build a large movement.

ARCI

The identification of the crisis of the anti-racist movement in 1998 suggests that Italian anti-racism, as a publicly visible activity of the large social movements, may be more concerned with the outward manifestation of anti-racist principles than with the inner consolidation of practices. This was already testified to in 1990 by Balbo and Manconi, whose book on the experience of the anti-racist research organisation, *Italia Razzismo,* notes the rise of an 'easy anti-racism' that risked being reduced to mere declamations. Large demonstrations tend to be held more often at periods generally perceived by the Left to be those of political crisis. Racism then becomes another outcome of the general situation of injustice brought about by the political turn to the Right, bringing with it an economic neoliberalist agenda, that is coupled with the tighter control of personal liberties. The increased concern of the Italian Global Justice Movement, now mainly represented by the local social forums, with immigration and racism indicates the extent to which racism in Italy is rarely the subject of singular attention. Rather, it is a constant in the formulation of a political response to the parliamentary right wing which assists in the marginalisation of racism by proposing immigration as an economic challenge whose social implications become apparent only when this line is crossed and migrants allowed to settle permanently in Italian society.

In contrast, the activities of many migrant associations, emerging over the last decade in Italian civil society, reveal an anti-racist dimension that remains constant over time. Despite the primary concern of many of these associations with the internal consolidation of the 'communities' or intercultural settings in which they operate, many of them are undeniably anti-racist. Unlike in France, there is no strong separation made between such 'communitarian' organisations and the action of the left wing due to the absence of any large, specifically anti-racist organisations. The anti-racist activities of the migrants' associations intervene on two levels. Firstly, they provide information and assistance to members in response to the practical situation regarding their status in Italy. This includes the development of an analysis of the regulation of immigration – permits to remain in the country and to work – and negotiations with health, education and housing authorities regarding the specific needs of these groups.

Secondly, such organisations act as a source of information for the development of a left-wing agenda on immigration and racism. Local migrant organisations such as in Florence, *Nosotras*, the Roma Association or the Senegalese Community are often invited to talk at meetings organised by social centres or social forums. These initiatives, however, are often beset by a solidaristic approach which paternalises migrants by focusing firstly on their experiences of racism, and secondly on their cultural traditions through the organisation of so-called 'multiethnic' dinners and concerts. Despite the political anti-racism in which several local migrants' organisations are involved, this focus often serves to depoliticise their action and, albeit unwillingly, creates a divide between 'communal activities' and political activism. The report of the 'Women's Culture Campus', an event organised by and for migrant women in 2000, notes the problematic nature of reducing the identities of new populations in Italy to their visible cultural characteristics. In particular, the process of culturalisation facilitated by the focus on 'multiethnicity' and cultural diversity of the Italian anti-racist Left leads to an explanation of the 'problems of integration as the product of pre-existing differences (those of the immigrants) and do not consider those imposed or constructed by institutional politics' (Nosotras 2001:54).

The Italian anti-racist arena is confounded by the disparity of the organisations loosely aggregated in this domain and the tendency, of the left wing in general, to organise protests and single-issue campaigns that are not followed-up by an identifiable movement. Mobilisation around the anti-racist cause is hindered by two further interrelated problems: the tendency of Italian social movements to generate holistic analyses of social problems that obscure their specific nature; and their preference for a highly theoretical approach that resists innovation. Both of these problems are represented in the current difficulty in establishing a coherent anti-racist response to the right-wing government's clampdown on immigration. The growing importance and visibility of the social forums, grounded in a new politics of 'globalisation from below', present an account of racism that relates it uniquely to the nature of contemporary migration processes and, consequently, to the larger problem of globalisation. This generalised and overly theorised account both obscures the localised realities of racism – the deportation and detention of immigrants and the institutional discrimination of racialised groups – and hinders the involvement of migrants' associations in social movement agendas. So-called 'migrants' working groups' established by the various social forums across Italy have found it difficult to attract the support of migrants' associations because of a refusal to treat racism as a complex of institutionalised practices that bear on the lives of individual black and 'minority ethnic' people rather than as part of larger and more intangible processes that, to be overcome, must be treated as a whole. The disunity that this creates pushes migrants' associations further towards both more localised forms of organisation and European initiatives, represented in Italy by the European Network Against Racism, and away from the construction of a cohesive national movement with adequate strategies for the campaign against the increasing institutionalisation of racism.

CONCLUSION

The four national arenas of anti-racist activism chosen for this study represent significant differences among them. These are born of the wide historical, political and cultural disparities between the four as states, that inevitably impinge upon the development of unique anti-racist discourses and means of political activism. Nevertheless, the accounts of anti-racism in each of these settings establishes a wider perspective upon the phenomenon of anti-racist activism in the political arena of western Europe. The varying histories of colonial domination and subordination, of societies of emigration or of immigration and of politics of assimilation or multiculturalisation are inextricable from an explanation of the political makeup of the European space as a whole. Public political culture in these various settings has been shown to be of equal importance to the establishment of anti-racist discourses. This is true both when the emphasis has been on the construction of a national way of doing anti-racism that mobilises the social myth of multiethnicity, such as in the British case and, as in the Italian and French cases, when patriotic discourses of nationalised struggles against racism are used by activists and become integral to anti-racist discourse.

What is also clearly evident from these accounts is that each national setting harbours its own diversity of anti-racist discourses and practices, many of which compete and even conflict with each other over what constitutes a more adequate representation of anti-racist concerns. This supports my epistemological inclination to draw comparisons at various levels that resist the dominance of national settings as the ultimate measures of comparability. The analysis in the next two chapters of public political culture in contemporary anti-racism and of the centrality of political representation as a means for interpreting it sociologically shall reflect this multiple approach. Anti-racism emerges out of the immediate concerns of politically conscious groups and individuals in a given national setting. Yet, as the examination of the legacy of anti-colonialism has revealed, it has consistently borrowed from beyond national frontiers. The implication of protagonists from a wide range of national, cultural and political origins contributes to anti-racism's heterogeneity and the inevitable finding that organisations across countries often find more similarities than those that share the national space.

4

Anti-Racism as
Public Political Culture

Anti-racism has come to be employed as a component of
national identity, a symbol of the benefits of national allegiance, and as a way of dismantling forms of prejudice that
militate against the mobility of labour and capital. These
forms of anti-racism are often of far more consequence than
popular or agitational movements. Nevertheless, they are
always, in part, provoked by such activism. In other words,
the anti-racism of the powerful tends to be initiated by factors that are not completely in their control, most importantly the pressure for change exerted by the struggles of
oppressed groups.

Alaistair Bonnett (2000:47)

An historicisation of anti-racism, such as that which has been my
primary objective to this point, reveals the extent of Bonnett's suggestion that anti-racism and conceptualisations of nation are far
more closely related than common-sense understandings allow us to
imagine. Nevertheless, we have also seen how the anti-racism standpoint in, for example, black self-organisation, influenced by the anti-
colonialist critique, counters the commemorative anti-racism of
constructed national tradition by placing racism at the core of an
analysis of the state's role in compounding racialisation and the
ensuing discriminations. The research reveals a virtual continuum of
proximity-to-distance from the public political culture of the nation-
state along which the various discourses of anti-racism as they
emerge can be theoretically placed in our effort to create a workable
sociology of European anti-racism. What is required, at this point, is
a fastening of such theoretical and historical elaborations to a political sociological examination of the discourse and practice of contemporary anti-racist organisations. In what way do anti-racist
activists compound the notion that anti-racisms are heterogeneous
with the effect of either complementing or critiquing the public

political culture of the states in which they intervene? Whereas the following chapter shall concentrate more centrally upon that critique, in this chapter greater emphasis shall be placed on the other extreme of the proposed continuum: a qualitative assessment of the discourses developed and the practices elaborated by anti-racist organisations, in juxtaposition with a look at the work of some key commentators on the subject, that elucidate the extent of the relationship between anti-racism and national public political culture.

The chapter shall discuss the identification of a crisis in anti-racism in the early 1990s and show how the elements of such a crisis, theorised by Pierre-André Taguieff and Paul Gilroy, are embodied in two dichotomies central to an analysis of anti-racism: majoritarianism or communitarianism and anti-racism or anti-fascism. The development of each of these notions shall proceed in recognition of their dichotomous nature but critiquing only majoritarianism and anti-fascism respectively. These are two discourses that are central to anti-racism, strongly reflecting national public political culture as an ideal or aspiration of anti-racist intentions. For the case of the majoritarian discourse of anti-racism, I shall focus on its denial of so-called communitarianism as a means of examining its hegemonic positioning within anti-racist discourses vis-à-vis the struggle for self-organisation, epitomal of an anti-racism grounded in the experience of racialisation. As regards anti-fascism, the commitment against the contemporary 'fascism' of the extreme Right shall be shown to construct itself in relation to a patriotism that recalls the past fight (of the nation) against Nazism. This stands in contrast to the anti-racism of black and 'minority ethnic' people which either does not share in this 'memory' or constructs it universally as detached from a discourse of national heroism. In each discussion, I shall use a 'key story' of two of the organisations interviewed – *SOS Racisme* and the Anti Nazi League – to further illustrate the nature of majoritarianism and anti-fascism. The concept of 'key story' refers to the ability of the discourse of each of these organisations to encapsulate the two notions I claim are central to a vision of anti-racism that relates to a valorisation of national public political culture.

ANTI-RACISM IN CRISIS

The claim that anti-racism was in crisis was made by both Paul Gilroy and Pierre-André Taguieff in 1992. The timing of these declarations should be seen as significant. They are made at the beginning of the 1990s marking the end of a decade of heightened neoconservatism in Britain and the rise in popularity of the extreme right wing in France. It was also a time when 'minoritarian' themes gained in popularity due to the consideration of ethnicity brought about by the explosion of ethnic conflict in eastern Europe (cf. Wilmsen and McAllister 1996). More specifically, the 1980s in both Britain and France was a decade in which anti-racism took an important turn. In Britain this involved the end of the autonomy of much of the politicised, self-organised black activism of the 1970s and the institutionalisation of anti-racism by Labour-controlled local government in direct defiance of the Thatcherite centre. This tendency in anti-racism, noted by Gilroy (1987, 1992) and Bonnett (1993) among others, does not belie the fact that the 1980s was also the time of a significant rise in black community organisations with a strong anti-racist dimension, largely in response to the treatment by the police and the government of blacks following the Brixton uprisings of 1981. During the 1980s, France witnessed the emergence of the *Mouvement beur* and its subsequent takeover by the determinedly youth-oriented, mediatised anti-racism of *SOS Racisme*.

Taguieff and Gilroy display marked differences in their approach to many of the central issues that bear on anti-racist discourse, such as nationalism and national identity, black and 'minority ethnic' representation and culture. Their stances are strongly determined by the specific nature of anti-racism in their respective countries, Britain and France. Gilroy is black British, a theorist of cultural studies and now a Professor of African American Studies. Taguieff is a French philosopher and *politologue* who espouses strong republican and secular views that shape his approach to anti-racism. They also share similarities in their identification of the changing nature of racism and in their critique of anti-fascism. Understanding the issues raised by these authors was a vital process in constructing the object of this research. The way in which both relate their critique of anti-racism to the way in which it has been understood by the institutions that claim to promote it was of interest to my concern with the relationship between anti-racism and the range of official discourses of public political culture (democracy, tolerance, equality, freedom etc.) with which it at times intersects.

Pierre-André Taguieff

In 1991, Taguieff addressed the French *Commission nationale consultative des droits de l'homme*. He claimed that despite the scientific community's historical agreement that racism is a false scientific theory and that different human 'races' do not exist, racism is deemed to be on the rise. This fact appears to be met with puzzlement by anti-racists who demand a response to the question of how it is still possible today to be racist. This question becomes the focus of anti-racist concerns, he argues, because racism has been constructed as irrational or phantasmic in contrast to the rationality, normality and stability of the anti-racist stance. The wonderment at the persistence of racism is said to be countered by rites of an exorcist nature that place racism in the realm of the magical. Against this, Taguieff argues that the question that should rather be asked is 'How is it possible not to be racist?' (Taguieff 1992:164). Asking such a question as an anti-racist is, for Taguieff, to profoundly question the racism of anti-racism itself. In his logic, anti-racism's attack on racism is carried out using the same racially discriminatory language ('Bloody racist!'; ibid.:165), that it decries, therefore showing that existing anti-racism is rather more similar to racism itself: 'The principles of anti-racism are in part the same as those of racism (according to anti-racism). The reasons are often shared, including the "good" reasons' (ibid.). In asking how it is possible not to be racist, Taguieff, as he does in his books on racism and anti-racism (Taguieff 1989, 1991a,b, 1995), intimates that it is the inappropriate nature of anti-racism's political comportment that creates hostility to the anti-racist message among sectors of society, leading ultimately to the growth in support for the far Right in France during the 1990s.

In Taguieff's terms, the growing failure of anti-racism as a convincing political message is rooted in the fusion of the various anti-racist traditions in France into a nebulous and misunderstood set of ideologies. This culminates in the anti-fascist and youth-oriented anti-racism of 1980s France, embodied by *SOS Racisme*. The crisis he identifies to have been facing anti-racism is primarily that of the problematic representation of racism in anti-racist discourse. Rightfully, he points to the paradoxical wording of the law on racial, antisemitic or xenophobic discrimination that, in France like in other countries, forbids discrimination on the grounds of belonging to a 'race', amongst other categories. However, Taguieff's polemicism – his many volumes take the form of essays rather than studies – does not allow him to empirically verify the extent to which anti-racist activists had a part to play in this wording of French law. The standpoint of many anti-racist organisations against the policies of their governments often means that their views are not considered in the drafting of law and policy. This is evidenced in the lack of access to funding experienced by many associations due to their criticism of government policy:

> If we want to organise a campaign to denounce the fact that the Republic's public prosecutors do not take action on complaints of discrimination or racism, clearly the Ministry of Justice or other ministries are going to refuse to have their financial statements declare that their money was used for paying for a campaign against the public prosecutors.
>
> *SOS Racisme*, France

Furthermore, as Taguieff himself concedes, the law may refer to 'race' in the socially constructed meaning of the term, rather than in the refuted biological sense. Transposed to the English-speaking context, Taguieff's objection concerns the ongoing debate on the political use by anti-racists, and specifically black people (Sivanandan 1990), of 'race' in the pragmatic sense, denounced by Paul Gilroy (1998, 2000). Whereas, in the US, it is in fact 'race' as a functioning category that is contested, in Britain as the previous chapter revealed, the question revolves much more around colour, epitomised by the discourse of political 'blackness' (McVeigh 1998).

The critique of the continued use of 'race' concepts (Voegelin 1933a) in anti-racist language remains internal to anti-racism, according to Taguieff. He identifies several points of criticism that claim to be external to anti-racism and qualifiable as 'objective'. Firstly, anti-racism can be said to have failed because, having set itself the objective of stopping the *Front national*, 'the party of organised hatred has not at all disappeared from the French political sphere' (Taguieff 1992:168). This is because French anti-racists have failed to recognise the new cultural racism of the *Front national* and have instead clung to a vision directly inherited from the ideological struggle against Nazism. Taguieff's judgement of the 'success' of French anti-racism in the 1980s in terms of its mission to eradicate the far Right finds resonance amongst contemporary anti-racist activists. It was, for example reflected by the *Sans-papiers* movement:

> We should admit that anti-racist organisations like SOS Racisme had existed in France for some fifteen years – since the beginning of the 1980s – and that that had absolutely not stopped the rise of racism seen, in particular, in the electoral results achieved by the Front National, the party of the extreme Right.
>
> *Sans-papiers*, France

Taguieff suggests that the political usage of anti-racism in France has two negative consequences. First, the perceived construction of anti-racism by the Left as uniquely 'anti-Lepeniste' creates competition between political parties as to who promotes the most authentic form of anti-racism. The use of anti-racism for political point scoring is, therefore, not grounded in a grassroots consensus. For Taguieff, the use of anti-racist polemic in the statements of political parties against the *Front national* may only lead to the suppression of individual freedoms and the reduction of anti-racism to a repressive force that

> not only causes the forgetting of its preventative mission, but also and above all contributes to nourishing the myth constructed by the *Front national*'s propaganda, the accusations and condemnations that sought to be exemplary became arguments that benefited the martyrdom of Le Pen.
>
> Taguieff (1992:170)

Above all, Taguieff sees the 'explosion' of ethnocentric 'communitarianism' as the primary threat to the coherence of the anti-racist movement, once inscribed in the values and traditions of republican secularism: 'Anti-racist mobilisations risk being imperceptibly transformed into modes of identitary self-reaffirmation, according to the principle: to each community (religious or ethnic) its own anti-racism, to each minority its mobilisation of self-defence' Taguieff (1992:171).

The debate on the possibility of organisations grounded in what are seen to be the concerns of a 'particularist', 'minority' community having a stake in anti-racism is still very much present in France. This is exemplified by *SOS Racisme*:

> From the moment that we would rely on a communitarian model, we'd lose all our power and all our force because we wouldn't be speaking to everyone's hearts. We would not be speaking to 60 million people, we'd be speaking to the victims concerned. And the victims concerned are not the main part of the activist force.
>
> *SOS Racisme*, France

Developing this argument further, Taguieff claims that a new 'fetishism' for ethnic origins has led to the advent of an 'imaginary racism', largely reflected by the media's reference to a person's ethnic origin or colour in reporting incidents which are then construed as 'race'-related or racist. He particularly objects to the victim's skin colour being mentioned in the reporting of what he refers to as 'pseudo-racist acts or racist pseudo-acts' (Taguieff 1992:172). He associates this with a strong objection to the 'communitarisation' of anti-racist organisations:

> Here again is an illustration of the communitarian impregnation of the very milieus of anti-racism: we define the 'victims of racism' according to their sole belonging to preestablished categories of victims, we identify them by reference to stereotypes of victims based upon ethnic or national origins.
>
> (Ibid.:172)

Such distaste for the public identification of the victims of racism may be contrasted with the contrary claim, made by some French anti-racists, that indeed racialisation and racism can be specified and attached to particular groups or individuals, depending on their origins, in turn assessed on the basis of their physical appearance. The targets are most often North Africans, among whom often no difference is made by those who discriminate against them:

> There is the whole second generation that came out of immigration who are French, who have French nationality. And often, when

> they are in the suburbs, Algerians, Tunisians and Moroccans under-
> stand themselves together. They undergo the same problems of
> racism, the same problems of discrimination whether they be
> Algerian, Moroccan or Tunisian. So, in the eyes of a quote-unquote
> 'French person of French stock' there is no difference.
>
> ATMF, France

Taguieff's critique rests on his disagreement with the proposition
that every attack on a person of colour – a Maghrebi in the case he
cites – is racially motivated. Against his opinion that this type of
'jumping to conclusions', as he would have it, has become the
norm, an interview with the Newham Monitoring Project revealed
the contrary. NMP holds that it is generally very difficult to have
attacks against black people, Asian people and asylum seekers recognised as racist:

> Quite often the police's approach to racial harassment is very, very
> shabby, it's very poor and they don't really see it as a priority. What
> they do is they tend to take incidents as isolated incidents and we get
> this a lot. Somebody is attacked – let's say Mr D., a shop owner who
> is attacked by three men who come into his shop and they threaten
> him, push him with a knife. This could be a scenario. Now what the
> police will do – a call will be made, 999 – police will come and treat
> it as an isolated incidence. As far as they're concerned – and this is a
> normal police response – it's a one-off, an attack on a shop keeper.
> What they don't take into consideration is, let's say, the perpetrators
> have been persistently, over a number of years, harassing the shop
> keeper – it's been racial harassment – what the police don't do is take
> that into consideration. So quite often the police will turn up, they
> won't be very sympathetic, they don't know whether there is a his-
> tory. Even when it's pointed out to them, they're not taking that into
> consideration: it's harassment, it's not a one-off. It often happens that
> they've been harassed for years and years and years and years and
> that when they do call the police, the police are not aware there is a
> history even when it's pointed out to them. They still don't recognise
> it as racially motivated even if it's pointed out to them.
>
> NMP, UK

Lastly, Taguieff claims that the anti-racism of the 1980s was largely an anti-racism 'from above' that suffered from being both too politicised and over-mediatised. The association between anti-racism and youth was limited by its elitist and apolitical dependence on the patronage of sporting and cultural 'stars': 'launched like a fashion, anti-racism could not but become unfashionable' (Taguieff 1992:173). The use by *SOS Racisme* of cultural icons as a means to spread the anti-racist message was indeed admitted to being a feature of the movement through its organisation of mass anti-racist concerts and other cultural events:

> Zidane kindly convinces all the French people that the mestizo Republic, mixing, is good for football. Cheb Khaled kindly convinces us that Raï culture in France is good. We started that. Before *SOS Racisme* world music was thought of as being very minoritarian music. We put it on the stage; all World Music has become majority music.
>
> *SOS Racisme*, France

The culturalist approach to anti-racism has also become one of the principle modes of action of anti-racists in countries in which this is a much newer political phenomenon. For example, ARCI in Italy, which has played a pivotal role in national anti-racism since the late 1980s, also cites the organisation of cultural events as one of its major contributions to the anti-racist project. Making visible 'other' cultural forms, primarily through the medium of music, is seen by ARCI to encourage intercultural awareness, principally among its own members:

> In '88 we organised the first musical concert of Youssou N'Dour in Italy. So, we began to work on rights with the councils, with the Italian state, but also to work within our organisation in order to promote the culture of immigrants' countries of origin but also to encourage exchange.
>
> ARCI, Italy

Taguieff's criticism of the French anti-racism movement of the 1980s can be seen as revolving around two central and interconnected points. Firstly, anti-racism has failed to counteract the new, culturalist racism of the far Right by reworking old themes (such as fascism and Nazism) that are of little contemporary relevance. Secondly, it is unable to do so because it relies to a growing extent on a 'communitarian' discourse that is exclusionary in its insistence on ethnic, national or religious group affiliation. In other words, basing anti-racism on the concerns of racialised groups, the actual or potential victims of racism in France, is seen by Taguieff as alienating those who, if its message was to be generalised, would more willingly join the anti-racist struggle. Taguieff's objection should be contextualised in the particular stance on anti-racism he has taken, since the publication, in 1989, of his *La force du préjugé* and his positioning vis-à-vis the French community of social scientists in the field. Despite the fact that it appears – on the basis of evidence from conference announcements and edited collections in France – that Taguieff has been marginalised by colleagues with interests in related themes, he continues to publish extensively and to be widely read both in France and beyond, in particular Italy. The intolerance he shows for an anti-racist project that seeks to ground its claims in the experiences of the racialised often goes unchecked by French social scientists who may write in an anti-racist perspective but who do not engage in specific studies of anti-racism, leaving the ground free for Taguieff. Furthermore, Taguieff epitomises the extent to which anti-racism is rarely deemed a subject worthy of serious study, instead becoming an issue for polemicism *par excellence*.

Finally, the outright refusal to countenance black and North African leadership of anti-racism in Taguieff's position must be related to his parallel work on antisemitism. His negation of the initiatives of the *Mouvement beur*, for example, as 'communitarian' and as ultimately dangerous for anti-racism, is linked to his perception that this type of activism encourages the rise in Islamic fundamentalism. This can be seen in Taguieff's criticism of 'anti-westernism' (1992:167) which he believes is a central tendency in anti-racism grounded in an anti-Zionist denouncement of the State of Israel as racist. The collective action of North Africans in particular, in Taguieff's formulation, becomes nothing other than a vehicle for a new anti-Semitism: 'The anti-racist racisation of the Jew as a Zionist, becoming an insult of the same type as racist or fascist. Such is contemporary anti-Jewish anti-racism' (ibid.). Beyond the racist assumption that paints all Arabs as antisemites, Taguieff reduces the critique of self-organised anti-racism to an argument over the comparative gravity of antisemitism over anti-Arab, anti-black and anti-immigrant racism in France. In so doing, he fans the flames of mistrust between the North African and Jewish communities in France, already lit by Jewish republicans such as Bernard Henri Lévi, and denies the possibility of interethnic solidarity in French anti-racism.

Taguieff's concern for the rise of a 'particularist' anti-racism is based upon the emergence, in the 1980s, of the *Mouvement beur*. However the fact that the groups that comprised this movement were denied the possibility to succeed at national level puts the legitimacy of his criticism into question. Indeed, organisations originally based in particular 'minority ethnic' communities, such as the ATMF, still experience difficulty in being accepted as part of a French anti-racist movement that distinguishes sharply between its own activism and those of the so-called 'communitarian' associations. It therefore appears that, far from becoming communitarised, the mainstream anti-racist movement in France refuses to extend itself to those whose perceived particularism clashes with its universalist, secular principles. This often leads to the distancing of anti-racist programmes from their primary audience and the entrenchment of a disunity which leads many to reject anti-racism, seen as disconnected from the reality faced by racism's targets, as a heading for their concerns.

Paul Gilroy

Paul Gilroy's identification of a crisis in British anti-racism departs from a similar perspective to that taken by Taguieff, yet works towards a different interpretation of the reasons for such a rupture. These differences should be interpreted both in terms of the varying national contexts from which both authors make their observations as well as the differing political orientations they represent. These two conditions intersect, as we shall see. The kind of political standpoint represented by Gilroy – against the top-down anti-racism of the British local authorities and for the self-organisation of black people – is almost untenable in the French context where mainstream anti-racism is defined by a Republican language that rejects difference and brands the activism of North Africans, in particular, as 'communitarian':

> There is a denial of any ethnic identity on the part of the state, by French associations that fight against exclusion and by those that fight against racism.
>
> ADRI, France

The historical conditions under which thinking on 'race' and racism developed in Britain differ widely from those of France. These differences are related by several anti-racists, in their analyses of the national contexts in which they work, to the colonial past of the two countries:

> Is the republican model, effectively based on French history, of the French nation which is completely unique, not simply an expression of a certain delay in the consciousness of problems that in other countries came about earlier, particularly in Britain, because British colonial history was made in another context that allowed the British government to react more quickly?
>
> ADRI, France

This is echoed by a British organisation:

> So that difference in approach which is also from the historical accident that Britain, because it was this great nineteenth-century imperialist power that colonised half the world had a much earlier migration into Britain than other European countries did.
>
> NAAR, UK

Despite the fact that both Britain and France experienced immigration before the collapse of the colonial system (Noiriel 1991), the effort made by these activists to place their action in an historical context that takes account of their countries' colonial legacy is revealing of the degree to which anti-racism is historicised and contextualised by organisations themselves.

Gilroy's identification of a crisis in anti-racism, like Taguieff's, centres firstly on its failure to coherently define racism and, secondly, on the move towards 'a belief in the absolute nature of ethnic categories and a strong sense of the insurmountable cultural and experiential divisions which, it is argued, are a feature of racial difference' (Gilroy 1992:51).

While Taguieff calls for a stronger centralisation of anti-racism under the auspices of the republican state, Gilroy critiques the 'dictatorial' anti-racism promoted by British local government in the 1980s. He separates clearly between the anti-racist and multiculturalist objectives promoted by municipal services in the realms of education or housing, for example, and the 'independent black defence organisations and authentic community groups whose actions go far beyond the narrow categories in which antiracism can operate' (Gilroy 1992:50). Therefore, while Taguieff sees French anti-racism as increasingly being taken over by the 'communitarianism' of particular 'minority ethnic' groups, Gilroy sees British anti-racism as moving further and further away from their realities. Indeed, Gilroy goes so far as to separate completely between antiracism – confined to municipal or 'white left' initiatives – and the political organisation of black communities for emancipation which he sees as encompassing much more than the fight against racism. Crisis hits the anti-racism that believes it can deal with racism in a vacuum that ignores other 'political antagonisms ... a limited project, defined simply, even simplistically, by the desire to do away with racism' (ibid.:51).

Gilroy bases his critique on what, during the course of the 1980s in Britain, became known as the 'race relations industry', mainly the activities of local government in the domain of multiculturalism. He claims that this brand of anti-racism both adds to the attack of the new Right against the anti-racist struggle and alienates 'community organisations and voluntary groups' (Gilroy 1992:51) whose political work is no longer supported by an anti-racism that prioritises tokenist cultural representation over the politicised linkage of racism to, for example, 'the contradiction between capital and labour ..., the battle between men and women' (ibid.). Gilroy identifies anti-racism as growing out of the uprisings of 1981, yet gradually becoming the exclusive enclave of activists and service providers 'now able to sustain itself independently of the lives, dreams and aspirations of the majority of blacks from whose experience they derive their authority to speak' (ibid.:52).

Gilroy, like Taguieff, accuses anti-racists of colluding with the nationalist new Right's project of installing a culturalist racism based on the 'definition of the nation as a unified cultural community' (Gilroy 1992:54). Nowhere has this been seen more clearly than in municipal anti-racism's approach to education. The introduction of multicultural curricula was the focus of attacks made by advocates of the cultural nationalism of the new Right (Palmer 1986). Gilroy (1992:56) argues that the 'boiling down of groups into their ethnic essences' that is encouraged by this form of anti-racism is compatible both with the essentialist politics of the new Right, the approach to anti-racism taken by the Left and certain forces within black communities. The eagerness with which the three encourage a reified view of culture, with each group sealed hermetically from contamination by the other, goes against what Gilroy seems to propose would be a just anti-racism. Both racism and anti-racism, in this respect, would lead to the conclusion that 'there is no possibility of shared history and no human empathy' (ibid.:57).

Gilroy further points to the growth of a black middle class, involved in anti-racism at local authority level and represented in three key strands, each playing a role in bringing anti-racism to crisis. Firstly, the 'equal opportunities strand' reduces anti-racism to policy making and produces 'general blueprints which can be universally applied' (Gilroy 1992:59). Despite Gilroy's assumption in 1992 that these types of anti-racism would diminish in importance with the demise of the power of the British local authorities, there is a sense in which they are still very much present. This is evident in NMP's criticism of policy research carried out by local government which appears to ignore key elements of the issue, in this case the problems posed by segregated housing:

There was a report that came out recently. It was researched over six months, it was the Commission for Racial Equality and the Federation of Black Housing Officers. They carried out a bit of research about social landlords and racial harassment. And in their recommendations they didn't address the issues of segregated housing. Particularly when you look at what's happened in Oldham and Birmingham recently, so it's an area that they didn't address at all. It's a very important area of work that needs to be looked at.

> These are very high profile organisations who are specialists of this area but they didn't address that issue.
>
> NMP, UK

Secondly, Gilroy notes the tendency formerly known as Black Nationalism which he claims has now replaced its political aims with culturalist ones. The danger in this strand is the 'coincidence' that the ethnic and cultural groupings it represents are often the same that common sense tell us are 'races'. Gilroy claims that the coexistence of this trend with 'old-style Labourism' (Gilroy 1992:59) means that a reified and culturally relativist view of 'minority ethnic' groups active in the left-wing political arena often determines the party's funding policies. Culturalist initiatives, in particular, received greater support following the uprisings of 1980 and 1985 marking a significant shift in the type of black activism visible in the political arena:

> Now, in terms of national politics in this country, things changed massively after the uprisings in 1980 and '85 and where you had a lot of money pumped into the initiatives and you had the emergence of a much stronger black middle class. So, the politics of the black communities isn't as one as it was in the 1970s where it was a race and a class politics; it was the struggle coming out of working-class black communities.
>
> CARF, UK

Lastly, Gilroy points to the tendency of reducing 'race' to class which sees the working class, in which it is assumed that 'race' differences become dissolved, as able to bring about an end to racism. While this approach served as a refuge from the growth of ethnic absolutism for some left-wing black and anti-racist activists in the 1980s, in Gilroy's opinion it is neither realistic, nor has it developed appropriate means of combating racism. He rightly observes that the arena of local authority politics in which the 'race' and class strand plays its role hardly provides the most radical locus for the action of organised labour. Its singular emphasis on 'race awareness training' has been criticised by many of the anti-racist organisations active in Britain today:

> There was a time in the 1980s after the riots here where different
> strategies for fighting racism were advocated like racial awareness
> training which is very much based on identity politics and was
> based on the idea that racism equals prejudice. So, the idea was
> that the way to get rid of racism was to actually get people who
> were working in the police force, in local government and to take
> them for racial awareness training and to basically, it sort of worked
> that white people were given a grilling about their own personal
> racism and so they were made to feel terribly guilty and break
> down and cry.
>
> CARF, UK

CARF, based at the *Institute of Race Relations*, itself promotes a
vision of anti-racism which strongly grounds the politics of 'race' in
that of class. However, the magazine makes a strong separation
between what it calls the anti-racism of the 'white Left' and the 'race
and class' approach, grounded in a perspective on the particular
experiences blacks may have as members of the working class.
Gilroy, although he does not state this clearly, presumably would
not support such a distinction:

> [W]e found at that time [1974] that many of what we call white left
> organisations, the anti-racist organisations coming out of left-wing
> politics here have a very, how would you say, Eurocentric or an
> orthodox view of struggle, of class politics and they didn't often
> recognise...for instance they didn't want to acknowledge the
> racism of the white working class. They didn't want to acknowl-
> edge that the trade union movement had a history of racism. So
> they tended to subsume the struggle of black people, immigrants
> under the class struggle.
>
> CARF, UK

Gilroy's central critique of anti-racism, as it is developed in the
three strands at work within the local government campaign

against racial discrimination, is that it 'seems very comfortable with this idea of blacks as victims' (ibid.:60). Essentially, this form of anti-racism reduces the political consciousness of black communities to the fight against racism as if it was that struggle that constituted the very identity of the diversity of individuals that comprise them. The crisis he identifies is brought about primarily by the 'white left' agenda of the local authorities which, it is suggested, used anti-racism as a vehicle for the attack against Thatcher's nationalist neoliberalism and, secondly, by the growing black middle class and the representatives of 'minority ethnic' communities. The latter joined forces with local government to promote a depoliticised, eth-nicised and equal opportunities-based vision of black communal activism.

Contrasted critiques

The main points made in both Taguieff and Gilroy's critiques of anti-racism pertain to the proposition that anti-racism is bound inextricably to the questions of national belonging or public political culture. The link between anti-racism and national public political culture was demonstrated by my interviews to be a feature of the discussion of anti-racism in all four countries, albeit in different ways. In the remainder of this chapter, I intend to build further on the factors, pointed to by Gilroy and Taguieff, that reveal the ways in which these dimensions of national public political culture are represented in anti-racist discourse.

Firstly however, it is helpful to briefly contrast the differences in Taguieff's and Gilroy's approaches. Both authors can be said to make three interrelated points that bear upon the link between anti-racism and the preservation or rejection of the elements of national public political culture with which it often intersects. Taguieff claims that the growing communitarianism of anti-racist discourse (1) and the demonisation of 'racists' as directly descended from Nazism (2) both actively reject the French republican values upon which anti-racism is based (3). Gilroy sees the disrooting of anti-racism from the interests of the black community in Britain (1) and the depoliticised ethnicisation of black activism through the vehi-cle of 'municipal anti-racism' (2) as leading it into crisis. Separately, he claims that the support for an anti-fascist vision of anti-racist politics marginalises the campaign against the real, institutional racism experienced by blacks and 'ethnic minorities', and rather construes racism as an attack on patriotism (3).

The main difference between both sets of propositions is that, for Taguieff, the crisis of anti-racism is brought about by the growing strength of the 'communitarian' strand of the movement which seeks to separate anti-racism from its real position as part of a set of democratic values inscribed in the French Republic. To a lesser extent, anti-racism's problems are contributed to by the promotion of a teleological perspective that connects racism to the history of fascism and Nazism and by the inevitable inability of a youth-oriented, fashionable anti-racism to sustain itself. The ensemble of Taguieff's critiques may be thought of as operating from the inside out. In other words, forces within the anti-racist community, and particularly racialised groups speaking on behalf of the victims of racism, have caused anti-racism's crisis. Gilroy's position, on the other hand, may in contrast be thought of as an outside-in position. Anti-racism is not the action of the racialised against the racism they experience or that carried out for their own empowerment. On the contrary, this has been appropriated, by either local authority officials or self-interested groups within black 'communities', leading to the depoliticisation of the anti-racist struggle and its disconnection from both the realities of racism's victims and the processes undergone in the wider political arena.

These two sets of critiques, although they effectively focus on the same problems, represent two wholly different visions of anti-racism. Following the direction in which they point, it is possible to elaborate upon the ways in which anti-racism and dimensions of European national public political cultures intersect. Based on the contributions of Gilroy and Taguieff, two main dichotomies may be identified around which the problems facing anti-racism are organised in their accounts. The first regards the proposed incompatibility of what are sometimes known as 'majoritarian' and 'communitarian' versions of anti-racism. Anti-racism is seen as grounded in a nationally inscribed set of values that insists on the potential for all members of the democratic nation to be anti-racist and which claims that the foundation of anti-racism upon the experiences of the racialised is detrimental to its popularisation as a social cause. The second relates to the debate between an anti-fascist vision of the struggle against racism, which focuses on the activity of the far Right and, it is proposed by its opponents, ignores the everyday, institutional racism experienced by black people, and anti-racism which, it is argued, recognises the insufficiency of relating racism solely to the activities of the far Right. Both dichotomies clearly point out the extent to which anti-racism, beyond the actual arena in which it directly intervenes, may inform understandings of nation and national belonging in contemporary Europe.

MAJORITARIANS AND COMMUNITARIANS

The use of the words 'majoritarian' and 'communitarian' to describe two approaches to anti-racism that I suggest are central to its understanding, is borrowed from the French context. It is in this country, although there are parallels in Italy, where the idea is most clearly formulated that anti-racism should be a discourse shared by all those believing in the values espoused by the nation-state. While I point to the dichotomy drawn by several theorists and activists between a 'majoritarianism' and a 'communitarianism' in anti-racism, I shall deal in this section with the former as it constructs itself in opposition to a 'communitarian' approach which it sees as restrictive and unrepresentative. The notion of a 'majoritarian' anti-racism may be seen as directly hereditary from the solidarity-based anti-racism of the 1950s and 1960s, founded upon a feeling of responsibility for taking action against the racism both of the colonies and, increasingly, the domestic towns and cities in which immigrants were beginning to settle in larger numbers than ever before. This consciousness was widespread among the socialist and communist parties and trade unions of the European metropolises.

The reference to 'communitarianism' is made by French activists, coming from 'majoritarian' organisations to describe the self-organisation of 'minority ethnic' or racialised groups themselves against racism. 'Communitarian' is also used by French activists to describe the type of anti-racism practised abroad, particularly in Britain. Anti-racism there is accused of not being anti-racist at all, but rather of being the ethnic politics of a vast range of communities based on a primordial conception of identity at direct odds with the egalitarian principles championed by the democratic state, particularly in France. Anti-racism activists often have recourse to 'national ways of doing things' – practices seen as legacies of anti-racist struggles fought, often over decades, in the national context – in order to explain and justify the principles they adhere to as anti-racists. Often, these principles differ widely from organisation to organisation, as well as across countries.

After establishing the key fundaments of the 'majoritarian'/ 'communitarian' dichotomy, I shall use a 'key story' to further illustrate the way in which the dichotomy becomes central to anti-racists' self-understandings and how this in turn bears upon possibilities for action. The French organisation *SOS Racisme* occupies the unique position of being a point of reference, not only for writers on the subject of anti-racism, but also for other organisations both in and outside France. It was therefore dealt with by several of my interviewees and often negatively compared with the principles and modes of actions of their own organisations. These discussions assist in reconstructing the way in which the clash between a 'majoritarian' outlook and a supposed 'communitarianism' come to take on such importance in contemporary debates on anti-racism.

The existence of 'communitarian' organisations assumed to participate in the growing ethnicisation of French society and the rupture between progressive and particularist collective action has been explored by several French sociologists (Lapeyronnie 1987; Baillet 1997). Specific reference is often made to the *Mouvement beur* which continued to capture French interest in the field rather euphemistically known as 'migration and inter-ethnic relations' (Simon-Barouh and De Rudder 1999) long after the movement itself had ceased to exist, at least on the national level (Poinsot 1993). For example, Baillet (1997) distinguishes between 'communalist' and 'societal' organisations in his discussion of political activism amongst young people of Maghrebi origin in France. Communalist organisations reinforce communal solidarity, generally amongst young people united by their common identity as (non-practising) Muslims originating from either Morocco, Algeria or Tunisia. They are contrasted with 'societal' organisations that first appeared in the 1970s with the aim of building a cultural and intellectual elite of Maghrebi origin. They serve as a mode for integrating young Maghrebis who may otherwise become unemployed, replacing the workplace as the primary locus for the integration of North Africans. They appeal to 'critical' activists who are able to take a stand due to their entry into the elite worlds of publishing, cinema and literature.

Baillet's comparison of these two types of organisation is relevant to the present discussion because, for analysts of French anti-racism, including the organisations themselves, there is little practical difference between the two. This is because, while the objective of 'communitarian' organisations, as it is seen from the outside, is to promote the values of particular national or religious traditions amongst its members and to protect their interests in relation to the French state, the aim of societalist organisations is to prepare individuals for integration who may relinquish their dependency upon communities. It is presumed, for example, that North African activists in 'majoritarian' anti-racist organisations intervene as concerned members of French society, or more realistically, as upholders of the ideals espoused by a certain current of left-wing political thought. Organisations such as the secular ATMF would most probably be seen by Baillet as 'societalist'. Nevertheless, the organisation identifies its origins as 'communitarian' yet insists on its independence and democratic nature, principles which mark it out from other organisations which it sees as being controlled, for example, by the embassies of the North African states in which their members originate:

> ATMF, if you wished to define it, is a secular, democratic and autonomous association. We uphold those three characteristics that mark us out from other so-called communitarian associations or those based on immigration, because most often those associations are manipulated, either by the local collectivities where they are based or by the relationship with the consulates of their countries of origin. So, they don't have the right, the liberty to say what they want and to say what they think.
>
> ATMF, France

'Majoritarian' organisations express their approach to anti-racism as differing to that of the 'communitarians' using two main arguments. Firstly, 'majoritarian' organisations see their involvement in anti-racism as inscribed in a long history of political commitment, generally on the left wing, which draws on specific legacies that are constructed as part of a national political heritage. Recurring themes in the self-description offered by these types of organisation include the histories of the resistance, the anti-slavery movement or that against colonialism. Importantly, such historical movements are upheld as fundamental steps in the building of democracy. For such types of anti-racist organisation, denying racism is not subversive, as it serves to remind the state of the values upon which it was founded and which it does not have to search beyond itself to find. This type of organisation often sees anti-racism as a responsibility and a means through which its own membership may be reminded of the values for which the democratic state stands. This is evident in the following quotation from a representative of ARCI. The organisation's involvement in anti-racism came about in response to the growth of racism in Italy and a feeling among its leadership that the large structure represented by ARCI could contribute both to a nascent Italian anti-racist movement and to instilling a sense of interethnic understanding within its own membership:

> We are not an association that, let's say, was born an anti-racist association. We are an association that was born out of the democratic culture of the Italian Left. So, we felt the necessity, in comparison to other anti-racist associations that are called anti-racist that were created in recent years, we need anchorage, to make our members understand – those who perhaps were partisans, or workers, or maybe had participated in the anti-fascist struggles of the seventies – to make them understand that they could not, on the grounds of their own history, be racist. We were very worried about this because the culture of intolerance is a culture that we felt ran the risk also of affecting our membership.
>
> ARCI, Italy

It is evident from the above that, for this 'majoritarian' organisation, anti-racist activity becomes as much about the sensitisation of its own members and the revalorisation of the history of the Italian left wing as about the campaign to oppose contemporary racism against immigrants in Italy. Anti-racism, therefore, becomes a vehicle for the promotion of a vision of the past, seen as formative of the political identity of ARCI activists, but in which many have lost interest. The relationship of the contemporary fight against racism to the heroism of the partisans – beyond the link made between racism and fascism – seeks to establish anti-racism as part of 'our' left-wing political heritage. This is further echoed by *SOS Racisme* for whom anti-racism should be based upon the education of the young generation in the lessons of past combats against anti-semitism or slavery which are now seen as inscribed in the history of democratic France:

> There was another struggle that we have waged since 1988 for an anti-racist education that values the cultures of immigration, that

teaches the memory of the Shoah, of that which led to Nazism in Europe, that, at the same time, teaches the great values of humanism and tolerance, the struggles waged around the Dreyfus Affair, around the abolition of slavery, the struggle for the declaration of human rights etc. We tried to make it almost compulsory within public education.

SOS Racisme, France

These organisations, which construe their anti-racism as a logical development of their commitment to democratic values more generally, do not try to avoid criticism of national policy making. On the contrary, because these organisations see themselves as legitimate political interlocutors, the conscience of the national political arena, they also value their right to develop a critique of the actions carried out in the name of the country's citizens. Both ARCI and *SOS Racisme*, for example, justify this taking of stands by placing great emphasis on their large membership:

ARCI is the largest Italian association. It has 1,200,000 members. ARCI is an old association; we were born in 1957 out of the experience of the society of mutual assistance, from the *case del popolo* [social clubs linked to the Communist Party]. So, ARCI has a real social basis, made up of clubs, cultural activities and recreational activities.

ARCI, Italy

Several million people said: I am here, I join the organisation *SOS Racisme* because I wear the hand 'Hands Off My Friend'. So, it was a form of membership of an association, of a struggle that was very obvious from the outside, that did not necessarily imply being a dedicated member with a card but which meant that this movement immediately became the leading movement in France. Within one year it had more informal members than all the other organisations that had existed for a century.

SOS Racisme, France

Their self-declared size and importance on the national political stage gives weight to these organisations' critique, both of the policy of current governments and of the misguided nature of public opinion. Such a critique is construed in two ways. According to the first, racism and intolerance are either the result of a misinterpretation or of a lack of knowledge of the democratic tradition and values, inscribed in the nation-state. In this account, as was demonstrated by *SOS Racisme*'s insistence on the importance of education, it is the organisation's responsibility to bring to light the truly anti-racist character of that public political culture. The discrimination experienced by 'minorities' is due, in this account, to a failure to apply the principles of the Republic to the whole of the population living in France. There is no need, in the organisation's view, to accord special rights to facilitate the disadvantaged. Rather a universalisation of the rights already accounted for by the republican vision suffices, both in order to ensure equality and to convince the French that the presence of 'immigrants' among them poses no real threat:

> We knew that this failure at school, this poverty, this delinquency had also contributed to the rise of the *Front national*. And we wanted both to come to the assistance of the problem neighbourhoods – so, to help minorities, to guarantee them access to the best conditions of life – but also, because we knew that to convince French people, tempted by the racist vote for the Front national, that there were solutions to poverty, to the violence in the neighbourhoods and that there were human solutions that would lead to better living conditions for everyone. And in fact, it was simply the application of the Republic that could stop the process of ghettoisation in the neighbourhoods.
>
> *SOS Racisme*, France

Another form of critique developed by 'majoritarian' organisations involves direct confrontation with the country's past failures and a linking of such with the emergence of contemporary racism. This was a position taken by ARCI for whom an engagement with anti-racism arose also out of a willingness to deny the prevalent view the Italian Left has of itself as blameless as regards fascism, racism and colonialism in the country's history. The organisation displays an openness to dealing with the cruelty of Italy's colonial past in recognition, more widely, of the paucity of debate on this issue in either academic or political circles (Burgio 2000). There is the sense that the criticism of Italians' view of themselves as 'always having been against racism' can only be made because the organisation speaks from the self-constructed standpoint of the largest, oldest – and, therefore, most representative – force on the non-party political Left. It is because the critique is made by the veritable 'insiders', social actors whose vision of political responsibility is built upon their – direct or indirect – connection to the history of Italian partisanship that this is possible:

> So, we initiated a permanent project also because in those years we challenged the – the demagogy of the Italian newspapers – that the Italians were great people, the Italians who had never... have never been racist. We contested that – look, Italy is a country that has lived through tragic experiences of racism. Colonialism in Africa is often depicted like the good colonialism... But, the use of gas in Libya is accepted, the use of torture by Italians in the colonies is accepted. But not only that, the burden of Italian history has also included the tragic experience of antisemitism, putting all the responsibility on Nazism, on Hitler. Somehow, the deportation of the Jews in Italy was in reality done by the Nazis, not by the fascists. We have also always contested this. Because it is true that the deportation of the Jews after the racial laws of '38, but in particular the deportations of '43, in particular the big deportation of the Jews of Rome, it is true that it was carried out by the Nazis, but the lists were prepared by Italian fascists, the coordinating structures for antisemitic persecution were laid down by Italians... So, we wanted an historical reading. We have always denied the demagogy of those years of the Italians as great people, the Italians that always stood up against racism. We said no. The Italians, in the history of our past, there are some large black marks. And so we somehow felt a duty, we felt a civic duty to work so that the first immigrant Italian citizens would have a strong basis of rights and, above all, to work for good relations between Italians and foreigners.
>
> ARCI, Italy

The second distinction that can be made between 'majoritarian' and 'communitarian' organisations is that the former concept judges the success of an anti-racism movement on its ability to generalise its message. Organisations which have developed a strong critique of the 'majoritarian' approach base their criticisms, in part, on the proposed weakness of the compulsion of making anti-racism attractive to everyone. Anti-racism, according to the 'majoritarian' approach, must be taken beyond the experiences of the racialised and elevated to the position of a universal value with which no fault can be found. This vision is clear in the explanation given for its formation by the Anti Nazi League. It proposes that opposition to the far Right can unite people from across the political spectrum:

You could see that there was actually lots of opposition to the Nazis but it was like from all different parts of society, so it wasn't just the Left, there was other people who were a bit more conservative who were against the Nazis and we wanted to bring that all into the one kind of group and we needed a group that had a very narrow, narrow remit so it doesn't stop people from fighting the Nazis. Because what you would see was there was people...there was revolutionaries and there was reformists and there was even people who were quite conservative and we wanted to unite all those people and that's when the Anti Nazi League was initiated with different kinds of MPs, different groups, celebrities and all that kind of thing.

ANL, UK

This type of anti-racism easily makes alliances with political parties in both the mainstream and on the far left wing. This is a factor strongly criticised by organisations who do not share the 'generalist' outlook. The search for party political alliances is seen by organisations grounded in the experiences of racialised 'communities' as a means of usurping the serious message of anti-racism and making use of it for political gains. The sentiment expressed by these organisations is that, while they remain consistent in their work on behalf of the black and 'minority ethnic' victims of racism, the political parties to which the generalisable principles of the 'majoritarian' message appeals are quick to relinquish responsibility once having gained power. This opinion was expressed particularly by the *Sans-papiers* movement, which remains vigilant of building alliances in the political sphere, as a result of its perception that many anti-racist organisations and political parties were quick to try and manipulate the success of its campaign.

The *sans-papiers'* very visible occupation of several Paris churches, beginning at Saint Ambroise in 1996, generated support in circles far beyond the political, including among celebrities. The *sans-papiers* insist on remaining independent from anti-racist organisations which are seen as being under the control of political parties with no real interest in the fate of those fighting for the regularisation of their status in France. So negative was the movement's experience in their dealings with established anti-racist organisations, that it does not define its own activism as anti-racist. The naming of anti-racism in the French context therefore becomes disconnected from its semantic meaning and comes to represent the activity of an elite group of overtly political actors, with all the pejorative connotations that this may have:

It was autonomy towards what were organisations with the implicit understanding that all organisations are almost always more or less linked to political parties. So you see, that was confirmed afterwards when there were the elections in France in 1997 when the Left came to power, there it was very clear. We saw which were the organisations that remained in solidarity with the struggle of the *sans-papiers* and which were the organisations that were too close to the Socialists, for example, to continue to come down on the streets, to go to demonstrations and to support the movement. So, there we saw very well the rupture between the two and that proved that the organisations were very closely linked to the political parties. So, linked to political strategies and when your party becomes the party of government, you don't have the same behaviour as … The *sans-papiers*, being completely independent from those kinds of problems, it guaranteed them to be able to continue their struggle in exactly the same way as before, without being concerned by the change in the political landscape.

Sans-papiers, France

The criticism of organisations as either directly or indirectly implicated in a party political agenda that bears little relevance to the situation faced by small local associations and the racialised groups they represent is heard across all four countries of the study. 'Majoritarian' anti-racism is seen by those critical of it – whom the former would call 'communitarian' – as manipulating the objectives of anti-racism or, as we have seen in some cases, as representing something altogether irreconcilable with their own activities. More generally, there is an acceptance on behalf of several localised groups that, out of necessity, they too belong to something that could be thought of as a national anti-racist movement. However, this is qualified by stressing the difference between their own approach – seen as anchored in the local reality of, for example, the black community or migrant women – and that of a publicity-seeking anti-racist movement, often spearheaded by a number of key individuals. This was clear in the view represented by the Newham Monitoring Project of its role in the British anti-racism movement:

> There are a lot of organisations out there who on the face of it are fairly much seen to be part of the British anti-racist movement and they are and they get involved in all the high profile issues and that's very good in a sense. But in another way, we're very critical of organisations we feel are not really addressing the real issues … Race politics is very sexy and there are certain people – it sounds like I'm slagging the whole thing off but it's not like that – there are certain individuals in race politics who like to be seen to be high profile, who like to be seen to be at the forefront.
>
> NMP, UK

The critique of 'majoritarian' anti-racism, developed by organisations who feel unrepresented by the view of anti-racism most visible in the public sphere, affords a more coherent perspective on the relationship between anti-racism and national public political culture. 'Majoritarian' organisations can be said to explicitly relate their activity to the democratic traditions of the states within which they act, generalise their scope to include the widest possible target audience and attempt to link their objectives to those of specific political parties. Often, such organisations refuse to accept the activities of others, founded in order to represent the interests of particular 'communities', as anti-racist due to the purported impossibility of universalising such an approach. In situations such as that of Britain, where even the anti-racism of the national movement prides itself on basing its action upon the specific experiences of the racialised, it is nonetheless denounced for not being reflective of the localised experiences of black victims, of police harassment or racial violence, as in the claim made by NMP. The differences between an anti-racist organisation which seeks to attack the racism experienced by the very group which constitutes it and the anti-racism which constructs itself as a movement at national level, speaking on behalf of a wide range of groups and individuals, often revolve around the relationship to public political culture. Whereas in some cases this means an active reinterpretation of values espoused by the French Republic or the Italian constitution, at other times this may refer to the 'national ways of doing anti-racism' often evoked by organisations which contrast their approach favourably with that practised in other countries.

SOS Racisme: 'Neither a minority nor a solidarity organisation'

No! Racism and discrimination are not fatal. No! it is not compulsory to see ghettos being multiplied, violence spreading, the fear of the other imposing itself. For us, France can succeed in becoming a mestizo republic. A nation loyal to its republican traditions, refusing communitarianism and respecting all those that live and make our country live. French or foreigner, black, white or *Beur*, the value of a woman or of a man is not judged by their appearance but by their qualities.

SOS Racisme leaflet

Since its emergence on the French scene in 1985, the protagonists of the SOS message have become extremely adept at concisely telling its story and, in so doing, addressing many of the key questions of my research. The SOS story is key in terms of the relationship I seek to draw between anti-racist discourse and the upholding of a certain vision of the responsibilities to be lived up to in the name of the democratic ideals contained within the nation-state. In what way does SOS Racisme embody a 'majoritarian' view of anti-racism by engaging both with its own self-description and that of others? How does SOS Racisme establish itself as an organisation with generalisable ideals that go beyond the concerns of the potential victims of racism? How does this relate to the organisation's insistence on the Republic as the proper framework within which anti-racist demands are most usefully made? The key story of SOS Racisme reveals that this involves an argument between universalism and particularism that attempts to reconcile the 'difference' of its public(s) with the colour-blind egalitarianism of its vision.

The 'majoritarian' ideals of the organisation were explained during the first minutes of the interview in the context of the larger story of *SOS Racisme*'s emergence onto the anti-racist arena in 1985. Relating to the context of *SOS*'s birth, parallel to the demise of the *Mouvement beur*, the organisation today describes itself as having reacted to the polarised situation facing French anti-racism brought about by the new movement of North African youth. The anti-racism of the established organisations, such as the MRAP or the LICRA, is portrayed as based on a Christian notion of solidarity. On the contrary, that of the *Beurs* is seen as 'minoritarian'. *SOS* explains its objective as seeking to bring the two together, thus introducing a new type of 'majoritarian' ant-racism into the political arena, one which could be equally embraced by 'immigrants' and those who wished to stand in solidarity with them, on equal terms:

In reaction to this idea of French people in solidarity with immigrants, a little bit like a Christian charity, the *Mouvement beur* was created by an immigrant minority. And *SOS Racisme* wanted to bridge the two by saying at the same time: we're not going to create either a minority organisation or a solidarity organisation, but an organisation which mixes the two: immigrants – the people who are the victims of racism – and those in solidarity with the victims. And so that was immediately the principle of the organisation. There is a majoritarian principle. And that majoritarian principle is always the characteristic sign that separates *SOS Racisme* at the level of all the movements that have been created since at the European level. That means that we remain the only organisation at the European level with a real political direction that constructs itself upon that model. With a political direction which says we are neither a movement of immigrants, nor a movement of solidarity, but we are a majoritarian movement that mixes immigrants and those in solidarity with them.

SOS Racisme, France

However, despite the organisation's wish not to prioritise the *solidaires* over the victims of racism among its membership, next to a picture of the symbol of the organisation – the yellow hand – the *SOS* membership leaflet reads 'I stand in solidarity with the victims.'

The novel idea of a 'majoritarian' anti-racist movement is further developed in *SOS* logic as founded upon a vision of equality:

> SOS Racisme was created in 1984 following the *Marche des beurs* that left from the problem neighbourhoods of Lyon to demand rights for the minority originated in the Maghreb. And *SOS Racisme* transformed that movement into a movement not of a *Beur* minority, into a movement of an anti-racist majority that wants to have the principle of equality in France respected. And so, we transformed a struggle that – some wanted to have a struggle for the right to difference – we wanted to transform that into a struggle for the right to equality: the right to equality of opportunity for all citizens living on French soil whatever their nationality or origin.
>
> *SOS Racisme*, France

Several points are contained within the vision expressed in the above statement. Firstly, there is the idea that the *Marche des beurs*, which called for minority rights, could be neither as effective nor as justified as a movement based on the demands of an anti-racist majority. There is the feeling that attaching the fight against racism to the specificity of the *beur* experience was to deny ownership of anti-racism to the 'several million people' who committed themselves to anti-racism by joining *SOS*. Secondly, it is claimed that the 'minoritarian' anti-racism of the *Mouvement beur* based its struggle upon the recognition of 'difference' or, in other words, the right of 'minority ethnic communities' to be recognised as such. Whereas there may certainly have been a current among the organisers of the *Marche des beurs* and the various organisations that sprang from it, that was more attached to either Muslim or Maghrebi identity as a common point around which to organise, this ignores what in fact triggered the movement. The *Marche des beurs* did not leave the *banlieues* of Lyon on a platform of classical identity politics. It responded, albeit in a manner often hindered by its internal disunities (Malik 1990), to the escalation of violent racism against the North African youth it represented. The atmosphere is described as follows:

> In the years 1983–1984, police blunders, murders of Arabs or West Indians, electoral alliance between the RPR and the Front National in Dreux, the glamorisation of Le Pen illustrated the xenophobic drift of

French society ... Worse still, the murderous crimes committed against Arabs, Turks or West Indians were claimed as 'acts of resistance'! That was the trigger.

Malik (1990:21)

SOS sought to replace the North African foundations of the movement, seen as espousing 'difference', with a 'majoritarian' anchorage in equality. The link made between equality, citizenship and nationality in the organisation's discourse implies that this egalitarianism comes from within the French Republic and need not be sought for elsewhere. The path to 'difference' is seen to lead furthest away from the equality guaranteed by adherence to republican values. The right to 'difference' perceived to be upheld by the *Mouvement beur* is little more than an affront to the equality provided them by their very existence as 'citizens who live on French territory'. This is clear also in the evocation of civilisation in the further description of *SOS*'s activity in the promotion of equality. The impression is given that both the 'majoritarian' nature of the organisation and the civilising egalitarianism of the French setting in which it intervenes justify the extension of the fight against racism beyond the narrow confines of those directly concerned to a range of interrelated campaigns for equal rights:

> The principle of saying, our battle is at the level of the equality of rights, the equality of opportunity, not only in the domain of racism but even in the domain of a civilisation that guarantees equality to people whatever their social origins.
>
> *SOS Racisme*, France

SOS's egalitarian discourse is clearly framed by a narrowly interpreted version of the debate between universalism and particularism. The organisation's 'majoritarian' stance promotes anti-racism as a universally comprehensible value. In other words, beyond the critique of 'difference', the intellectualism of the established anti-racists is rejected for a youth-oriented approach that makes it possible for all young people to agree in principle that racism is harmful. This is the principle contained in the slogans that appear on *SOS* leaflets: 'Black, *blanc*, *beur*: One youth, many colours' and

'Victory is within you', accompanied by a photograph of young black, brown and white faces each with a tricolour face-painted on one cheek. The universalisation of anti-racism and its equal embracing by youth of all backgrounds, according to *SOS*'s account, is also attached to the notion that equality of 'black, *blanc, beur*' and the fight against racism extends out of it and in to other struggles for equality. This is evident in the organisation's links with other progressive youth movements and the claim made that, as a result of its intervention and the support given by these groups to *SOS Racisme*, a much greater political impact may be achieved:

> One of the tools for demonstrating the power of the anti-racist youth – because that is the principal characteristic of *SOS Racisme*, that is to have been created on the basis of the youth and it is always created on the basis of the youth – was its very strong involvement in the secondary school and student movements of 1986 that led to the fall of the Chirac government, that made it fall on the principle of the defence of equality for all students, whatever their social origins, to access a quality university.
>
> *SOS Racisme*, France

The foundation of *SOS Racisme* with the support of Mitterrand led to the widespread scorning of the organisation as no more than a puppet of the Socialist government. The history of its governmental connections is well known. It includes that of the financing that enabled the production of the badges that out-gimmicked the seriousness of the *beur* marchers, too full of rage (Jazouli 1986) and too feared by the establishment to mobilise similar resources. Yet this history no longer tells the full story of *SOS* today. The passage of its founders to electoral politics – two ex-*SOS* presidents hold seats in the European parliament – and, significantly, the election of Malek Boutih as President in 1999, the first *beur* to hold the position, means that it no longer retains relations in the party political arena. Today, *SOS* expresses anger at the manipulation by the French Left of anti-racists, and the organisation in particular:

> The Left is the specialist of anti-racist swindles and we have served the swindling Left too much. That means that *SOS Racisme* made the

Chirac government fall. Mitterrand arrived, so we largely contributed to Mitterrand's victory in '88 and then we were had. We were had because we didn't get the right for immigrants to vote when he had promised it, we didn't get the arrangements we wanted in urban policies and so on. So, we say we are not here to serve politicians who want our voters but not our ideas.

SOS Racisme, France

SOS's separation from its political supporters is significant because it appears to have played a role in reinforcing its majoritarian stance, based on republican values. The wariness of being manipulated for political vote winning is translated into the organisation's view of itself as the true vanguard of egalitarianism. While the Left talks about extending equal rights to all, as seen in the above, when this comes to nothing but vote seeking, the reaction of *SOS Racisme* is to harden its resolve as the protector of the true values inscribed in the Republic. This notion of a certain burden which *SOS* leaders undertook to shoulder is implied by Boutih in his 2001 book when he explains that, following the departure of the then *SOS* President, Harlem Désir:

the people in power did not have an answer to the changes in French society. For an activist, the situation was even more worrying, because we couldn't put our heads in the sand and wait for better days, it was necessary to build the better days...

Boutih (2001:26)

In *SOS* terms, the problems faced by French society with regards the racism against blacks and *beurs* was realised as being resolvable only through a determined embracing of the undeniably French negation of difference. Hence, the title of the first chapter of Boutih's book: '*SOS Racisme*: From Differentialism to the Republic'. While the organisation went through a period during which it employed concepts of multiculturalism, in Boutih's account, today it clearly states that 'in France, minorities don't exist!' (Boutih 2001:30). The way towards ridding the society of racism consists of refusing any discourse which dilutes the Frenchness of anyone of non-French origin. The important fact for Boutih is that those still often seen as 'immigrants' are citizens of France and that this citizenship must, for equality to be installed, be disconnected from any religious, national or ethnic sense of belonging: 'Being French is being a citizen. That implies an equality of rights and duties within society, and means participating in the life of that society. And after, everyone, individually, can be what s/he wants' (ibid.:31–2).

This is echoed by *SOS*'s belief in the importance of secular education. While separate schools for different communities are strongly opposed, the organisation values the education of everyone about non-French culture within the framework of the national curriculum. The emphasis is placed on the value that 'immigrant' cultures have brought to France so that French culture, in *SOS*'s interpretation, is now one that equally reflects a diverse range of traditions. There is no reason, therefore, for those of non-French origin to demand any special rights on the basis of cultural or religious belonging.

> French society is a society which, culturally, has completely integrated minority cultures, much more than the countries that accuse France of being an assimilationist country...The French culture is a culture which has integrated massively, in terms of language, style, lifestyles, music, sport etc. The valorisation of immigration and the enrichment brought by immigration is a pedagogical process which we have been responsible for. Now, as we are now French whatever our origins: the generation that is 30 today, 25 per cent of it is of immigrant origin...The young people say, I am now French and I don't have to seduce people the whole time to try to have a place. I claim my rights, I have the right to a place and you don't have the right to question me about my origins.
>
> *SOS Racisme*, France

However, this view of the facility with which different cultures are accepted into the mainstream is contradicted by *SOS*'s account of its struggle for the inclusion of the knowledge of non-French cultures into the educational curriculum: its proposals on education have not, to date, been taken up. Here, the organisation finds it difficult to integrate its insistence on the primacy of the public, secular school system and the need to reflect the diversity that now constitutes French culture, as it would have it:

> Why teach the culture of one community to that community? We think that there shouldn't be specific teaching for Algerians of their Algerian culture at the secular schools but that there should be an education for everyone about Algerian culture. The problem is that we didn't get it through. The struggle that we still wage today at this moment so that the history curriculum, the civic curriculum etc., values the culture of immigrant communities more. But we don't want each community teaching its culture without the others being able to benefit. We don't support the idea that in a classroom they say: ok, the Algerians, you go to school with Mr A.N. Other who's going to talk to you about your culture of origin while the Chinese go with Mr Wong who's going to talk about the culture of the Chinese ... It's against communitarianism. In fact, there is a real stake to stop communitarianism in school.
>
> *SOS Racisme*, France

SOS insists that to differentiate between French people of different cultural origins would be to have failed in the struggle to make the egalitarian provision of the Republic functional for all. Boutih claims that to uphold the right to 'difference' is to fail to invest in the possibility of constructing a better France: 'At each step, differentialism is nourished by decomposition. And in fact, it is easier to adapt to decomposition than to create an ambitious project for society' (Boutih 2001:33). The notion that difference encourages disunity is as true for the anti-racism movement as it is for French society. *SOS Racisme* strongly resists the notion of affirmative action, for example, as it sees it, not as a tool for remedying institutional racism but as a means to visibly divide between blacks and whites:

> We are against [affirmative action] because, in fact, it is a tool for dividing the youth: the blacks on one side, the whites on the other, each one defending their rights, in their own way, using their own methods. We are for unifying the youth. We do not support saying we are going to create different rights; these for some and those for others.
>
> *SOS Racisme*, France

Nonetheless, the strong stance taken against what is thought of as being a 'communitarian' model, often ascribed to an Anglo-American 'way of doing anti-racism', is not necessarily borne out by *SOS*'s activities. One of the central campaigns around which *SOS* has reorganised itself since the election of Boutih in 1999 is 'testing': a means of bringing to light the everyday experience of discrimination suffered by non-white people in France. The testing method consists of collecting 'proof' of discrimination against non-French job and housing applicants or nightclub goers. They are carried out in the presence of witnesses, sometimes journalists, who record the dialogue between the two parties. Situations involving non-white applicants are compared to those in which a French person undergoes an identical 'test':

Today we are going in the direction in which France has to clearly show that whether your origins are in Europe, France or the Maghreb or Africa or Asia, we have equality of rights. So that has to be the objective of an offensive battle to ensure respect for republican law that guarantees equality of rights, that forbids quotas. That is the biggest change we have made, that is to take a very concrete sense of verifying the application of the equality of rights. So, it's the whole method of testing in the discos, it's the whole method of testing in employment ...

SOS Racisme, France

However, the method, as it is described in the *SOS Racisme* study on discrimination (2000) cannot avoid referring to people's ethnic or national origins. Indeed, the method encourages an essentialising of the participants through its comparison of the attitudes of Europeans and non-Europeans. For example, the report describes one of the potential outcomes of 'testing' in the following way: 'If someone who wishes to rent accommodation fills all the requirements (income, deposit ...) and s/he finds that s/he is refused accommodation, we may estimate that the refusal is linked to his/her nationality or ethnicity' (*SOS Racisme* 2000:7).

Furthermore, 'there must be participants of extra-European type and others of European type in order to show the reality of the discrimination' (*SOS Racisme* 2000:8). Nevertheless, *SOS Racisme* does

not seem to see any contradiction between, on the one hand, refusing to recognise the right of some to claim their 'difference' and, on the other, pointing out that very difference in order to campaign against their discrimination. Boutih sees this as part of the necessary realisation that to be French does not mean to be white and emphasises the proposition that republicanism – unlike nationalism – cuts across colour and cultural background:

> The right to physical difference is not anti-republican, on the contrary, it is perhaps a chance to reinvigorate the republican fabric...We must drive home that the Republic is not the Republic of whites. There are very white people, very upstanding, who go to church every Sunday but who are extremely anti-republican. You can have Maghrebi, African or Asian origins and be 100 per cent French, without having always to be questioned about our intentions because it is assumed we are a little less republican or a little less good republicans.
>
> Boutih (2001:38)

Finally, *SOS Racisme* justifies its position against 'difference' and 'communitarianism' by contrasting republican values with those it sees as being espoused by anti-racism in the UK. Efforts to introduce multiculturalism to the French context are seen as borrowing from a British or American politics of multiculturalism which, in *SOS's* estimation, has disastrous effects, most notably the ghettoisation of 'minority ethnic' groups who are unable to integrate into society. Anti-racism in Britain is anti-racism in name only as it refuses, in *SOS's* terms, the 'majoritarian' stance it upholds as unique in Europe:

> The youth organisations or the anti-racist organisations are not the same size nationally as *SOS Racisme*. That's because in England there are 400 anti-racist organisations, so-called anti-racist – 400 organisations of minorities...because each association is communitarian: the Surinamese association, the Caribbean association...
>
> *SOS Racisme*, France

However, *SOS's* self-description as being ahead of its times is refuted by the British organisations with which it has come into contact, for example NMP, for which *SOS's* insistence on the benefit of

integration revealed its failure to understand the historically derived complexities of placing vulnerable communities in situations of potentially acute racial violence:

I met SOS Racisme because the Council called me up to get some-body else's number, a youth worker who'd done some work in Tower Hamlets...In the end they did see us and I went to meet a couple of the people and told them about the work on the ground. Apparently they said we were one of the best organisations they saw. But I was a bit wary of some of the work that they do. They seem to think that they're dealing with racism and I really don't think that they are. I don't know enough about them but they seem to be very like 'we're in the forefront and you seem to be ten years, twenty years behind us'. What was interesting about that was I thought actually that wasn't the case and they were washing over a lot of the issues and thinking that they were dealing with them... There is a large Bangladeshi population in Tower Hamlets and in a lot of the estates you'll find that one will be predominantly white, one will be predominantly black African, Afro and African-Caribbean, and one will be predominantly Bangladeshi... There's a lot of anti-Bangladeshi feeling in Tower Hamlets... *SOS Racisme* did-n't really understand why, they said, 'these communities, why are they all in one area? The key is integration, they need to be mixing.'

NMP, UK

The key story of *SOS Racisme* clarifies the notion of the 'majori-tarian' anti-racism it embodies. It has had a significant impact upon the understanding of contemporary anti-racist discourse, both in France and beyond. Like the writings of Pierre-André Taguieff, *SOS* bases its ideology upon a resistance to cultural relativism. This is indeed a feature of anti-racism that merits holding up to scrutiny, especially where it reifies the groups on behalf of which it claims to speak. Nonetheless, *SOS Racisme* cannot be unambiguously under-stood as countering relativism and reification. When it speaks of blacks and *beurs* living in the *banlieues* does it not reinforce the image of the non-white that many French people have of blacks and North Africans? This aside, it is the means used to tackle both racism and the danger identified in the relativist stance that should be questioned. *SOS Racisme* denies the principle that anti-racism should be led by the racialised ('people are made responsible as a function of their work and not as a function of the colour of their skin. Malek is President because he's the best'). Secondly, racism is not analysed according to the principles that governed the thought of anti-colonialism or black emancipation. It is construed as a series of discriminations that operate in defiance of republican laws. For example, in the March 2000 edition of the *SOS Brochure*, racial discrimination is defined as: 'an undermining of the principle of equality according to which men are born and live as free and equal under law (Art. 1 Declaration of Man and the Citizen – 1789)'. Finally, by orienting itself exclusively towards the youth, *SOS* chooses to neglect several more complex arguments against racism which elsewhere have been central to the development of anti-racist discourse, most notably the critique of racism as it intersects with capitalism or sexism.

ANTI-RACISM OR ANTI-FASCISM?

The difference between organisations that characterise themselves as anti-racist and those which view their action as grounded in a history of anti-fascist resistance further reveals the nature of the interconnections between anti-racism and national public political culture. The 'majoritarian' discourse of *SOS Racisme* was shown to promote an anti-racism based on the right to equality as a provision of the French Republic. Anti-fascism, on the other hand, tends to ground itself more squarely in a patriotic discourse inspired by past struggles waged in the name of national liberation from Nazism or fascism. The self-descriptions of organisations, either expressly established to campaign against the activities of the far Right, or those of others with a more general orientation, but for whom the anti-fascism of the past serves as a central point of inspiration, shall be used to show how 'opposition to racial oppression has long been formulated as a national boast' (Bonnett 2000:50).

Having recourse to the Left's heroic anti-fascist past or, in the case of Britain, of the nation *tout court* in the war against Nazism, is a common feature of European anti-racist discourse. Seldom can the external observer differentiate between the general anti-racist movement and the organisations within it that are based upon a specific anti-fascist agenda. However, within the anti-racist arena in any given European setting, a strong distinction is made between anti-racism and anti-fascism. While being anti-racist does not imply neglecting the campaign against the rise in far-right activity, contrary to anti-fascism it generally goes beyond equating racism exclusively with the activities of the extreme Right. Anti-racism conceives of racism multiply, as wearing different guises and emerging both from within the institutions of the state to cause discrimination and as the often violent expressions of hatred by individuals, sometimes on behalf of a far-right grouplet and, as often, with no political affiliation or ambition. This generates an anti-racist discourse that mobilises a wide definition of racism and a campaigning strategy on several levels:

> We have a multilevel attack, you know, form of attack. Institutions, individuals, organisations...it's endemic...We know it's multifaceted so we have to deal with racism in the same way. We have to, first of all, we have to recognise that there is a racial problem in that area and then we confront them.
>
> The 1990 Trust, UK

In contrast, two central problems have been identified as characteristic of anti-fascism, both of which bear upon the discussion of the relationship between anti-racism and public political culture; anti-racism understood here in its broadest sense to include also those approaches organised exclusively around the fight against right-wing extremism. Firstly, anti-fascism seeks to relate present-day racism back to the genocidal project of the Nazi *Shoah*. This engenders a dilution of the contemporary experience of racism, relativised in relation to the extremes in which racism, it is claimed, may result. Therefore, the fight against racism becomes generalised to represent a continuation of the country's historic banishment from its midst of Nazism and fascism. Secondly, anti-fascism often employs a patriotic discourse that builds upon the aversion of the nation's citizens to the excesses of fascism. This results in the principle of establishing a resistance to the far Right within the broadest possible base of support, an approach which, as Gilroy (1987, 1992) argues, fails to make sense of the complexity of racism.

The recalling of the atrocities of the Nazi past, as a lynchpin of their discourse, is strongly observable among organisations that may be referred to as 'majoritarian', in the sense evoked in the previous section. Therefore, beyond the specificity of the anti-fascist stance, the recourse to the *Shoah* as a means of legitimating their activities is a common feature of anti-racism more generally. While this is clearly noticeable among organisations with strong links to the Jewish community, such as in France the LICRA or the LDH, it is also the case for several others, in both France and Italy, more so than in Ireland or Britain. In Britain, the consistent reference to the *Shoah* is more markedly the preserve of organisations that categorise themselves as anti-fascist, such as the ANL or *Searchlight*, the anti-fascist magazine. In France and Italy, the predominance of this type of discourse in mainstream anti-racism is also due historically to the proximity of the experience of Nazism.

ARCI represents a fitting example of the means through which anti-racism becomes part of the organisation's commitment, both to a critique of Italy's fascist past and to a valorisation of the engagement of the resistance fighters it counts among its members. The account of Italy's past, examined in the discussion of 'majoritarian' anti-racism, may in part be used once more to show how, beyond self-criticism, it emphasises Italian solidarity with the Jews during the Second World War. Contemporary commitment to anti-racism is construed as both a continuation of the responsibility assumed in the past in the face of fascism and Nazism and as a rectification of the failure of others to take such responsibility:

> It's true that in those years there was a big demonstration of solidarity with the Jews, many priests hid them in their own houses, many Italian citizens... That Italian history was born of important moments of solidarity but also of important moments of tragedy. The Italians were shown to be indifferent or to have participated.
>
> ARCI, Italy

In practical terms, the emphasis placed on linking present-day racism to that of the Nazi past is achieved through anti-racist education, a central dimension of the activities of many mainstream anti-racist organisations. This is constituted by reference to the notion of 'memory'. In particular, among French anti-racist organisations, for example the LICRA, the expression 'education for memory' refers to the teaching of the *Shoah*. *SOS Racisme* also prioritises this form of anti-racist education and makes the link between the teaching of the histories of the *Shoah* and immigration and the values of humanism and tolerance. While in the previous section, this excerpt was used to show how *SOS* emphasises values seen as granted by the French republic, its use here points to the link made between the *Shoah* and the valorisation of immigrant cultures. Beyond the obvious importance of recalling the horrors of the *Shoah*, such an easily made transition from the reference to the post-war immigration of blacks and North Africans to the Nazi genocide is not mindful of the problems incurred by the neglect of the qualitative differences between present-day racism against black people and immigrants and antisemitism in western Europe (Memmi 2000).

> Another struggle that we have waged since 1988 was for an anti-racist education that values the cultures of immigration, that teaches the memory of the Shoah, of that which led to Nazism in Europe, that, at the same time, teaches the great values of humanism and tolerance, the struggles waged around the Dreyfus Affair, around the abolition of slavery, the struggle for the declaration of human rights etc. We tried to make it almost compulsory within public education.
>
> *SOS Racisme*, France

The emphasis placed on the valorisation of the memory of the *Shoah* as a central ideological guiding point for several 'majoritarian' anti-racist organisations may compromise the attention to racism in the present day. The presentation of the raison d'être of anti-racism as beginning and ending with *Shoah* memory mobilises a public for whom the *Shoah* is neither a common point of reference, nor often is its history very familiar. In other words, the attempt to connect the contemporary realities of racialised young people to the past atrocities of the *Shoah* often does so in neglect of any real feeling of connection among such publics. However, rather than engendering the solidarity upon which a movement could be constructed, this sometimes leads to the further alienation of anti-racism's target group. Furthermore, due to greater emphasis being placed on the Jewish *Shoah*, often in neglect of the sufferings of other peoples under Nazism – Roma, lesbian, gay and black people in particular – the tendency, within a certain current of anti-racist discourse, to teleologically view racism as culminating potentially in a variant of the Nazi 'final solution' belies the failure of many groups to identify with what is often portrayed as the unique suffering of a single people.

Lastly, the relation often made between an insistence on the primacy of *Shoah* memory, as the ultimate in anti-racist lessons, and the justification of the Zionist project often creates deeper rifts between groups which otherwise may share a similar position on racism. The case of *SOS Racisme* in the 1980s reveals how the leaders of the *Mouvement beur*, invited to discuss affiliation to *SOS*, remained powerless in the face of the dominant Zionism of the organisation's allies, the French Union of Jewish Students (UEJF):

> The young people of the UEJF, Zionists for the most part, are steadfast in their ideas on the Israeli – Palestinian conflict. They often even place themselves at the limit of provocation ... If [the *beurs*] attack *SOS*, they are attacking the Jews and Israel. If they talk about the *beurs* in the housing projects and the problems of integration, they must accept the mediation of their discussions by Jews, to be represented by *SOS* and therefore by UEJF and its Zionist doctrine. The squaring of the circle. By showing their incapacity to discuss with the Jews of *SOS* the *beurs* were ensnared in the trap that was set for them.
>
> Malik (1990:32)

Beyond the mobilisation of the history of the *Shoah*, what specifically distinguishes anti-racism and anti-fascism? Gilroy (1992) proposes that the distinction concerns the relationship between the discourse of anti-fascism and that of patriotism. For Gilroy:

> a tension exists between those strands in antiracism which are primarily antifascist and those which work with a more extensive and complex sense of what racism is in contemporary Britain. This simplistic antifascist emphasis attempts to mobilise the memory of earlier encounters with the fascism of Hitler and Mussolini. The racists are a problem because they are descended from the brown and black-shirted enemies of earlier days. To oppose them is a patriotic act; their own use of national flags and symbols is nothing more than a sham masking their terroristic inclinations.
>
> Gilroy (1992:51)

Anti-racism often evokes a 'national way of doing things' which relativises the way anti-racists in other countries work and constructs a view of anti-racism as inscribed in national public political culture. Anti-fascism, on the other hand, opens its discourse to a wider public that may be mobilised around a specific objection to fascism, and Nazism. These may include those whom the Anti Nazi League labels 'soft racists'. In the ANL's terms, convincing a mass public to support campaigns against institutional racism, for example, would be difficult as a large proportion of its target audience falls into the category of so-called 'soft racists', today most generally those who support the widespread anti-immigration discourse promoted by the British media. However, even these people may be won over by making a connection between contemporary far right-wing politics and Hitler, whose defeat is a principal element of British patriotic discourse:

> A lot of the ground that the Nazis want is – the kind of disillusioned, white working class – is people that we want to win as well. We want them to become anti-Nazis so we don't just see them as soft racists and write them off, we try and win them to not go out on NF marches, BNP marches, not supporting them in any way whatsoever.
>
> ANL, UK

The anti-fascist approach is conducted on two fronts. The first attempts to appeal to the widest range of possible adherents. This also connects with an ideology positioned in the leftist politics that go hand-in-hand with the anti-fascist standpoint; that the working class that is won over by the arguments of the neofascist parties is a victim of 'false consciousness'. The second front concentrates on what I have already referred to as the 'natural' anti-racist/anti-fascist audience; those traditionally involved in the trade unions, left-wing political parties or, in Italy, the social centres. In the Italian case, the lack of a distinct anti-racist movement means that anti-fascist discourse cuts more widely across a range of left-wing movements. In the case of ARCI for example, a strong link is made between what is considered to be a decrease in strong national identity and the acceptance of difference. The existence of a strong consciousness of

anti-fascist history, on the other hand, is seen as a means of rebuild-
ing the weakened national identity upon which, later, an anti-racist
consciousness may be constructed:

> We felt that there was a weak Italian national consciousness, a per-
> ception of history that was also weak. Luckily, the consciousness of
> the partisan fight against fascism was strong, on the other hand.
> So, that great struggle of the people was strong, one of the great-
> est stories of Italian history: the anti-fascist resistance. And beneath
> that anti-fascist fight is, therefore, the Italian constitution which
> was written on the basis of an encounter between Catholic culture,
> Liberal culture, Communist culture, Socialist culture: it is still a con-
> stitution that stands by those who suffer. It is a constitution that
> refuses war and refuses racism because the experience of anti-
> semitism was seen by the partisans – and so by its authors – as a
> risk from which Italy could no longer hide.
>
> ARCI, Italy

Linking to the argument made in the previous section, this
excerpt shows how an anchoring in anti-fascist history shifts easily
into a discourse in support of the anti-racist character of elements
of the national public political culture, in this case the Italian constitution. According to such logic, anti-fascism is seen as incompatible with contemporary racism. The influence of the partisans upon
the writing of the Italian constitution therefore sustains both existing state provisions as satisfactory mechanisms for confronting
racism and the anchoring in anti-fascist heroism as an adequate
means of mobilising for anti-racism in the present day.

Gilroy (1992) argues that, beyond the patriotism mobilised by
the anti-fascist stance, the focus of anti-fascism on the activities of
the far right wing, as the most pernicious of racism's countenances,
fails to place racism within the centre of national politics. This claim
relates directly to the argument in Chapter 2, that the anti-racism
that emerges in the aftermath of the Second World War, and before
the critique generated by the anti-colonial movement, fails to
engage with the centrality of racism to the pasts and presents of the
European states. For Gilroy (1992:51) therefore, 'race' and racism
must not be treated as 'fringe questions but as a volatile presence at

the very centre of British politics, actively shaping and determining the history not simply of blacks, but of this country as a whole at a crucial stage in its development'. The key story of the Anti Nazi League shows how it effectively reflects both the teleological and the patriotic dimensions of anti-fascism by uniquely grounding them in a view which links the campaign against the far Right to a left-wing politics, based on the notion of class consciousness.

The Anti Nazi League: 'People opposing the Nazis, confronting them on the street'

My research into the Anti Nazi League was carried out during and after my participation in one of its protests against the National Front in South Bermondsey, in the East End of London in April 2001. During the day I spent with the ANL, I participated in the protest, recorded the speeches made by the organisers during the rally held afterwards, and followed the group to a 'safe' pub where I conducted an interview with one of the organisation's full-time employees. This key story was constructed by adding this material to the significant amount said about the ANL by other British anti-racist organisations and to the writings of several authors on the subject.

The combination of these various research materials allows me to make three main points. Firstly, the ANL, founded by the Socialist Workers' Party (SWP) in 1977, builds a class analysis of what it calls Nazism (the activity of the British far Right). Most important in this perspective is the insistence upon the 'natural' alliance of the black and white working class. Secondly, its singular attention to the attack on the far Right is linked to a teleological view of racism which identifies Hitlerism as the specific form of racism to which British extremists aspire. It constructs a unidimensional portrayal of racism which is consciously neglectful of the latter's heterogeneity. Furthermore, despite its firm grounding in the class politics of the SWP, it seeks to appeal to individuals from across the political spectrum and, most significantly, to the apolitical, particularly in its earlier period during the late 1970s, by means of mass concerts that built on the legacy of Rock against Racism (Gilroy 1987; Renton, www.dkrenton.co.uk/anl.html). Lastly, it relies on a form of patriotic discourse which legitimates the fight against 'the Nazis' by recalling the heroism of Britain's defeat of Hitler.

The ANL's origins in the SWP are often played down in importance by the organisation's supporters. The SWP has been accused by several authors (e.g. Tomlinson 1981) of manipulating the anti-racist cause through its establishment of the League, an organisation that, both at the time of its emergence and since the early 1990s when it was rebuilt, has enjoyed a level of support unknown to the majority of European anti-racist/anti-fascist groups. As Renton points out, 80,000 people attended the first of the ANL carnivals in 1978 with tens of thousands participating in events it has organised including carnivals, concerts and protest marches. The League's critics imply that the SWP had 'dishonest motives' (Renton, www.dkrenton. co.uk/anl.html) for creating the ANL: to recruit members for itself. Renton cites Tomlinson's invocation of the SWP's control over the ANL as based on the former's 'drive avowedly against racism and fascism, but also by its own ideological implication, against state racism and state fascism, and ultimately the state itself' (Tomlinson 1981; cited in Renton ibid.). The ANL's foundation from within the SWP is seen by other British anti-racist groups as ensuring that it enjoyed stronger structural support, in the form of a 'party machine', than was available to most of the independent self-organised black organisations in existence until the late 1970s:

> In the '70s an organisation came along called the Anti Nazi League which was very sort of populist and managed to bring the whole issue of Nazis standing in elections to national prominence. But at the same time a lot of the grassroots organisations who formed part of CARF, sort of smaller groups, were actually swept aside by these sort of bigger organisations that have more effective party machines but was very much just looking at the whole question of the Nazis and not tying up the whole issue of the return of Nazism to the growth of racism.
>
> CARF, UK

There is certainly a strong tendency within ANL discourse to attack governmental policy and the individual representatives of government – as true for today's Labour government as it was during the days of Conservative rule. However, it has no developed stance on institutional racism, for example. Its purported anchorage in the class politics of the 'old' Left relies on a romanticised discourse that promotes the necessity of black and white people from local communities – understood to be members of the working class – uniting to root out fascism. This focus on the working class and the local community results in a problematic construction of the anti-racist public which takes no account of the rise in Britain, since the 1980s, of significant middle-class groups among the racialised, which nonetheless continue to experience racism, nor of the dominant numbers of white, middle-class members of the ANL itself. Furthermore, the continual reference to the binary black–white configuration simplifies the complex nature of the various racialised groups who make up the purported black working class. This has become particularly problematic in light of the racism experienced by white migrants, such as the East European Roma, in recent times.

Criticisms of the ANL have focused on the impression that it is mainly made up of outsiders, people who do not live in the areas heavily populated by blacks and asylum seekers where the far Right is active. Nevertheless, the organisation insists on the link between opposing the 'Nazis' and protecting the interests of local community members, black and white. It insists that it is legitimate to highlight the rise of 'fascist' activity in an area such as South Bermondsey, whether or not campaigners live in that area or have sought the support of local residents. That support is seen as necessary, but only in order to back up preexisting ANL mobilisation, rather than the latter emerging out of the impetus of local residents:

It's really important to win black people who feel unconfident. On the streets round here last week black people weren't coming out of their houses and we have to show that there is opposition in the streets and it'll be even better if you come out. If your community comes out, the Nazis are nothing. You've seen it today: there's twenty Nazis. We need a thousand people out on the streets next week, two thousand to really stop it and that has to be the local community which is black and Asian and Chinese and Irish and everything really.

ANL, UK

The assumption of alliance between blacks and whites, living together in local 'communities' and suffering the same problems is problematised by other British anti-racist groups. The ANL is seen as successful in mobilising large numbers of people but as rarely bearing the consequences of a highly visible protest in an area where tensions between blacks and whites are high or in places lived in by asylum seekers, often at risk of attack if further attention is drawn to their presence. The proposal that anti-racism and anti-fascism should be grounded in a left-wing politics of class is seen by several black anti-racist organisations as ignorant of the realities of institutional racism faced by racialised people. The following statement, although it does not directly name the Anti Nazi League, is representative of the critique often waged against the call for unity between the black and white working classes:

A lot of black people and individuals joined these organisations because these organisations said that they work fighting against racism but that they didn't tell them at what level they were fighting racism or what kind of stance or angle they were fighting it from. They could be a very left-wing group for example who think Marx was certainly against race and we follow Marx and, you know ... Two years ago there was a demonstration in Brixton against the police. A lot of black organisations were involved, very good, very peaceful, very well coordinated. The problem is one group – I'm not going to name – came up, a white-led group and started causing trouble, started harassing the police, started fighting the police. This group was a white-led group basically and it ended up tragic. They hijacked the whole thing, the whole demonstration. The police reacted very badly as usual. They reacted. These people ran away immediately. The black community were blamed, the black community were arrested. I was there ... I saw it and I thought that's so disgusting what they do or what they've done. They didn't really care, they didn't give a shit about these people in the community. They were there for their own political means and gains and that just drove me crazy. I was just very wound up. It's the community who has to take the backlash not these people who are middle-class, white people living in suburbia. That's a fact.

The 1990 Trust, UK

The Anti Nazi League bases its discourse both on the importance of unity between black and white people from working-class communities and upon the need to singularly focus on the emergence of fascist groups in these areas. The ANL's targeting of such groups is concentrated around its equation of the activities of extreme right-wing groups in the British political arena, no matter how small in size or importance, with the event of Nazism. It puts forward a teleological anti-fascism that focuses on the primacy of the *Shoah* and insists on labelling British right-wing groups as Nazi. The organisation's members engage with the history of the Second World War and the *Shoah*. For example, the ANL employee whom I interviewed had recently returned from a visit to Auschwitz. The significance of this for the League is evident in the following:

> We very much go on their history as well about the Nazis taking power in Germany and the Holocaust and you learn from that, you learn from what the Nazis did. And a famous quote of Hitler is 'if our adversaries knew what we were from the beginning and smashed us when we were small this would never be a problem.'
>
> ANL, UK

According to Gilroy (1987), the focus on the 'Nazism' of parties such as the British National Party and the National Front reflects a significant shift in British anti-racist politics of the 1970s away from the youth-oriented focus of Rock Against Racism and towards an older public. Whereas RAR had been involved in the production of new cultural forms that reflected the growing diversity of the British population and created common reference points for youth of different backgrounds, the ANL's focus on the 'Nazis' connected the campaign back to the anti-fascist struggle of the 1930s and 1940s. As Gilroy (1987:131) points out, 'the League's leaflets were illustrated with imagery of the war – concentration camps and Nazi troops – and were captioned with the anti-fascist slogan "Never Again".' He claims that the use of the word 'Nazi' to label the British far Right strategically sought to mobilise both those who had lived during the time of Nazism and young people concerned for their futures.

The emphasis placed on the link between contemporary far-right racism and the Nazism of the past, in Gilroy's analysis, led directly to the 'creation of a host of mini organisations' (Gilroy 1987) within the Anti Nazi League. Whereas Gilroy claims that the purpose of these splinter groups was to transfer the locus of anti-racism from the dancehalls to the workplace, and therefore to the heart of traditional working-class politics, Renton's (www.dkrenton.co.uk/anl.html) description of these 'mini organisations' presents a different picture. Whereas it is certainly true that the ANL does mobilise what it views as being a politics of class, its labelling of the British far Right as Nazi in the 1970s, on the contrary, contributed to popularising the anti-fascist struggle beyond its traditional left-wing audience. Some of the groups named by Renton include Aardvarks Against the Nazis and Left-handed Vegetarians Against the Nazis, indicating the extent to which the Nazi appellation popularises and, above all, depoliticises anti-racism for many of those attracted by the ANL message.

The organisation explains its use of the label 'Nazi' in a way which clearly demonstrates its underpinning by the teleological logic I have proposed shapes much anti-fascist discourse:

> The National Front and the BNP today both try and stay away from using the word 'Nazi'. When you see them, if it's like an interview or on television, they try to stay away. If you look at their web pages and guest books and where they come from it's really quite obvious they are Nazis. What we label as Nazi is that they're Hitler admirers. Their politics are the same as Hitler's were and the National Socialist Nazis were in Germany. So I think it's really important to label them with that because they try and shy away, particularly the British National Party at the moment who are trying to repackage themselves as a respectable political party.
>
> ANL, UK

The ANL suggests that an emphasis on the Nazi-like features of the British far right-wing parties generates greater public support. The appeal to fight the 'Nazis' unites individuals from a wide range of political allegiances and strengthens its commitment to the 'legacy' 'that you have to have a united front against the Nazis' (ANL, UK). ANL origins are portrayed as based upon a common opposition to British 'Nazism':

> What it was saying was, whatever your arguments are politically – there might be political arguments you can have here and there – but

> when it comes to the Nazis, we oppose the Nazis and we want groups set up in all the local communities, we want to get the local communities involved and we want to confront them physically.
>
> ANL, UK

The use of the term 'Nazi' is seen by Gilroy as directly linked to the recourse had by the ANL to patriotism as a means of mobilising support. Indeed, in the interview I conducted, the naming of the far Right as 'Nazis' was seen as deterring patriotic British voters from supporting the NF or the BNP. Gilroy cites the leaflets produced by the League during the 1970s to show how the ANL played upon the vision of Nazism as intrinsically German and, therefore, inassimilable to the British way of life:

> Why should you oppose the National Front? ... They say they are just patriots. Then why does Chairman Tyndall say 'the Second World War was fought for Jewish, not British, interests. Under the leadership of Adolph Hitler, Germany proved she could be a great power.'
>
> (Gilroy 1987:132)

Gilroy's argument is that the ANL, by associating the National Front with Hitler's Nazism – 'pictures of the NF leaders wearing Nazi uniform were produced' (Gilroy 1987:132) – constructed the latter as a foreign body. The 'Nazis' had to be defeated because, while they spoke in the name of British patriotism, in reality they stood for the Hitlerian ideals against which Britain had gone to war. Although Gilroy concedes that the League's actions contributed to the defeat of the far Right at the end of the 1970s, he claims that 'this was achieved ironically by reviving the very elements of nationalism and xenophobia which had seen Britannia through the darkest hours of the Second World War' (ibid.:134).

Renton (www.dkrenton.co.uk/anl.html) opposes the relationship Gilroy draws between Anti Nazi League discourse and British patriotism. He sees the use of the appellation 'Nazi' as merely the simplest way of mobilising large numbers among the public to take action against the far Right. Renton bases his claims on interviews he conducted with ANL members active in the 1970s. For example, he (ibid.) cites one such member as saying:

> I'm sure if you went through the files carefully enough, you may find bits of Anti Nazi League propaganda that do use a nationalist rhetoric that I wouldn't be wildly happy with, but in general this isn't the case. By focusing on the Nazis, the ANL showed people the logic of racism, and raised the general question of racism.

Gilroy disagrees directly with this last statement: for him the so-called logic of racism is almost completely neglected in ANL discourse. The far Right, though dangerous, is only a tiny factor in the overall picture of British racism, according to Gilroy. Focusing on its activity is to marginalise racism and to uphold the view of it as nothing but the perversity of the few.

Although the writings of Gilroy and Renton refer to the ANL's earlier period of activism, during the late 1970s, the attachment to the discourse of patriotism, observed by Gilroy, seems to have remained integral to the League's position. The recourse to patriotism operates on two levels. Firstly, the organisation's discourse evokes the horrors of the *Shoah* as a means of separating the sentiments of what it calls 'soft racists' from the ideals of the British far Right, seen as lauding the 'final solution' and suggesting a similar end to Britain's 'immigration problem'. By recalling Nazism, the ANL seeks to divide between everyday racism, or 'common-sense racists', and real fascism, seen as much more pernicious. The following excerpt demonstrates how the organisation believes in appealing to British patriotism as a means of winning over the 'soft racists' by strongly delineating the racism of the Conservatives, for example, from that of the National Front or British National Party. The ANL seeks to win back those who may be attracted to the far Right's nationalism. It fails, therefore, to problematise nationalism or to define it in relation to fascism in any way. To an extent, the Anti Nazi League distinguishes between three levels of political identification: harmless nationalism, soft racism and dangerous fascism:

> Actually being a Nazi isn't popular in Britain today. So they [the far Right] say they are nationalists, they call themselves nationalists. What's the problem with that? I campaign on the streets against Nazis, not nationalists but they hope to win the white working class

who is proud of being British. It's like the Nazis are going to march next week for St George's Day. The reason we're opposing that march is because the National Front have called it and they're the Nazi party. If any other party had called it and if it was locals marching for St George's Day, we wouldn't oppose that because I don't see those people as Nazis. Then you're caught calling a lot of the population Nazis. Now there might be another argument to have with those people. They might be racists but a lot of people that are proud to be British aren't racist. A lot of people proud to be British are quite proud to be multicultural and multiracial as well. Not always, but Nazis are something very significant and if you start calling everyone to the Right … if you start getting into an argument, saying the Tories are Nazis or people like that, well then you alienate a lot of people. And they aren't Nazis. They're not people who stand for the concentration camps, the horrors of the Holocaust, they're just a minority … And as soon as people hear it's Nazis, people are appalled by it. Because I think most people associate Nazis with Hitler and something that's abhorrent, it's anti-Jewish, it's concentration camps. Even people who are slightly racist do not want to kill people.

ANL, UK

Secondly, the patriotic language employed by the ANL appeals to those old enough to remember the Second World War and builds on this memory in order to encourage younger generations to confront contemporary 'Nazism'. In particular, the type of language used to rally older people around the anti-Nazi cause relates to Gilroy's perspective on the ANL's patriotism. Beyond the problematic stress on 'Nazism', described in Gilroy's account, he shows how the ANL sought to compare the apparent patriotism of the far Right with the real patriotism of the Britons who fought against Hitler:

The idea that the British Nazis were merely sham patriots who soiled the British flag by their use of it was a strong feature of ANL leaflets. This inauthentic patriotism was exposed and contrasted with the genuine nationalist spirit which had been created in Britain's finest hour – the 'anti-fascist' 1939–45 war.

Gilroy (1987:131)

The premium placed by the ANL on those who remembered that war is demonstrated by the following. The strategy used by the organisation is to play on people's personal recollections and require them to ascertain their own patriotic allegiance:

> I think people can be fooled by some of their arguments unless there is quite a clear opposition and an alternative to be able to say 'do you want these people here?' and to expose them. Even in South Bermondsey last weekend there was some white pensioners saying that the Anti Nazi League rally was just as bad as the Nazis, actually the Nazi rally was better. They weren't saying these people were Nazis. Now, try to get a discussion with them and you try to say 'what do the Nazis stand for? You must remember the Second World War, you remember what Hitler's about' – they're kind of half listening to you – 'and they're against the welfare state but you're a pensioner, you'd be slung into a concentration camp. They don't think that you should have the right to have a pension.' So, it kind of makes people stop and listen.
>
> ANL, UK

In conclusion, the discourse promoted by the Anti Nazi League on three interlinking levels: a populist discourse of class politics, a teleological view of the contemporary activity of the British far Right as grounded in Nazism and the recourse had to a patriotism that challenges the authentic Britishness of fascist groups is explanatory of several of the major differences between anti-racist and anti-fascist discourse. Nonetheless, as has been stressed throughout this section, it is not possible merely to see the former as upholding a critique of nationalism, patriotism or public political culture while the latter embraces it. My discussion of the centrality of teleological explanations of racism has demonstrated the extent to which this is integral to what I have referred to as 'majoritarian' or 'mainstream' anti-racism. Differences in such reflections of the collective memory of suffering or struggle differ across countries. A reflection upon the link between the *Shoah* and anti-racist activism is more obviously significant in the French and Italian contexts, societies with a more direct experience of both the *Shoah* and the resistance than Britain and, especially, Ireland.

However, despite the reliance of some organisations on an idealised account of the importance of incorporating national public political culture into anti-racist discourse, anti-racist organisations in general do operate a more complex understanding of racism than do anti-fascists. This is undoubtedly because the latter choose to focus on a single issue whereas anti-racist organisations are often forced, as we shall see in the following chapter, to confront racism in a variety of more or less apparent forms. However, as the key story of the Anti Nazi League has revealed, the unique focus on the growth of so-called British 'Nazism' often fails to build on what is undoubtedly a successful and powerful movement for the campaign against racism in its different guises.

CONCLUSION

The discussion of the 'majoritarian' and 'anti-fascist' conceptualisations of anti-racism has dealt with the integration of dimensions of public political culture into the language of much anti-racist activism. Anti-racism is considered to be without benefit if unable to appeal to as large a number of individuals as possible. The way of achieving a 'generalist' anti-racist commitment is consequently considered to be the mobilisation of a discourse of national tradition and historical legacies which makes citizens proud of their country's struggle for democracy. These forms of anti-racist patriotism are generally neglectful of the exclusion of the racialised, the non-national or 'minority ethnic groups' that this often entails. The recourse to history in particular is immediately questioned by the parallel narratives of colonial domination, fascist regimes or Nazi collaboration which complete accounts of the histories of the states of western Europe and cast doubt over the utility of an anti-racism which singularly mobilises a discourse of humanism or anti-fascism that overlooks the origins of the racialisation process.

The declaration of a crisis in anti-racism by Pierre-André Taguieff and Paul Gilroy at the beginning of the 1990s revolved centrally around these two issues. Each author represents a respective end of the continuum that the research has revealed may be a useful way of conceiving of the heterogeneity of anti-racism. Anti-racism is deemed to be in crisis because of its purported rejection of the humanistic values of democratic egalitarianism that is assumed are provided by recourse to the political traditions of the modern nation-state. In sharp contrast, a crisis has also been said to have afflicted anti-racism because of its over-association with the bureaucracy of the state and with the mythology of the European nations' past. As the next chapter shall demonstrate, the recourse to public political culture in anti-racism coexists with an evolved critique of the perceived failure of such an approach to effectively counter the implications of institutionalised racism. Do Taguieff and Gilroy really account for the full extent of anti-racism's variety in their identification of its crisis? Or do both, for widely differing reasons, pinpoint specific dimensions of anti-racism that, to serve their political-theoretical argumentation, are used to illustrate the need for anti-racism's transformation, or indeed for its dismantling? The continuum of proximity-to-distance along which anti-racism may be said to be arranged, being constructed as I develop my analysis, serves to demonstrate the untenability of treating anti-racism as either a unitary or a linear component of modern politics.

5

Who Says What, for Whom and from Where? Anti-Racism and Political Representation

The chasm between the colonised and the colonialists, for instance, was often so large that even the White Europeans of good will could not imagine what was happening in the souls of their domestic servants ('they are impenetrable'). For the oppressed, there exists a sense of despair and of futility that conditions and tempers every feeling and mood and which does not exist for the non-oppressed. The non-oppressed can, by definition, remove themselves from any situation. As heart-warming as the undertakings of the American writer Griffith were, in staining himself dark among the Black people of the South, he knew that he could, whenever he so desired, return to the North, rean-nounce his whiteness to the world and put an end to his vol-untary nightmare. One could never completely put oneself in the place of the Black person, or in that of the Jew who has lost his family to the crematoria.

Albert Memmi (2000:162–3)

By this final chapter, the full extent of the heterogeneity of anti-racism in Europe should be apparent. It includes the establishment of educational programmes to battle against entrenched notions of racial hierarchy; the struggle of black people and immigrants to Europe, inspired by an anti-colonialist vision of emancipation, against the racism of the state; the determination of a class-conscious left politics to harness the historical struggle of the work-ing class to that of the racialised; and, underlying it all, the project of humanitarian solidarity to bring a universalist, colour-blind, merit-based utopia to fruition. It is this plurality, and the lack of unity it engenders, that has led some to draw the conclusion that anti-racism has reached an impasse. As Bonnett (2000:116) notes, the inability to clearly pinpoint a singular anti-racism has led to it (depending on one's viewpoint) being concomitantly seen as either ' "winning the day" or "coming to an end" '. Bonnett goes as far as to say that the tensions in anti-racism work positively to 'animate its debate and provoke the heterogeneity of its activism' (ibid.). Seen from a perspective that prioritises the collective action dimension of anti-racism, this may well be the case.

On the other hand, from the point of view of this book that regards anti-racist practices and the discourses which have come to shape them as existing in tandem, anti-racism's tensions may relate a more complex, and certainly less optimistic, message. The fragmentation of anti-racism, to the extent that some objectively anti-racist practices refuse the appellation due to the pejorative connotations it may imply, has resulted in dramatic disunities, based on both hierarchies of victimhood and a breakdown in communication between the oppressed and the *solidaire*, as most clearly seen in the United States. Nonetheless, anti-racism's diversity also means that 'while one tradition is being overlooked and forgotten, another is likely to be gathering momentum' (Bonnett 2000:116). The temporal differences between anti-racisms in different settings, their varying speeds, the diversified conceptualisations of 'race' and racism and the radically different standpoints of activists, both across countries and between organisations in a single society, contribute to ensuring that something is always 'going on'.

These variations can be attributed to the positioning of anti-racisms along our continuum of proximity-to-distance from the public political culture of the nation-state. It is not only in order to explain discourses – such as 'majoritarian' anti-racism's construction of 'communitarianism' as its polar opposite, or the reinvigoration of Nazism as timelessly symbolic of all racisms – that the continuum becomes significant. If we construct a fuller account of the development of these discourses, as I have concentrated on doing, and draw connections between the rise of their importance in anti-racism and political projects that became significant at specific times during the history of post-war Europe, we may begin to see how positioning and agency work to challenge or uphold them, thus gradually increasing the heterogeneity of anti-racism.

This chapter shall bring such positionings into focus by examining the praxis of contemporary European anti-racist organisations, juxtaposing it with an analysis of the political theoretical relevance of the central questions posed by this anti-racism to established theorisations of political participation. I shall examine those dimensions of political participation that impinge directly on the principal elements of public political culture that intersect with the variety of anti-racist standpoints identified. Specifically, in contrast to the previous chapter which positioned its lens at one end of the continuum – the anti-racist embodiment of public political culture – here the focus shall be turned to the other extreme. Based on the themes structuring their work, prioritised by the activists interviewed, the chapter shall map the ways in which they call into question the assumptions about the political possibilities open to anti-racists made by an anti-racism that sustains the importance of public political culture.

More than any other theme of anti-racist discourse, the examination of the notion of representation is revelatory of the positioning of the variety of anti-racisms vis-à-vis public political culture. The extent to which anti-racists deem it either necessary or possible for anti-racism to be representative of the actual experience of racism defines conceptualisations of its political ownership. Schematically – and at this stage in terms only of ideals rather than practices – anti-racists who position themselves within public political culture generalise the ownership of anti-racism. However, based as their ideas often are on an ideal of equality, they nonetheless fail to problematise the capacity of the racialised to become involved in the actualisation of anti-racism. Challengers of 'mainstream' anti-racism's idealisation of public political culture seek to disconnect their discourse from the nationally defined boundaries of political participation and, in so doing, question the very presumption that the inclusion of the racialised in the polity (or, indeed, the anti-racist community) is an unproblematic possibility. Moreover, such a challenge also questions the ability of an anti-racism that is ideologically generalised beyond the tangible experiences of the actual or potential victims of racism, to effectively counter it and to go beyond the level of principles.

On these grounds, the chapter shall proceed as follows. The political theoretical construction of the concept of representation (Pitkin 1967) shall be contrasted with the specific meaning of representation in anti-racist terms. I shall ask how the varying positions taken within anti-racism on the concept of representation embody the differential relationships towards public political culture across varieties of anti-racism. The ensuing discussion shall focus on three central dualistic positionings within anti-racism that go towards more concretely establishing representation as a means through which to qualify the extent of anti-racism's contemporary heterogeneity. These three pairs may respectively be termed 'authenticity or experience', 'right or independence' and 'localised or globalised'.

The first of these pairs shall examine the tension between a reified view of 'community', constructed both from within and without, and the grounding of anti-racism in a first-hand knowledge of racism. The second pair focuses on the relationship of anti-racist organisations with the institutions of the state. The last conceptual coupling examines the differences between an anti-racism rooted in the local – often the neighbourhood – and one which seeks to internationalise its action, particularly at the European level. The analysis of the meaning of representation for anti-racism, deepened by the discussion of these three dualistic strands, shall be related both to the discourse produced by contemporary anti-racist organisations and to an historicisation of the evolution of the political ideals that are formative of it.

ANTI-RACISM AND POLITICAL REPRESENTATION: BEYOND VISIBILITY

In the end, the issue of representation is related directly to the question of who is being represented by whom to whom, and under what auspices.

Ioan Davies (1995:105)

Political theoretical discussions of political representation see it as fundamental to the procedures of political deliberation: 'Representation then becomes a key concept, referring to the rules of making "present" in political deliberations those citizens who cannot directly participate themselves, who are in fact absent' (Wagner 1994:91). Although Pitkin (1967:2) points out that both the concept and the practice of representation have 'had little to do with democracy or liberty', clearly representation has been linked to the notion of political participation that comes about with modern citizenship, mainly in democracies. While representation can take place in a variety of settings, it is the role of the elected representative that has been at the centre of the discussion of the concept of representation. The basic assumption, made by Weber (cited in Pitkin), is that a group authorises a representative to act on its behalf, a process which is both binding on the actor and legitimates her autonomous actions. This view, which came to the fore with the rise of mass parties of class-based politics, assumes, as Wagner makes clear, that all individuals identify with a social class that is represented by an organisation that, in turn, represents them to the political institutions. Historically, the success of what became the project of social democracy, during the expansion to universal suffrage, was to make mass support (portrayed as representativity) a condition for political success, expanded to all parties. This in turn created a 'tension between the objective of truly representing and that of success in the competition' (Wagner 1994:94). The shift from the mass party to that which Wagner terms the 'electoral-professional' (ibid.:95) and the growing influence of corporate interest seems to be enabled by the ability of elites to maintain the view that the party system is grounded in the relationship between representative and represented.

Visibility and humanisation

Readings of racial conditions that reify race in fixed and unchanging terms presume that racially coded invisibility is restrictive, that it essentially, and so necessarily, delimits possibility and opportunity. On these assumptions, visibility is taken as a virtue, a norm of whiteness amid the night of blackness. Visibility, then, should always be pursued, protected, cherished; invisibility is to be avoided, derided, denied.

David Theo Goldberg (1997:81)

Beyond the obviously problematic nature of accounting for representation almost exclusively in terms of the modern democratic system of electoral politics, Pitkin's discussion, covering the gamut of writings on the subject, assumes that no matter the quality of the representation, in theory, the representation of individual interests is always a possibility. However, to follow Goldberg, human visibility is always a minimum condition for representation to take place. When anti-racists discuss the notion of representation, they rarely refer to the electoral system per se, although this may be one target of their concerns. They rather, more complexly, refer to the process of making visible something (someone) which has formerly been kept invisible. Drawing on the histories of anti-racisms as we are by now familiar with them, the invisibility of the racialised, in the political project of anti-racism, has not been the simple consequence of institutional domination by the state and capital (e.g. poor working conditions or education hindering possibilities of political involvement). It has also been, and continues to be, the inability, or the refusal, of the 'majoritarian' or the 'white left' approach in anti-racism to relinquish the representation of its principles to those for whom racism has been, or risks being, a first-hand experience. This is evident in the following recounting of opposition to black representation in the history of the British anti-racist movement:

I think that through the '70s and most of the '80s there was blacks of organisations on the one hand and there were black people of black communities organising and sometimes in alliance with other organisations around specific issues. But, the anti-racist organisations that existed, of which there were a number, did not have as part of the principles of their organisation or even as a very conscious fact that the black communities and the people who suffered racism had a very ... had a predominant role to play in how it was confronted. And that was sometimes consciously rejected, as in the case for example of the Anti Nazi League, or in some cases just hadn't been really thought about and so, although it's not that the black communities weren't organised and didn't fight racism, the majority white organisations of the society that was concerned about racism did not give priority to those black organisations and didn't bend over backwards to involve them and certainly didn't see them as playing the leading role in the fight against racism.

NAAR, UK

The contrast between the visibility of anti-racist action and the invisibility of the self-organisation of racialised groups, encapsulated by the claim made in the interview that it wasn't that the black communities weren't organised, has been one of the central means by which action has been defined as anti-racist – and thus political – or 'merely' communitarian, and therefore belonging to the private sphere. We can understand representation, as it relates to anti-racism, as encompassing the politicised nature of such action and, necessarily therefore, its visibility in the public sphere. Always understanding anti-racism as comparable across time as well as location, as a project of solidarity or the upholding of a universalised principle, abstracted from experience, 'majoritarian' anti-racism felt, albeit unconsciously, that the possibility of 'passing' publicly (for whites and, some contexts, for the proponents of a colour-blind approach) was what would influence the success of the anti-racist message. Therefore, an anti-racism that seeks to be representative – in the democratic terms of the concept proposed by Weber – needs firstly to make visible those who were to be represented (the racialised) as a precondition for participation in the formulation of anti-racist strategy. The process of making visible their very existence was deemed fundamental for the *Maison des ensembles*:

> About a month ago we went on the beaches to clean the black oil slick. And when we were in Brittany ... the surprise was that at the beginning they were suspicious of us and that suspicion, we understood afterwards that there was a very destructive job done and a very damaging role played by the media especially. Because they wanted to demonise immigrants. They wanted to demonise the *sans-papiers*: they are criminals, they are this, that and the other. So, in whatever region, it is that impression that the people immediately have of us. But when they approach us they understand that it is completely the other way around.
>
> MDE, France

In a second step, visibility is insufficient on its own. This is true for two reasons. Firstly, negatively, because opinion has often connected the public attempts of the racialised to question racism with violence and, as a consequence, with fear. While American examples abound, in Europe this is made clear by the public reaction to the Brixton uprising and those more recently, still known as riots, in Bradford and Oldham; to the publicly expressed rage of the marchers of the *Mouvement beur* in 1980s France; and, more passively, to the arrival of asylum seekers (some as corpses) to Lampedusa or to the Irish coast. Secondly, as Goldberg points out, in his discussion of Fanon on the invisibility of the colonised, visibility is often of little use without self-determination. Although clearly Fanon refers to the necessity of gaining national freedom from colonial domination, the relevance of this claim to the context of European anti-racism becomes clear in Goldberg's (1997:81) statement that 'being recognised, whether as self-conscious or as Other, and thus being visible, requires that one be outside the Other's imposition, free of the Other's complete determination.' The qualification of visibility with self-determination is evident in the claim that mere recognition is insufficient in order for preconceived mappings of power, especially those within organisations or a movement, to be displaced.

The visibility upon which the principle of representation in anti-racism is based goes beyond the mere action of 'causing one to see'. This is evident in Fanon's discussion of the invisibility of the colonised when he talks of unveiling as a process that humanises black people (Goldberg 1997). Transposed to the context of anti-racism and politics, if we take humanisation to symbolise the potentiality of the racialised to speak for themselves and – once deinfantilised – to become agents in their own right, the process of unveiling takes on a profound meaning, beyond the metaphorical connections with the colonial situation described by Fanon and others. The importance placed on visibility by the *Sans-papiers* movement is described in the following, both in terms of the simple process of making public and the implied humanisation brought about by the act of speaking on one's own behalf:

> Suddenly you saw people like Madjiguène Cissé who spoke on TV, who had an extremely sophisticated political discourse, very well thought out, in which she didn't just say anything, and it wasn't at all the image of the *sans-papiers* that rape women ... But it's very important as a change and I think it contributed a lot to what people said: 'Because the *sans-papiers* are able to talk on the television and say politically interesting things it's true, why shouldn't they have the right to vote and why shouldn't they even be able to have political responsibility at least at the local level?'
>
> *Sans-papiers*, France

However, the notion of visibility in this also implies that the *sans-papiers'* unveiling process sought not only to humanise or personalise them, but also to prove their intelligence against the myth of fear constructed around them and, therefore, to justify their presence as well as their actions.

So the condition of visibility is not sufficient for ensuring that anti-racism be representative of the standpoint of the actual or potential victims of racism. Visibility cannot be said to be representative in this sense if it involves either tokenism, leaving underlying power arrangements unchanged, or if coupled with a discourse of justification that induces a questioning of the legitimacy of those intervening in the political arena to do so. Yet, both these scenarios are realities of certain forms of anti-racist practice, past and present. Under what circumstances, therefore, may the 'visibility plus self-determination' formulation advocated by Fanon become a principle of anti-racist organising? In order to more deeply explore the centrality of the concept of representation to anti-racist self-understandings and the type of relationship with public political culture that this implies, I shall now turn to the discussion of three conceptualisations of political representation. I emphasise how each provides for the key notion of possibility, in terms of political participation, as a central means for examining the relationship between varying anti-racist perspectives on representation and concomitant positionings vis-à-vis public political culture.

Representation as 'standing for'

Pitkin (1967) proposes that representation as 'standing for' may be conceived as either descriptive or symbolic. Pitkin's discussion of the literature, mainly of proponents of the electoral system of proportional representation, sees descriptive representation as 'mirroring' 'the people, the state of public consciousness, or the movement of social and economic forces in the nation' (ibid.:61). Such a position, following John Stuart Mill, insists on the right of minorities to be politically represented, for example, based on the conviction of the advocates of representation as 'standing for', that true representation should amount to an accurate reflection of the characteristics of the represented. Of interest for anti-racism is Pitkin's critique of this approach. Firstly, this type of descriptive representation is inadequate because it does not account for any type of action on behalf of the representative. This clearly conflicts with the view, of for example Mill, that while every citizen has the right to representation, this does not equal a 'right of decision'. When it comes to decision making and what Pitkin calls 'effective government' (ibid.:64), action is all-important and the principle of majority rule overrides the ideal of equal representation. Secondly, Pitkin points out that being representative does not necessarily imply accuracy of depiction. Linking back to my previous discussion of the limitations of visibility in anti-racist conceptions of representation, she notes that 'what is necessary to make a representation is not accuracy of depiction of something visible, but simply depiction of something visible, the intention to depict' (ibid.:67).

Therefore, representation as 'standing for' – be it descriptive or symbolic – requires neither that the represented be involved in decision making nor that they be accurately characterised in the representation. When transposed to the context of anti-racism, this critique is mirrored in two of its main problems of representation: the hegemony of principles and that of tokenism. The role played by tokenism within the representative structures of anti-racist organisations over time is significant for understanding how anti-racism becomes aware of the problematic nature of a representation that is denied the possibility of action.

Early purposefully anti-racist organisations, such as CARD in Britain, were plagued by the problem of tokenism. Often the 'white left' activists and intellectuals behind the will to create the first national anti-racist organisations were not completely aware of the tokenism involved in establishing an anti-racist organisation for the racialised to participate in that did not necessitate the latter's involvement in initiating it. Tokenism appeared at both the symbolic level and at the concrete level of individuals' involvement. The tokenism of symbols in anti-racism has often been linked to the attempt to embed – rather than ally – the struggle against racism within the class struggle or, more recently, within the anti-globalisation cause, at times simplistically conceptualised as the fight against American imperialism. For many black and 'minority ethnic' anti-racists the symbols of these generalised left-wing approaches were unable to represent the specificity of the oppression caused by racism. This is reflected in the following comment on organisations grounded in a 'race' and class perspective in Britain:

> They thought it was class, they put a political angle on it or a political stance in the society on 'race'. But you don't need politics to be a racist. You don't need to follow any political party, you just have to be uneducated and racist ... When they put a class slant on it or a political slant on it, you don't dilute the issue to make it less worthy. It's so much in the background it's not even worth going into it.

> A lot of black people and individuals joined these organisations because these organisations said that they work fighting against racism but that they didn't tell them at what level they were fighting racism or at what kind of stance or angle they were fighting it from.
>
> The 1990 Trust, UK

In the contemporary situation, we may see how several far left-wing organisations with an interest in anti-racism informed by their more general commitment to a wide range of radical political causes hinder the formation of alliances because of their concern with linking anti-racism to other ongoing campaigns. This is evident in the following account of the attempt to establish a national anti-racist network in Italy, hindered by the predefined agenda of several left-wing groups and social centres:

> I discovered after a year in the organisation that there is a formal structure that legitimates the decisions taken by a smaller group of people – no more than eight – and of this, six out of the eight come out of the former militants of one of the old splinter groups of the Left. In Florence here, one of the groups who had participated in the 1995 attempt to set up a national network was a group known as *Socialismo Rivoluzionario*, and when we finally set up the National Commission in Naples in October 1995, we set up a formal structure, a national anti-racist network, this group refused to join it because on that occasion, the campaign on demilitarisation was abandoned and they didn't like it together with other groups, they call them *centri sociali*. They decided they were not going to join the national network. They founded a second one called the *Tre febbraio*. The *Tre febbraio*, I read in the papers some weeks ago that they have set up a trade union of immigrants.
>
> COSPE, Italy

The above situation is characteristic of a form of tokenism, displayed by the emphasis on symbols that do not originate within anti-racism but are harnessed to it, that in fact tokenises the anti-racist cause as a whole. Anti-racism is no longer an end in itself but becomes a means towards the achievement of what is perceived to be a more wide-reaching, revolutionary goal. The following comment describes the means used to tokenistically 'include' immigrants and to establish an organisation that is outwardly representative of their concerns:

> We have a very active group – the *centri sociali*. What happens is that they will organise a party, a dinner which many immigrants will attend. They'll make a list of participants at the party and these participants will become members and supporters of the anti-racist organisation *Tre febbraio*.
>
> COSPE, Italy

A second form of tokenism, usually attributable to organisations with a specifically anti-racist remit, is characteristic of the descriptive representation in Pitkin's account. In the terms of her treatment of visibility, those concerned by racism are 'depicted', with the emphasis having been placed on intention rather than accuracy. When this is coupled with the preclusion of the possibility to take action in 'standing for' representation, the relevance to anti-racism is acute: variants of anti-racism have given, and in some situations continue to give more weight to their intention to give the racialised visibility than to involving them in action against racism. This is particularly problematic in the relationship of trade unions, political parties or social centres, with the contemporary organisations of asylum seekers, migrants and refugees. The tokenism of such encounters is related in the following description of the British situation and compared to situations in which successful autonomous action has been taken by new immigrants to Europe themselves:

> Here when they bring asylum seekers to speak they usually get them to speak about their bad experiences at home and how they became asylum seekers ... They're not recognised as a political force here. And I think that needs changing. Because that worked very well in Germany and in France with the *sans-papiers*. So in that sense having refugees and asylum seekers and immigrants

> confronting the issue as a force, as a political force, to become a legitimate partner in the debate. This is what I seek for all immigrants and refugees, not only for myself. This is my first experience as a token voice, an alternative voice.
>
> NCADC, UK

This form of tokenism seeks the visibility of the racialised purely as victims of racism, without a concomitant recognition of the sophisticated strategies they develop independently of the 'support' of organisations which see themselves as standing in solidarity with immigrants. But as Madjiguène Cissé, a spokesperson of the Saint Bernard Collective of the *Sans-papiers*, in her book on the movement's experience, remarks in reaction to the many French anti-racist and left-wing groups who sought to appropriate it, 'Those of us who manage to arrive in Europe generally have a real history of struggle under our belts' (Cissé 1999:175).

Representation as 'acting for'

To what extent can adding the dimension of action to the concept of representation go towards redressing the failure of descriptive or symbolic representation, to use Pitkin's terms, and go beyond the tokenism clearly visible in several strands of anti-racism and inter-related politics? Representation as acting for, in Pitkin's account, differs from the classical Hobbesian theory of representation, in which the representative is authorised by a group to act on its behalf, and 'standing for' representation which fails to account for agency. It is defined as 'an acting for others, an activity on behalf of, in the interest of, as the agent of, someone else' (Pitkin 1967:113). The discussion of 'acting for' representation attempts to answer the question of what the act entails. Clearly, what is of most importance is how well the representative, through actions, 'acts to further the objectives of those he represents' (ibid.:116). 'Acting for' representation is relevant for anti-racism because it refers to the agency of some 'on behalf of' (ibid.:117) others. For Pitkin, the reference to agency suggests that the action involved in representation is not autonomous but entails acting 'in place' (ibid.:119) of another.

Representing as 'acting for' has been a major feature of anti-racist action, most clearly evident in the type of solidaristic organisations accounted for in Chapter 2, and the paternalism resultant from speaking on behalf of the victims of racism. Because of the action entailed, this form of representation is more problematic than 'standing for' which, as either a principle or a symbolism, does not involve participation in decision making, the criterion Pitkin employs to distinguish between the two. Decisions that are taken, affecting anti-racist strategy and the formulation of an organisation's discourse, in which the actual or potential victims of racism have played no part may not be said to characterise Pitkin's description of this form of representation as 'acting "as they would have themselves" ' (Pitkin 1967:119). Often in anti-racism, representation has been constructed on the basis of assumptions by white anti-racists, made without consulting the populations whose interests they feel themselves to be representing. Such assumptions have been coupled with reasonings that constructed the racialised as either too inexperienced or too fearful to express themselves. Such reasonings were nevertheless an improvement on those of the far Left for whom black people's failure to join the class struggle was symbolic of 'false consciousness', so that their true interests had to be given voice.

An anti-racism that speaks on behalf of the victims of racism is clearly evident in the contemporary Irish situation, dominated by the community development approach discussed in Chapter 3. The approach, initiated in the work with Travellers and extended to refugee and migrant groups, such as the Bosnian community, is constructed upon the notion of partnership between settled and Traveller people or more generally, to use the terminology of its advocates, between 'majority' and 'minority' populations. As I have shown, such partnerships have generally been balanced in favour of the 'majority' members of the organisation. Arguments made by the creators and supporters of the partnership idea rely on the supposition that the education denied to Travellers, as well as the intolerance against them in the public sphere, necessitate an initiation period in which negotiations over funding and representation at institutional meetings for example, are undertaken by their 'settled' supporters. Nevertheless, despite the increased visibility of several members of the various Traveller organisations at national and international meetings as spokespersons, this fact belies the failure of the advocates of community development to relinquish their power as a function of the increased competency of those they work on behalf of. This was revealed in an interview with the Bosnian coordinator of the Bosnian Community's women's project, *Žena*, in Dublin:

> Most of the time it's actually Irish people who are running refugee projects ... Most of the time you'll have refugees say working in a project as part time or very smaller positions only to give those projects credibility but they are not given themselves a chance. And very often the argument is that there aren't educated refugees around which is a not good argument because there are plenty with university degrees and experience.
>
> *Žena* Project, Ireland

Attempts to represent racialised groups, by speaking on their behalf, have also been made by anti-racist and other progressive groups in reaction to the former's self-organisation. This was particularly obvious in the case of the *Sans-papiers* movement in France whose spontaneous and autonomous action engendered a series of attempts of appropriation on behalf of the established French 'majoritarian' groups:

> When they did that, immediately all the organisations in existence – and particularly the anti-racist organisations – came to the church, to Saint-Ambroise, and wanted more or less to take control. And it didn't work because, precisely, what the *sans-papiers* have always insisted on since the beginning was the autonomy of their movement. That is to say, the fact that the movement should not be controlled by ... What the organisations said when they came to the church, they said, 'we, we have experience, we know the French legal system with regards to foreigners and so on. So, we're going to help you to prepare your dossiers.'
>
> *Sans-papiers*, France

The most revealing part of this statement is that the French organisations felt a need to take control of the *sans-papiers'* action because of their longer experience. This relates clearly to the positioning of anti-racisms in relation to public political culture in the following way: Firstly, as Cissé (1999) makes clear, the existing organisations assumed that the *sans-papiers'* main concern was to obtain the papers necessary for them to stay in France and that, therefore, they should not draw attention to themselves. On the contrary, Cissé (ibid.:175) remarks, 'the movement was begun by the *sans-papiers* themselves, who did not want to listen to those who advised them to entrust them with their dossiers and to go and wait at home'. The organisation's assumption reveals an uneasiness about non-citizens independently taking highly visible, politicised action that directly challenges implicit understandings of nationally defined rights of political participation.

Secondly, Cissé claims that 'this desire to control, to speak instead of the people actually concerned, to relegate the *sans-papiers* to second class, grew with the return of the Left to power' (Cissé 1999:177). Those of the *sans-papiers'* supporters close to the Socialist Party no longer saw their support as being due to their belief in the progressiveness of their party, another facet of proximity to public political culture: that which sees egalitarian principles as central to government by the Left. With the Socialists in power, the organisations and the parties themselves pressured the *sans-papiers*, if it insisted on remaining autonomous and continuing its action, to organise itself in a traditionally recognisable form that they felt would facilitate communication. On the contrary, the establishment of a national coordination of *Sans-papiers*, by removing its spontaneity, is described by Cissé as a compromise and by one of its principal supporters as having resulted in the reduced efficiency of the movement. Therefore, although those who wished to 'act for' the *sans-papiers* never quite managed to do so, the imposition of a formalised structure on what was 'precisely the opposite of an organisation. It's first of all an event.' (*Sans-papiers*, France), led to a reduction in its autonomy:

I think that when the *sans-papiers* are less efficient is exactly when they begin to organise. And I think that was quite clear with the National Coordination of the *Sans-papiers* because all the French political or associative organisations – anti-racist – have always demanded to have an interlocutor representing the *sans-papiers*. They didn't want to work with small groups, collectives you see, that were very badly defined. They wanted a general representative

> of the *sans-papiers* in France. So the organisations encouraged the
> *sans-papiers* to create this national coordination. The problem is
> only that now that we have a National Coordination of the *Sans-papiers*, the more organised and institutionalised it has become, the
> less efficient and representative it is too ... So, as soon as they
> wanted to organise with a single representative that caused prob-
> lems and I think that where they are really efficient is precisely
> when it is spontaneous, when it's in a particular place, that there
> are too many problems and that people decide at that moment to
> regroup and take action.
>
> *Sans-papiers*, France

The implication that the movement's formalisation and institutionalisation led to it being less representative is indicative of the
inability of 'acting for' representation, even among individuals and
groups with shared interests, to truly reflect the needs and wishes of
those it seeks to represent. The installation of a national coordination of the *sans-papiers*, above the myriad of localised collectives
throughout France has led to several of the latter splintering off
from the official national movement and organising independently.
Such is the case of the *Maison des ensembles*, a collective of 300
sans-papiers men:

> You have collectives who don't identify themselves with the
> National Coordination or, in any case, if they identify with it they
> don't care, it's not their problem. For example, one of the collec-
> tives that has been mentioned recently is the *Maison des ensembles*,
> which is in Paris in the 10th district, where there are around 200 or
> a little more *sans-papiers* who have installed themselves, who sleep
> there, who created a collective. But they don't want contact with
> the National Coordination of the *Sans-papiers* for example.
>
> *Sans-papiers*, France

Self-determination: representation as 'acting as'
Hannah Pitkin herself does not provide an alternative to the two
possible forms of political representation she proposes: 'standing

for' or 'acting for' representation. Nevertheless, the means she uses to conceptualise these types of political representation may be carried through into a third possible formulation, specific to self-organised anti-racism, that I would like to call 'acting as' representation. Pitkin does not foresee the possibility of this last formulation of representation because her perspective, based upon the study of elected representatives, creates a natural distinction between the representative and the represented. No matter to what extent the interests of the two may be shared, the representative is the one who acts because she has more competency to do so, on the grounds both of objective criteria such as experience or skills, but also of her privileged positioning vis-à-vis the political system of representation. In the domain of anti-racism, however, as the case of the *Sans-papiers* reveals most clearly, the gap between representative and represented is initially insignificant due to the situation faced by both; that of being *sans-papiers*. We have seen that 'standing for' representation in anti-racism often affords the racialised visibility but denies them the possibility of participating in decision making. Indeed, anti-racism as a cause may, as a whole, become symbolic of struggles conceived of at a more generalised level. Representation as 'acting for' has often not even entailed visibility, preferring to act on behalf, often of a public of whom the group acting has no personal knowledge. When the victims of racism are seen to be acting for themselves, the impetus to 'speak on behalf of', through the declaration of its superior competencies, implies that political participation is determined by membership of the (national) public sphere, dependent on knowledge of the system – or, in my terms, familiarity with public political culture – and, thus, not immediately open to the non-inducted.

Under what circumstances have certain strands of anti-racism been able to rupture the boundaries of possibility, to determine strategy and politicise their action? What precisely does Fanon's prescription of the necessity of visibility coupled with self-determination imply for the case of anti-racism? Before attempting to answer, I first want to argue that, although writings on black emancipation and anti-colonial liberation lend valuable insights into the link between representation and power or powerlessness, they are not directly translatable to the case of anti-racism. This is because anti-racism, as distinguished from what I have called 'identity politics', and despite my critique of paternalist solidaristic or 'majoritarian' efforts, has not historically involved an either/or relationship between 'white' and 'black' styles. To be sure, anti-racism has been confounded by identity politics and even separatism. However, in Europe, despite the important influence of US developments on Britain in particular, its allegiances have always been more complex.

What, therefore, can be characterised as 'acting as' representation in anti-racism? Three levels may be identified, only one of which can be seen as self-determinant in the sense implied by Fanon. Each of these levels reveal the complexity involved in the defining of an anti-racist and, on the basis of such, determining with whom the right of representation lies. This problem relates also to the further question of whether anti-racism – as opposed to community politics for example – involves the self-representation of the racialised, or whether it more simply involves the representation of anti-racists and their beliefs writ large. I have tended to state that anti-racism should reflect the experiences of the actual or the potential victims of racism as a more precise formulation. However, this, as we have seen, clearly conflicts with a 'majoritarian' approach according to which 'The victims concerned are not the essential part of the activist force' (*SOS Racisme*, France). In light of this problem, it is clear that, in anti-racism, representation as 'acting as' may, in some instances, have more in common with 'standing for' representation than with Fanonian ideals of self-determination.

The first level, in which the above problem is most clearly the case, is best exemplified by the 'majoritarian' anti-racism discussed extensively in the previous chapter. The emphasis placed on the ability to generalise the anti-racist message, to popularise it in public opinion, beyond the limited concerns of those affected by racism, means that the issue of *who* represents is considered unimportant. For *SOS Racisme* the fact that today the organisation is said to be made up of 'three-quarters blacks and beurs' (*SOS Racisme*, France) is seen as merely reflective of the general situation of politically motivated youth in France:

> Today, the activist school-going youth will be three-quarters black and *beur*. So *SOS Racisme* is going to be three-quarters black and *beur*. Let's say that in the composition of our leaders it's more or less that but it could be three-quarters, it could be 50 per cent ...
>
> *SOS Racisme*, France

What is deemed to be of greater importance is that representation be adequately reflective of the interests of the organisation, along the lines of the criterion of 'accurate depiction' in Pitkin's account of 'standing for' representation. Secondly, representatives should be appointed on the basis of merit and not on the grounds of experience. The importance placed on this principle can be seen in *SOS Racisme's* construction of its ideals in opposition to those of the British anti-racist organisations with which it has had contact:

> *SOS Racisme*, at national level like at local level, it is the force of conviction of the people that creates their responsibility, the strength of engagement and people's efficiency. I argued with the English because they said that some guy didn't have the right to answer because he wasn't black. I said 'Wait, do you hear all the stupid things he's saying, the one who's black?' Between a guy who only talks rubbish, who defends the small minority of rich blacks and a white person who is going to say, 'I think that everyone has the right to everything,' excuse me but I prefer the white person, even if he hasn't personally been a victim. But at least he's not just watching his own back, he's not there for his own self-interest. We are very realistic. People are responsible as a function of their work and not as a function of the colour of their skin. Malek is President because he's the best.
>
> *SOS Racisme*, France

Indeed, the contrast between a meritocratic approach and one which emphasises 'a principle of black representation' (NAAR, UK) is often perceived as being a matter of national divergence, mainly British and French. Nonetheless, as my discussion of 'majoritarianism' and anti-fascism revealed, these differences are rather born of the more complex understandings established by varieties of anti-racism of the elements of public political culture – most notably egalitarianism in this instance – which it upholds as part of its action:

> At the founding conference of the European Network, Britain as usual had been the people who had fought quite hard for a principle of,

we would say black but that's not the common terminology in Europe – but a principle of black representation, ethnic minorities and those that directly experience racism, that's the form they adopted in the end on the NAAR committee. And there are two reps in each EU country and we said one – at least one – must be from a minority community which was fought against so violently by some people particularly the French, the Danish and one or two others. They just wouldn't have it and then even when it was adopted constitutionally they still elected two white people.

NAAR, UK

The result of this account – the election of two white representatives – is indicative of the way in which 'acting as' representation is formulated by 'majoritarian' anti-racists, with the importance placed on merit-based representation as the most viable means to adequately put forward anti-racist demands. This ideal clearly practices anti-racism as 'acting as' by interpreting the act of representation in anti-racism as adequately reflecting its membership: all anti-racists, regardless, as the SOS representative puts it, of skin colour. The fact, however, that in the NAAR account, quality representation was equated with white representatives directly questions the extent to which skin colour may in fact, albeit unconsciously, be relevant for the political choices made.

Second-level 'acting as' representation may be thought of as a pragmatic strategy. I generally came across it in Ireland and Italy where anti-racism is a relatively new phenomenon, and where organisations dealt specifically with the rights of asylum seekers, migrants and refugees. As in the first level, pragmatic representatives 'act as' anti-racists and in this sense represent themselves as (mainly white) citizens concerned by the racism they witness against immigrants. The fundamental difference is that these activists seek neither to act for others, nor do they see the fact of their status as representatives as unproblematic. Nonetheless, while some express the difficulty of acting as anti-racists in the absence of a grounding in the experience of racism, they fail to problematise the lack of alliance with racialised groups in relation to their own action. This appeared to be the case of *La rete d'urgenza contro il razzismo*, a legal advocacy organisation for immigrants in Turin:

> We are Italian in the majority. The girl who works part-time here is Venezuelan and then the cultural mediators are foreigners ... But we are, yes, we are predominantly Italian ... It's a problem not to be able to involve foreigners because then, when we want to take action, because one side is the consultancy work, information, research, and that's ok, that is we can do it, but when we want to carry out an action it is difficult to do it if we are all Italians.
>
> *La rete d'urgenza contro il razzismo*, Italy

When asked why it was difficult to involve non-Italians, the answer was reflective of the belief among several anti-racists, either that the majority of new immigrants prioritise material needs over political involvement, or that intercommunal rifts make participation in anti-racist initiatives difficult for many immigrants. Both reasons given problematise the inaction of the immigrants without questioning the role of the organisation in either the problem or the solution:

> I think it is difficult to involve them because ... it may be that many people who are here in Italy as foreigners have problems to resolve, questions of mere material necessity, and so they have little time to become involved in political activities. And so I think that a main reason is that, then maybe also these same foreign communities are divided – that is not all foreigners – therefore the various communities are divided between themselves, so maybe Moroccans don't go where there are Albanians, and vice versa.
>
> *La rete d'urgenza contro il razzismo*, Italy

The activists of *La rete d'urgenza* recognise that their action, albeit of practical use to the immigrants who use their emergency hotline, cannot be representative of the latter's concerns. However, they have been unable to propose reasons for the lack of immigrant participation due to an inherent lack of dialogue between the organisation and the recipients of its services. This problem is more consciously approached by the Irish National Federation of Anti-Racist Campaigns (NFARC). Here the pragmatism of the 'acting as' representation of white anti-racists, representative of and responsible for only their own anti-racism, is clearly articulated, grounded in a more reflective reasoning than that of *La rete d'urgenza*:

> Quite aside from the fact that I think it is a very different scenario for someone who has arrived in Ireland as a refugee or an asylum seeker and then they subsequently, after probably a long disturbing process, successful or otherwise, at the end of it or still locked into it, for their concerns to be very personally focused and wanting to have a life and get on with that. So, it's very different for people like ourselves who are campaigning in a very different way. There's no threat to my position by doing this. I will not face a harsher interview in the Department of Justice than some people possibly have because of being vocal in their opposition to the policies of the government. I mean someone coming from an ethnic minority or asylum seekers background.
>
> NFARC, Ireland

In this account, the action taken by NFARC members, which includes protests at airports in attempts to physically stop deportations, is explained in pragmatic terms. The organisation holds that immediate action needs to be taken to draw attention to the gravity of governmental measures against asylum seekers and immigrants. Such action cannot be taken by the latter, whose position is too fragile to risk exposure and arrest and must, therefore, be taken by those in the privileged position to do so, namely the country's white Irish citizens. The NFARC representative directly responds to the criticisms waged against the organisation as speaking on behalf of immigrants and asylum seekers rather than 'acting as' Irish anti-racists, aware of the problematised nature of their positioning:

> There were some who felt that we were doing an injustice by doing that. It took me a while to work out in my head but I still didn't feel

it was wrong. I'm aware of this great gulf that is there and I would love the day to come when all I would have to do was go out in support of the asylum seekers rather than us trying to think of what the fuck we're going to do. But I still think that, as an Irish person, I am perfectly entitled in my own right – or we are in our own right – to challenge policies of the Irish government which are enacted on our behalf. I am perfectly entitled to go out and voice a virulent opposition to that merely as an Irish person who is horrified that we should be going down that road.

NFARC, Ireland

Indeed, the current critical situation facing anti-racism in light of the consolidated European politics of anti-immigration has led to a renewed emphasis on the importance of this type of role, played by citizens on behalf of refugees, asylum seekers and immigrants. The British organisation NCADC emphasises that added to asylum seekers' personal involvement in the campaign against deportation, the visible involvement of British people is vital for fostering a sense of community and constructing networks of support on which asylum seekers can rely:

When members of the community, when British people get involved that makes the news. It's very important to show that these people have lives here, that they're not just passing through ... the whole point of showing support is that the local community, the host community gets involved. The neighbourhood, the churches, other parents in schools because when British people get involved they're crucial for the campaign because they know the system.

NCADC, UK

The third level at which 'acting as' representation is developed relates directly to the original questions posed as to the feasibility of Fanon's call for the necessity of black people's visibility and self-determination in the quest for emancipation. While anti-racism, even in its most radical forms, is not a synonym for black emancipation, the movement for racialised self-organisation has been fundamental to the growth of anti-racism as a political idea. It has also been one of the grounds upon which the attack on self-organised anti-racist strategies has been built by a 'majoritarian' anti-racism that seeks to uproot it from a basis in experience and abstract it to the level of universalist ideals. How then are principles of the self-representation of the racialised formulated in contemporary anti-racism? Firstly, the feeling is expressed that the involvement of racialised groups themselves, most notably asylum seekers and immigrants, is a necessity today. Such a view sees it as impossible to effectively run a campaign based purely on principles that depersonalise it, and ultimately disconnect it from the realities of the individuals concerned:

> They [asylum seekers] have to be involved; we cannot run a campaign for somebody. If they do not want to be involved, we don't have power of persuasion of another people. If you personally are affected and you don't want to do anything for yourself then how can you expect anybody else? That's one point of view. The other point is that it's important for them to get involved because it's very empowering. It's very healthy in terms of the state in which they are, so they should break ... And I know it's very difficult because people are very scared, they're being increasingly criminalised through the right-wing press in this country so it's very difficult for them but it's very important. Once when they face deportation many of them actually do get involved and prior to that they wouldn't because they have nothing to lose.
>
> NCADC, UK

This view is corroborated by the Newham Monitoring Project (NMP), whose work with the victims of racial and police harassment is motivated by a concern to involve those who seek their assistance in the decision-making process.

> We do talk on behalf of our cases but we're very careful not – when I say speak on behalf it's with the express permission. One of the things that we do through our case work at NMP is try to empower

> individuals to make decisions themselves, to take a stance. We offer advice but we don't make decisions for individuals. We help them with the decision-making process. What we do is we tend to empower individuals to get involved in campaigns. What NMP do is we show people that it's actually possible to do something about it.
>
> NMP, UK

Self-representation is, therefore, a fundamental means both of anchoring anti-racist campaigning in a personification of the victims of racism that incorporates that which Fanon calls the process of humanisation, and of empowering those affected to take action on their own behalf. Seen in such a way, we begin to see how the adherence of 'majoritarianism' to principles of public political culture is unable to adequately reflect what – in terms of the realities of the daily lives of individuals – localised anti-racism seeks to embody. Goldberg (1997) makes clear the problems involved in denying the racialised the possibility to independently generate their own principles by remarking that 'denied self-determination, denied the freedom to choose one's principles, one is denied self-definition and so the visibility self-definition makes possible and marks' (Goldberg 1997:101).

The failure to recognise the importance of 'acting as' representation for black and 'minority ethnic' groups is what has led to the current stalemate of local anti-racisms in Florence, where a 'majoritarian' left-wing political arena has failed to create meaningful alliances with anti-racist and migrants' organisations:

> If you speak to a couple of people in ARCI, they will say to you that I say that to be anti-racist it has to be black-led. That's not what I said. What I always told them is that they cannot call themselves an anti-racist organisation if there is no anti-racist dimension in their day-to-day work, in the way they function. Their method of organising what they call the anti-racist camping once a year, that does not in any way make ARCI an anti-racist organisation. One could argue exactly the opposite, because last time I was there the only few black people, apart from those who came from the UK and from other countries, the blacks living in the country they were

> only, or moving things from cars or cleaning and me and some-
> body else and that was that.
>
> > COSPE, Italy

Several interviews accounted for the development of self-representation by the racialised, as those best placed to reflect the experience of racism and, therefore, to build strategy to counter it. The growing acceptance of such, as a principle adopted by anti-racist organisations, albeit established by alliances of individuals from a range of backgrounds, is depicted as being grounded in a struggle against generalised approaches to anti-racist activism. NAAR locates the acceptance of 'black representation' in the campaign against the election of a British National Party member to the local council of the borough of Tower Hamlets in London in 1994. The attack on the local racialised communities in the area, mainly Bangladeshi, symbolised by the election necessitated, in NAAR's estimation, that the response come from those against whom the attack was waged, visibly backed by a wide alliance of supporters. However, this understanding was in fact shown to have been the product of two decades of the gradual acceptance of the role played by black British people in the organisation of their political demands:

> The role of the black community in fighting racism, black organi-
> sations in fighting racism had begun to filter through and was hav-
> ing an effect because you'd had changes in those organisations
> through the '80s – you know in the '80s the trade unions had
> largely established race committees, started to have race officers –
> so it was a growing understanding in those organisations of race
> issues and anti-discrimination issues so that had definitely been
> having an effect. So, those two things came together in a very
> broad movement where those organisations accepted and under-
> stood that they had to take the lead from the black communities
> and the black organisations, local community organisations in this
> case largely Bangladeshi. And that meant, for example, the TUC
> organised a demonstration in April 1994 which was the biggest
> anti-racism demonstration there probably has been in this country.

And even though it was the TUC who organised it, paid for it, you know got the TUC all round the country, trade unions paying for coaches and transport, they wanted the local Bangladeshi community and their organisations to actually lead the demonstration. So, the whole front part of the demonstration was led by black people although the main people from TUC were up there with them as well and so on. The local organisation that was really the leadership of that was something called Tower Hamlets Anti-Racist Committee.

NAAR, UK

The type of alliance described in the above is the result of decades of struggle, by racialised, politically organised groups, to claim ownership of the fight against racism. The ability of mainstream progressive organisations to recognise the self-representation of the actual and potential victims of racism as a principle and to adhere to it through their actions is born of a shift in the conceptualisation of the possibility of political participation and, thus, representation. It would be simple to depict attitudes of acceptance or denial of the importance of self-representation across the organisations interviewed as being merely due to the different national settings in which they operate. A national comparativist approach could argue for a fundamental difference in attitude to public political culture between France and Britain, most notably. However, examples of the *Mouvement beur* in 1980s France and today's *Sans-papiers* break the linear view of France as unerringly republican in the approach of its social movements to the relationship between their action and the public political culture espoused by the state. Similarly, British insistence on representation by the racialised, emerging as points of conflict in international settings, is indicative of the formulation of a 'national way of doing things' which is equally embedded in a variety of public political culture: the centrality of 'race relations' as an institution of British society.

Above all, representation in anti-racism is inextricable from the notion of possibility as it pertains to the accessibility of various groups and individuals to participate in processes of political deliberation, be they within the anti-racist arena or in the political sphere more generally. I have mapped the various means through which this possibility has been articulated in anti-racist discourse, demonstrating how the way in which the relationship to representation is expressed by different organisations indicates their positioning in terms of public political culture. The belief in the ability to 'stand for' anti-racist principles regardless of the individual's positioning in society is inextricably bound to a belief in the fundaments of public political culture in democracies, most notably those pertaining to liberty and equality; a vision which upholds colourblindness as a practice rather than an ideal. On the other hand, where the objective of what Patricia Williams (1997) has called a 'colour-blind future' is mismatched to the reality of racialised existence, self-representation becomes a key both to the formulation of an anti-racist strategy that is reflective of that existence and to the empowerment of those 'acting as' themselves.

In the remainder of the chapter, I shall further elucidate these tensions by examining the specific ways in which the key issue of representation is articulated, through the discourse and practice of organisations, in the relationship to experience, of the interaction with the local and national institutions of the state and through the choices to internationalise their activities or to remain on the local territory in which the politics of 'race' are most frequently played out.

KEEPING IT REAL: AUTHENTICITY OR EXPERIENCE?

[I]mages of past humiliations flickered through my head and I saw that they were more than separate experiences. They were me; they defined me. I was my experiences and my experiences were me, and no blind men, no matter how powerful they became, even if they conquered the world, could take that, or change one single itch, taunt, laugh, cry, scar, ache, rage or pain of it.

Ralph Ellison (1952:408–9).

The debate on representation in anti-racism, summed up by the question 'who says what for whom?', is epitomised by the relationship to experience expressed through the discourse and practices developed by diverse anti-racist organisations. As the discussion of representation as 'acting as' suggests, the importance placed on Fanonian visibility plus self-determination is dictated by the extent to which strands of anti-racism deem it necessary to ground their politics in the 'lived experience' (Fanon 1967) of the actual or potential victims of racism. The call for such self-representation, however, raises a key problem that has confounded students of the politics of 'race' and ethnicity more generally; that of the difference between a reified claim of authenticity and a grounded politics of experience. I shall argue that choices made in one or another direction are definitive of whether or not an activity can be named anti-racist. However, the extensive confusion between authenticity and experience in this domain (Taylor 1992) has conveniently led the defendants of a 'majoritarian' approach to label any discourse that resists colour-blindness as illegitimately 'communitarian'. Where can we draw the boundary to enable a more fruitful sociological account of anti-racisms that is nonetheless cognisant of the decades of struggle that have led both to the entrenchment of authenticity and the liberating possibilities of experience?

Taylor (1992) claims that the notion of self-determining freedom, as it is found in Rousseau, has often been confused with that of authenticity as the two have conceptually grown together in political philosophy. If we keep in mind that, in the way I am using it, self-determination is closely linked to a grounding in experience, it is possible to observe the growth of confusion between the two ideas. Paradoxically, in that authenticity is increasingly considered, in North American thought on multiculturalism, to contravene the ethics of liberty, it originated as a modern ideal of individual 'self-fulfilment or self-realisation' (ibid.:29). However, for Taylor, authenticity, pushed to extremes, embodies a subjectivism in which 'things have significance not of themselves but because people deem them to have it' (ibid.:36). This endows it with a strong degree of what Taylor calls 'soft relativism' and accounts for the contemporary understanding of authenticity as related to the valorisation of difference and the acceptance of diversity. Making the link to his later writing on multiculturalism, Taylor then relates authenticity to the importance placed on recognition. Whereas authenticity emerges as a lynchpin of modern individualism, it also proposes 'models of society' (ibid.:44) according to which the right to be oneself is proposed to be universal, based on the relativist dictum that 'no one has the right to criticise another's values' (ibid.:45). The obvious relation between authenticity and identity has further cemented the link with recognition according to which, as Taylor's (1994) argument also tells us, the refusal to recognise the identity of a group or individual can be a form of oppression.

Taylor separates between a culture and an ideal of authenticity. The first is almost narcissistic in its embracing of 'self-indulgence and egoism' (Taylor 1992:56); the second, more positively, works towards self-fulfillment as an ideal which may benefit society. However, in trying to understand the way in which authenticity has been applied to the discussion of anti-racism, it seems that Taylor wrongly interprets the relation between the first variant of authenticity and the notion of self-determination. He sees the latter as embodying a call for freedom that 'pushed to its limit, doesn't recognise any boundaries, anything given that I *have* to respect' (ibid.:68). In his chapter 'The Politics of Recognition' in *Multiculturalism* (1994) Taylor borrows his meaning of contemporary authenticity from Fanon's invocation of negritude. However, he misinterprets Fanon's highly ambivalent attitude to negritude which is aware of the reification that this claim to an authentic blackness implies. For Fanon, negritude is essentially a transitory stage of the process of decolonisation. In Taylor, it is a value to be pursued along the lines of a belief in the universal right to equal dignity. As Hesse (1999) demonstrates, Taylor's emphasis on a compatibility between the demand for the recognition of 'authentic identities' and the humanist notion of universal equality, belies the historical fact of the unevenness with which these rights are extended. According to Hesse, Taylor is reluctant to let go of the idea that universalism may be disconnected from the cultural and historical situatedness that gave it its hegemonic status in the hierarchy of political ideals. The failure to locate the historical and cultural origins of the universal ideal itself makes Taylor unable to conceive of the claim to authenticity as itself reessentialising an 'identity' once imposed by the colonial relationship and now constrained within a system of fixed positionings within the regime of equality.

Taylor's misinterpretation of Fanon's treatment of authenticity reveals his confusion between authenticity and self-determination. If the culture of authenticity is taken to imply a complete separation from the duties of life in society and, therefore – importantly for anti-racism – from cooperation with others beyond the self or the identitarian group, then it cannot be thought of in the same terms as those in which Fanon employs the concept of negritude. Therefore, while one may argue that claims to authenticity have at times been harnessed to the politics of anti-racism, these do not mirror other demands for the self-determination of anti-racist strategies by the racialised, based upon the primacy of their experience. Indeed Taylor, by initially pointing to the confusion between the two, ends up falling into his own trap by linking authenticity to (positive) self-fulfillment and self-determination to (negative) self-indulgence.

The exclusion of so-called 'communitarian' anti-racisms, seen as incapable of generalising their message beyond a particular 'minority ethnic' community is based on the negation of an imagined discourse of authenticity. The fear displayed by 'majoritarian' organisations of those who demand the right of the racialised to self-representation is related to the supposition that these demands reflect an unwillingness of such groups to cooperate according to the dictates of society, or in this case the anti-racist arena. While groups have, and some continue, to invoke separatism, such an operationalisation of authenticity cannot be categorised as anti-racism. Indeed, it is vital to clarify the differences between a truly anti-racist politics, initiated by racialised communities which, nonetheless, is not confined within their boundaries, and a politics of authenticity which seeks to preserve a traditional 'self', 'secure behind the closed shutters of black particularity while the storms rage outside' (Gilroy 1993:188). Gilroy (2000) furthermore introduces the notion of 'black fascism', pointing to the cooperation between black separatist groups and their white neofascist counterparts, citing African-American ultranationalist Osiris Akkebala's support for the British National Party. Despite the obvious differences between the mobilisation of racism involved in the politics of black and white fascism and the rage and mistrust that have often characterised anti-racist negotiations, but which have always been expressed as a negation of racism, the argument against authenticity has often been mobilised to deny the racialised inclusion in anti-racism. This was clearly the reaction in France to the *Mouvement beur*, one which, according to the French association for the development of intercultural relations (ADRI) has continued to be formative of anti-racist possibilities to date:

During the '80s there was a very strong mobilisation of young people of Maghrebi origin – which we called the *Mouvement beur* – that was founded upon the fight against racism. The problem is that in France these movements were not accepted in and of themselves ... There was a denial of public recognition of this anti-racist movement, founded on both strong political and cultural identities. The anti-racist arena today does not want to take up

> that process again. It is a process of openness towards a concept of anti-racism that in fact integrates the notion of French cultural diversity without being based on the mobilisation of people who are effectively discriminated victims of racism.
>
> ADRI, France

From a view of some of the writings influential upon the formulation of self-determinant anti-racist thought, we are able to further elucidate the nature of the confusion between authenticity and self-determination, and the reason why 'communitarianism', as it is also possible to label authenticity, has generated so much fear. In particular, it is by returning to Fanon that a solution to the problem may be proposed. Clearly Fanon has been misunderstood as much by some of those who sought to emulate him (the more radical black separatist groups of 1960s America in particular), as he has been by Taylor himself. Taylor sees Fanon's call for native violence in response to colonial domination, coupled with his mobilisation of the concept of negritude as proof of the latter's quest for authenticity and, ultimately, recognition. If we recall Goldberg's discussion of Fanon on visibility, it becomes clear that recognition is insufficient and that self-determination as self-fulfillment, as I have chosen to turn around Taylor's interpretation, should not be reliant on the view of the Other but wholly grounded in knowledge of self, only achievable through engagement with lived experience.

It is here that the true difference between authenticity and the politics of experience as the outcome of a self-determinant stance begins to become clear. Negritude, for Fanon, cannot be the embodiment of the strivings of the colonised because the consciousness of her blackness and its embracing as emblematic of her authenticity are brought about only in the antagonistic relationship with the colonised. As Fanon remarks in *Black Skin, White Masks* (1967:110), 'in the white world the man of colour encounters difficulties in the development of his bodily schema. Consciousness of the body is solely a negating activity. It is a third person consciousness.' This is echoed by Paul Gilroy in his discussion of the Africentric movement in which, he claims, the stress on black biological and cultural superiority that desperately allocated whites an inferior place betrayed it 'as merely another symptom of white supremacy's continuing power' (1993:191). What is much more important for Fanon is how negritude could be mobilised as 'a moment in the process of achieving absolute freedom, but not its force' (Judy 1996:64).

Reflecting on the importance Fanon places on experience,[1] it appears that the consciousness involved in negritude evolves 'with experience and is not a consciousness of experience' (Judy 1996:63; emphasis in original). The fight against oppression must therefore reflect the truth that is born of experience epitomised by Fanon's claim that 'the *fellah*, the unemployed man, the starving native do not lay claim to the truth; they do not *say* that they represent the truth, for they *are* the truth' (Fanon 1963:49; emphasis in original). The contrast between the truth of experience and claims to authenticity in the decolonising process is revealed in Fanon's attitude to the nationalist politicians, who 'make the people dream dreams' (ibid.:68). The subversion the leaders allude to in their speeches incites the masses still further when it employs a language of authenticity: 'and sometimes these politicians speak of 'We Negroes, we Arabs', and these terms which are so profoundly ambivalent take on during the colonial epoch a sacramental signification' (ibid.).

The ambivalence of the invocation of authentic we-ness epitomises the contrast Fanon continually draws between words and actions; or authentic ideals and lived experience. The primacy of the experience of suffering is also clear in the NMP's classification of their action. The 'community' referred to is the local area, populated by people from a diversity of backgrounds:

> NMP has always been at the forefront in East London and that's because we're a community-led organisation. So our work comes out of case work, our campaigns come out of case work, our case work comes out of attacks on the ground.
>
> NMP, UK

Similarly, the spontaneity with which the *sans-papiers* movement created itself, through the decision to occupy the Saint Ambroise church, is emblematic both of the extent of the desperation that enabled such radical action to be taken and the strength to do so, emerging from the shared experience of precariousness. The movement produced a blurring of the boundaries between the experience of daily living (in the churches) and strategic politics:

> It's spontaneous. It was born outside of any type of political or anti-racist organisation, it was born rather in the hostels for African workers, in particular in a hostel at Montreuil in the East of Paris where there are many Africans. And it's above all in these hostels that the idea of holding this sort of event was born, an event which was a little bit spectacular because as soon as you put 300 Africans with women, children and all that in a church in Paris, well, immediately everyone looks and asks questions.
>
> *Sans-papiers*, France

To develop his ideas about experience, Fanon drew on the existential philosophers Sartre and Merleau-Ponty (Macey 2000). Sartre's differentiation between reflective and prereflective consciousness appears to be at the nub of the dispute between authenticity and experience/self-determination. Prereflective conscious ness is embodied by the individual who claims to be denied choice in what she is or what she does. This is considered to be 'bad faith', a concept used by Sartre to encapsulate the notion of a lie to oneself which nonetheless 'implies in fact that the liar is in complete possession of the truth which he is hiding' (Sartre 2001:207). 'Bad faith' is seen as an evasion of the responsibility that comes with freedom (Priest in Sartre 2001) because the consciousness of the self is aware of living in bad faith, or ultimately, of living a lie (Sartre 2001). Prereflective consciousness is inextricable from the individual's attempt to construct an identity. The quest for authenticity is always built upon the search for an identity which the individual cannot find within herself, given that 'pre-reflective consciousness is a *nothingness*; it has no content but is simply a relationship to what is outside' (Craib 1998:35).

In contrast, reflective consciousness is based upon taking responsibility for one's place in the world and what one does with it (Craib 1998). This responsibility, which comes with the condemnation of persons to freedom and thus, to carrying the weight of the world on their shoulders (Sartre 2001), is born of the 'consciousness (of) being the incontestable author of an event or of an object' (ibid.:194). The individual's responsibility is both for the world and for himself, both of which he has created in that 'he is the one by whom it happens that there is a world; since he is the one who makes himself be' (ibid.). It is only through the consciousness of experience that we live truly, according to Sartre, in full responsibility to both ourselves and to the world. As Craib notes, the lack of responsibility involved in the prereflective attempt to construct one's social role, and thus avoid a true engagement with experience, is evident in the fact that 'identity politics are never as satisfying as they promise to be' (Craib 1998:34). The search for identity which is at the heart of the claim to authenticity is, for Sartre, ultimately impossible to achieve. This is made more concrete in Merleau-Ponty for whom consciousness becomes important in its interaction with the existing material world, a realm he calls the life-world. Consciousness for Fanon is activated in relation to lived experience and the nature of experience is qualified by the individual's positioning.

This point relates fundamentally to that made by standpoint theory (Calhoun 1995). The emphasis on standpoint, or the importance placed by Spivak on 'making visible the assignment of subject-positionings' (Scott 1992:33), does not propose an a priori access to knowledge that is open, prereflectively to some but not to others. Scott advocates caution in the recourse to the 'truth' of experience in the writing of history which must be accounted for in my separation of authenticity and lived experience, and which reveals the tendency to amalgamate them which dominates the literature. For Scott, references to the 'evidence of experience' (ibid.:25) which do not at the same time explore the conditions under which such experience has been constructed, notably the uneven relations of power which define the variable possibilities for action of women, blacks, gays and lesbians, reproduce the dominant idea that 'the facts of history speak for themselves' (ibid.). Experience is understood to be commensurate with the notion of 'full active awareness' (ibid.:27) which, in turn, equates it with 'authentic truth'. We can see here how authenticity and experience come to be considered as exchangeable concepts. In this form, 'authentic experience' 'naturalises categories such as man, woman, black, white, heterosexual, or homosexual by treating them as given characteristics of individuals' (ibid.).

In opposition to the essentialising of experiences to which their unproblematised usage gives rise, Scott advocates an historicisation of the process of experience which connects between words and things, or the way in which 'concepts and identities' (Scott 1992:33) have emerged and how they have been written about historically. Subjects have to be considered, not merely as existing 'out there', but as interacting with others and as agents of their experience. This, for Scott, means that they must be 'constituted discursively' (ibid.:34) in a way that also recognises the conflicts and contradictions among discursive systems. To do justice to experience and to separate it from the claim to authenticity, several narratives have to be used in parallel in order to reveal the complexity of experience and to deindividualise it in a way that is aware of the multiple processes that are enacted in the construction of the historical knowledge that is later presented as 'truth'.

When related back to anti-racism, it is clear that what is in fact a working through of the experience of racism in the praxis of the struggle against it, is interpreted by some as being an invocation of the superiority of prereflective or authentic identities in the determination of who has a right to speak about it. The confusion between reflective consciousness in such a situation, born of the responsibility to interpret the experiences lived (*vécues*) in the lifeworld, and prereflective assumptions of privileged knowledge is to a certain extent understandable. However, although authenticity, and specifically negritude, have been, as Fanon predicted they would be, vital in the construction of the racialised consciousness that was then able to build a response to racism, they have never stood for the whole story. Rather, disunities borne of the inability to overcome essential identities, on the one hand, or constructed images of the unicity of such imagined identities on the other, have most often resulted from a lack of dialogue. 'Majoritarian' or old 'white left' anti-racisms that bemoan the particularism of self-representative initiatives have been mainly to blame for the long periods of mistrust in anti-racist circles. Similarly, contemporary 'progressive' approaches, such as community development with its reification of 'minority' and 'majority' groups, risks reproducing such authenticities before the fact.

Speaking of the importance of an anti-racism that is grounded in experience but which rejects authenticity as bad faith should enable us to envisage the development of discourses and practices which deny the levity of abstracted 'majoritarian' principles without making anti-racism the exclusive domain of the victims of racism. On the contrary, the replacement of authenticity with a self-determining politics of experience may endow the racialised with the strength to work in alliance with supporters who are ready to listen to those experiences, to gain access to their 'truth' and to counter its implications. It is through the recounting of lived experience that this 'truth' is stripped of the uniqueness of authority critiqued by Scott and becomes instead a political tool that redresses the disguising of these other narratives, long obscured by generalist anti-racism.

SELLING OUT? CLAIMING RIGHTS OR ASSERTING INDEPENDENCE

If it is nevertheless true that the welfare state was intrinsically a national and social state (national *because* social, social *because* national), one might wonder whether the evolution of its crisis will not lead to an accentuation of this imbrication of the *national* and the *social*, which would end up in the (minimally viable) paradox of societies that are economically 'open' to the world, but that are 'closed' from the point of view of social rights and the organisation of citizenship.

Etienne Balibar (1994:208)

A second central tension in anti-racist interpretations of representation concerns relations between anti-racist organisations and the institutions of the state. The position taken, in varieties of anti-racist discourse, on issues of funding and interaction with state agencies at the level of service provision and policy making, further uncovers their location vis-à-vis public political culture, as it is embodied by these institutions. Differences between organisations on the nature of state–social movement interaction, often an important part of the discourse of organisations, may be conceptualised as either one of 'right' or as one of 'independence', although both engender a significant degree of ambiguity in the attitudes of individual organisations. The basic difference between the 'right' position and that of 'independence' can be quite neatly captured by an examination of the sources of financial support that sustain anti-racist work. A stance of 'right' is taken by organisations that regard receiving public funding as an entitlement due to them as citizens and tax payers. One of 'independence', on the other hand, argues that to be allocated state funding would deny organisations the ability to criticise state policy and practice. Furthermore, those holding this stance see the position of 'right' as one of hypocrisy which is counterproductive to the purported aim of anti-racism to expose the inadequate or directly inciteful nature of state practices in relation to racism. In return, advocates of the 'right' position distinguish between material support and their ability to critique state praxis, and indeed, sometimes mobilise such funds in the campaign against institutionalised racism.

The question of the source of material support for the practice of anti-racism is a tool for examining the wider implications of the development of an anti-racist discourse that regards racism as fundamentally shaped by the practices of the state or one which prioritises the singularity of events over an analysis of deep structures. The positioning of organisations with regard the racism of institutions is tied to the way in which they conceive of representation. Organisations that, by not seeking government funding, claim an independent stance vis-à-vis its various agencies also tend not to seek representation within state initiatives against racism at either local or national level. Others that, on the contrary, although pointing to the racially prejudiced nature of institutional practices, do not view the racism of institutions as structurally embedded, regard alliances with the state as important in bringing about changes in policy. Whereas the 'right' perspective often reduces racist policies to bad government, the 'independence' stance tends to see racism as transcending the practices of individual governments; rooted rather in the historical discrimination of the racialised in western states.

Beyond the specificity of the anti-racist domain, the cleavage between a position of 'right' and one of 'independence' must be seen in light of its wider social theoretical implications, namely in debates on the crisis of the welfare state. The holding of a position of 'right' or one of 'independence' goes towards empirically assessing the role of non-governmental organisations – in this instance anti-racist groups – in what Hardt and Negri (1994) have described as the subsumption of civil society under the state. Essentially, the insistence on a position of 'independence' from the state, which necessitates the search for alternative funding, is grounded in the realisation of the neoliberal state's increased reliance on the voluntary sector for the organisation of citizens' social needs that accompanies the collapse of the welfare state. Hardt and Negri (ibid.) oppose North American communitarian thinkers, such as Michael Walzer (1999), who argues for strong state intervention for the facilitation of an efficient civil society. Such proposals are made on ethical grounds that focus on the importance of civil society for solving problems once dealt with by the state. The role of the state, therefore, is to establish the conditions in which 'self-help' and 'mutual aid', to borrow Walzer's terms, among groups in society may emerge. His choice of such terminology, directly taken, in the US context, from the Black Power movement, clearly reveals the extent to which this discourse has been appropriated by the 'centre'. 'Civil society' loses significance because the resolution of social conflicts no longer requires mediation between polarised state, on the one hand, and society on the other, because 'civil society is absorbed in the state' (Hardt and Negri 2000:25).

Taking the ongoing crisis of the welfare state and the effects on civil society – or more specifically the domain of non-governmental organisations – into account, the distinction between a position of 'right' and one of 'independence' implies the following. Beyond the myriad of practicalities that engender the greater or lesser degrees of organisations' coinvolvement with state bodies, the taking of a principled stance of 'right' or one of 'independence' is dependent upon the image of the state constructed in the discourse of one or another organisation. Such an image is concomitantly formed by the view of public political culture formulated in that discourse. In other words, organisations that insist on their 'right' to accept government funding and/or to participate in state initiatives against racism develop a view of the state as neutral at a level beyond the specific practices of individual governments over time. For such organisations, the fact that they were not established by the state and are not ostensibly controlled by it is proof enough of their independence no matter the degree of interaction at the level of financing or decision making. On the other hand, those which maintain an autonomous stance do not see the state as a neutral interlocutor on issues of 'race'. The 'independence' stance tends to mobilise an historicisation of racism that places the state, rather than individual governments, at the centre: the primary locus for the production of bio-political control as it specifically shapes and perpetuates racialisation.

The position of 'right' as opposed to that of 'independence' is one of ambivalence because, unlike the latter, while insisting upon its rights, it maintains a discourse of autonomy from state control. Nevertheless, an examination of this discourse reveals that this control is epitomised rather by the behaviours of particular political parties, governments or individual agencies of state bureaucracy. The degree of autonomy is based on making precise political choices which relativise these organisations' claim to independence. For example, several organisations originating in specific migrant communities, such as the ATMF, insist upon their independence, both from the French state and from their countries of origin. Such a position indicates the stress placed by these organisations on the politicised – rather than the solely cultural – nature of their action, and on their concern for the recognition of their democratic and secular nature. They wish to be seen as respectful of French norms rather than those of North African states which contravene human rights:

> In Morocco, like in Algeria, like in Tunisia, political regimes are dictatorships. There were many human rights crimes in these countries and so ATMF has always denounced this state of affairs and it has also always been autonomous, independent whether that be in relation to the countries of origin but also towards the French state. ATMF, if you wished to define it, is a secular, democratic and autonomous association. We uphold these three characteristics that mark us out from other so-called communitarian associations or those based on immigration, because most often those associations are manipulated, either by the local collectivities where they are based or by the relationship with the consulates of their countries of origin. So, they don't have the right, the liberty to say what they want and to say what they think.
>
> ATMF, France

This stance indicates the extent to which independence may also be conceived of separately from the sources of financial support. In such analyses, the standpoint of independence is constructed in more abstract terms that distinguish between the possibility of being funded by and participating in state-sponsored bodies and, despite this, retaining independent political principles, grounded in the concerns of the association's membership. This interpretation leads the ATMF to describe its sources of funding as follows:

> Presently, we have the support of the local authorities, the regional councils, the town, the state, the police, the social welfare. So, all the institutional partners support one or other of ATMF's projects.
>
> ATMF, France

The position of the ATMF, as of several French organisations, is one of 'right' in terms of the dualistic relationship I want to describe here. Independence is conceptualised in the absence of a profound historicised account of the state's role in the promulgation of racism. Or, in the case of organisations such as the ATMF, where such analyses have taken place, they focus more heavily on the racism of the colonial regime in the country of origin without complementing it with one of the inequalities 'race' produces in the ex-colonialist metropolis. This is compatible with the difficulty with which the term 'racism' is used in the French public sphere, euphemistically referred to collectively as discriminations. This enables the stance of 'right' to be formulated as one which positions itself both within and without the state's relations to both racism and anti-racism. Racial discrimination at the level of the state, in education, service provision, policing and the like, is explained in terms of singular events, based on mistaken practices that, through the involvement of anti-racist organisations in policy making may be remedied over time. This is demonstrated by the ATMF's principal role in the local government's establishment of a consultative committee on the affairs of 'foreign residents':

> Here in Strasbourg particularly, the Consultative Council was created in '92 and then, in '97, a charter was signed with the Mayor of Strasbourg, Catherine Trautmann, who is now Minister of Culture. And this charter, article 7 for example, there is an article that says that the municipality will do all it can to support the participation of foreign residents in public life. Basing ourselves on this charter, which is a political advancement for the municipality, we are trying to make the articles of this charter concrete.
>
> ATMF, France

In such a way, independence as a value, conceived of in terms of the 'freedom of expression' granted by democracy, is provided for by a grounding in public political culture. *SOS Racisme* for example rejects the proposal that by accepting public funds it is in fact working in 'partnership' with the state. The organisation adopts a pragmatic approach to its financial relationship with the French public sector. Juxtaposed with my description of the 'majoritarianism' of

SOS, the belief that it has a right to receive public funds further elucidates the organisation's construction of its ideological role as one of returning France to the basic political principles of the Republic. Therefore, state praxis is completely severed from an historicised view of the development of republicanism as a domain from which the (non-white, non-male, non-French ...) Other has been systematically excluded (Balibar 1991a):

> We believe in public funds. It's not a question of partnerships, they like using that term partnership. I wouldn't use that term. I would say, here we are, there are public funds, I pay taxes. These public funds are there for such and such an activity. The activities paid for by the state are fulfilled either by public administration, or by local authorities, or by NGOs. We are an association like any other. We demand that these public funds be allocated to us, at either local or national level, if our activity is relevant to the public programme that was voted for.
>
> *SOS Racisme*, France

The space *SOS Racisme* claims to occupy vis-à-vis the French municipal and national authorities demonstrates its generalist stance. It describes its acceptance of public funds for projects which are 'relevant to the public programme' as compatible with its search for independent sources of income to fund campaigns that openly criticise government policy. The organisation aspires beyond connections with either particular communities and localities or a party, a government or the authorities of the state. Instead, it harnesses itself to principles with which neither side, nor the French population in general, can have any argument, thus legitimising all sources of material subsistence. Again, the search for alternative funds is a purely pragmatic choice:

> Now we are doing a membership drive in which people are going to have 20 francs a month withdrawn from their bank account that will be transferred to the organisation's account. It's because we want to acquire sufficient financial autonomy to carry out campaigns that the government won't subsidise.
>
> *SOS Racisme*, France

We may see the extent to which the discourse of 'right' as it is formulated by some anti-racists enters the larger debate on the interaction of state and civil society in light of the erosion of the welfare state. Whereas at a first glance it would appear that a belief in the right to public funding signals an organisation's strong support for the welfare state system, the alternative view (Hardt and Negri 1994) makes a different argument. A strong interaction between organisations and state bureaucracies leads the former, although perhaps unwittingly, to facilitate the work of the traditional welfare state and to gradually take over its functions. Organisations that view the acceptance of government funding as hypocritical pose the argument that any degree of dependency gradually furthers the subsumption of the non-governmental sector under the state, denying all possibility of critique and taking over the state's role of care for society.

SOS Racisme comments on its right to receive public funds as a non-governmental organisation, one of the legitimate recipients of these funds for the carrying out of 'public campaigns'. This conflicts significantly with the argument that views the public funding of NGOs by neoliberal governments to carry out functions that replace those traditionally performed by the state as indicative of the collusion of such organisations with this policy. Furthermore, it proposes that, by emphasising the organisation's status as a 'service provider', such a process fundamentally transforms the role of oppositional social movements. Rather than positively releasing society from the 'standardisation of social behaviour' (Wagner 1994:98) that the collectivist welfare state imposed, and increasing the freedom to choose, as the neoliberal agenda would have it, the transferral of duties from the state to the 'community' results in the imposition of further restrictions on the independence of the non-governmental sector. The enlarged role of the 'community' in the provision of services – from education and training to care for the elderly and the mentally ill – has led to their professionalisation. This means a curbing of the possibilities for critique and a distancing of these organisations from their roots in neighbourhoods and communities. This was particularly emphasised as a problem by CARF:

> Even though I wouldn't consider CARF as a voluntary sector organisation we would certainly link up with voluntary sector organisations and those groups are finding it very, very difficult, both under the Tories and under the present Labour, to actually keep having a

> campaigning role because what's happened is that the voluntary sector is increasingly being incorporated into services. When you've seen the decline of the welfare state and the cuts to the welfare state, the government are coopting the voluntary sector to be an arm of the welfare state. So, it's very difficult to campaign against racism because what you're doing is being told that you've got to service black communities because you're actually doing a welfare state role so all the groups are becoming welfare organisations now.
>
> CARF, UK

The increased professionalisation of the non-governmental sector is accompanied by its institutionalisation. In the current approach of European governments to the question of asylum and immigration this can be witnessed in the role envisaged by the British government in 1999 for organisations active in the domain:

> So, with the vouchers[2] and the hostels and all these new things that are being proposed they're saying that refugee networks can actually provide those services for the refugee groups. And those groups that get coopted are going to find it very difficult because they're going to have to work with the Home Office, with the government and it's going to raise all questions of confidentiality: how to best serve their clients when they're serving the government. So that is a big debate here.
>
> CARF, UK

For Shukra (1998), black radicalism in Britain has, to a large extent, been incorporated into the state. This is so due to a belief, brought about by the rise of a black professional class, that the state is no longer 'a source of repression and inequality but ... a vehicle of anti-racism' (ibid.:111). The effect on the politics of anti-racism, for Shukra, is that the insistence of black political leaders on official investigations and state compensation for racism has led to the view of the state as a neutral party. By encouraging victims to seek compensation through the judicial system, black leaders put the initiative for responding to racism in the state's hands. Furthermore, the tendency to view cases of racism, such as the deaths of black people in police custody or the detention of asylum seekers, as individual incidents does not allow for reflection on the reform of the system that permits racist practices to form.

In contrast to the voluntary mobilisation of 'unpaid campaigner[s]' (Shukra 1998:118) in the 1970s, Shukra claims that, by the 1990s, the black activist is 'typically a professional or politician who uses his or her job to contest racial discrimination at an attitudinal and institutional level, usually through the Labour Party, employers and the state rather than against them' (ibid.). This view is mirrored by CARF which stresses the importance, against the growing phenomenon of professionalised 'activism', of retaining a view on the everyday effects of racism on the racialised:

> The politics of the black communities isn't as one as it was in the 1970s where it was a race and a class politics; it was the struggle coming out of working-class black communities. Now it's very, very different and the political priorities of more middle-class organisations of immigrants if you like are not the political priorities necessarily of communities who are really at the bottom of society. So where a number of organisations – immigrant, black organisations – may be more concerned by looking at questions of equal opportunities, discrimination in careers we've always said that is not our level of interest; we are starting at what's happening at the bottom of society, we're starting at the shop keeper who's a victim of racial violence, you're talking about the young black man who's beaten up by the police. Those are our interests and we're not getting sidetracked into those other things and there are other groups who can do that anyway.
>
> CARF, UK

In Shukra's view, the recourse to the judiciary and to the formal mechanisms of the party system taken by contemporary black activists in Britain is indicative of their adoption of a relationship with the state that is conceived of in terms of 'right'. In this instance, it is manifested through the declaration of the right to involvement in decisions taken by the state that concern black people. For Shukra however, what may have begun as a process of empowerment has ended with the 'attempt to reconcile black power values with British institutions' (ibid.:119).

One crucial episode through which the debate about the institutionalisation of anti-racist politics may be observed is the campaign in the UK for the recognition of institutional racism. Although the notion of institutional racism was formulated by black and anti-racist organisations during the time of the Scarman inquiry into the Brixton uprisings in the early 1980s (Solomos 1999), it has principally come to the fore in light of the MacPherson report on the inquiry into the death of black teenager, Stephen Lawrence in 1993. As Solomos argues, the definition of institutional racism given in the report, by dwelling on 'unwitting prejudice' and 'racist stereotyping', is unable to encapsulate 'both the historical processes and the contemporary realities that shape relations between the police and black minority communities' (ibid.:3). Solomos wonders to what extent the imprecision of the report's definition[3] is due to the consultation of both official bodies, notably the Commission for Racial Equality and campaigners for the Lawrence family. Relating this to Shukra's comments, it may be the case that the weakness of the definition was resultant from the overemphasis of what he calls 'black political organisers' on 'showing people how to take their grievances through the courts' (Shukra 1998:118). This, he claims, is evidenced by the failure of the Lawrence family's private prosecution to bring about the condemnation of Stephen's killers in 1996.

The full extent of the tension between a position of 'right' and one of 'independence' with regard to the relations that anti-racist organisations develop with the agencies of the state is embodied by the question of institutional racism and the quest, in Britain, to remedy it. The quality of the difference that Shukra, albeit slightly crudely, makes between radical anti-racism and what he terms black 'perspectivism' is elaborated upon by a brief look at the approach taken by The 1990 Trust to institutional relations. The organisation, although not funded by the state, has been integral to several government-initiated campaigns on racism, including the MacPherson report:

> We were quite heavily involved in the Stephen Lawrence inquiry, where in fact the definition of institutional racism was actually born out of the definition we introduced to the inquiry.
>
> The 1990 Trust, UK

Beyond its role in the domain of anti-racism, the organisation focuses on increasing the representation of black people vis-à-vis the official structures of British society; representation, although grounded in the specificity of black experience, is conceptualised by the organisation in the formalistic terms introduced by Pitkin:

> The 1990 Trust was born out of the National Black Caucus and the information and policy unit and its objective was to increase the participation role of our communities – black communities. By the term 'black' I mean that generically to mean African, Asian and Caribbean people and the policy was to improve the access of our communities in all aspects of society whether that's in academic, political, economic whatever, where there's a lack of representation of black people.
>
> The 1990 Trust, UK

This position encapsulates the difficulty for organisations constructed upon the quest for political inclusion and representation in political decision making to take a wholly autonomous stance. The 1990 Trust appears to oscillate between asserting the need to influence policy making and acute wariness of the hidden agendas of those who seek to cooperate with it. It therefore emphasises communication with state institutions and sees its role as the representative of black communities for too long excluded from the decision making that concerns them:

> One of the things we do is to look at legislation and have a look at how things will affect our communities and then we can go to decision makers and tell them how it is going to affect our communities, are you going to do something about it or what can you do about it?
>
> The 1990 Trust, UK

On the other hand, it displays an awareness of too widely opening its alliance. The organisation's involvement with the private sector is motivated by an interest in reducing discrimination at the workplace but may expose it to the risk of manipulation. The characterisation of this fear demonstrates the ambivalent position that The 1990 Trust holds, between a discourse of 'right', based upon a quest to redress the exclusion of black people from the political sphere, and one of autonomy that remains fully aware of the dangers of 'being subsumed in [the] official mechanisms' of the state (Shukra 1998:118).

> If people who want to work with us will use us through whatever means, perhaps accessing our net for their own gain we're not going to allow them. If people are more philanthropic about it and want to help and have got money to help us with our cause then fair enough, we'll work with them but we're not going to let them exploit us because that's the exploitation of black people that goes back hundreds of years. We're not going to go back to the 19th century and start being used as puppets or as slaves.
>
> The 1990 Trust, UK

This ambivalence appears to mark many organisations central to anti-racism that concomitantly retain a strong commitment to a particular 'minority ethnic community'. The strength of Shukra's critique may therefore be tempered by a recognition of the internal pressures in several such organisations to get 'the best deal' for the community, an endeavour that may not allow for complete independence.

A stance of complete 'independence' is more easily taken by several of the anti-racist organisations based upon alliances of black and white people with a wide range of support from social forces, in particular, as we saw in the case of NAAR, trade unions, social centres or the smaller political parties. The principled choice of such a standpoint is grounded in a recognition of institutional racism that believes that 'you can't take money which is from the government and keep your independence because it becomes impossible to criticise national "race" policy or national asylum policy if you're taking money from the government that's creating the problem' (CARF, UK). This is echoed by Residents Against Racism which relies on donations rather than applying for public funds because:

> We feel that we would then be beholden to the state and we're crit-
> icising the state. We'd be against it because it's immigration
> authorities, customs who have impounded people's goods that
> were being imported, the Gardaí. It's state racism that Residents
> Against Racism ... that's our particular agenda because we feel that
> if racism is endorsed by the state it gives every petty little racist ...
> you know, they feel justified in the nasty things that they do.
>
> RAR, Ireland

The approach to the sources of funding is generally extended to
the issue of cooperation with state agencies, deemed to hinder the
independent mobilisation by anti-racists against governments'
operationalisation of the power of state racism. This is experienced
particularly strongly by groups protesting against immigration
policy:

> It's not that racism is a separate thing out there and then you have
> the anti-immigrant policies over here: the two are so closely con-
> nected because in order for a government to effect a policy of
> deportation or exclusion in effect, in order to effect a policy like that
> they cannot paint asylum seekers in Ireland in a very positive light
> because in order to deport them you must ensure that levels of pub-
> lic sympathy for them remain low. And the way that's achieved in
> my view is by presenting negative images of how much it's costing
> the state, that they're on the dole, they're spongers, in effect, and
> allowing all sorts of myths to emerge about how much more they're
> getting than, say, our socially deprived, indigenous Irish groups.
>
> NFARC, Ireland

The centrality of the 'independence' stance to organisations
established to monitor racial harassment, particularly that of the
police, such as the Newham Monitoring Project is embodied in the
organisation's belief that 'racism can only be altered by community
self-organisation and action' (NMP 1988:5). The efficiency of that

action precludes the need, in NMP's thought, for involvement in institutional arrangements. On the contrary, it believes that 'as a practical result of community action and campaigns, institutions and agencies have been forced to respond to racism and racist attacks in a serious, non-tokenistic way' (ibid.). The role of anti-racists, beyond the espousal of principled positions against discrimination, for the fair treatment of immigrants and for equality of rights, in finding solutions to problems faced on a daily basis by racialised individuals further highlights the choices involved in retaining a stance of complete independence. In the case of the monitoring of policing or that of other state institutions – housing, education, immigration etc. – what some see as their 'right' to participate in and shape decision making is rejected by others as hypocritical. This is so, not only because of the dependency generated by the acceptance of funds, as has already been made clear, but also because by cooperating with the state's agencies, anti-racist and other non-governmental organisations are increasingly coopted to fulfil the state's role; a role many anti-racists are determined not to succumb to:

> What we do is we don't sit on the police board. We refuse to do that. We don't work with the police. We never have police officers visiting our premises here. There is a conflict of interest. If we do go out on cases, interviews with the police etc., we'll do that outside. As a political organisation, our job is not to investigate a case of racial harassment on behalf of a case or on behalf of the police: it's the police's job to do that. So what we do is, we pressurise the police into doing what they should be doing and taking action they should be taking in the first instance. In terms of our involvement with the police, obviously there is a dialogue. There has to be a dialogue. I have to talk to police officers. And normally it's to make demands more than anything.
>
> NMP, UK

BRINGING IT ALL BACK HOME: LOCALISED OR GLOBALISED ANTI-RACISM?

Backyards are where grand narratives of race, nation and empire come down to earth, are relayed or contested in small talk, in nationalisms of the neighbourhood or racist rumour-mongering; here gossip gathers strength, and moral panics put down roots, cultural guerrilla wars are waged, and all kinds of personal negotiation and resistance flourish; across the backyard fence even public enemies can sometimes be private friends.

Phil Cohen (1998:12)

The physical location of anti-racist praxis in Europe, the arena in which it acts, takes on a rising significance with the concomitant consolidation of political Europe. However, anti-racism's awareness of the growth in importance of a transnational approach at the level of the European Union to issues that affect it profoundly, most notably immigration, has not brought about a greater level of effective cross-national cooperation. Although individual organisations express the importance of participating in Europe-wide initiatives, this may be motivated, as the Italian case testifies, by the need for external legitimation of a movement waning at the domestic level. Furthermore, beyond the international arrangements of the European institutions, anti-racist organisations have been both unable to access the increasingly globalised sphere of progressive politics and reluctant to privilege this new movement of 'counter-empire' (Hardt and Negri 2000) over a 'politics of location'.

Anti-racism thus occupies a compelling theoretical position, in light of contemporary scholarly and social movement trends, between two central domains of political engagement with transnational implications (Vertovec 1999): that of the 'ethnic diasporas' (ibid.) and that of the movement for a 'globalisation from below'. Seeing anti-racism as an alternative here may appear confusing both because most writers on the rise of the transnational movement against economic globalisation view diasporas and migrants as being central to it (cf. Mezzadra 2001) and because, often, no separation is made between the latter and anti-racism per se in this new body of thinking. The failure to draw such distinctions is the very reason for which it is probable that, for the time being at least, the three will remain quite separate. The discourse of organisations with regards the internationalisation of their action reveals both the nature of the actual possibilities open to anti-racist activists and, at the level of ideas, the problems attached to the equation of the ideal of anti-racism with that of contemporary anti-imperialism.

Before looking at the consequences of the anti-racist aspirations of the proponents of left-wing anti-globalisation, what possibilities does anti-racism have to develop its agenda beyond the national, and more often the very local, level? In the majority of cases, such opportunities have arisen due to the proliferation of structures established by the European institutions, most notably those that emerged from the 1997 EU Year Against Racism. Interestingly, several organisations that display a stance of autonomy vis-à-vis their own governments accept cooperation with institutions of the EU as legitimate, sending delegates to various meetings of the European Network Against Racism (ENAR) or similar bodies. This was recognised as problematic by CARF for example, which pointed to the depoliticised approach to anti-racism of the EU institutions, demonstrated by the restriction of their support to activities prioritising a culturalist approach to the problems posed by racism and by their unwillingness to include action on behalf of migrants and asylum seekers, non-citizens of the EU:

> They're [the EU] increasingly unwilling to fund anything that has to do with asylum seekers or people who would like citizenship rights which means that basically they are institutionalising, I think they're institutionalising racism in their funding policies because they're saying that we are only going to fund those people who are European, are European citizens.
>
> CARF, UK

Nevertheless, the opportunity to participate in initiatives such as ENAR was seen as an important means of widening the level of exchange with other European anti-racists, often while recognising the probable eventual inability of the body itself to impact upon European bureaucracy. This was noted by COSPE, the official Italian delegate to the ENAR, which also situated the importance of the experience gained from international encounters within a perspective upon the specific problems faced by non-majoritarian anti-racists in Italy:

> When more and more organisations get experience from other countries, in this case taking place through the European Network

> Against Racism sponsored by DGV [of the European Commission] then that doesn't change it, the learning process is still there, the exchange of experience is still there. It also brings closer the European dimension in this work.
>
> COSPE, Italy

The experience of meeting a British delegate at a European conference is seen as having been formative in questioning fixed notions of representativity held, according to COSPE, by many active Italian anti-racists:

> One of the most active people in anti-racism in this country, a woman from Pisa, when I first discussed with her the need for blacks to be, if not in the forefront of anti-racism then intimately involved in it, she didn't get it. When I met her two years later, I realised there had been a great change in her because she had meanwhile come in contact with Lee Jaspar somewhere in Sweden. She said, 'the British delegates, amongst them there was a black guy – he was really nuts, he was a racist.' I said, 'really, what did he say?' 'He stood up and questioned why in a conference like that called an anti-racist conference in Sweden, 95 per cent were white. Were black organisations invited? He challenged everything.'
>
> COSPE, Italy

Cross-national encounters are also initiated by organisations independently of such institutions. Several organisations recognise an importance in constructing a European approach to anti-racism in response to the Europeanisation of racism itself, both of the far Right and of the mainstream anti-immigrationism of EU governments:

> We try to get involved as much in Europe as possible. Even more so now because we have to get our foot into Europe. The fascists, the far Right have got a very strong hold in Europe.
>
> The 1990 Trust, UK

> We founded, with six European associations, the association Youth Against Racism with which we do some common projects in schools in the six countries. Last year together, we created a platform that we brought to the Amsterdam summit. We think that this European dimension is decisive, fundamental today. These years have contributed to making us take a step in the direction, of thinking of ourselves as a piece of the Italian anti-racist movement but also as a piece of the European anti-racist movement.
>
> ARCI, Italy

Beyond such principles of commitment, actual cross-national encounters are often marked by significant tension between national approaches to anti-racism. The example of NAAR's yearly participation in ARCI's international anti-racist meeting, for example, demonstrates the possibility of cross-national projects, conceived by organisations from highly diverse national anti-racist arenas, to strengthen a discourse of 'national ways of doing anti-racism'. The tension experienced by NAAR in this cooperative attempt results both in an insistence upon the supremacy of the 'ways of doing things' developed by British organisations and an historicisation of the reasons for these specificities in a comparative perspective:

> One of the things we were involved in was this Overcome Racism Now initiative which was done by ARCI which is an Italian operation. At the initial discussions into that it was almost impossible to engage with it because they wanted images of ... the use of the term immigrant which we don't use. We do not for example say that the Bangladeshi community is an immigrant community because most of them now have British passports and they're a black British ethnic minority community of Bangladeshi origin and to talk about them as immigrants sets the wrong framework. But secondly the kind of images, the kind of discussion ... their whole thing was to say people are making an exaggerated fuss about this because there are actually very tiny numbers of black people in these cities so they wanted the figures to show there's only really

> 2 per cent. I said, 'well, excuse me, you know in London there are 33–34 per cent black and ethnic minority people.' And our point is not that this is small, it's big and therefore London and government and London government have to change to reflect the reality of London not to try to push it into a corner.
>
> NAAR, UK

The self-reflection induced by these types of cross-border initiatives indicates the significance of references to different national societies which has long been a key feature of anti-racist discourse. As American and anti-colonial struggles served as formative points of reference in the construction of self-determinant anti-racism in the 1960s and 1970s, negative images exported by the media are mobilised to encourage the society in which the organisation is active to learn from the mistakes of others. Often the organisations that have recourse to cross-national examples are those that hold a weaker position within the national anti-racist domain, as in the case of the ATMF in France:

> Why are immigrants always confined in ghettos with housing conditions, education conditions, working conditions and so on that can only threaten social peace because at a certain moment there will be ... we haven't learnt the lesson of what has happened in the United States. Can you imagine if arms were sold in the supermarket like in the United States in France or in Italy?
>
> ATMF, France

On the other hand, cross-national dialogue may lead to the construction of the anti-racism of other national movements as wholly incompatible with one's own due to the proposed inadequacy of that country's policies on 'race'. This attitude, displayed by *SOS Racisme*, is indicative of that organisation's strong association of anti-racism with public political culture and its assumption therefore that, in the British case, state policies against racism must be reflective of the approach taken by anti-racist organisations:

> I went to discuss last weekend in Birmingham, in London over there. They're not there yet, they're still talking about intentions: we're going to guarantee that there will be larger proportions of immigrants in public services, larger proportions in the police etc. But everyone claims that it is not applied. There is a whole host of states that have taken decisions like that – the Netherlands, England etc. ... as they don't have the same culture in England and in Germany to be able to do something coherent. If we don't manage to have an understanding with the English and the Germans, we'll do it with the others.
>
> SOS Racisme, France

The evident tension produced by cross-national anti-racist exchange raises important questions regarding the location of anti-racism within the general sphere of progressive politics. Such questions concern both the physical location of anti-racist action – the sites in which it takes place and the events in reaction to which its discourse is elaborated – and its virtual location vis-à-vis the purported relevance of social movement politics on a globalised plane. Anti-racism is shaped profoundly by the space in which it evolves. Even those organisations active at a national level relate their discourse to the lived experiences of racism of the individual and mobilise an often sophisticated analysis of the conditions of racism engendered in neighbourhoods, schools or working environments structured by poverty and often violence.

This body of experience is also unquestionably urban in origin (Gilroy 1987) and sets the racialised subject against the backdrop of the city, divided as it is into localities, each with its own cultural distinctions (Brixton, La Goutte d'Or and, increasingly, Dublin's Parnell Street and the Roma Camps of Florence), and socioeconomic markings. The different rates at which these sites grow in importance as major locations for the acting out of anti-racism problematise the ability to find a common ground. The contrast drawn between Turin and Amsterdam in the following reveals the extent to which these two cities, for clear historical reasons, are incomparable in terms of anti-racist experience. The problem confronting communication thus goes beyond differences in the approach of individual organisations and instead is shaped by the vast contrasts between the two cities as tangible sites of anti-racist action:

> For European projects on occasion we have made contact with other associations in other countries ... It's quite difficult, especially with the Dutch organisation for example. Because, probably we didn't seem very professional to them and so there was a certain difficulty in cooperating, in the sense that probably they weren't very interested in what we do because it appeared to them as something that for them existed in the past but which couldn't offer them anything new. And on the other hand, for us the situation is so different ...
>
> *La rete d'urgenza contro il razzismo*, Italy

It is the centrality of 'place' to the evolution of an anti-racism grounded in a self-determinant politics of experience that sets it apart from both the 'old' New Social Movements and today's rising movement against globalisation. Clearly the diversity of anti-racism means that various organisations see their aims as more or less compatible with elements on the spectrum of such progressive politics. Several groups equate the set of political problems they seek to overcome with those indicated by the movement against economic globalisation, for example pro-immigration organisations such as NFARC:

> The script I suppose or our stated objectives to which all the groups subscribed were we take quite a radical position on immigration controls, i.e. we argue for their complete abolition. Now we haven't argued for their abolition unilaterally or that Ireland must do it in advance of everybody else. But our argument being really that in a world where it's becoming increasingly easier for capital and money, goods, services etc. to move in a virtually borderless world and at the same time becoming more and more difficult for people to actually cross frontiers.
>
> NFARC, Ireland

Nevertheless, such shared analyses have not generally furthered workable, long-term alliances due to experience-based anti-racism's attachment to physical space and the contrast this yields between a particularist grounding and one with determinedly universalist aspirations. The particularism of an anti-racism based on the experiences of the racialised seeks not to harness it to the ethnic, national or religious particularism often referred to in differentiations made between types of social movement. Particularism here may be thought of precisely in terms of the 'politics of place' which anti-racists evoke when they speak of the local community, meaning the area or neighbourhood. This community, as Back (1996) or Gilroy and Lawrence (1988) show us, yields the alliances between black and white working-class youth, that, despite cultural differences, mobilise shared lived experience as grounds for internal solidarity.

Anti-racism's ability to overcome the cultural cleavages of modern societies demarcates it, as we have seen, from the domain of identity politics. For the same reason, namely by operationalising a 'politics of place', neither can it be seen to easily fit the niche of globalised politics opened by the transnational 'ethnic diasporas'. Although Gilroy (1987) has proposed that black British culture, and particularly the anti-racism of young black Britons, is shaped by their belonging to a black diaspora, I want to argue that this means something very different than the notion of diaspora mobilised by contemporary students of transnationalism (Portes 1999; Vertovec 1999). Gilroy (1987:154) claims that, in Britain, the 'conversation over the meaning and significance of "race" ' is shaped by 'a history that shows the necessarily complex relationships which have existed between blacks and the cultural and political institutions of the white, urban, working-class communities that are transformed and reoriented by their presence' (ibid.:155).

Gilroy argues that the feelings evoked by belonging to the black diaspora do not inspire an 'aspiration to a homogeneous African culture' (Gilroy 1987:158). Rather, solidarity with Africans demonstrated most clearly in the opposition of European blacks to Apartheid, is evidence of the force of a shared burden of powerlessness. Citing Ralph Ellison, Gilroy reminds us that 'it is not culture which binds the people who are partially of African origin now scattered throughout the world but an identity of passions' (Ellison 1952; cited in Gilroy 1987:159). This empathy does not seek to uproot experience-based anti-racism from its base; it serves, on the contrary, as a symbol for home-grown anti-racism, the motivation to create a space for the racialised in Europe in the societies which, for most, are the only ones they know.

Vertovec (1999) argues that 'ethnic diasporas' are central to the notion of transnationalism, compounded by the ability of new information technologies to heighten the individual's awareness of her diasporic condition through communication with like others. What are known as the 'politics of homeland' are increasingly engaged in at the level of the transnational, mobilising the hyper-modern tools of the information superhighway to communicate their message to the globalised community of campaigners for whom such causes are an expression of the new anti-imperialism. However, as Vertovec also reminds us, the diasporic nature of the liberatory campaigns of such 'transnational ethnic communities', immigrants in other lands, does not vouch for their ability to over-come essentialisation. Appadurai (1995) describes such politics as the 'new patriotisms' (cf. Anthias 2002). If experienced-based anti-racism, as I argue, evolves out of a more complex series of ques-tionings regarding the position of the racialised in contemporary European societies, beyond the relationship with a purported home-land, then it cannot be expected to find its place at the 'global' level of politics, alongside the 'ethnic diasporas'. Although on the ground, the demands of Palestinians or Kurds may find resonance with the protagonists of anti-racism, as a movement, the objectives of a 'politics of homeland' which, by definition, set their sights else-where, conflict significantly with the diversified realities of those who, as Castles (1984) puts it, are 'here for good'.

On the other hand, neither may anti-racism easily access the cur-rently forming movement against globalisation, as has been evident from the experience of several of the organisations interviewed. This appears to be due to the operationalisation of a transnational or glob-alised conception of politics that abstracts them from the primary level of experience so central to anti-racist praxis. By equating anti-militarism with the struggle against neoliberal policy, the protection of the environment and the resistance to the 'imperialism' of the international institutions, the Global Justice Movement univer-salises the applicability of its discourse. While at a level of abstraction, these struggles are related, they cannot be so at the level of practical action. The tendency of the 'anti-globalisers', identifiable in Italy for example by the social forums, to collectivise these campaigns before enabling their internal consolidation is alienating of anti-racism. For example, the preparation by the organisers of the protests against the G8 meeting in Genoa in July 2001 of a pro-immigration demonstration involved only a small number of the immigrant groups active in the politics of anti-racism in Italy themselves.[4] Similarly, the failure of the 'migrants working group' established by the Florence Social Forum to increase the participation of migrants in it indicates the significant lack of dialogue between the established migrant organisations and the social forums.

The universalisation of the Social Forum's remit to include immigration and racism in the absence of the participation of the racialised and in denial of the preexistence of several effective organisations is further proof of the tensions engendered by such an approach. Uprooting such politics from the location in which they are grounded and attaching them, still at the level of the resolution of practical difficulties, to a discourse of global processes, is ultimately to suppress them before they have had the opportunity to develop. In the countries of Europe where immigration as a recent phenomenon is coupled with an anti-immigrationist politics of unprecedented vigour, the objectives of the anti-racism constructed by these new immigrants and their European supporters are firstly concerned with survival and resistance. The practical obstacles, of internal diversity and external stigmatisation, facing such groups in the effort to self-organise are explained by NCADC:

> Before it used to be benefit scroungers but now they're all illegal immigrants and the interchangeable use of the words 'illegal' and 'asylum seekers' confuses people all the time because the majority of people in this country, and I think in the rest of Europe, do not have any personal experience of refugees and asylum seekers and the only images that they get and perception and feeling that they form is through the mediation of the press ... So it's quite difficult for asylum seekers who are not an organic group, so we're not talking about a powerful, strong organic group with resources that can fight for itself. They are people who come from 120 different countries and speak the same number of languages and have most of the time nothing in common, in fact they have more differences among themselves than with the host community most of the time.
>
> NCADC, UK

The increasingly cross-national manifestations of globalisation 'from below' disable the participation of this new public, despite the fact that it is considered by its organisers as fundamental to its ideals of open borders for people rather than capital:

> We're not involved in European level things because most of our people can't travel, we don't have budget. For example, last year we wanted to send two people to Caravan but it turned out that Germany doesn't take these persons' travel documents.
>
> NCADC, UK

Dal Lago and Mezzadra (2002), two central figures in the Italian intellectual response to globalisation particularly concerned with migration embody the rapidity with which the movement for a 'globalisation from below' seeks to engender the 'migrant' as the symbol par excellence of its ideals. Evoking the culturalism of anti-immigrationist arguments, Dal Lago and Mezzadra (ibid.:153) point to the new migratory movement into Europe as symbolic of the universalism of the migrant as against 'western "racism", understood to be the politico-cultural expression of the material predominance of the more developed countries'. For these writers, the 'migrant' represents a new figure of the universal that poses a fundamental critique to the 'modern political project' (ibid.) and which resists its multiculturalisation in favour of an equality that supersedes 'difference'. For Dal Lago and Mezzadra, this still embryonic tendency is matched by what they think of as a movement of bottom-up globalisation and its emphasis on the displacement of localised conflicts in reaction to 'capitalistic globalisation' (ibid.:154).

For these writers, the displacement of the localised refers to the effort to connect local and global which seeks a common project of intellectual and activist resistance against a consolidated transnational counter-force: globalisation. Nevertheless, their failure to confront the immediacy of the extremely localised difficulties faced by the 'migrant' – conceptualised as a symbol or a movement rather than as an individual – and the negotiations which must take place at the level of the locality in the interests of survival is indicative of the failure of anti-racism to be fully included in the new politics they describe. Hardt and Negri (2000) call for the politicisation of what they call the 'mobile multitude', namely migrant workers and asylum seekers. Like Dal Lago and Mezzadra, these authors' fundamental concern with the effects of globalisation – or empire – views migrants as one of its principal victims, but also as a primary counter-force. For them, the 'multitude' is politicised when 'it begins to confront directly and with an adequate consciousness the central repressive operations of Empire' (Hardt and Negri 2000:399).

They give as an example of such a politicisation the demands of the *Sans-papiers* for *papiers pour tous*: 'residency papers for everyone means that all should have the full rights of citizenship in the country where they live and work' (Hardt and Negri 2000:400). It is also, if we recall the discussion earlier in this chapter, a struggle that was autonomously engaged in by *Sans-papiers* with assistance from supporters but without being subsumed under a wider movement simply because of the relevance to such of their demands. In sum, anti-racists, and above all migrants involved in the anti-racist project, recognise what Hardt and Negri call the 'repression and incessant territorial segmentations of Empire' (ibid.:399). This is evidenced in the following statements, each from refugees active in anti-racism in two different countries: France and Britain:

> Political dependency, economic dependency are in the hands of France and the other European countries that colonised Africa. As long as there is this notion of dependency, there will always be immigration. As long as we don't manage to develop a real policy of cooperation with Africa there will always be immigration.
>
> MDE, France
>
> That's basically what's happening here: it's globalisation. Globalisation is the polite term for colonisation, you know, imperialism. It's fine as long as it works for western government going and destroying the third world but when the third world comes and knocks on your door, either through human rights abuses or economic abuses …
>
> NCADC, UK

However, this shared recognition is insufficient for the construction of a homogeneous movement that, due to the greater resources – most crucially that of citizenship – accessible to the protagonists of anti-globalisation, may result in the subsumption of the myriad of causes it espouses under its overarching ideology of renewed universalism. NCADC recognises that, despite the great utility of uniting the various strands of progressive politics, it is difficult to achieve.

> Generally it's difficult to bring positive social and progressive social campaigns together because I think that Green people, you know environmentalists, as well as anti-racists and immigration campaigners they have loads in common. As well as the stability campaigners, human rights campaigners, AIDS campaigners.
>
> NCADC, UK

The inability to explain this difficulty is itself indicative of the lack of dialogue between anti-racists and 'anti-globalisers'; one apparently engendered by the constant strain on local anti-racist groups to merely respond to racism at neighbourhood level, leaving little opportunity for the mind to envisage a globalised future; seemingly, for the time being at least, so far removed from everyday realities:

> Because NMP's work is so localised ... we don't work around European issues. We have to keep our work localised. Because we're so short-staffed it's very difficult to work out of that remit. NMP will always be a localised group ... There are a lot of conferences by European organisations or national organisations and it's all about political discussion and intellectualism and not very real. That's what I mean about organisations being out of touch with reality. Until you do case work, until you work with the people on the ground, you're not aware of the intricacies of the problems that are faced by people on the ground.
>
> NMP, UK

CONCLUSION: THE POSSIBILITY OF ALLIANCE

I have proposed that anti-racism's ability to adequately reflect the lived experiences of the actual or potential victims of racism is crucial to the development of anti-racism in Europe. The history of the shift from solidarity-based, tokenist anti-racism to self-representation, however, is the history of only one end of our proposed continuum of proximity-to-distance from the public political culture of the nation-state. As has been made clear, the universalist aspirations of a significant body of anti-racist activists mobilise a colour-blind discourse that elevates the representation of the struggle against racism beyond the lived experience that Fanon (1967) stressed so strongly in his quest to rid black people of the effects of the processes of epidermilisation. The fears of 'majoritarian' anti-racism are that the linking of racism to experience will result in a politics of authenticity that denies the broadening of dialogue beyond what are seen as being the cultural enclaves of particularist 'minority ethnic' communities.

I have argued that, contrary to these fears, the prioritisation of lived experience over cultural essences has marked the anti-racist involvement of the racialised in Europe. Organisations based upon the experiences of the actual or potential victims of racism and, crucially, their supporters, often mobilise a questioning of public political culture that engenders a distance between anti-racism as a form of contestatory social movement politics and the state. I have proposed that, in light of the transformation of the notion of the role of such movements, brought about by the subsumption of civil society under the state, a stance of independence allows for the development of a critique that fundamentally questions the view of the state as a neutral interlocutor. The grounding in experience and the stress placed on autonomy are also reflective of 'non-majoritarian' anti-racism's insistence upon a politics of location. Beyond the material constraints that often restrict participation in transnational social movement arenas, anti-racism resists the elevation of its concerns to what is often perceived as being a level of abstraction that mobilises univeralist aspirations that fail to capture the uniqueness of the cosmopolitan localism into which the anti-racism I am describing taps.

Much of this, particularly the new activism of migrants, refugees and asylum seekers, is tentative and incomplete. To be sure, localised, experiential anti-racism must contend with the increased determinacy of 'identities' that proliferates communities and gives rise to 'minority ethnic' leaders that claim to speak on their behalf, an act of attempted homogenisation which rejects the diverse understandings of both culture and politics amongst 'members'. It is for this reason that the notion of alliance has emerged as fundamental to the anti-racist discourse I have examined in the course of the research. The importance of alliance building, between diverse organisations and racialised groups, may be traced back, particularly in the British context, to the identification of a crisis in anti-racism at the beginning of the 1990s. The crisis which both Taguieff and Gilroy identified as emerging in the course of the 1980s must be situated in the particularity of the rapidly changing political conditions brought about during that decade and the first half of the 1990s. The collapse of state socialism and the outpouring of ethnic determinism that ensued is undeniably connected to the identification of a neoracism which both writers see as to some degree responsible for the crisis in anti-racism, in particular due to its inability to find responses adequate to it. The predominance of culturalist perspectives engendered by the crisis in the Balkans most notably, gave more shape to the right-wing project to shift the attention away from biological hierarchy to the cultural incompatibilities brought about by immigration: it seemed to be borne out by the Soviet experience.

On the grounds of this acute preoccupation with cultural incompatibilities, anti-racism, confounded by significant problems of organisation and direction, was faced in the early 1990s with a rise in racism and, in particular, the growth of the far Right. Whether this was on a grand scale, as was the case in France with the rise of the *Front national*, or whether, as in Britain, events were rather more low-key is immaterial to the fact that it was perceived symbolically by the anti-racist movement. Moreover, the growing acceptability of Le Pen's politics, like for Haider in more recent times, was felt by anti-racists across Europe as being indicative of a growing European trend that could not but have an effect in other countries, due notably to the growing consolidation of a European far Right, not least within the European Parliament. The return of the far Right, absent from the political arena in any serious form since the late 1970s, was the impetus for a challenge from within the anti-racist movement in various European countries to the disunity which traditionally characterised it. In Britain, the trigger for this challenge was the 1993 election of a BNP member to the Tower Hamlets local council. The event later led to the birth of the National Assembly Against Racism:

We were actually formally established in, we began in 1994 ... And it developed out of the fact that at a by-election in Tower Hamlets which is the part of London that we're in, in September 1993 a candidate of the BNP got elected and a very broad campaign – community-led

> campaign – was established in Tower Hamlets. But it was an issue of such national significance that a wide range of national and non-Tower Hamlets organisations got involved in particular the TUC [Trades Union Congress] and the churches and lots of other kinds of organisations.
>
> NAAR, UK

The initial campaign against the BNP led to the planning of a national assembly against racism, an event bringing together a wide range of anti-racist organisations and others with shared objectives. The importance of creating alliances between organisations is seen by NAAR as superseding the disunities that continue to divide strands of anti-racism. Such a view promotes a pragmatic approach to anti-racist practice that attempts to counteract the perceived growth in the efficiency of the new Right:

> The anti-racist movement in this country – and I suspect across Europe – has tended to be very divided with different organisations reflecting different people's views about the relationship between race and class, whether or not they agree with black self-organisation, whether they think local campaigning is more important than national campaigning or whether they think that you should just fight the neo-Nazis or whether you have some broader agenda. So, our approach is very much, well these are all legitimate discussions in the anti-racist movement but the anti-racist movement ... and they should take place – but the anti-racist movement cannot be held up or divided from doing things – according to what your analysis is – of what the Labour government is doing with the Immigration and Asylum Bill, you have to if you agree that this is a racist piece of legislation, that it will whip up racism, then you have to build the broadest possible alliance on that basis and leave the discussion, for example, on what immigration policies should actually be to a different time.
>
> NAAR, UK

Nevertheless, the primacy of alliance building stressed by NAAR in the guise of a national movement is criticised by groups active at local level, such as the NMP. While the organisation does not resist alliances, it insists on the prioritisation of local work and points to the distancing of the protagonists of a national movement from what it thinks of as the daily realities of 'race' politics:

> We're a localised organisation but we have wider alliances: we have alliances with the Monitoring Group, we have alliances with NAAR, we know all of these people and we support those organisations as well. But we do localised work.
>
> NMP, UK
>
> Obviously we are involved in national issues but our work is so localised and it's very important that it is, it's grassroots work. We do contribute, we do make criticisms of policy etc. etc., we have our opinions but we're not policy makers. We change things on the ground for people on the ground. There are a lot of anti-racist organisations who are really out of touch with the realities of what is going on because they don't do case work and they're not a grassroots organisation, it's as simple as that. The only people who are really going to know what's happening on the ground are people who work for grassroots organisations.
>
> NMP, UK

In contrast, not all organisations believe that the degree of unity is sufficient. This is particularly the case for those such as NCADC, a new face of anti-racist activism in need both of the support of established organisations and of a link between its activism and a wider sphere of progressive politics, beyond strict anti-racism:

> It's important to join all the forces. At the moment it's very difficult because all the organisations are quite small, under-resourced, fighting in their own little backwater. I think there's a lack of unanimous cry, a lack of a united front because of the way people are working ... To get that strong alliance, we need to have a strong movement.
>
> NCADC, UK

The increase of alliance building as a general reaction to the crisis in anti-racism of the early 1990s is undeniable. Nevertheless, there is a tendency for the issues around which such unity is called upon to reflect the traditional interests of anti-racism without wholly taking stock of the profound changes in racism since the identification of the crisis. As we saw in Chapter 3's analysis of French anti-racism, organisations in that country were quick to unite in reaction to antisemitism but remained divided over the *'foulard* affair'. Similarly, following the initial success of the *Sans-papiers* movement which, by occupying the churches, mobilised the ensemble of the French progressive sphere, its consolidation and the amnesty awarded the movement's main protagonists led to a cooling of interest from mainstream anti-racist organisations. Throughout Europe, particularly in light of the advent of the West's 'war on terrorism', several organisations, notably the Institute of Race Relations in Britain, have noted the threat posed by Islamophobia. In light of the Afghan and Iraq wars, this issue is today posing itself as one of potential divisiveness amongst anti-racists, some of whom mobilise a simplistic separation between faithfulness to the memory of antisemitism and to the general rejection of any form of racism.

As noted by *SOS Racisme*, 'We have to organise common actions to increase the movement's strength ...'. Nonetheless, the heterogeneous nature of anti-racism revealed in this study may question the possibility for anti-racism to, in real terms, embody a movement at either national or international levels. The alliances stressed by anti-racist organisations may be more modestly activated at the level of specific campaigns rather than engendering the creation of a viable anti-racist movement with a united approach, a future that, it appears, would be unrealistic to predict. On the contrary, the lack of homogeneity characteristic of anti-racist politics reflects the importance of the ongoing struggle internal to anti-racism; a struggle of impulses to institutionalisation against those of autonomy, of culturalisation against politicisation and of generalisation over localisation. In sum, such tensions remain the product of the continuum along which anti-racism appears to organise itself, a diversity of approaches and political standpoints which, paradoxically, itself reflects the 'universalisation' of racism as a problem against which a wide range of political and social groupings feel it right to take action, in turn dictating the possible degree of lived experience shaping the varieties of anti-racism it produces.

Conclusion
Anti-Racist Futures: A Sense of Déjà Vu or a Journey into the Unknown?

To meaningfully conclude this work, it is necessary to ask, firstly, what has been accomplished in its course to engender a more complete understanding of what is, ultimately, a much spoken-about but little studied phenomenon. Secondly, how it may help us to reflect upon the challenges facing anti-racism in the near future. My aim is not to repropose the prescriptions that have hindered a sociologically significant approach being taken to anti-racism to date. Rather, in light of the contemporary political atmosphere of increased antagonism against racialised outsiders described in the introduction, it is important to ask, what are the possibilities open to anti-racism? How can the approach taken in this study, of an historicised working through of the complexities of the evolution of anti-racist discourse and praxis, assist in evaluating the as yet unresolved problems facing anti-racism? To what extent does the creation of both national and European enclaves of multiculturality, closed off from those clamouring to get in, represent for anti-racists little more than a sense of déjà vu? Or does the necessity of balancing ongoing racism against those already on the inside with the rights of those to be detained and expelled present anti-racism with both a new set of racisms and the necessity of reinventing the terms with which to combat them? Undoubtedly a mixture of both is the case. Yet, what appears to be certain is that the creation of a heuristics of racialisation that separates insiders (the tolerated) from outsiders (the detritus) forces a reevaluation of anti-racist possibilities and a critical choice of an adequate vocabulary with which to explain what may be considered as a third phase in the history of European racism; a new era of 'race' thinking in Europe.

What has been revealed in this work that may equip anti-racism with a degree of the historical hindsight necessary for approaching this novel situation, which nonetheless borrows successfully from the discourses developed in European 'raciology' (Gilroy 2000) in the post-war period? My work began from the premise that anti-racism, with some notable exceptions (e.g. Lloyd 1998), has been the subject of little empirical study in any of the social scientific disciplines. On the other hand, it is a subject that inspires considerable passions among the intellectual left wing, leading in scholarship, as Bonnett (2000) points out, to a predominance of polemics either in support of existing discourses and practices or in their condemnation. However, Bonnett's own work, like that of several other authors (Gilroy 1992; Lloyd 1998), while based on considerable engagement with texts, including those produced by organisations themselves, has not tended to treat anti-racism as an object of sociological research grounded in a direct engagement with its protagonists. This failure to approach anti-racists as the most apt interlocutors for uncovering the full extent of anti-racism as a social and political phenomenon has engendered prescriptive conclusions that do not necessarily reflect the complexity of the problems facing it (Anthias and Yuval-Davis 1992; Bonnett 1993). It has also led to anti-racism often being equated wholly with only one of its component discourses at the expense of an analysis of its multiplicity. Gilroy's (1987, 1992) separation of municipal anti-racism – seen as the embodiment of anti-racism writ large – from black resistance obscures the fact that many of the organisations, based in Britain's 'black communities' to which he refers, define their work as anti-racist and that they have been central to establishing the agenda upon which much of the contemporary activism of independent organisations is based.

In a different way, Taguieff's (1991a,b) equation of all anti-racism with what he considers are the negative influences of the far Left, third-worldism and 'communitarianism' confuses the interrelations between the three, in a dangerous reinterpretation of anti-racist and anti-colonialist history. By reducing anti-racism to this fictitious triad, he denies the dominance of the republican anti-racism, that he in fact espouses, over the French anti-racist arena. Taguieff's polemicism, in particular, reveals the way in which anti-racism often awakens strong reactions, both in scholarly work and in the discourse of the Left, that when examined more closely demonstrate the tenuousness upon which such arguments are based (cf. Gallissot 1992). The authority which his numerous volumes on racism and anti-racism have been accorded is testimony to the paucity of empirical work on anti-racism with which to compare them and, specifically, to the weakness of historical knowledge of the evolution of anti-racisms, even among those who claim to be committed anti-racists.

A principal starting point for this study was, therefore, the felt necessity of redressing this lack and, secondarily, of bringing to account those for whom anti-racism is little more than a vehicle for an attack on the Left and social movements more generally. Within the literature that did exist, my main point of departure was the declaration, in the early 1990s, that anti-racism was in crisis. Both Gilroy's and Taguieff's arguments, and those of others who alluded to it (Lloyd 1996b), were compelling in that they appeared to note the transformation of the challenges facing anti-racist activists and to point out several of the reasons for which anti-racism as a political discourse may be unable to deal with them. Nevertheless, the theorisation of cultural racism as an entirely new phenomenon which, in Taguieff's terms, was facilitated by anti-racists and with which they were unable to cope effectively according to both authors, appeared too straightforward. Barker's (1981) study of neoracism a decade previously, which noted the continuing links with biological 'science', and the critique of the newness of neoracism proposed by Balibar (1991a) questioned the uniqueness of the argument. Particularly in the terms introduced by Taguieff, racism was being presented ahistorically, while anti-racism was being endowed with a factually questionable history that was deemed responsible for the overnight transformation of racism, from a focus on biological 'race' to one on incompatible cultures. The emphasis on the newness of cultural racism rejected the historicisation of racism necessary for an analysis of the former's origins. By turning instead to anti-racism for its explanation, these writers indeed recognised a central flaw at the origin of anti-racist thought: its failure to historicise the interrelationship between racism and the European nation-state as the vehicle through which racisms, in their various forms, are created and sustained.

The link made between the crisis facing anti-racism, as a viable form of collective action and as an influential political discourse, and the advent of cultural racism necessitated an historical analysis of the evolution of the notion of culturalism in anti-racist thought. Far from being the anti-racism of the racialised 'minorities' whom Taguieff accuses of transforming anti-racism into a communitarian, left-wing enclave of rabid anti-Zionism and primitive anti-humanism, culturalism was fundamental to the establishment of an institutional response to racism in the aftermath of the *Shoah*. The discovery of the relations between anthropological cultural relativism, the UNESCO tradition, and ultimately the policies of several western states with regard to immigration, put into question the idea that anti-racism exists in a relationship of antagonism towards the state. On the contrary, anti-racism as it evolved in the post-war years, despite precedents such as the Pan-African Conference, initially relied upon a mobilisation of a renewed notion of humanism that replaced the 'civilising mission' towards progress with the notion of equal but different cultures that was wholly compatible with the policies of the international institutions. Despite the persistence of colonialism in the first post-war decades, combining repression with 'civilisation', the notion that human beings are divided according to cultures rather than 'race' came very quickly to dominate European political language. This allowed for the understanding of human differences that had become ingrained in politics since the Golden Age of racism to continue unharmed in many respects, while outwardly, any invocation of human superiority or inferiority was condemned.

The confusion with which the origins of culturalism as a specifically anti-racist project was met is in turn connected to the lack of historicisation of anti-racism as a whole. The undoubted basis of the argument for cultural relativism in the left-wing and anti-racist intentions of a minority of anthropologists in the inter- and post-war years was assumed to connect this argument to the more subversive versions of anti-racist activism. In fact, the adoption by UNESCO of a culturally relativist approach, which eventually motivated the reification of culture that epitomises multiculturalist policy making, shows how this has been a dominant rather than a subordinate trend. What led to the ability for some to deny the undoubtedly hegemonic origins of culturalism, and instead to make a connection between the current emphasis on the cultural and ethnic exclusivities of identity politics and the history of self-organised anti-racism (Taylor 1994)? Over the course of the research, my growing realisation of the extent of anti-racism's heterogeneity and the conflictual nature of its various discourses made it apparent that it was anti-racism itself, or at least one variant within it, that was responsible for these interpretations.

One of the principal arguments upon which this work rests therefore is that a hegemonic, culturalist anti-racism that emerges in the aftermath of the *Shoah*, based on the need to explain the persistence of racism in the absence of 'race' (Goldberg 2002), fails to historicise the connection between racism and the modern European state. Both the earlier need to explain the differences between human groups, without evoking racially hierarchical theorisations of superiority and inferiority, and the later description of racism as cultural rather than biological are historically rooted in the depoliticisation of racism for which this type of anti-racism is responsible. Racism, according to the legacy of the UNESCO tradition which came to dominate mainstream and official responses to racism, is a behaviour born of individual prejudice. Although such attitudes may be conditioned by situations of colonial domination or racist repression, they may be overcome only with greater education and individual knowledge. A total separation is made between the racism of the Nazi era and that of the post-*Shoah* period. While the Nazi regime perpetuated racism and married 'race' to politics, the racist sentiments that continue to be expressed towards racialised others following this aberration in the course of modern European history are mired in ignorance. Never is the source of this 'ignorant prejudice' related to the actions of the state.

What was it precisely that these forms of undoubtedly well-intentioned, education-centred anti-racism omitted in their account of racism? Why did competing anti-racisms emerge, following the eruption of anti-colonialism, that targeted the state as the main courier of the spread of racist thought? In order to account fully for the multiplicity of anti-racism's evolution, I needed to develop an analysis of its competing understandings of racism. This could be achieved only by returning to the history of the rise of the 'race' idea and its gradual connection to the language of politics by the latter half of the nineteenth century. By examining the extent to which a vocabulary of 'race' became embedded in the practices of politics by the First World War, it clearly appears that racism had become the norm rather than the exception. Although the genocidal levels of the *Shoah* were indeed an unimagined extreme, the possibility to think racially about human populations had entered political discourse indefinitely and has since proved almost impossible to eradicate. Anti-racism since the *Shoah* has consisted of a struggle between a view of racism as radically transformed in the post-war era, and one which, on the contrary, sees it as a seamless, if qualitatively different, continuation of a process begun in the nineteenth century. A central means of assessing the viability of this assumption became the notion of public political culture. Just as racism could be differentially conceived as either fundamentally opposed to the ideologies of the state or undeniably grounded within them, so too anti-racism could be interpreted as either upholding the values of the West incorporated in the state or as a challenge to their usage in practice. These values – democracy, freedom, fraternity, human rights, equality – could at once be seen as the very principles upon which the modern state was built and, therefore, the ideals that an anti-racism that seeks widespread public support should uphold, or alternatively, as the hypocritical anchorings of the state in principles of equality and rights that belie the selective nature of their application.

The construction of the continuum of proximity-to-distance to the public political culture of the nation-state along which I proposed anti-racism could be seen to be arranged was not, therefore, a preconstructed theoretical framework into which I attempted to insert my 'findings'. On the contrary, this formulation was settled upon quite late in the course of my research as a result both of a reading of the often contradictory histories of 'race', racism and anti-racism and an engagement with the discourse produced by anti-racist organisations through conversations with their protagonists. The extent of the disparity between versions of anti-racism in a contemporary perspective could not be merely arbitrary, nor solely a matter of national differences. The stress placed on representation or institutional independence, upon the possibility of alliance building or that of internationalising anti-racist mobilisation could all be shown to have precedents in the evolution of anti-racism since its beginnings. In turn, the often widely differing approaches taken to these matters were related to the extent to which public political culture was incorporated into anti-racist discourse or rejected by it. Representation by the actual or potential victims of racism, perhaps the most important concern of contemporary anti-racists, is considered an important aim by those who recognise the continuing power of the state to marginalise and exclude the racialised. For those who reject its importance, anti-racism may succeed only if it adopts a colour-blind approach based upon the universal aspirations of a western conceptualisation of fairness.

POLICING STRANGERS: ANTI-RACISM IN CONTEXT

How does the heterogeneity of anti-racism, brought about by its evolution following widely differing political legacies, shape the possibilities of combating racism today? While the various national contexts focused on in this study reveal specific problems, born of the temporal and political differences in the anti-racist practices they have given rise to, the consolidation of European raciology means that they are all faced with a similar set of challenges. The states of western Europe, particularly those with a longer history of immigration, are developing a discourse of discrimination that separates increasingly between in- and out-groups. The in-group, however, is no longer merely the indigenous, culturally dominant majority; it now includes the racialised minorities who, in current political discourse, have contributed to the makeup of diverse, multicultural societies. Keeping those who wish to enter European societies today out is portrayed as equally beneficial to preexisting 'minority ethnic' groups. Beyond the obviousness of the fact that reliance on such discourse coexists with a persistence of racism against second- and third-generation 'minorities', its use nevertheless denotes a significant shift.

SOS Racisme's claim that 'We have to organise common actions to increase the movement's strength,' or the ANL's insistence that 'a lot of people proud to be British are quite proud to be multicultural and multiracial as well' demonstrate how 'majoritarian' anti-racism promotes the inclusion of the racialised as a seamless part of national society. This language has increasingly become that of governments in the attempt to impose a policing of 'illegal' immigration that claims to be non-racial, and so to have no effect on existing 'race relations'. The control of immigration is, on the contrary, proposed as the only means of curbing the rise of the far Right. Using a language that is as old as Europe-bound immigration itself, centrist parties which connect the 'crisis' of immigration to the recent electoral successes of the extreme Right in Europe, themselves claim to promote an anti-racist stance. The ability of this glaring contradiction to pass unnoticed in public opinion, beyond the success of anti-immigrant rhetoric to filter through to societal consciousness, is based upon the fundamental division between the familiar and the strange. Whereas even casual observation informs us that complete 'integration' has not been fulfilled, 'strangerhood' has shifted by degrees, no longer to define those we have come to know and tolerate. Strangers, 'the solid leftovers of the productive process called "social spacing"; [who] posit the perennial problems of recycling and waste-disposal' (Bauman 1995:181) have become the new Others, those just, or not yet in. 'Our own' familiar Others have been culturalised and tamed; the strangers are still racialised in the completeness of their inassimilability. Yet behind the externally expressed pride in the success of 'integration' is the message that the management of internal difference is teetering on a brink whose balance is controlled by the politics of immigration. Allowing their numbers to rise, it is alleged, will unbalance the carefully measured equilibrium of 'normality' to 'difference' upon which contemporary societies have been painstakingly constructed.

Further, the emphasis on the interrelationship of immigration and criminality is an attempt by governments to place the issue beyond the realm of human relations; policing immigrants removes the possibility of coming to know them in a way that existed for an earlier generation. The reciprocity between discourses of 'race' and those of criminality, the sliver of a dividing line between security and segregation, ensures that the association of bio-power with the politics of exclusion has been sustained. The success with which the language of security has currently woven itself around and interconnected major political themes – terrorism and immigration in particular – is evidence of the persistent ability of 'race' to continually don new guises. Without needing to evoke unspeakable references to biological difference, the new politics of 'race' replaces them with the vocabularies of dangerosity that, it has long since been forgotten, originally compounded the success of 'race' as a viable political idea. Imprisonment and expulsion have consistently served as the tools for creating society in the image of the holders of power: 'vibrant multicultural communities' must not be allowed to become sources of sinister internal enmity.

'GLOBALISING' CULTURE? ANTI-RACISM'S RESPONSE

Anti-racism's response in the face of this new era of 'race' thinking continues to mirror its internal diversity. Despite the establishment of new organisations specifically focusing on the rights of asylum seekers, migrants and refugees and the preoccupation of several established groups with the issue, anti-racist practice, not altogether surprisingly, on the contrary reflects the mundane familiarity of today's racism. Whereas the target of institutional racism and racist violence may have enlarged to incorporate new immigrants, the effects on activists have undergone relatively little change. In countries such as Britain and France, the current climate of anti-immigrationism can be related to its many precedents over the decades following the large-scale arrival of non-Europeans. In Ireland and Italy, the recently established anti-racist organisations experience for the first time what will become a well-known repertoire of repression and violence. The almost banal nature of the racism that continues to affect racialised groups and new immigrants across Europe is experienced by anti-racists as a conveyor-belt of incidents, only periodically interrupted by qualitative shifts in the language of 'race' and the preferred targets of racism.

Bhattacharyya and Gabriel (2002:149) argue that 'sadly, for those trying to organise resistance, the issues troubling black communities in Britain remain tediously familiar and unchanging. Poor housing and healthcare, inadequate access to education and training, high unemployment, low incomes – such ills are nothing new.' They make the point that the failure to consider the persistence of these problems in the current preoccupation of scholarship with questions of 'identity' and 'globalism' is to ignore what are increasingly thought of as 'less glamorous issues' (ibid.). In considering the future of anti-racism, I would like to suggest that the problems to which this gives rise do not only have an affect upon scholarship. Both the preoccupation with notions of culture and identity, as well as the transnationalisation of the sites of social movement politics in reaction to the processes of globalisation are profoundly significant for assessing the possibilities facing anti-racism as both discourse and praxis. As I argued in Chapter 5, with regard to the contrasts between a localised and a globalised approach to anti-racism, the predominance of the latter as a new formation for the expression of the concerns of progressive social movements often reifies the racialised in its efforts to reformulate the terms of the discourse on racism as transnational. While it would be impossible to claim that the increased globalisation of capital has had no effect on the regimes of racism of European states, the process of homogenisation that accompanies the call to 'think globally' carries consequences for the building of lasting anti-racist alliances.

Echoing Bhattacharyya and Gabriel (2002:149) again, the contemporary interlinking of what is perceived to be the wider context of globalisation with the micro-level proliferation of culture has led to discussions of 'hybridity, fragmentation, performative identities and strategic essentialisms'. The undoubted scholarly usefulness of these concepts must however raise questions as to their interpretative capacity in the consideration of the everyday resistance of the racialised and immigrants in today's Europe. The relation made by the movement for 'globalisation from below' of such microcosms to what are portrayed as intangible, giant, all-encompassing processes at 'global level' also passes through the use of these terms. Activists employ a renewed language of universalism in the attempt to deal with local realities involving real people. The tentative links made between established anti-racism, specific pro-immigration campaigns and the wider Global Justice Movement, through its local networks, run the risk of once again disconnecting racisms from their institutionalised roots in the politics of states. By viewing racism only as part of a spiralling process of uncontrollable 'globalisation', and largely failing to draw coherent connections to lived experience, these discourses and forms of activism cannot but re-reify the racialised subjects of their concerns.

By examining these evolutions we may see the extent to which they overlap with what Hesse et al. (1998) call 'academicism' to obscure the situation facing anti-racism: the coexistent persistence of familiar racisms with the reformulation of both their terms and the locations in which they are enacted. The contemporary emphasis in academic writing on issues of 'race' and racism, upon a language of hybridity and transnationalism as a means for understanding the changing nature of post-colonial racialised existence often obscures the roots of racism. Hesse (ibid.:145) notes the concomitant dehistoricisation and depoliticisation of racism that this involves:

> Somehow the end of the twentieth century has constructed a position in which the history that produces racism has been sanitised, such that we can no longer speak of a history producing racism. In order to begin to talk about racism, we cannot anchor that in a historical discussion at all ... So we get to a position of what I call political relativism, which is that people are simply in different racialised positions, and the politics arises simply from being in a different position.

An insistence upon the newness of the context in which racism emerges and is promulgated in contemporary times involves this very process of dehistoricisation. Whereas the political future faced in an era of 'globalisation' is undoubtedly uncertain, and to an extent unknown, explaining racism in terms that are completely disconnected from the history of its evolution throughout the course of modernity is to deracinate it from its origins in the politics of modern states and to unwittingly participate in the separation of bygone racism from the proposed urgency of curbing 'criminal' immigration.

The subtle ways in which racism is disconnected from its historical roots, even by some of those who challenge it, is not unrelated to the contemporary usages of a language of culture in the connection of anti-racist concerns to globalised social movement politics. As made clear in Chapters 2 and 5, the renewal of culturalism in the approach of the new movements to work with 'migrants' demonstrates the divide drawn between the political usefulness of the critique of racism against new (global) immigrant populations and the latter's own politicisation. The essentialisation of migrants through their assignment to cultural communities belies the questionable utility of the concepts of either culture or community for describing, or making politically coherent, these diverse groups and individuals. My research has revealed the sophistication of the political analysis developed by these new anti-racists themselves and yet, conversely, the reliance of several groups on a culturalist politics in a clear attempt to gain access to both progressive political arenas and the public eye. The predominance of identities as all important for finding one's place in a globalised transnational, diasporic world – the language promoted by both scholars and new movement activists – poses these new self-organised activists with a challenge to either conform or risk isolation.

Anti-racism is caught, therefore, between a recognition of the need to build alliances that take account of the changes in 'race' thinking that accompany the globalisation of migration and the stark reality of the familiarity of racism at the level of the city or neighbourhood. Renewed reifications of 'minority ethnicity' and 'immigrant groups' run the risk of returning anti-racism to the squabbles over the importance of 'difference' or 'multiculturalism' which, particularly in the French and British contexts, albeit in different ways, locate the concerns of anti-racism within the shifting definitions of national societies around which competing political discourses are constructed. The persistence of the depoliticising forces of culture and identity is now channelled through both governments and progressive politics with the effect, once again, of marginalising racism from the centre of politics where, as Gilroy (1992) reminds us, it has always belonged and where, unfettered, it continues to lurk. The confusion of the reality of post-colonial racism with the misconstrued assumption that 'we're living in a post-racist condition' (Hesse 1998:143) is undeniably linked to the success of both post-colonial studies and new movement politics, as well as the 'anti-racism' of the European centrist governments, to capture contemporary imaginations.

As his biographer David Macey notes in relation to Frantz Fanon, who has been a central figure to this work, his reception in contemporary post-colonial studies stands at direct odds with the ' "revolutionary Fanon" of the 1960s' (Macey 2000:29):

> The Third Worldist Fanon was an apocalyptic creature; the post-colonial Fanon worries about identity politics, and often about his own sexual identity, but he is no longer angry. And yet, if there is a truly Fanonian emotion, it is anger. His anger was a response to his experience of a black man in a world defined as white, but not to the 'fact' of blackness. It was a response to the condition and situation of those he called the wretched of the earth. The wretched of the earth are still there, but not in the seminar rooms where the talk is of post-colonial theory. They came out on the streets of Algiers in 1988, and the Algerian army shot them dead...Had he lived, Fanon would still be angry. His readers should be angry too.
>
> (Ibid.)

As Fanon himself reminds us in the closing of *Black Skin, White Masks* (1967:227), 'it was not the black world that laid down the course of my conduct. My black skin is not the wrapping of specific values.' Anti-racism faces the serious task of transporting the message contained in Fanon's words into the consciousness of European societies. Whether with the exclusionary purposes of European states or the progressive mission for social change and an end to national exclusivities of the social movements, to essentialise the 'Other' is to dehumanise her. But racism affects human beings, profoundly, and in ways which cut across all we have been taught. To culturalise is not to endow one with humanity, but – sadly – to shirk responsibility by circumventing the political. Anti-racism must repoliticise the origins and the stakes of racism and, for this, its allies shall be few.

Notes

INTRODUCTION

1 All translations of texts in either French or Italian, including interview citations, unless otherwise stated are my own.
2 'Communitarianism' in the French context is used to describe community politics, seen as conflicting with the values of republican secular individualism. It has no relation to communitarian theory in political philosophy.

CHAPTER 1

1 These writers are principally Hannah Arendt, Etienne Balibar, Zygmunt Bauman, Oliver Cox, Frantz Fanon, Michel Foucault, Neil MacMaster, Gérard Noiriel, Enzo Traverso and Eric Voegelin. The fact that the work of these highly diverse authors has never been read together means that it may not have been possible to reveal the full complexity of the historical and theoretical interlinkedness between 'race' and state that this chapter intends to theorise. The various disciplinary and political traditions that each represents should not disguise the utility of their being used together, a project that reveals the high degree of compatibility between the theorisations bred of otherwise almost always separate intellectual trajectories.
2 African-American authors (cf. Cox 1943) critiqued the relationship of colonialism to capitalism and proposed a political analysis of racism as early as 1940. However, in the inter-war years W.E.B. Du Bois, possibly inspired by the work of the anthropologist Franz Boas, carried out cranial measurement as a means of disproving racial science (Harrison 1995:54). Such work, as well as that of Julian Huxley et al. (1935) 'which explained modern genetic theory in layman terms to show that biological races did not exist' (MacMaster 2001:170) circumvented a critique of the politicisation of 'race'.
3 In 1684 François Bernier published the *Nouvelle division de la terre par des différents espèces ou races qui l'habitent*.
4 Note that the belief in polygenesis existed before the advent of nationalism and the displacement of the primacy of the Creation by the variety of the species. Voltaire for example compared 'men' to varieties of trees (Todorov 1989). However, nationalism was required to facilitate the complete shift to polygenesis, beyond the intellectual sphere, and its incorporation into the language of politics.
5 Bio-power emerges after the end of sovereign power which, above all, was concerned with discipline. This new power, not disciplinary in itself, nonetheless does not suppress disciplinary power because it exists on a

different level. Bio-power is addressed to living beings and, more specifically, to their global mass. The technology of bio-power is directed at all
the processes that are proper to this mass of humans such as birth, death,
sickness etc. 'Bio-politics' consist of demographics and statistics, the
gathering of information about the lifecycles of populations to ensure
their control (Foucault 1997:215–17).

6 Whereas in France, the Jews were emancipated in 1790 and 1791 and
Napoleon's army emancipated Jews in many of the countries it conquered
(Traverso 1996), in Germany they were not granted full emancipation
until 1869 with Bismarck's rise to power (Meyer and Brenner 1996).

CHAPTER 2

1 Originally a lecture given at the invitation of UNESCO to open the
International Year of Struggle Against Racism.

2 The Roma community of Florence, whose members mainly originate
in the former Yugoslavia, have been settled in poorly equipped camps.
The racism against them is epitomised by this decision based on an ignorance of the tradition of the Roma of eastern Europe and their historical
abandonment of the nomadic lifestyle.

CHAPTER 3

1 Slogan of *SOS Racisme*: 'Hands off my mate.'
2 This information is taken from an unrecorded interview with the LICRA.
3 This Lyon-based organisation later became the *Jeunes arabes de Lyon
et banlieues* (JALB).
4 *Droit et Liberté* 29/10–4/11/1949. *Droit et Liberté* is the MRAP's journal.
5 The so-called *double peine* refers to the possibility of those of immigrant
origin being judged twice for a crime committed in France. This generally
results in the attempt to deport an individual, after having served a sen-
tence for the crime in France, for trial in his/her country of origin. In
many cases, the individual concerned has never been to that country nor
speaks the language.
6 The importance of the notion of community is its ability to analytically
join together the fight against racism and issues of class struggle (Gilroy
1987).
7 This view is typified in British history by the Conservative MP, Enoch
Powell, the first mainstream politician to call for repatriation (CARF
1998). In 1968, Powell made his infamous 'rivers of blood' speech in
which he constituted black people as alien and warned that Britain
would be swamped by immigrants.
8 The Asian Dub Foundation has been active in the campaign to free Satpal
Ram, a Bengali man sentenced to prison for defending himself during a
racist attack in a restaurant in 1986.
9 The slogan appears on the *Anti Racist Campaign* (ARC) website (http://flag.
blackened.net/revolt/arc).

10   Lentin and McVeigh (2002:22) estimate the current number of 'ethnic minorities' in Ireland, North and South, at 200,000 but add that 'we must re-emphasise, these figures can only be guesstimates.'

11   The speaker is referring to the reports on a court case taken by a Traveller family who were denied access to a hotel that they had booked for a wedding reception when the managers saw that they were Travellers.

12   One of the first black Irish players to play for the Republic of Ireland soccer team.

13   Quotation from *Che Fare*, the magazine of the *Organizzazione Comunista Internazionalista*, handed out at a demonstration against Italian detention centres in Florence: 'Immigrant workers, break the chains of blackmail of the Italian bosses and government.'

14   ARCI describes itself as the largest association in Italy and has been involved in anti-racist campaigning since the early 1990s.

15   '*Straniero*' is the Italian word for foreigner whereas '*extracomunitario*' is used, both offically and colloquially, to refer to someone from outside the European Union.

CHAPTER 5

1   Judy (1996) usefully shows that the English translation of Chapter 5 of Fanon's *Black Skin, White Masks* as 'The Fact of Blackness' misrepresents his meaning in the French '*L'expérience vécue du noir*' which should be translated as 'The Lived Experience of the Black'.

2   The voucher scheme, whereby asylum seekers could only purchase goods at designated shops using special coupons rather than cash, was brought in by the Labour government and has since been abolished. The hostels referred to, more commonly known as detention centres, have been developed with several new premises built in the UK and across Europe since the time of the interview in 1999.

3   The report defines institutional racism as 'the collective failure of an organisation to provide an appropriate and professional service to people because of their colour, culture or ethnic origin. It can be seen or detected in processes, attitudes and behaviour which amount to discrimination through unwitting prejudice, ignorance, thoughtlessness and racist stereotyping which disadvantage minority ethnic people' (The Stephen Lawrence Inquiry 1999:6.34).

4   This information was taken from a seminar with Sandro Mezzadra, an organiser of the pro-immigration demonstration at Genoa; European University Institute, February 2002.

Bibliography

Adorno, Theodor W. and Horkheimer, Max. 1979. *Dialectic of Enlightenment*. London: Verso.

Aimiuwu, Sonia and Balsamo, Franca. 2002. *Il colore sulla pelle: Attitudini e aspettative di minoranze etniche femminili in Europa*. Turin: L'Harmattan Italia.

Amalvi, C. 1984. 'Le 14 juillet', in Pierre Nora (ed.), *Les lieux de la mémoire*. Paris: Gallimard.

Amnesty International. 2001. *An Information and Action Pack on Amnesty International's Campaign for Leadership Against Racism in Ireland*. Dublin: Amnesty International.

Anthias, Floya. 2002. 'Diasporic Hybridity and Transcending Racisms: Problems and Potential', in Floya Anthias and Cathie Lloyd (eds), *Rethinking Anti-Racisms: From Theory to Practice*. London and New York: Routledge.

Anthias, Floya and Lloyd, Cathie. 2002. *Rethinking Anti-Racisms: From Theory to Practice*. London and New York: Routledge.

Anthias, Floya and Yuval-Davis, Nira. 1992. *Racialised Boundaries: Race, Nation, Gender, Colour and Class and the Anti-Racist Struggle*. London and New York: Routledge.

Appadurai, Arjun. 1995. 'The Production of Locality', in Richard Fardon (ed.), *Counterworks: Managing the Diversity of Knowledge*. London: Routledge.

Arendt, Hannah. 1966. *The Origins of Totalitarianism*. New York and London: Harcourt Brace Jovanovich.

Back, Les. 1996. *New Ethnicities and Urban Culture: Racisms and Multiculture in Young Lives*. London: UCL Press.

Back, Les and Solomos, John (eds). 2000. *Theories of Race and Racism: A Reader*. London and New York: Routledge.

Back, Les and Solomos, John. 2001. 'Doing Research, Writing Politics: The Dilemmas of Political Intervention in Research on Racism', in Harry Goulbourne (ed.), *Race and Ethnicity*. London and New York: Routledge.

Baillet, Dominique. 1997. 'Jeunes d'origine maghrebine dans l'éspace associatif et politique'. *Migrations Societé* 9, no. 49: 7–22.

Balbo, Laura and Manconi, Luigi. 1990. *I razzismi possibili*. Milan: Feltrinelli Editore.

Balibar, Etienne. 1991a. 'Is There a "Neo-Racism"?', in Etienne Balibar and Immanuel Wallerstein (eds), *Race, Nation, Class: Ambiguous Identities*. London: Verso: 17–28.

——. 1991b. 'Racism and Nationalism', in Etienne Balibar and Immanuel Wallerstein (eds), *Race, Nation, Class: Ambiguous Identities*. London: Verso: 37–67.

——. 1991c. 'Class Racism', in Etienne Balibar and Immanuel Wallerstein (eds), *Race, Nation, Class: Ambiguous Identities*. London: Verso: 204–16.

——. 1992. *Les frontières de la démocratie*. Paris: La Découverte.

——. 1994. *Masses, Classes, Ideas: Studies on politics and philosophy before and after Marx*. New York: Routledge.

Balibar, Etienne. 2003. *Europe: Vanishing Mediator? We, the People of Europe? Reflections on Transnational Citizenship*. Princeton: Princeton University Press.

Balibar, Etienne and Wallerstein, Immanuel. 1991. *Race, Nation, Class: Ambiguous Identities*. London: Verso.

Balsamo, Franca. 2002. 'Introduzione', in Sonia Aimiuwu and Franca Balsamo (eds), *Il colore sulla pelle: Attitudine e aspettative di minoranze etniche femminili in Europa*. Turin: L'Harmattan Italia.

Barkan, Elazar. 2003. 'Race and the Social Sciences', in Theodore R. Porter and Dorothy Ross (eds), *Cambridge History of the Social and Behavioral Sciences*. New York: Cambridge University Press.

Barker, Martin. 1981. *The New Racism: Conservatives and the Ideology of the Tribe*. London: Junction Books.

——.1983. 'Empiricism and Racism'. *Radical Philosophy* Spring: 6–15.

Barot, Rohit and Bird, John. 2001. 'Racialization: The Genealogy and Critique of a Concept'. *Ethnic and Racial Studies* 24, no. 4: 601–18.

Barthes, Roland. 1957. *Mythologies*. Paris: Editions du Seuil.

Bauman, Zygmunt. 1989. *Modernity and the Holocaust*. Cambridge: Polity Press.

——. 1991. *Modernity and Ambivalence*. Ithaca: Cornell University Press.

——. 1995. *Life in Fragments: Essays in Postmodern Morality*. Oxford: Blackwell.

Bhattacharyya, Gargi and Gabriel, John. 2002. 'Anti-Deportation Campaigning in the West Midlands', in Floya Anthias and Cathie Lloyd (eds), *Rethinking Anti-Racisms: From Theory to Practice*. London and New York: Routledge.

Blatt, David. 1995. 'Towards a Multi-cultural Political Model in France? The Limits of Immigrant Collective Action, 1968–94'. *Nationalism and Ethnic Politics* 1, no. 2: 156–77.

Body-Gendrot, Sophie. 1998. ' "Now You See, Now You Don't:" Comments on Paul Gilroy's article'. *Ethnic and Racial Studies* 21, no. 5: 848–58.

Bonnett, Alastair. 1993. *Radicalism, Anti-Racism and Representation*. London and New York: Routledge.

——. 2000. *Anti-Racism*. London and New York: Routledge.

Bourdieu, Pierre and Wacquant, Loic J.D. 1992. *An Invitation to Reflexive Sociology*. Chicago: University of Chicago Press.

Bourne, Jenny. 2001. 'The Life and Times of Institutional Racism'. *Race and Class* 43, no. 2: 7–21.

Boutih, Malek. 2001. *La France aux français? Chiche!* Paris: Mille et Une Nuits.

Burgio, Alberto. 2000. *Nel nome della razza: il razzismo nella storia italiana, 1870–1945*. Bologna: Il Mulino.

Bush, Barbara. 1999. *Imperialism, Race and Resistance: Africa and Britain, 1919–1945*. London: Routledge.

Calhoun, Craig. 1995. *Critical Social Theory*. Oxford: Blackwell.

Campaign Against Racism and Fascism (CARF). 1998. 'The Powell Effect'. *CARF*, no. 43: 6–7.

Castles, Stephen. 1984. *Here for Good: Western Europe's New Ethnic Minorities*. London: Pluto Press.

Césaire, Aimé. 1972. *Discourse on Colonialism* (trans. Joan Pinkham). New York and London: Monthly Review Press.

Chaterjee, Mary Searle. 1987. 'The Anthropologist Exposed: Anthropologists in Multi-cultural and Anti-Racist Work'. *Anthropology Today* 3, no. 4: 16–18.

Cissé, Madjiguène. 1999. *Parole de sans-papiers*. Paris: La Dispute.

Cobb, Nina Kressner. 1979. 'Richard Wright: Exile and Existentialism'. *Phylon* 40, no. 4: 362–74.

Cohen, Phil. 1998. 'Who Needs an Island?'. *New Formations* 33: 11–38.

Cohen, Phil and Bains, Harwant, S. (eds). 1988. *Multi-Racist Britain: New Directions in Theory and Practice*. Basingstoke: Macmillan.

Collins, Martin. 1992. 'Racism and Participation – The Case of the Irish Travellers', in Dublin Travellers Education and Development Group (ed.), *Irish Travellers: New Analysis and New Initiatives*. Dublin: Pavee Point Publications.

Comas, Juan. 1961. ' "Scientific" Racism Again?'. *Current Anthropology* 2, no. 4: 310–40.

Connell, R.W. 1997. 'Why Is Classical Theory Classical?'. *American Journal of Sociology* 102, no. 6: 1511–57.

Court, Artelia. 1985. *Puck of the Droms: The Lives and Literature of Irish Tinkers*. Berkeley: University of California Press.

Cox, Oliver Cromwell. 1943. 'Race Relations'. *Journal of Negro Education* 12, no. 2: 144–53.

——. 2000. 'Race Relations', in Les Back and John Solomos (eds), *Theories of Race and Racism*. London and New York: Routledge.

Craib, Ian. 1998. *Experiencing Identity*. London: Sage.

Dal Lago, Alessandro. 1999. *Non-Persone: L'esclusione dei migranti in una società globale*. Milan: Giangiacomo Feltrinelli Editore.

Dal Lago, Alessandro and Mezzadra, Sandro. 2002. 'I confini impensati dell'Europa', in Heidrun Friese, Antonio Negri and Peter Wagner (eds), *Europa politica: ragioni di una necessità*. Rome: Manifestolibri.

Davies, Ioan. 1995. *Cultural Studies and Beyond: Fragments of Empire*. London and New York: Routledge.

Du Bois, W.E. Burghardt. 1946. 'Colonies and Moral Responsibility'. *Journal of Negro Education* 15, no. 3: 311–18.

Dummett, Michael. 1973. 'CARD Reconsidered'. *Race Today* 5, no. 2: 42–4.

Ellis, J. 1991. *Meeting Community Needs: A Study of Muslim Communities in Coventry*. Monographs in Ethnic Relations No. 2. Coventry: Centre for Research in Ethnic Relations, University of Warwick.

Ellison, Ralph. 1952. *Invisible Man*. London: Penguin Books.

Fanon, Frantz. 1963. *The Wretched of the Earth*. New York: Grove Press.

——. 1967. *Black Skins, White Masks*. London: Pluto Press.

Fay, Ronnie. 1992. 'Minorization of Travelling Groups and their Cultural Rights – The Case of the Irish Traveller', in Dublin Travellers Education and Development Group (ed.), *Irish Travellers: New Analysis and New Initiatives*. Dublin: Pavee Point Publications.

Fekete, Liz. 2002. *Racism: The Hidden Cost of September 11*. London: Institute of Race Relations.

Foucault, Michel. 1978. *The History of Sexuality, Volume 1*. London: Random House.

——. 1997. *Il faut défendre la société: Cours au Collège de France, 1976*. Paris: Gallimard Seuil.

Fysh, Peter and Wolfreys, Jim. 1998. *The Politics of Racism in France*. Basingstoke: Macmillan.

Gallissot, René. 1992. *Razzismo e antirazzismo: La sfida dell'immigrazione*. Bari: Dedalo.

Gilroy, Paul. 1987. *'There Ain't No Black in the Union Jack': The Cultural Politics of Race and Nation*. London: Unwin Hyman.

——. 1992. 'The End of Anti-Racism', in James Donald and Ali Rattansi (eds), *'Race', Culture and Difference*. London: Sage/Open University.

——. 1993. *The Black Atlantic: Modernity and Double Consciousness*. Cambridge, Mass.: Harvard University Press.

——. 1998. 'Race Ends Here'. *Ethnic and Racial Studies* 21, no. 5: 838–47.

——. 2000. *Between Camps: Nations, Cultures and the Allure of Race*. London: Allen Lane.

Gilroy, Paul and Lawrence, Errol. 1988. 'Two-Tone Britain: White and Black Youth and the Politics of Anti-Racism', in Philip Cohen and Harwant S. Bains (eds), *Multi-Racist Britain: New Directions in Theory and Practice*. Basingstoke: Macmillan.

Girard, Patrick. 1980. 'Historical Foundations of Antisemitism', in Joel E. Dinsdale (ed.), *Survivors, Victims and Prepetrators: Essays on the Nazi Holocaust*. Washington, DC: Hemisphere Publishing.

Glean, Marion. 1973. 'Whatever Happened to CARD?'. *Race Today* 5, no. 1: 13–15.

Gobineau, Arthur comte de. 1915. *The Inequality of Races*, trans. Adrian Collins, introd. Oscar Levy. New York: G.P. Putnam's Sons.

Goldberg, David Theo. 1997. *Racial Subjects: Writing on Race in America*. New York and London: Routledge.

——. 2002. *The Racial State*. Malden, Mass. and Oxford: Blackwell.

Goldhagen, Daniel Jonah. 1996. *Hitler's Willing Executioners: Ordinary Germans and the Holocaust*. London: Abacus.

Gumplowicz, Ludwig. 1875. *Rasse und Staat*. Vienna.

Hall, Stuart. 2002. ' "In but not of Europe": Scattered Speculations about "The Myths of Europe" '. Paper given at the conference *Figures d'Europe – Figure d'Europa, Images and Myths of Europe*, jointly organised by the EUI, HEC Department and the City of Florence, 11–13 April 2002, European University Institute, Florence.

Hannaford, Ivan. 1996. *Race: The History of an Idea in the West*. Baltimore: Johns Hopkins University Press.

Hardt, Michael and Negri, Antonio. 1994. *Labour of Dionysus: A Critique of State Form*. Minneapolis: University of Minnesota Press.

——. 2000. *Empire*. Cambridge, Mass. and London: Harvard University Press.

Harrison, Faye. V. 1995. 'The Persistent Power of "Race" in the Cultural and Political Economy of Racism'. *Annual Review of Anthropology* 24: 47–74.

Hesse, Barnor. 2000. 'Diasporicity: Black Britain's Post-Colonial Formations', in Barnor Hesse (ed.), *Un/Settled Multiculturalisms: Diasporas, Entanglements, 'Transruptions'*. London and New York: Zed Books.

——. 1999. ' "It's Your World": Discrepant M/multiculturalisms', in Phil Cohen (ed.), *New Ethnicities, Old Racisms*. London: Zed Books.

Hobsbawm, Eric and Ranger, Terence (eds). 1983. *The Invention of Tradition*. Cambridge: Cambridge University Press.

Huxley, Julian, Haddon, A.C. and Carr-Saunders, A.M. 1935. *We Europeans: A Survey of 'Racial' Problems*. London: Jonathan Cape.

Jazouli, Adil. 1986. *L'Action collective des jeunes maghrébins de France*. Paris: Editions Harmattan.

Judy, Ronald A.T. 1996. 'Fanon's Body of Black Experience', in Lewis R. Gordon, Renee T. White and T. Denean Sharpley-Whiting (eds), *Fanon: A Critical Reader*. Oxford: Blackwell.

King, Jason. 1998. 'Porous Nation: From Ireland's 'Haemorrhage' to Immigrant Inundation', in Ronit Lentin (ed.), *The Expanding Nation: Towards a Multi-ethnic Ireland*. Dublin: Trinity College.

Koselleck, Reinhart. 1985. *Futures Past: On the Semantics of Historical Time*. Cambridge, Mass. and London: MIT Press.

Kundnani, Arun. 2001. Commentary: 'From Oldham to Bradford: The Violence of the Violated'. *Race and Class* 43, no. 2: 105–10.

Kushnik, Louis. 1998. *Race, Class and Struggle: Essays on Racism and Inequality in Britain, the US and Western Europe*. London: Rivers Oram Press.

Lapeyronnie, Didier. 1987. 'Assimilation, mobilisation et action collective chez les jeunes de la seconde génération de l'immigration maghrébine'. *Revue Française de Sociologie* 28: 287–318.

Leach, Edmund. 1970. *Lévi-Strauss*. London: Fontana Press.

Lentin, Ronit and McVeigh, Robbie (eds). 2002. *Racism and Anti-Racism in Ireland*. Belfast: Beyond the Pale.

Lévi-Strauss, Claude. 1975. 'Race and History', in *Race, Science and Society*. New York: Whiteside and Morrow, for UNESCO.

——. 1983. 'Race et culture', in *Le Regard Eloigné*. Paris: PLON.

—— and Eribon, Didier. 1991. *Conversations with Claude Levi-Strauss*. Chicago and London: University of Chicago Press.

Lindqvist, Sven. 1992. *'Exterminate all the Brutes'*. London: Granta Books.

Lloyd, Cathie. 1996a. 'Antiracist Ideas in France: Myths of origin'. *The European Legacy* 1, no. 1: 126–31.

——. 1996b. 'Anti-Racist Strategies: National identity and French Anti-Racist Discourses and Movements', in Y. Samad, T. Ranger and O. Stuart (eds), *Culture, Identity and Politics*. Aldershot: Avebury.

——. 1998. *Discourses of Antiracism in France*. Aldershot: Ashgate.

——.1999. 'Universalism and Difference', in M. Bulmer and J. Solomos (eds), *Racism*. Oxford: Oxford University Press.

Mac An Ghaill, Mairtín. 1999. *Contemporary Racisms and Ethnicities: Social and Cultural Transformations*. Buckingham: Open University Press.

Macey, David. 2000. *Frantz Fanon: A Life*. London: Granta Books.

MacMaster, Neil. 2001. *Racism in Europe 1870–2000*. Basingstoke: Palgrave.

Malik, Kenan. 1996. *The Meaning of Race: Race, History and Culture in Western Society*. London: Macmillan.

Malik, Serge. 1990. *Histoire Secrète de SOS Racisme*. Paris: Albin Michel.

McVeigh, Robbie. 1992. 'The Specificities of Irish Racism'. *Race and Class* 3, no. 4: 31–45.

——. 1998. 'Is Sectarianism Racism? The Implications of Sectarian Division for Multiethnicity in Ireland', in Ronit Lentin (ed.), *The Expanding Nation: Towards a Multi-ethnic Ireland*, Dublin: Trinity College.

——. 2002a. 'Nick, Nack, Paddywhack: Anti-Irish Racism and the Racialisation of Irishness', in Ronit Lentin and Robbie McVeigh (eds), *Racism and Anti-Racism in Ireland*. Belfast: Beyond the Pale.

McVeigh, Robbie. 2002b. 'Is There an Irish Anti-Racism? Building an Anti-Racist Ireland', in Ronit Lentin and Robbie McVeigh (eds), *Racism and Anti-Racism in Ireland*. Belfast: Beyond the Pale.

Mason, Philip. 1968. 'Ten Years of the Institute', *Race* 10, no. 2.

Memmi, Albert. 2000. *Racism*. Minneapolis and London: University of Minnesota Press.

Meyer, Michael A. and Brenner, Michael. 1996. *German-Jewish History in Modern Times, Volume 2*. New York: Columbia University Press.

Mezzadra, Sandro. 2001. *Diritto di fuga*. Verona: Ombre Corte.

Modood, Tariq. 1992. 'British Asian Muslims and the Rushdie Affair', in James Donald and Ali Rattansi (eds), *'Race', Culture and Difference*. London: Sage/Open University.

——. 1997. ' "Difference", Cultural Racism and Anti-Racism', in Pnina Werbner and Tariq Modood (eds), *Debating Cultural Hybridity: Multicultural Identities and the Politics of Anti-Racism*. London: Zed Books.

——. 1998. 'New Forms of Britishness: Post-Immigration Ethnicity and Hybridity in Britain', in Ronit Lentin (ed.), *The Expanding Nation: Towards a Multi-ethnic Ireland*, Dublin: Trinity College.

Mosse, George. 1978. *Towards the Final Solution: A History of European Racism*. London: J.M. Dent & Sons.

Mullard, Chris. 1985. *Race, Power and Resistance*. London: Routledge and Kegan Paul.

Newham Monitoring Project (NMP). 1988. *Still Fighting: Annual Report 1988*. London: Newham Monitoring Project.

——. 1989. *Into the 1990s from Strength to Strength: Annual Report 1989*. London: NMP Publications.

Ní Shúinéar, Sinead. 2002. 'Othering the Irish (Travellers)', in Ronit Lentin and Robbie McVeigh (eds), *Racism and Anti-Racism in Ireland*. Belfast: Beyond the Pale.

Nicholson, Philip Yale. 1999. *Who Do We Think We Are? Race and Nation in the Modern World*. Armonk and London: M.E. Sharpe.

Noiriel, Gérard. 1991. *La tyrannie du national: Le droit d'asile en Europe, 1793–1993*. Paris: Calmann-Lévy.

Nosotras. 2001. *Prendiamo la parola: Il campus delle culture delle donne un anno dopo*. Florence: Nosotras.

O'Connell, John. 2002. 'Travellers in Ireland: An examination of discrimination and racism', in Ronit Lentin and Robbie McVeigh (eds), *Racism and Anti-Racism in Ireland*. Belfast: Beyond the Pale.

O'Toole, Fintan. 2000. 'Green, White and Black: Race and Irish identity', in Ronit Lentin (ed.), *Emerging Irish Identities: Proceedings of a Seminar*. Dublin: Trinity College.

Palmer, Frank. 1986. *Antiracism: An Assault on Education and Value*. London: Sherwood Press.

Pitkin, Hanna Fenichel. 1967. *The Concept of Representation*. Berkeley, Los Angeles and London: University of California Press.

Poinsot, Marie. 1993. 'Competition for Political Legitimacy at Local and National Levels Among Young North Africans in France'. *New Community* 20, no. 1: 79–92.

Portes, Alejandro. 1999. 'Conclusion: Towards a New World – The Origins and Effects of Transnational Activities'. *Ethnic and Racial Studies* 22, no. 2: 463–77.

Race Today Collective. 1976. 'Editorial: Self-Organisation vs. "Self Help" '. *Race Today* 8, no. 3: 51.

Ratzel, Friedrich. 1887. *Völkerkunde, Volume 1.*

Rawls, John. 2001. *Justice and Fairness: A Restatement.* Cambridge, Mass. and London: Belknap Press of Harvard University Press.

Redecker, Robert. 2002. 'Taguieff, avertisseur d'incendie'. *Le Monde,* 25 January 2002.

Renton, Dave. 'The Anti-Nazi League 1977–82'. www.dkrenton.co.uk/1970s.html

Rex, John. 1975. 'Racialism and the Urban Crisis', in *Race, Science and Society.* Paris and London: UNESCO Press/George Allen & Unwin.

Roy, Arundhati. 2002. *Guerra e pace.* Parma: Ugo Guanda Editore.

Runnymede Trust. 1997. *Islamophobia: A Challenge for Us All.* London: Runnymede Trust.

Said, Edward. 2002. 'Waiting on a Countervailing Force: Europe Versus America'. *Counterpunch* www.counterpunch.org/said1116.html

Sartre, Jean-Paul [Stephen Priest (ed.)]. 2001. *Jean-Paul Sartre: Basic Writings.* London and New York: Routledge.

Schneer, Jonathan. 1999. 'Anti-Imperial London: The Pan-African Conference of 1900', in Felix Driver and David Gilbert (eds), *Imperial Cities: Landscape, display and Identity.* Manchester and New York: Manchester University Press.

Schneider, Jane. 1998. 'Introduction: The Dynamics of Neo-orientalism in Italy (1848–1995)', in Jane Schneider (ed.), *Italy's 'Southern Question': Orientalism in One Country.* Oxford: Berg.

Scott, Joan Wallach. 1989. 'History in Crisis: The Others' Side of the Story'. *American Historical Review* 94, no. 3: 680–92.

——. 1992. ' "Experience" ', in Judith Butler and Joan W. Scott (eds), *Feminists Theorize the Political.* New York and London: Routledge.

Shukra, Kalbir. 1998. *The Changing Pattern of Black Politics in Britain.* London: Pluto Press.

Simon-Barouh, Ida and De Rudder, Véronique. 1999. *Migrations internationales et relations interethniques: Recherche, politique et société.* Paris: L'Harmattan.

Sivanandan, A. 1976. 'Race, Class and the State: The Black Experience in Britain'. *Race and Class* 17, no. 4.

——. 1982. *A Different Hunger: Writings on Black Resistance.* London: Pluto Press.

——. 1983. 'Challenging Racism'. *Race and Class* 15, no. 2.

——. 1990. *Communities of Resistance: Writings on Black Struggles for Socialism.* London: Verso.

Small, Stephen. 1994. *Racialised Barriers: The Black Experience in the United States and England in the 1980s.* London and New York: Routledge.

Solomos, John. 1999. 'Social Research and the Stephen Lawrence Inquiry'. *Sociological Research Online* 4, no. 1: 1–7.

SOS Racisme. 2000. *Etude de SOS Racisme sur les discriminations.* Unpublished report.

Spire, Alexis. 1999. 'De l'étranger à l'immigré: La magie sociale d'une catégorie statistique'. *Actes de la Recherche en Sciences Sociales* 129: 50–6.

'The Stephen Lawrence Inquiry'. 1999. *Report of an Inquiry by Sir William MacPherson of Cluny.* Presented to Parliament by the Secretary of State for the Home Department by Command of Her Majesty. London: The Stationery Office.

Stolcke, Verena. 1995. 'Talking Culture: New Boundaries, New Rhetorics of Exclusion in Europe'. *Current Anthropology* 36, no. 1: 1–24.

Taguieff, Pierre-André. 1989. *La force du préjugé: Essai sur le racisme et ses doubles*. Paris: La Découverte.

——. 1992. *La lutte contre le racisme et la xénophobie*. Rapport de la Commission Nationale Consultative des Droits de l'Homme Presenté à Madame le Premier Ministre le 21 mars 1992. Paris: La Documentation Française.

——. 1995. *Les fins de l'antiracisme*. Paris: Michalon.

——. 2002. *La nouvelle judéophobie*. Paris: Milles et Une Nuits.

Taguieff, Pierre-André. (ed.). 1991a. *Face au racisme 1: Les moyens d'agir*. Paris: La Découverte.

——. 1991b. *Face au racisme 2: Analyses, hypothèses, perspectives*. Paris: La Découverte.

Tannam, Marian. 2002. 'Questioning Anti-Racism in Ireland', in Ronit Lentin and Robbie McVeigh (eds), *Racism and Anti-Racism in Ireland*. Belfast: Beyond the Pale.

——. 'Developments in Anti-Racism in Ireland'. Unpublished.

Tannam, Marian, Smith, Susan and Flood, Suzie. 1998. *Anti-Racism: An Irish Perspective*. Dublin: Harmony.

Tarrow, Sidney. 1994. *Power in Movement: Social Movements and Contentious Politics*. Cambridge: Cambridge University Press.

Taylor, Charles. 1992. *The Ethics of Authenticity*. Cambridge, Mass. and London: Harvard University Press.

——. 1994. *Multiculturalism: Examining the Politics of Recognition* (ed. and introduced by Amy Gutmann). Princeton: Princeton University Press.

Todorov, Tzvetan. 1989. *Nous et les autres: La reflexion française sur la diversité humaine*. Paris: Seuil.

Tomlinson, John. 1981. *Left–Right: The March of Political Extremism in Britain*. London: J. Calder.

Touraine, Alan. 2000. *Can we Live Together? Equality and Difference*. Cambridge: Polity Press.

Traverso, Enzo. 1996. *Pour une critique de la barbarie moderne: Ecrits sur l'histoire des Juifs et de l'antisémitisme*. Lausanne: Editions Page Deux.

UNESCO. 1968. 'UNESCO Statement on Race and Racial Prejudice'. *Current Anthropology* 9, no. 4: 270–2.

Urbinati, Nadia. 1998. 'The South of Antonio Gramsci and the Concept of Hegemony', in Jane Schneider (ed.), *Italy's 'Southern Question': Orientalism in One Country*. Oxford: Berg.

Van den Berghe, Pierre. 1967. *Race and Racism: A Comparative Perspective*. New York: John Wiley & Sons.

Varikas, Eleni. 1998. 'Sentiment national, genre et ethnicité'. *TUMULTES* 11: 87–97.

Vertovec, Steven. 1996. 'Multiculturalism, Culturalism and Public Incorporation'. *Ethnic and Racial Studies* 19, no. 1: 49–69.

——. 1999. 'Conceiving and Researching Transnationalism'. *Ethnic and Racial Studies* 22, no. 2: 447–62.

Vinen, Richard C. 1994. 'The End of an Ideology? Right-Wing Antisemitism in France, 1944–1970'. *The Historical Journal* 37, no. 2: 365–88.

Voegelin, Eric. 1933a. [2000]. *Race and State*. Baton Rouge and London: Louisiana State University Press (trans. Ruth Heim).

——. 1933b. *Die Rassenidee in der Geistesgeschichte von Ray bis Carus*. Berlin: Junker & Duennhaupt.

——. 1940. 'The Growth of the Race Idea'. *The Review of Politics* July: 283–317.

Wagner, Peter. 1994. *A Sociology of Modernity: Liberty and Discipline*. London and New York: Routledge.

Wallerstein, Immanuel (with Arrighi, Giovanni and Hopkins, Terence K.). 1989. *Antisystemic Movements*. London: Verso, 1989.

Walzer, Michael. 1999. 'Rescuing Civil Society'. *Dissent* Winter: 62–7.

Watt, Philip. 1998. 'Reporting on Refugees'. *Focus* Winter 97–8, no. 57/58: 29–30.

Wieviorka, Michel. 1994. 'Ethnicity and Action', in John Rex and Beatrice Drury (eds), *Ethnic Mobilisation in a Multi-cultural Europe*. Aldershot: Avebury.

——.1997. 'Is it So Difficult to Be an Anti-Racist?', in Pnina Werbner and Tariq Modood (eds), *Debating Cultural Hybridity: Multi-cultural Identities and the Politics of Anti-Racism*. London: Zed Books.

Williams, Patricia J. 1997. *Seeing a Colour-Blind Future: The Paradox of Race*. New York: The Noonday Press.

Wilmsen, Edwin N. and McAllister, Patrick (eds). 1996. *The Politics of Difference: Ethnic Premises in a World of Power*. Chicago: University of Chicago Press.

Young, Robert. 1992. 'Colonialism and Humanism', in James Donald and Ali Rattansi (eds), *'Race', Culture and Difference*. London: Sage/Open University.

Zincone, Giovanna. 1994. *Uno schermo contro il razzismo: Per una politica dei diritti utili*. Roma: Donzelli Editore.

WEBSITES CITED

Anti-Racism Campaign (Ireland)	http://flag.blackened.net/revolt/arc.html
Asian Dub Foundation	www.asiandubfoundation.com
CARF	www.carf.demon.co.uk/
David Renton	www.dkrenton.co.uk
Institute of Race Relations	www.irr.org.uk
MIB	http://mibmib.free.fr
RAR (Ireland)	http://flag.blackened.net/revolt/rar.html

OTHER WEBSITES CONSULTED

Anti Nazi League	www.anl.org.uk/
Anti-Racism Crosspoint	www.magenta.nl/crosspoint/
ARCI	www.arci.it
Associazione Alma Terra	www.arpnet.it/~alma/

ATMF	www.atmf.org/
Blink	www.blink.org.uk/
C.L.R. James Institute	www.clrjamesinstitute.org/
Deportation Alliance	www.deportation-alliance.com/
Eric Voegelin Institute	www.ericvoegelin.org/
La rete d'urgenza contro il razzismo	www.unimondo.org/reteurg/
Sans-papiers	www.bok.net/pajol/
Metro Eirinn	www.metroeireann.com/
NAAR	http://ourworld.compuserve.com/ homepages/aa_r/
NCADC	www.ncadc.org.uk/
Pavee Point	www.paveepoint.ie
Searchlight (Anti-Fascist Magazine)	www.s-light.demon.co.uk/
SOS Racisme	www.sos-racisme.org/
The Stephen Lawrence Inquiry	www.archive.official-documents.co.uk/
UNITED for Intercultural Action	www.unitedagainstracism.org

Index